ENGRAVED BY SARTAIN.

HISTORY

OF

JEFFERSON COLLEGE:

INCLUDING AN ACCOUNT OF THE

EARLY "LOG-CABIN" SCHOOLS,

AND THE

CANONSBURG ACADEMY:

WITH BIOGRAPHICAL SKETCHES OF

REV. MATTHEW BROWN, D. D., REV. SAMUEL RALSTON, D.D., REV. MATTHEW HENDERSON, REV. JAMES RAMSEY, D. D., REV. JOHN H. KENNEDY, AND REV. ABR'M. ANDERSON, D. D.

BY JOSEPH SMITH, D. D.

Author of "OLD REDSTONE."

PITTSBURGH:

PUBLISHED AND PRINTED BY J. T. SHRYOCK,

GAZETTE BUILDING, FIFTH STREET.

1857.

STEREOTYPED BY W. S. HAVEN, PITTSBURGH, PA.

CONTENTS.

CHAPTER I.

INTRODUCTION—LOG-CABIN SCHOOLS.

Page.

Character of First Western Ministers—When and by whom "Log-Cabin" Schools begun—Mr. Dodd's School on Ten Mile and in Washington—Mr. Smith's School at Buffalo—Dr. M'Millan's School at Chartiers.......... 5

CHAPTER II.

THE CANONSBURG ACADEMY.

By whom the Academy founded—David Johnston, first teacher—Dr. M'Millan's position at first—His "Log-Cabin" School merged into Academy—Movement of Synod of Virginia—Redstone Presbytery selected Canonsburg—Interesting ceremony of opening Academy—Persons engaged in it—First student, Robert Patterson; sketch of his life and character—Notice in Pittsburgh Gazette—Contributions for Academy—Specimen of their character—Charter in 1794—First Trustees—Petition to Legislature in 1796—Teachers, Mr. Johnston, Mr. Samuel Miller, Mr. Mountain and Mr. Stockton—Action of Presbyteries—Literary Societies—Contests—Secret affiliated Societies.......... 17

CHAPTER III.

THE ACADEMY BECOMING A COLLEGE.

Trustees and Officers—Another Petition to Legislature—*Judge Edgar*—Presbytery of Redstone—Old Mr. Patterson's account of Academy in 1798—Rules and Regulations—Colonel Canon's death and character—Legislative aid—New Movement to get College Charter—Act of Trustees, about conditions of preaching in Academy—Members added to the Societies—Change of Constitution in 1798—Names of Trustees—Charter of Jefferson College, in 1802—Why called after Mr. Jefferson—Good reasons for the name—New Trustees—New rules—*Mr. Watson*, first President; his death and character—*Mr. Dunlap* elected President; his character.......... 45

CHAPTER IV.

HISTORY OF JEFFERSON COLLEGE FROM 1804.

Graduates of 1804—*Ross' Latin Grammar*—Account of *Ross*—*Book-case* for the Societies; reminiscences about it—Graduates of 1805 and 1806—Presbyterian and Associate Presbyteries successfully appealed to for aid—Gen. Hamilton's success at Congress—Injunction of the Board upon Drs. M'Millan and Dunlap—Graduates of 1808—First communication from Board of Washington College; result—Dr. Ralston chosen President of Board—Dr. Murdock's report about conference with Washington Committee—Graduates of 1809—State of Finances—Death and character of *Judge M'Dowell*—Trustees' rule for order of procession at commencement—Description of an "*Exhibition*," or College Commencement, in "old times.".......... 69

CHAPTER V.

NEW PRESIDENTS AND "COLLEGE WAR."

Page.

Dr. Dunlap and the Board—Graduates of 1810—Dr. Dunlap resigns—Graduates of 1811 and 1812—*Dr. Wylie* elected Principal—About Ezekiel Hannah's will—Graduates of 1813, 1814 and 1815—New negotiations with the Board of Washington College—Various conferences—Final failure in attempt to unite the colleges—Much sharp shooting, on both sides, but none killed, and few wounded—Reflections on the whole case—*Rev. R. Johnston*, a trustee for seventeen years—Sketch of his life—Dr. Wylie resigns—*Dr. Wm. M'Millan* succeeds him—*Dr. Matthew Brown*—Remarkable circumstances connected with his election.......... 85

CHAPTER VI.

DR. M. BROWN'S PRESIDENCY.

A new era in the state and prospects of Jefferson College—Dr. Brown's extraordinary character and qualifications—Connection of Jefferson College with Jefferson Medical College in Philadelphia—*Jacob Green, Esq.*—Literary Societies in difficulties—Theological Seminary of the Associate Presbyterian Church established at Canonsburg—New College building in 1829-32—Crisis in the life of Dr. M'Millan; Death of his old friends, *Prof. Miller* and *C. Ritchie, Esq.*; their lives and character—Agricultural labor provided for students by a College farm; its ultimate failure; reflections about it—Recent movement by Synod of Pittsburgh for *Ecclesiastical supervision*—Its failure; reasons—Aids to be sought in investigating that whole subject—General conclusion of the whole history,...... 111

CHAPTER VII.

SOME ACCOUNT OF THE LITERARY SOCIETIES OF JEFFERSON COLLEGE.

History of Philo Literary Society.. 139
History of Franklin Literary Society.. 154

BIOGRAPHICAL SKETCHES.

Biographical sketch of the late Rev. Matthew Brown, D. D................................. 180
Biographical sketch of the Rev. Samuel Ralston, D. D.................................... 192
Biographical sketch of the Rev. Matthew Henderson...................................... 234
Biographical sketch of the Rev. James Ramsey, D. D...................................... 252
Biographical sketch of the Rev. Abraham Anderson, D. D.................................. 283
Memoir of the late Rev. John H. Kennedy, A. M... 353

APPENDIX.

The origin of Jefferson College.. 373
Dr. M'Millan's Manuscript.. 413
Importance of Colleges and of Classical Education—Early history of Collegiate Institutions.. 418

HISTORY OF JEFFERSON COLLEGE.

CHAPTER I.

INTRODUCTION—LOG-CABIN SCHOOLS.

Character of First Western Ministers—When and by whom "Log Cabin" Schools begun—Mr. Dod's School on Ten-mile and in Washington—Mr. Smith's School at Buffalo—Dr. M'Millan's School at Chartiers.

THE early history of most nations, ancient or modern, is obscured and deformed by incredible traditions and monstrous legends. The laborious researches of Niebuhr, Arnold, and others, have contributed much to separate the precious from the vile, and to ascertain, with some precision, where true history begins. The American people have this great advantage, in regard to the story of their rise and progress, that no fabulous period belongs to the outset of their history. This is especially true in respect to that portion of them who first sought homes and formed settlements in the eastern part of the Valley of the Mississippi. Though much obscurity rests upon the unimportant details of the first years of trial and sorrow, through which those who succeeded the hunters, trappers and Indians traders of Western Pennsylvania, were compelled to pass, the prominent features of the men of those times, and of the measures they pursued for elevating their physical, intellectual and moral condition, are now well ascertained, and rest on no uncertain tradition. The Scotch-Irish emigrants, who began to pour out on the Western frontier, a little before the last quarter of the 18th century, and to form settlements through Western Pennsylvania and Virginia, were a remarkable race. They brought with them a deeply cherished love for the *House of God* and the *School House.* The ministers of the gospel of the Presbyterian Church, and of the Associate, or Secession body, were well educated men, most of them graduates of the college of New Jersey; and devoted their untiring efforts to organize and build up churches in the new settlements. They also co-operated with their people in organizing schools; and in most cases took them under their own care, becoming teachers themselves, or providing adequate instructors. This may have been, possibly, in some instances, with a view, in part, to eke out a scanty support. But we have no doubt that this part of their labors, was in a measure forced upon them. Their poor people, living in log-cabins, and surrounded by constant harassings and perils from their savage foes, and doomed to very exhausting toils, in order to support their growing families, threw this responsible work on the hands of their ministers. Yet they, without exception, were compelled to work too, and to work hard, on their little patches of cleared land. There was not one of them, who did not become familiar with the axe and the maul, the plow and the hoe. Almost coeval with the period of their settlement west of the mountains, these ministers got up schools near their dwellings. As such dwellings would be generally as near the centre of their congregations as practicable, this location of the school houses would be most convenient to their people. Such a school was probably first established by Dr. M'Millan, near his own house, about two miles east of the present location of Canonsburg. Another was formed by the Rev. Thaddeus Dod, who settled on Ten-mile, in the southern part of Washington county, in the fall of 1779. Mr. Dod's school was begun as early as 1782 or 1783,—as we shall presently see. That Dr M'Millan's school, in its earliest form, preceded Mr. Dod's, seems highly probable, both from general tradition,* and from his language in a letter to Dr. Carnahan, dated March 26th, 1832, which we shall presently quote. This remarkable man, whose whole subsequent life was intimately associated with the cause of education, and with the history of Jefferson College, came out and settled in Western Pennsylvania, in November, 1778, though his first visit and labors as a minister of the gospel in the West, date back to 1775. This school, under the immediate care of Dr. M'Millan, seems to have been for the first few years, simply the English school of the neighborhood, with occasionally some Latin scholars. About the time of its organization, or soon after, the services of James Ross, Esq., were secured, who taught the general branches of English education, boarded with Dr. M'Millan, and pursued or completed his own classical studies, under the tuition of the Doctor, in compensation for his services in the school. This statement, we are aware, disturbs a current tradition, but is supported by the testimony of a letter of Dr. Carnahan, Ex-President of Princeton College, now before us.†

That Dr. M'Millan had in view the ultimate development of this school into the more distinctive form of a *Latin school* for young men having the gospel ministry in view, there is no reason to doubt. But that it possessed this form from

---

* "That Dr. M'Millan had a school at his own house, soon after he went to Western Pennsylvania is *undoubtedly true*. This corresponds with the tradition I heard."—*Letter from Dr. Carnahan.*

† We give the following extract from a letter of the Rev. Dr. James Carnahan, to the Rev. Dr. Charles Hodge—dated, "Princeton, N. J., May 13th, 1851." "The tradition I heard was, that Ross taught the English school; and that Dr. M'Millan taught him Latin, Greek, and Mathematics. Mr. Ross was undoubtedly a man of uncommon talents, an able lawyer, and of high standing as a Senator of the United States. But I never heard him spoken of as a distinguished Latin and Greek scholar. Judge Addison and Judge Brackenridge, of Pittsburgh, were always spoken of as first rate classical scholars. But this was not the reputation of Mr. Ross."

the beginning, seems highly improbable. The harassed and troubled state of the country, for the first four or five years after the Doctor's settlement at Chartiers, renders it very unlikely that materials could be found for getting up this department at his school. But we have stated at large, in "Old Redstone," our reasons for questioning the accuracy of the tradition which has assigned to him the honor of opening the first *Latin school* in the West, the substance of which may be seen in the note below.*

But though we question the early date of Dr. M'Millan's school as a *Latin* school, it seems almost certain to us that he made the *first* movement in the cause of education. And again, his school became what the Doctor had, perhaps, always contemplated from the beginning—a classical school; and it was the *sole classical* school, west of the Monongahela river, for young men preparing for the gospel ministry, after others of a similar character were discontinued. This school was the immediate predecessor of the Academy at Canonsburg, which was founded in 1791. But the manner in which the one preceded the other, and was merged into it, we shall see hereafter. In the meantime, soon after Dr. M'Millan's school commenced, in its primal form, Mr. Dod opened his school at Ten-mile. His son has recently given,

* The records of the Presbytery of Redstone show that there were no licentiates under their care, who had received their previous scholastic or theological training from Dr. M'Millan, till after 1785. Their first candidates, Messrs. *Hughes, Brice, Patterson and Porter,* were first under the instruction of Messrs. Dod and Smith, from 1783 to 1786. Dr. M'Millan enumerates them among the first who were trained and brought into the ministry in the West. He mentions none before them The Rev. Joseph Patterson, who studied, with a *few others,* under the direction of the Rev. Joseph Smith, at Buffalo, in 1785, was *afterwards,* along with *some of these,* at Dr. M'Millan's school; and the Doctor, in his letter so Dr. Carnahan, writing of his first movement to prepare young men for the ministry, mentions *these persons* as forming the materials of his first Latin school. There are some other facts stated in "Old Redstone," pages 7* and 78, serving to confirm the view then taken.

in the *Presbyterian Magazine* (for September, 1854), an interesting statement, which, though somewhat extended, will be read with interest. The following is the Rev. Dr. Cephas Dodd's account of his father's efforts in the cause of education:—"He (the Rev. Thaddeus Dod*) felt the importance of a better common school education, and, in order to promote it, visited the schools, and counseled the teachers as to the best manner of performing their duties. For the special purpose of educating young men for the gospel ministry, he had a building erected within a few steps of his own dwelling, in which he opened a classical and mathematical school, in the spring of 1782. The students present at that time were Messrs. James Hughes, John Brice, Daniel Lindley, Robert Marshall and Francis Dunlavy. These were all young men, and avowedly pursuing a course of education, preparatory to the ministry, excepting Mr. Dunlavy, whose intention is not certainly known. He was a young man of superior talent, of amiable disposition, took an active part in social worship, and, it is thought, Mr. Dod and others felt some disappointment when he took a different course. He was afterwards a Judge in the State of Ohio. Daniel Lindley, in consequence of the failure of his health, was compelled to relinquish his undertaking. John Hanna, also having the ministry in view, came probably in 1783. The Rev. David Smith, young at that time, was also one of the students. Whether he came with the first, or at a later date, is not recollected. With what view his father sent him, we may easily imagine; and his hope was not disappointed. Another young lad, son of Col. James Marshal, entered the school about 1783. The Rev. Jacob Lindley, D. D., the early friend and companion of the writer, (and to whom he is indebted for much aid in calling to recollection and establishing these particulars), was also an inmate of the family, and though but from eight to ten

* The Rev. T. Dod and Rev. C. Dodd. The son added a *d* to his name.

or eleven years of age, was reading Latin, and we are assured that his father placed him there with the hope that he might, in due time, be prepared by divine grace to take part in the work of the ministry. It may also be noted that some three or four men were taught surveying. There is no reason to think that for any other purpose than that of educating men for the ministry, the building would ever have been erected, or the school opened. After having been in operation three years and a half, it was closed in the fall of 1785, either because Mr. D. had sold the farm on which he lived, and was about removing from it, or for other reasons. Doubtless after boarding such a number in the family, with the few conveniences of house-room, &c., they enjoyed, both he and Mrs. Dod needed a little rest. Here, then, on an exposed frontier, we find the first classical school in the West, and might claim for Mr. Dod the precedence in efforts to promote the cause of education for the ministry. Such claim, however, we do not make, though the above facts show that it cannot belong to any other. It is true that Mr. D. took upon him the labor of teaching, years before it was entered upon by any of his brethren; but it was not his own private enterprise. He, with Messrs. Smith and M'Millan, felt deeply the need, both present and prospective, of a faithful and able ministry to supply the wants of our Western Zion. The harvest was great, and the laborers were few. When they met, it was often the subject of their conversation, and instead of waiting for ministers to come from abroad, they wisely resolved to endeavor to raise them up in their midst. Who can say which of them first proposed or acted on this plan? They sought for young men of piety and talents who would be willing to devote themselves to the work, and undertook to prepare them by a thorough education. One was found at Ten-mile, two at Buffalo, and some in other places; and Mr. Dod was first employed in teaching for reasons which it is not for us to assign. Each of the above named ministers were employed more or less in teaching at his own house, but finding it inconvenient and interfering too much with their pastoral duties, their next movement was the getting up an Academy at Washington, for which a charter was granted September 24th, 1787, with a donation of five thousand acres of land. Without entering into any detail of argument to show that the aforesaid ministers were first to move in this matter, it may be sufficient to call attention to the names of the Trustees. They were the Rev. Messrs. John M'Millan, Joseph Smith, Thaddeus Dod, John Clark, Matthew Henderson, (of the Associate Presbytery,) and John Corbly, (Baptist.) Here were five Presbyterian ministers, being all who were west of the Monongahela river, and with them, seven or eight elders of Cross Creek Buffalo, Chartiers, &c.; and one of them in an extreme part of what was then Washington, but now Green county. The other trustees were, with a few exceptions, in connection with the Presbyterian church. Two of them, (Judges Allison and M'Dowell,) who were elders of Chartiers, were at that time in the Legislature, and aided in obtaining the charter. The land appropriated by the State, lying north of the Ohio, would, of course, be unproductive for a long time. Nevertheless, the trustees resolved to go forward. After some unsuccessful attempts to obtain a Principal, Mr. Dod was urgently solicited to take the place. He was unwilling to leave his people, but, after some conference on the subject, informed them, that, provided the appointment were made but for one year, he might, for the sake of getting the institution into operation, think it his duty to accept; but, if for a longer term, he should reject it at once. The appointment was made accordingly, and after consulting his people, he signified his acceptance, and at the same time resigned the office of trustee. There being no available funds wherewith to erect a building, the upper rooms of the Court House were hired for the purpose, and the Institution went into operation, 1st of

April, 1789. There were about twenty or thirty students, of whom five afterwards entered the ministry. While in Washington, Mr. Dod preached there one-third of his time and divided the remainder between the two places at Ten-mile. At the expiration of the time for which he had engaged, he was prevailed on to continue three months longer. Mr. Johnston, who had been teaching in the English department, was appointed his successor. Some time in the next winter the Court House was burned; and there was no suitable building to be had in town. The Rev. Messrs. M'Millan and Henderson went together to Washington, and requested J. Hoge, Esq., who was the proprietor, and also trustee, to make a donation of a lot on which to erect a building. Discouraged by his refusal, they went and asked the same of Col. Canon, of Canonsburg, who not only gave the ground, but otherwise contributed liberally to the cause. An Academy was erected at Canonsburg. Mr. Johnston was made its principal; and Washington Academy suspended operations for a number of years. Dr. M'Millan was one of the principal agents in getting up the Academy at Washington, was one of a committee to solicit subscriptions for its support, and continued his patronage till, by the circumstance above related, he was induced to abandon it; after which he became the most efficient supporter of the institution at Canonsburg. He does not seem, however, to have considered the latter as growing out of his Latin school, for we find he wrote to Dr. Carnahan: "I had still a few with me when the Academy was opened at Canonsburg, and finding that I could not teach and do justice to my congregation, I immediately gave it up and sent them there." Such was the origin of the two literary Institutions in Western Pennsylvania.

The Rev. Joseph Smith, of Buffalo, Washington county, who came out to the West in the year 1780, early distinguished himself by his efforts to aid in preparing young men for the ministry. The following statement, given to the public, some years ago, in "Old Redstone," may not improperly be again introduced in this place, though we have cheerfully modified it, with the desire of bringing it into harmony with the foregoing account of Mr. Dod's school. Mr. Smith was anxious from the first, after he settled in the West, to look out for, and aid in preparing young men to preach the gospel. He was among the first who moved in this matter. The first school that was opened *exclusively* with a view to the training of young men for the sacred office, is believed to have been begun by Mr. Smith, at Upper Buffalo, as early, at least, as 1785. The Rev. Joseph Patterson says, in a note, on a small package of letters, written principally to his wife, found among his papers after his death: "In the fall of 1785, being thirty-three years old, it was thought best, with the advice of the Presbytery of Redstone, that I should endeavor to prepare for the gospel ministry. There being no places of public education in this country, I, with a few others, studied with the Rev. Joseph Smith, of Buffalo congregation, Washington county, Pa., being partially absent from my family," &c.

The subject of opening such a school had pressed heavily on Mr. Smith's mind for some time. There was one difficulty in his way; he had no suitable house. But he had recently erected a house adjoining his dwelling house, to serve as a kitchen and outhouse. If his wife would be willing to surrender that, for a while, and fall back on their former hampered domestic system, it could be done. He stated the case to her. She cordially acquiesced in the plan, and warmly seconded his views. Almost immediately this Latin school was begun. Messrs. M'Gready, Porter and Patterson began their course. Soon after, James Hughes and John Brice, who had already been with Mr. Dod, joined them. This school for the languages and sciences was continued some time; and then, by some mutual arrangement, was transferred and surrendered to the care of Dr. M'Millan, near

Canonsburg. This we regard as the period when Dr. M'Millan's school took its more distinctive form as a *Latin school;* or rather, perhaps, was enlarged, so as to include a course of classical and scientific studies, as its more prominent feature. This view of the case harmonizes with Dr. M'Millan's statement to Dr. Carnahan, given in a previous note, and with a passage in a manuscript in his own handwriting, where, speaking of the origin of his *ministerial school*, and not of the school in its previous state, he says: "Accordingly, I collected a few who gave evidence of piety, and instructed them in the knowledge of Latin, Greek, &c., viz: James Hughes, John Brice, James M'Gready, Samuel Porter, &c." These were a part of the materials with which he says his school began, and he mentions none that *preceded* them. Indeed this list corresponds with what he mentions about the *second set* of ministers in the West, and with the records of the Redstone Presbytery, that gave no account of any earlier licentiates. Now as all the persons that are here mentioned were either with Mr. Dod, or Mr. Smith, before they were under the instructions of Dr. M'Millan, it is thus ascertained that though Dr. M'Millan's school may have been first organized, as we believe it was, it did not assume the more distinctive form of a Latin school for training candidates for the ministry, until his colleagues had been for some time giving instructions with that view, and perhaps until they both ceased to teach their schools. The statement given to us, some years ago, by Mrs. Irwin, an aged, but very intelligent lady, then residing in Marysville, Ohio, since deceased, respecting Mr. Smith and his school, is too remarkable to be omitted here, though already published in "Old Redstone," p. 77. It is in substance, as follows—(and her pastor, the Rev. Mr. Smith, testified that it has been her unvaried statement for many years, and he has no doubt of her memory being perfectly good in this case,)—"That she was between twelve and fifteen years of age, living near Mr.

Smith's, one of his spiritual children, took a great interest at the time in what Mr. Smith did in this matter, and all her life after familiarly remembered the following facts: that in 1785, Mr. Smith opened a small school, for assisting and training young men for the gospel ministry; that Messrs. M'Gready, Brice, Porter and Patterson began their course with him, Mr. James Hughes soon after joining them; that Mr. M'Gready came from Dr. M'Millan's, with whom he had been living, not as a student, but as a laborer on his farm; that five congregations, through the ladies, united in furnishing these students, (with the exception of Mr. M'Gready,) with clothing, viz: Buffalo, Cross Creek, Chartiers, Bethel and Ten-mile; that they made up summer and winter clothing, for several of these young men (coloring linen for summer wear, in a dye, made of new-mown hay, and sending woolen cloth, by merchants, east of the mountains, to be *fulled* and *dressed*, and brought back with them on their return,) that this was the *first movement* made for preparing young men for the ministry; that there was no *such* school, at this time, at Chartiers, nor until after the one at Buffalo was discontinued; that Mrs. M'Millan and the Chartiers ladies took their share in this effort to sustain this school at Buffalo, Mr. M'Gready coming from Dr. M'Millan's to the school." This is very explicit testimony. If it conflicts with the account given of Mr. Dod's school, it may easily be supposed that she was not aware of what Mr. Dod had done, as his place of residence lay at some distance from Buffalo. It may be thought, indeed, that Mr. Smith's school was rather a *divinity hall;* but the period at which the several persons Mrs. Irwin mentions, were licensed to preach the gospel—which was some years after—much longer than students for the ministry, in those days, studied theology—shows conclusively that preparatory studies were embraced in Mr. Smith's school. The interesting fact, brought to light by Mrs. Irwin's narrative, of the efforts of the ladies in those days, to assist in the cause of education, is a striking feature of those early times. We are here reminded of the testimony borne by the Rev. Robert Patterson, in his letter to Dr. Brown, (to be hereafter referred to,) to the generous piety of the wives of the Rev. Messrs. Smith and M'Millan. "It should be here stated," says Mr. Patterson, "that for want of suitable places elsewhere, the students generally lodged in the minister's family, without profit and sometimes at considerable expense to the household. In this service and toil, the wives of these two godly ministers heartily concurred. I knew them well; and they were both eminently mothers in Israel."

We cannot learn that either the *Rev. Matthew Henderson*, or the *Rev. John Clark*, of Lebanon and Bethel churches, had any personal charge of a school. They doubtless lent their special attention in promoting good schools in their congregations. But no other schools than those of which we have now given some account, existed at that early period, in Washington county. We speak, of course, of those above the grade of common English schools. Having now related the first efforts made in the cause of education west of the mountains, we have cleared our way to an entrance upon the history of the first school at Canonsburg.

NOTE.—A very able and elaborate paper, furnished to us by Prof. Robert Patterson, of Oakland College, Miss., in which the claims of Dr. M'Millan's "Log Cabin" school to priority as a *Latin school* are defended, will be found in the Appendix.

CHAPTER II.

THE CANONSBURG ACADEMY.

By whom the Academy founded—David Johnston, first teacher—Dr. M'Millan's position at first—His "Log-cabin" school merged into Academy—Movement of Synod of Virginia—Redstone Presbytery selected Canonsburg—Interesting ceremony of opening Academy—Persons engaged in it—First student, R. Patterson; sketch of his life and character—Notice in Pittsburgh Gazette—Contributions for Academy—Specimen of their character—Charter in 1794—First Trustees—Petition to Logislature in 1796—Teachers, Mr. Johnston, Mr. Samuel Millar, Mr. Mountain and Mr. Stockton—Action of Presbyteries—Literary Societies—Contests—Secret affiliated Societies.

The precise date of the first movement towards the formation of a school at Canonsburg, above the grade of a common English school, cannot be ascertained. There were living in and near what afterwards became the village of Canonsburg, several respectable, public-spirited gentlemen, such as *Col. John Canon*, (on whose land the town was laid out and thence took its name,) *Judge James Allison*, *Judge John M'Dowell*, *Alexander Cook*, *Esq.*, *Messrs. James Foster*, *Thomas Brecker*, *Robert Ralston*, and others; who, perhaps, some time before 1789, held frequent conferences about getting up such a school. These gentlemen were then generally living in log cabins, and wore hunting shirts. Some of these conferences were very possibly held at log-rollings, house-raisings, or corn-huskings. The country was still comparatively a wilderness. William Darby, Esq., whose memory was remarkably tenacious as to dates, has stated in a letter which he wrote in 1850, that "through 1789 and 1790 the Academy

2*

was in operation." Through both these years the Indians were still giving much annoyance to the western settlements of Washington county. And these troubles reached their greatest height during the following year. But this future home of science and literature was even then begun. It was, of course, in its most embryo state. It is ascertained that during 1791, that eventful year of trial and sorrow in Western Pennsylvania, the services of *Mr. David Johnston*, who had, during a part of that and of the previous year, taught at Washington, were secured. At this time Dr. M'Millan's school, in the celebrated *Log-cabin*, near his own house, two miles from Canonsburg, was still in operation. This school was continued for some time after the Canonsburg school was set on foot, under the patronage of some, if not all, of the persons named above. Dr. M'Millan was, up to this time, and for a year or two before, interested in behalf of the Academy at Washington, of which he was a trustee, along with Rev. Messrs. Henderson, Joseph Smith, and others; and was therefore committed to its interests. But he and others soon became discouraged in that enterprise. In an important paper found on the Records of the Trustees of Jefferson College, dated December 29, 1817, in the Doctor's own handwriting, it is stated as follows: "In the year 1787, the Legislature of this State granted a donation of lands, for the purpose of erecting and supporting an Academy in the town of Washington. The Rev. Messrs. Matthew Henderson, Joseph Smith, John M'Millan, and others, used their influence and best endeavors to get this Academy into operation, for the purpose of promoting literature among the inhabitants of the Western counties in general; and also, with the fond hope that the loud calls and repeated demands for preachers of the of the gospel might be supplied from that institution. But so indifferent were the inhabitants of that town to the interests of literature in general, and to the demands of the church in particular, that, notwithstanding the State donation, an Academy could not be supported. The Rev. Mr. Dod, and after him Mr. David Johnston, made the attempt, by engaging as teachers; but were forced to give up the benevolent design, through the indifference and inattention of a majority of the trustees. When the hopes of Mr. M'Millan were blasted by the indifference and inattention of the trustees of the Academy at Washington, he turned his attention to Canonsburg, as a place of greater hope and more suited to his views. He solicited donations from private individuals for erecting an Academy at that place, and succeeded. The Legislature granted a charter in 1794. A house was built; and a Latin and Greek school, which he had kept at his own house for the purpose of supplying the churches, as far as practicable, was translated to this infant Academy." We have given this extract, not to endorse some of the rather severe and caustic reflections on the trustees and people at Washington, but as a historical testimony, as to the period when Dr. M'Millan's school coalesced with and was merged into the school at Canonsburg. That this latter school had a prior existence, in some humbler form, and was not merely an out-growth from the Log-cabin school, is proved, *first,* from Mr. Darby's statement, ("Old Redstone," page 193.) "I often passed there on week-days. Though the Academy was then established in Canonsburg, the school (at Dr. M'Millan's,) was still in operation, but when discontinued I cannot state." Secondly, from Dr. M'Millan's own language, in an original manuscript of the Doctor's in our possession: "I had still a few with me when the Academy was opened; but, finding that I could not teach and do justice to my congregation, I immediately gave it up and sent them there." Thirdly, from the Rev. R. Patterson's statement this is also inferred. In a letter to the Rev. Dr. M. Brown, dated October 1, 1846, he states that a conference of ministers and citizens took place in July, 1791, to determine the locality of an institution on a more enlarged scale, commensurate with the growing demands of the church and the country. The two points respectively advocated by Dr. M'Millan and Col. Canon, were the Log-cabin, near Dr. M'Millan's, and the town of Canonsburg. Into which of the already existing schools should the other coalesce and be merged, with a view to a larger academy, was the question. It was decided in favor of Canonsburg; and the two schools were *very soon*, thus united. This is our view of the whole case. And the above stated facts and testimony are adduced in its support.*

---

* It will be seen in the progress of our account, that, according to the Rev. R. Patterson's recollections, Professor Miller was then teaching and conducting this original school; and that *Mr. David Johnston*, about the middle of the summer, was also engaged, not to supersede, as we suppose, Professor Miller, who taught the English branches and the mathematics, but to teach the classical department. Our view of the whole matter is, that there was, *first*, Mr. Miller's school, sustained by the gentlemen in and around Canonsburg—then this school, enlarged by the employment of Mr. Johnston, still, in fact, under the direction and control of these gentlemen. Messrs. M'Millan, Henderson, and Smith, at this time, when the school was enlarged, heartily co-operated with them in this movement, not officially as trustees, nor as members of the "Academy and Library Company," which was the name they gave themselves about this time. Perhaps the relations of these three ministers to the Washington Academy were still such as to render a formal relation to the "Company" improper; perhaps they regarded the whole enterprise as much better to be left in the hands of those gentlemen, and more likely to succeed in finding favor with the Legislature of the State. But they lent their hearty agency in enlarging the foundations of the school, and starting it on its new career. Dr. M'Millan may, at this time, have fully made up his mind that it should supersede and take the place of the "Log-cabin" school. And so it might have been understood by all parties concerned. But we think that in the strict history of the case, there was here, soon after, a coalescence between the Institution already begun at Canonsburg, and now further enlarged, and the "Log-cabin" school—rather than as has often been asserted, that "the Canonsburg Academy grew out of the Log-cabin," and was simply an enlargement of it. That the merging of the "Log-cabin" school into the Canonsburg Academy, and the active co-operation of Dr. M'Millan and of the Presbyteries and churches, gave life and vigor to the Academy, cannot be doubted: and this will be made apparent in the progress of this history. Though there was no formal recognition of the facts above stated on the part of the "Academy and

Another important event about this time occurred. The Synod of Virginia, October 1st, 1791, took measures to get up two institutions, one in the bounds of the Presbytery of Lexington, Virginia, and the other in the bounds of the *Presbytery of Redstone*, (then including all Western Pennsylvania and Virginia,) for the purpose, especially, of aiding poor and pious young men in their preparation for the gospel ministry. For a full account of this matter, the reader is referred to the note below.* The latter institution was placed under the immediate care of the Presbytery of Redstone. And Dr. M'Millan was appointed by the Synod to take the

---

Library Company," or their trustees, we have no doubt they well knew the Academy would have speedily gone down but for these main elements of its life. Why there was not a greater prominence given to these features of the case, it may now be difficult to say. Perhaps, as we have already intimated, it may have been thought wiser and more prudent. With such men as Col. Canon, Judge M'Dowell, Judge Allison, and others, some of them ruling elders; Messrs. Henderson, M'Millan and Smith, may have rightly thought the whole enterprise, in this way, would be perfectly safe and would succeed better.

* The Synod of Virginia, at their session in Winchester, October 1, 1791, appointed a committee, of which the *Rev. Joseph Smith* was chairman, to form a plan for promoting the education of persons for the ministry of the gospel, and to bring in an overture on the subject. Upon the report of this committee, the Synod having considered the same, and made such amendments and additions as were judged necessary, agreed to it—as follows: "As the supplying of churches with a pious and well qualified ministry is of acknowledged importance—overtured—1st. That the Synod of Virginia undertake the patronage of a seminary of learning for the purpose of educating young men for the gospel ministry. 2d. That they devise means for supporting or assisting young men of piety and genius in procuring an education, who may not be possessed of sufficient property for the purpose. The 'Synod highly approve of the proposition contained in the overture, as they are well convinced of the necessity of extending the opportunities of acquiring knowledge, and especially the knowledge of the doctrines of religion, to all who intend to preach the gospel of Jesus Christ to the world.' Taking this measure therefore into serious consideration, the Synod recommend that there be two general institutions for learning conducted under the patronage of this body; one to be established in Rockbridge county, Virginia, under the care of the Rev. William Graham, as the president; the other in Washington county,

management and direction of it. The Redstone Presbytery, a few weeks after the action of the Synod of Virginia, (October 18, 1791,) having met at Pigeon Creek, approved of the recommendation of their Synod, and appointed Dr. M'Millan their treasurer, and "ordered their members to use their best endeavors to obtain contributions for the purpose and put

Pennsylvania, under the care of the Rev. John M'Millan. The principles upon which those institutions are to be conducted are as follows:

"1st. The learned languages and usual circle of sciences shall be taught in them, to as many as shall be sent there for instruction.

"2d. During the course of academical education, and from the first initiation of the students into the seminaries, a course of religious instruction shall also be entered upon, and continually adhered to during their residence there, according to the principles of our church. Books of a practical and doctrinal nature shall be put into their hands at once. Catechetical lectures shall be established and examinations entered into, upon their progress in this kind of knowledge, from time to time. The attention to these studies shall be kept up during the whole of their academical course, and suited to the capacities and progress of the youth.

"3d. The Presbyteries of Lexington and Hanover shall be the trustees of the seminary in Rockbridge, to cherish it by their influence, and pointedly to attend the examinations of the students, either in a collective capacity, or by committees from their respective bodies, duly appointed. The Presbytery of Redstone shall, in like manner, superintend the seminary in Washington county.

"4th. In one or other of these institutions, it is the advice of the Synod, that all the youth within our bounds who intend to engage in the ministry of the gospel, shall be instructed.

"5th. As there are a number of pious youth in our country who might be serviceable in preaching the gospel, but, through want of sufficient ability, are unable to obtain an education; it is the intention and desire of Synod that the ministers in their respective Presbyteries shall seek out such, and that they, being examined and approved by the Presbytery, shall be placed in the respective seminaries, at the expense of the Presbytery who shall approve them.

"6th. In order to obtain the proper supplies for such indigent students, the Presbyteries are exhorted to use their influence, in their respective bounds, with the pious and benevolent, to make annual contributions for raising a fund for this purpose: this fund to be placed in the hands of the treasurers appointed by the Synod, who are to return annual accounts of receipts and expenditures; and from it the youth, upon the foundation, are to draw their

them into the hands of Dr. M'Millan as soon as possible, and of their diligence therein to render an account at the next spring meeting."

No precise location, otherwise than Washington county, was determined by the Synod as to the Western Institution. The probability is, that the Synod, though leaving that matter entirely open for the action of the Presbytery of Redstone, supposed, or took it for granted, so far as they knew the views of Messrs. Smith and M'Millan, and the course pursued by those brethren, that the location would be either Washington or Canonsburg, just according as these places and their vicinities might evince the more decided practical co-operation. These two remarkable men were the most prominent movers in the whole business at Synod. Mr. Smith was chairman of the committee who reported the whole paper on the subject. But they were both trustees of the Academy at Washington. Mr. Smith lived comparatively in the vicinity, and his congregation included some then living in or near Washington. But he, sharing with Dr. M'Millan in desponding feelings about the further prospects of Washington Academy, had united with *Messrs. M'Millan, Henderson, and others*, but a few months before, in a memorable transaction at Canonsburg, which we shall presently relate. But though he had aided in a movement to get up the Canonsburg Academy, as he was still a trustee at Washington, and he had not yet lost his interest in that place, or his hope of reviving that suspended school, it was, perhaps, his special desire that the Synod should leave the precise location of the Presbyterial

---

supplies, by an order from their respective presidents. And those youth, upon their obtaining their education, at the expiration of one year, after being settled in some line of business, shall begin to refund to the treasury the expenses of their education, in such time and manner as the Presbytery may direct.

"7th. The rules of these seminaries and the mode of education therein, shall be submitted to the Presbyteries for their respective approbation."—"*Old Redstone,*" *pp.* 423–5.

school undetermined. He soon after finished his course by a triumphant death. Had he lived, it is hard to say, what his influence might have been in determining the place of the school, and in modifying its whole character. We have already seen that Dr. M'Millan lost his confidence in the institution at Washington. He considered it as dead. The Presbytery, perhaps, partook largely of his views and feelings. At their next three meetings, however, they took no decisive action on the subject. It was a time of unusual trouble, from the Indians. The country was in a state of great distraction. Perhaps, also, they thought it prudent to take time sufficient to enable them to determine wisely what they would do as to the *manner* and *place* of carrying out the recommendation of the Synod. At length, when they met at Pigeon Creek, October 18, 1792, the question of location, as to the institution intrusted to their care by the Synod, was fully considered, and the several places—Washington, the Log-cabin, and Canonsburg, were, perhaps, advocated by their respective friends. "*The Presbytery unanimously agreed to appoint Canonsburg to be the seat of that institution of learning, which they are appointed by Synod to superintend; and that all the young men, taken upon the fund for the support of poor and pious youth, shall be educated there.*" An attempt was made, subsequently, to get the Presbytery to reconsider their action. But it resulted only in a kind of compromise, by the adoption of the following resolution, viz: "That if it should appear, at a future day, most conducive to the good of the church, that another seminary of the like nature should be erected in our bounds, we will not oppose a division of the funds." This was at Rehoboth, April 18, 1793. This determination of the Presbytery to make Canonsburg the seat of their institution, though it did not result in securing to the Presbytery any control over the Academy, or any right or power to sit, as a co-ordinate branch of the Board of Trustees, or to elect or even nominate any of the trustees or teachers, was, nevertheless, so adjusted, or led to such arrangements with the trustees, as to answer, in their view, the design of the Synod, in *fact*, though not in *form*. There is, indeed, a singular minute in the records of the Board, for 1796, hereafter to be noticed, in which the *Presbytery of Ohio* is mentioned, as uniting with the trustees in agreeing to *support* two teachers of the languages. But otherwise, we have found not the faintest trace of anything like ecclesiastical supervision ever exercised over the Academy. Having given this account of the doings of the church, through her judicatures, in reference to our institution, we must now turn back a little.

It appears that in July, 1791, it was settled, at a conference of citizens and ministers, numerously attended, that the incipient steps should be taken, for getting the Academy under way. Col. Canon made a donation of a lot for the erection of a suitable building. He undertook to put up, immediately, a large stone edifice, and have it prepared as soon as possible; his expenses to be reimbursed afterwards, as the trustees might be able to provide. In the meantime, it was thought proper to open the Academy at once, *on the ensuing day*. The Rev. Robert Patterson's account of the proceedings of that day is so graphic and life-like, that we shall let him tell the story:

"An appointment was made to meet the next day, Tuesday, 10 o'clock, A. M., in a small English school house, near Canon's mill, about half a mile from the village; and a general invitation was given to all friends of learning and of their country, to attend; and then and there to see the Canonsburg Academy opened. Meantime, Mr. David Johnston, a graduate of the University of Pennsylvania, who had, without success, been trying to open a Latin school in the town of Washington, was invited to attend, and take charge of the young Academy. At 10 o'clock, on Tuesday morning, many citizens were present on the ground, to witness the opening of the first academy on the west side of the Allegheny mountains. Of the inhabitants of the town and vicinity, there were present, Judges M'Dowell and Allison, Craig Ritchie, Esq., and Rev. Matthew Henderson, living at a few miles distance. Mr. Henderson was a Scotch seceder clergyman, blessed with Scotch talents, Scotch education, Scotch theology, and Scotch piety; his memory is still highly cherished, as a worthy cotemporary of Messrs. M'Millan and Smith. These three ministers, with Mr. Johnston and two pupils, William Riddle and Robert Patterson, who had recited a few lessons to Abraham Scott, took their position under the shade of some sassafras bushes, growing in a worm fence, near the English school house, which could not be vacated for a short time. And here, under the pleasant shade of the green bushes, protected from the rays of a July sun, (*corona populi parva circumstante,*) the two pupils, with '*Corderii Colloquia*' in their hands, were just about to read '*Quid agis,*' when Mr. M'Millan, addressing his two brethren, and the small assembly, remarked in substance, as follows: 'This is an important day in our history, affecting deeply the interests of the church, and of the country in the West; affecting our own interests for time and for eternity, and the interests, it may be, of thousands and thousands yet unborn.' And, turning to Mr. Henderson, asked him to engage in prayer, seeking the blessings of God on the institution now to be opened. And I must say, the broad vernacular pronunciation of the Scotch tongue never could be more delightful and impressive than it was then; while every thing proper to the occasion appeared to be remembered in prayer, by this good man.* The first lesson in the Academy was soon recited. *Robert Patterson,*† being the senior, led, beginning the first

---

* For a sketch of the Life of Mr. Henderson, see Appendix.

† The *Rev. Robert Patterson*—the *first student* of Canonsburg Academy, was born April 1, 1773, at Stillwater, New York, near the spot afterwards celebrated as one of the most obstinately contested fields of the Revolution.

sentence as above, '*Quid agis.*' After a short lesson was recited, and before they were dismissed, Mr. M'Millan requested Mr. Smith to close the exercise with prayer. Mr. Smith, in conclusion, was as solemn and appropriate as Mr.

Soon after his birth, his parents removed to Germantown, Pa., and the subject of this sketch distinctly remembered the battle of Germantown, which occurred when he was in the fifth year of his age. After a brief residence in York county, on the farm of George Ross, father of the late Hon. James Ross, his parents emigrated to the West, and took up their residence in Washington county, in 1779. About this time the attention of the Pioneers of our church was directed to the importance, not to say necessity, of training up a ministry for the Western churches from the West itself. In 1785, the Rev. Joseph Patterson, father of the deceased, commenced a course of theological study with the Rev. Joseph Smith, of Buffalo congregation, was licensed in 1788, and soon afterwards became pastor of the churches of Racoon and Montour's Run. In the Spring of 1791, the Rev. Robert Patterson commenced his studies at Canonsburg Academy, then just opened, reciting the first lesson in that institution, which has since grown up into Jefferson College. His interesting letter, given above, descriptive of the opening scene in the history of the Academy, and its organization under the shade of the sassafras bushes in a fence corner, on the banks of Chartiers, has been widely read. After prosecuting his studies for three years and a half at Canonsburg, Mr. Patterson, in the Fall of 1794, entered the senior class of the University of Pennsylvania, Philadelphia, where he graduated in 1795. On his way to Philadelphia, a journey then performed only on horseback, he met the forces sent out by Government to quell the Whisky Insurrection. After his graduation, Mr. Patterson was engaged, for nearly five years, as tutor in the University, and in the further prosecution of his classical and mathematical course. He returned to his father's residence, at Racoon, in April, 1800, and was licensed to preach in April, 1801, having pursued his theological studies with the Rev. Dr. Ashbel Green, one year in Philadelphia, and one year afterwards with the Rev. Dr. M'Millan. In August, 1801, he was united in marriage to Miss Jane, daughter of Col. John Canon, of Canonsburg; and in the Fall of 1802, was installed pastor of the congregations of Upper and Lower Greenfield, in the bounds of the Presbytery of Erie. In this pastoral charge, supplementing at the same time, a slender ministerial support by the working of a farm, he continued four and a half years; when, in April, 1807, he accepted an invitation to take charge of the Academy at Pittsburgh, now the Western University of Pennsylvania. During the three years he presided over this institution, he numbered among his pupils many who afterwards filled prominent public stations, and who often spoke in grateful terms of his care and faithfulness as an instructor.

Henderson had been in the beginning; and the little assembly retired much gratified, and with high expectations, which have been abundantly realized. The English school was soon vacated, and served for a place of recitation till autumn, when Col. Canon had so far progressed with a fine large stone building, as to afford convenient accommodation, both to teachers and students. Mr. Miller, who had been the teacher in the English school, was retained, and employed as professor

From 1810 to 1836, Mr. Patterson was engaged in the business of bookselling, and for a portion of the time in paper manufacturing, having been one of the proprietors of one of the first paper mills established in the West. His business operations carried on, more or less extensively, for more than a quarter of a century, and causing him to be widely known in this capacity, throughout the Western country many years ago, were attended with many changes and severe reverses. During the greater part of this time, Mr. Patterson was pastor of the Highlands congregation, in the Presbytery of Ohio. The people of this charge have often affectionately remembered his faithful ministrations through a long series of years, and the recollection of the relationship he had sustained to them, with its many pleasing associations, was a theme of grateful acknowledgment, on his part, to the latest period of his life. In 1840, Mr. Patterson removed from Pittsburgh a few miles into the country. So long as the infirmities of increasing age would permit, he manifested his continued interest in the service of his Divine Master, by preaching or lecturing occasionally in the congregation with which he worshiped. For many years the things unseen, and eternal, formed a prominent subject in almost every conversation in which he took part. Scarce an acquaintance, or even an entire stranger, who, in passing his late residence, has ever had with him the briefest interchange of friendly greeting, but could add his testimony to that of the Rev. R. Lea, who, in conducting the religious exercises at his funeral, remarked that he did not remember a single conversation with him for years, were the interview long or short, in which the subject of religion had not been introduced. But in his own home, his spirituality of character, and his heavenly mindedness, shone with their brightest lustre. On his death bed, he enjoyed great peace. His remarks and broken sentences showed that whilst affectionately regarding those around him, his thoughts were with that Saviour he was so soon to see. On Sabbath afternoon he lapsed into a state of almost lethargy, which continued with little interruption until Tuesday, September 5, 1854, when, without a struggle or a sigh, he fell asleep in Jesus. Thus died that excellent man, who, when a boy, under the sassafras bushes, read the first lesson in Corderii, at the opening of Canonsburg Academy.

in the mathematical sciences, and proved to be an instructor of the highest order, and continued to fill the place thirty or forty years; as long as he was able to discharge its duties. His memory is greatly cherished by hundreds, who were taught by him. In a short time, more students came from the region of country around than could have been generally expected, in a land that, a few years before, had been an Indian wilderness. On the roll, in a few weeks, were entered Abraham Scott, Robert Patterson, William Wylie, Thomas Swearengen, James Snodgrass, Ebenezer Henderson, James Duncan, James Allison, Joseph Doddridge, Darsey Pentecost, James Dunlavy, Daniel M'Lean, William Kerr, Philip Doddridge, and Alexander Campbell." *

The institution was got up by an association of ministers and citizens. They called themselves "Contributors to the Academy and Library;" and about the time above indicated, by previous appointment, they met, and chose by ballot, trustees. The charter, which they afterwards obtained, designated them "The Academy and Library Company." Their constitution required nine trustees, to be elected annually, by those who had contributed to the Academy and Library, and who were entitled to enjoy the benefits of the Library, agreeably to certain regulations. But of their earlier meetings, previous to the date of their charter, and of their mode of proceeding, nothing but tradition now remains. We do not know with certainty who were the *nine* first trustees. There can be little doubt, however, that they were nearly, if not quite, the same that we find in the recorded minutes in 1796. †

---

* Extract of a letter from Mr. Patterson to Dr. M. Brown, in 1845.

† When the academy was fairly under way, and the new building finished and opened for instructions, the trustees inserted in the Pittsburgh Gazette, in 1792, the following notice:

"The building for the Academy at Canonsburg is now finished, and the institution under good regulations. The Grammar School is taught by *Mr.*

The contributions for the support of the Academy were gathered from the congregations of the Presbyterians and Seceders through the Western country. The ministers were, in many cases, very active in gathering these offerings from their people. They consisted not solely in money, but in produce and articles of every description. These offerings, (chiefly by promise or subscription,) were made by nearly all Presbyterian congregations in the West, for the purpose both of refunding Col. Canon the cost of the Academy, and of aiding in payment of teachers, besides occasionally with a view of raising means to support, in part, young men who were candidates for the gospel ministry. The history of the proceedings of one minister, the *Rev. Joseph Patterson*, will suffice for a sample of what was generally done in the congregations west of the mountains. It appears, by the dates of the payments made by him, sometimes to Mr. M'Millan,

---

Johnston; and the English, Euclid's Elements of Geometry, Trigonometry, Plain and Spherical, with the latter's application to Astronomy; Navigaion, Surveying, Mensuration, Gauging, Dialing Conic Sections, Algebra, and Book-Keeping, by *Mr. Miller;* both well known for their attention and abilities. Boarding in the neighborhood to be had at good houses, at the low price of ten pounds, payable, principally, in produce. The situation is healthy, near the centre of Washington county; the fund raised by the Presbytery, and to be applied for the support of a certain number of scholars, annually, is directed by the Synod of the district to be appropriated to this Academy. It is hoped the public will regard with a favorable eye this institution, and give it all the encouragement that it may deserve.

"Nov. 2, 1792.

"N. B. The printers in the different States will please insert the above in their newspapers."

This is truly an interesting paper, proving that science and literature were opening their stores, on the very outskirts of civilization, at a period when the savages of the forest had not yet ceased to prowl around the borders of western settlements, and even to cherish the hope of repossessing Washington county as a hunting ground. If they could have read and understood this advertisement, they must have felt somewhat as *Hanibal* felt, when he found that the Romans were selling the lots on which his army was encamped at their gates. The above notice may be seen in the Lyceum, at Jefferson College.

as treasurer, and sometimes to Col. Canon, that the cost of the Academy was not all refunded for several years—some of the receipts being as late as 1794–5. There are found among the papers of Mr. Patterson, two subscription rolls of different date, but containing in part the same names; the latest of the two being dated in June, 1794; the last also stating that it was for the purpose both of finishing the Academy, and for aid to poor and pious students. One of the papers has about one hundred and twenty names, and the other not quite one hundred. But little was paid at the time of subscribing; and but little, at any time, in money; great part in grain, wheat, rye; and no small portion in linen; the linen, chiefly by the ladies: some by widows, and some by wives and daughters of the men who had subscribed. The sums were in Pennsylvania currency; and a large portion of them did not exceed 3s. 9d.—7s. 6d., and a few advanced to 10s. and 15s., and still fewer to £1. The grain was delivered in mills, and then sold. The linen was sometimes delivered to the Treasurer, to be disposed of as he could, at 1s. 1½d., per yard, or 25 cents. One subscription was to be paid in *Whisky!* All are reported on the papers to have been fully paid; and the amount of both subscriptions reached nearly $350.

The following subscription paper will be found very interesting:

"June 9th, 1794. We, whose names are hereunto signed, desirous to forward the Academy building, at Canonsburg, do promise, for that purpose, to pay, or deliver into some mill, in the bounds of the Rev. Joseph Patterson's congregation, the quantities of wheat or rye annexed to our names, and deliver the receipts thereof to said Patterson, on or before the end of this present year."

The following may be selected among the long list of names found on this interesting paper:

James Ewing, 5 bushels of wheat, at 2 shillings.
William Flanegan, 1 " " " "
Robert Moor, 2 " " " "
John Logan, 2 " " " "
James Laird, 4 " " " "
Samuel Riddle, (in money,) 7s. 6d.
John M'Millan, cash, $1.
Joseph Patterson, cash, $6.
Mrs. Vallandingham, 6 yards of linen.
Mrs. Elenor Thompson, 3 yards of linen.
John Kelso, 4 bushels of wheat.
John Thompson, 4 " "
James M'Bride, 3 bushels of rye.
Hugh M'Coy, 4 " "
Alexander M'Candless, 2 bushels of wheat.
John Cardike, (a pious negro,) 2 bushels of wheat.
George Vallandingham, cash, 7s. 6d.
Mrs. Nesbit, 3 yards of linen.
Widow Riddle, 3 " "
Her daughter Mary, 3 " "

"The value of these old papers," says Professor R. Patterson, who furnished them to Dr. Brown, "consists in their exhibiting the spirit of the enterprise, the objects for which the institution was founded, and the humble resources of its patrons. Such unassuming donations as two or three yards of linen, four or five bushels of wheat, rye or corn, four pounds of tea, would astonish the present race of students at Canonsburg." In this manner, for the noblest purpose, among a simple and hard working people, in the seclusion of the valley of Chartiers, was laid the foundation of a retreat for learning, whose halls would be resorted to, and whose influence felt, when the country, at that time a wilderness, would be teeming with a busy and enterprising population. May the far-sighted sagacity and wide-reaching philanthropy of its sires descend upon its sons. Then and there commenced an institution whose pupils were thereafter to be found in every honorable profession in their native country—in the sacred desk, at the bed-side of the sick, in the courts of justice, and in legislative halls. Others bearing the everlasting gospel to distant shores, exerting their abilities, acquired or strengthened here, to elevate and enlighten the infidel European, the superstitious Hindoo, the degraded Chinese, and the wild Indian of our own land. In view of the circumstances attending the formation of this institution, the sons of Jefferson College need not fear that their Alma Mater will be like

> "The tower which builders vain,
> Presumptuous piled on Shinar's plain."

Thus began the Canonsburg Academy, and such the history of the first years of its existence. It began in prayer and was supported by religious patriotism; and, therefore, no wonder it has remarkably flourished and gained a noble rank among the literary institutions of the United States.

In the year 1794 a charter was granted, incorporating the trustees of "The Academy and Library Company, in the town of Canonsburg." This charter or act of incorporation was granted by the Supreme Court of Pennsylvania, of which Judge M'Kean was the Chief Justice, agreeably to an act of the Legislature, April 6, 1791, entitled, "An act to confer on certain citizens of this Commonwealth, the power and immunities of bailies, politic and law." This gave it a legal existence. This charter the venerable founders did not get till the institution was some years advanced in its glorious career. But, as Dr. Brown says, "They had a charter from a higher authority than the Legislature of Pennsylvania, or the Supreme Court, venerable as it then was. They sought and obtained a charter from the Court of Heaven." It is obvious that neither the Presbyteries, nor the church as such, acted officially, or were, in any way, recognised in the whole proceedings. It was the "Academy and Library Company."

We do not believe that those good men would have had the smallest objection that the Presbyteries of Redstone and Ohio, and the Seceder Presbytery of Chartiers, should hold whatever relation, officially, they might have preferred. But it was, perhaps, regarded as wiser, on all hands, that the institution, being a candidate for an act of incorporation, for Legislative aid, and eventually for a College charter, should be divested of an ecclesiastical character. There was, at that time, much inveterate prejudice, in reference to ecclesiastical endowments, by legislative enactments. If the Academy had assumed the name and form of such an institution as was contemplated by the Synod of Virginia, it would have probably been refused a charter and all legislative aid, and, in that event, could scarcely have been sustained. Our forefathers, both lay and clerical, were, in these matters, wise and good men.

From 1796 down to the period to which we propose to extend this historical sketch, we shall derive our principal aid from the records which were kept by the trustees. Previous to that time no minutes of their proceedings are to be found. These old records begin in this form: "January 25, 1796. The trustees of Canonsburg Academy met at Col. Canon's, according to appointment. Members present Robert Ralston, John M'Dowell, Thomas Brecken, John Canon, James Foster, James Allison, and Alexander Cook." Mr. Allison was chosen president, and Mr. Cook, clerk. On the opposite page there is a statement without any date, as to the year, "of a meeting, on the first Tuesday of October, of a number of contributors, who proceeded to vote, by ballot, for trustees of the Academy and Library, the result of which was, that John Canon, John M'Dowell, Craig Ritchie, Robert Ralston, Thomas Brecken, James Allison, James Foster, David Gault, and Alexander Cook were duly elected." But as no date of year is given, we cannot tell whether it was in October, immediately previous to the January meeting, above noticed, or back, some years before, at the original formation of this first literary association of the West. The latter, we are inclined to suppose from the prominent place this minute occupies—being entered on the blank leaf which precedes the regular recorded minutes. At this meeting, in January, 1796, the trustees prepared and adopted a petition to the Legislature of the State, praying, that if they should establish a College on this side the mountains, they would fix it at Canonsburg. As it may be read with interest by many, we will here insert it:

"That your petitioners, confiding in your patriotism and good wishes, for the interest and advantage of this extensive Western country, whose population is daily increasing with an astonishing rapidity—having also much at heart the education of our youth, and understanding that a law was in some forwardness, last year, for the establishing of a College on this side the mountains—humbly beg leave to request, that if such a pleasing event may take place, due regard may be had to the most convenient place and other local advantages, hence deriving our hopes that this village will attract your favorable notice. That your petitioners are firmly persuaded this town merits a decided preference, on many considerations. The situation is remarkably healthy. The inhabitants of the town and its vicinity are generally sober, orderly and religious. Being in the heart of a very fertile country, and at a considerable distance from any public market, produce must necessarily continue low. There was, some time since, a handsome stone building erected, and nearly finished, wherein a respectable number of youth have been instructed in classical literature and the mathematics, and in which one hundred students may be commodiously taught. Boarding and lodging may be obtained in decent families, at from £12 to £15 per annum. That any fund appropriated by the Legislature, for the erection of suitable buildings, for a College, would thus, in some measure, be anticipated, should the honorable House think fit to give this place their sanction, and might be converted to its interest some other way. From these considerations, and others that might be mentioned, we humbly hope you will grant this to be the place for a public institution. And your petitioners, as in duty bound, will ever pray, &c., &c.

"Signed by order of the Board,

"JAMES ALLISON, *President.*

"*Test—*

"ALEXANDER COOK, *Clerk.*"

They notice, also, that their clerk had received and paid over to Mr. Ritchie, two pounds, sixteen shillings and seven pence, for the use of the Academy, from Mr. Saunders, being the half of the proceeds of two nights exhibition. Of the nature of this gentleman's performances, nothing is recorded.

At the next meeting of the trustees, May 3, 1796, after electing Mr. Ritchie, treasurer, they directed him to call upon the students to receive their respective sums, quarterly, or what part of a quarter may be due, when the general payments shall be made; and to keep an accurate list of the names of the students, together with their entry and departure from the school. These lists to be furnished by the "masters." They also fixed the price of tuition at five pounds per annum, and directed the treasurer to pay the "masters" quarterly. There is then introduced this interesting minute, out of chronological order; and why so, is no where explained:

"Whereas this day, being the 28th of April, 1796, it is jointly agreed by the Reverend Presbytery of Ohio and the Trustees of the Canonsburg Academy, to employ two masters to teach the Latin and Greek languages, in the said Academy, to commence from the 2d day of May, 1796, viz.: *Mr. David Johnston* and *Mr. James Mountain;* each master aforesaid to receive the sum of ninety pounds specie for one year; and to be paid quarterly, in equal dividends; for which we jointly and severally become bound, as witness our hands the day and date above written

Presbytery	*Trustees.*
"JOHN M'MILLAN,	JAMES ALLISON,
"JOSEPH PATTERSON,	JOHN M'DOWELL,
"JAMES HUGHS,	JOHN CANON,
"JOHN BRICE,	THOMAS BRECKEN,
"THOMAS MARQUIS,	ALEXANDER COOK,
"THOMAS MOORE,	JOHN FOSTER,
"BOYD MERCER.	CRAIG RITCHIE."

At the adjourned August meeting of the Trustees, they appointed a committee to adjust the balance due Col. Canon, on behalf of the Academy, and give him assurance of payment, in three months, upon receiving from him a legal conveyance of the Academy lot, and appurtenances. In October, of the same year, a number of contributors met, pursuant to their rule, selected by ballot, as Trustees for the ensuing year, the Rev. Messrs. Joseph Patterson, Thomas Marquis, and Boyd Mercer, and Messrs. James Allison, John Canon, Alexander Cook, James Foster, John M'Dowell, and Craig Ritchie. These Trustees met November 14, 1796, and elected Judge M'Dowell, President; Mr. Ritchie, Treasurer; and Mr. Cook, Clerk. They also took measures for surveying and securing the Academy lot, appointed an usher to assist Mr. Mountain, and increased his salary ten pounds, for the present year. *Mr. David Johnston*, who had been absent, and out of their employment for some time, wrote to the Trustees to inquire whether they wished again to employ him as teacher. This, they informed him, the state of the school would not permit them to do; assuring him, at the same time, that no man would be more acceptable. Some service of the county, perhaps in one of its public offices, then engaged the time of Mr. Johnston; and the Trustees intimated to him, as another reason for declining to employ him, that the county would probably still engage his services. (Perhaps he had formerly withdrawn from their service, on account of more lucrative employment; and they would now give him a mild hint of it.) They agreed, however, that his family might still occupy the house belonging to the Academy property; in which they resided till the first of May.

The last meeting of the Trustees, during this year, occurred December 1, 1796. They authorized the President to give Col. Canon a bond for one hundred pounds, as the balance due him, on sundry accounts, incurred by building the Academy, making the Academy responsible for the above sum to the present Trustees, with interest upon the same until paid. *Joseph Stockton*, (afterwards the Rev. J. Stockton,) was continued an assistant tutor, with a salary of £25 per annum.

During this period, the two Presbyteries of Ohio and Redstone, as appears from their records, continued to watch over this institution with sedulous care. The Presbytery of Ohio, at their usual Spring meeting, recorded that, "it was found upon inquiry, that something considerable had been collected towards defraying the expenses of the building of the Academy in Canonsburg; but, as enough had not yet been raised, it was again recommended to the members to continue their endeavors, and make report at their next Fall meeting." And at that meeting they renewed their recommendation, stating that "necessity now required vigorous efforts for the purpose." The Presbytery of Redstone sent their commissioners to attend upon the examination of the students; who, at their following meeting, made a favorable report. The Academy was rising in reputation, and increasing in number of students. The employment, for some time, of *James Mountain, Esq.*, as teacher of Languages, was propitious to the school. He was a thorough classical scholar, a polished gentleman of the old school in his manners, and afterwards became a very respectable lawyer. He also became, in subsequent years, a trustee; and we well remember, in our college days, of dreading his presence, when about to be examined on Latin or Greek. It was said he had nearly the whole of Homer's Iliad in his memory, and could recite long passages of it, with great fluency. His services as an instructor in the classical department of the Academy ended with April, 1797, as he insisted upon a higher salary than the Trustees felt warranted to give. There was then a successful effort made to secure the services of Messrs. *Carnahan* and *Stockton,* for £25 each, for six months. Mr. Carnahan, however, made it a condition that he should be at liberty to withdraw at any time after the space of three months, upon his giving two weeks' notice. This arrangement was made in April, 1797. *Mr. Watson,* who was then in his senior year, and about to graduate the ensuing Fall, at Princeton College, was probably already in the eye of the Trustees, and especially of Dr. M'Millan, for the arduous work of conducting the most important department of their Academy. Mr. Patterson had already jotted down in his Diary, (March 14, 1796,) "I hear Mr. M'Millan intends visiting Princeton, in May, in order to the return of Messrs. Watson and Hughs." The Trustees, in anticipation of Mr. Watson's coming, had resolved, and entered it on their minutes, "that they would employ him as Teacher." On September 27, 1797, they agreed with him, "To teach the Academy for twelve months, beginning from the first Tuesday of November next; and the money arising from the students under his care, he accepts, as full compensation for his labors; and to be collected in the same manner as usual." He was also to employ an usher, when they might think it necessary. The Trustees were re-elected October 3d, for the ensuing year.

During the session of the Legislature, nothing was done for the Academy. The number of students was thirty-five, and five in Mr. Miller's department. It was a period of much religious prosperity also: for the Rev. Joseph Patterson notes in his Diary: "I hear that there is not one student now in the Academy, but appears to have religion, or is a subject of sharp awakenings." This was June 29, 1797. The following persons are mentioned, as regular members of the two literary societies, (the Philo and Franklin,) then formed among the students, for that year. We give their names, with the titles they bore in after life, just as they are given in the catalogues of the Societies.

PHILO SOCIETY.

Rev. John Watson,
Ex-President of Jefferson College,
Rev. Jno. Boggs, Pa.,
Rev. Robert Lee,
Rev. Robert Johnston, Pa.,
Rev. Wm. M'Millan, D. D.,
Ex-Pres't. of Jeff. and Frank. Colleges,
Rev. Wm. Moorehead,
Rev. James Satterfield,
Rev. Samuel Tate,
Rev. J. Smith,
Wm. Fowler,
Rev. Elisha Macurdy,
Rev. John M'Lain,
Rev. Joseph Stockton,
Rev. Abraham Boyd,
David Rennalls,
William Carr,

FRANKLIN SOCIETY.

Rev. James Carnahan, D. D.,
Ex-President of Princeton College,
Rev. Cephas Dodd, Amity, Pa.,
Rev. J. Galbraith, Clarion Co., Pa.
Rev. T. E. Hughs, Darlington, Pa.,
Rev. Jacob Lindley,
Ex-President of Ohio University,
Rev. Stephen Lindley, Ohio,
Rev. Wm. Wood, Mercer, Pa.,
Rev. Wm. Wick, Pa.,
Rev. Johnston, Eaton, Erie Co., Pa.
Dr. James Power, Pa.,
Rev. Alex. Monteith, Pa.,
James Marshall,
Rev. James Hughs.

It is probable that in both these lists there are some errors, but we suppose they are substantially correct. They were not all students of the college, but some of them were members of the faculty. They present a noble set of names. There are several still living—the Rev. Messrs. Robert Johnston, James Satterfield, James Carnahan, D. D., Cephas Dodd, J. Galbraith, Jacob Lindley, and Dr. James Power. As this year is memorable, in the history of the Academy, for the organization of the above mentioned literary societies, it may be more proper here than elsewhere to give some further account of them. They were founded by graduates of Princeton. The *Philo Literary Society* was founded by the Rev. John Watson, the first President of the College, August 23, 1797; and the *Franklin Literary Society* was founded, November 14, 1797, by Dr. James Carnahan, who had been a pupil of Watson's, and afterwards teacher for some time, in the Academy, in connection with the Rev. Thos. E. Hughs, who we know was also a graduate of Princeton. Some of the founders and earliest members of these societies still survive; and the names of those who have gone to their rest, will be remembered with honor and affection, by numerous friends and relatives. They were generally ministers of the gospel; and surviving friends will be gratified to find their names recorded among the founders of these two fraternities. "As the charter, constitution, and laws of Jefferson College," says Dr. Brown, in an unpublished life of Dr. M'Millan, "were evidently formed on the model of Princeton, so it may be presumed that the constitution, rules and exercises of the Literary Societies, were formed on the plan of the societies at Princeton. The founders had been members of the Cliosophic or Whig Societies at Nassau Hall, and of course would introduce into the new societies, whatever they deemed most valuable, adapting them to the condition and habits of the students, and state of society, in the new settlement of the country. * * * These societies have been greatly useful. They have been important auxiliaries to the College in discipline, in maintaining good order, and in training the minds of the students to habits of attention, accurate discrimination, and argumentation, so as to improve in composition and oratory, to an extent not to be attained in the ordinary exercises of the college. Here, too, young men, accustomed to observe the strictest parliamentary rules, in their discussions, if called to the halls of legislation, or to act a part in popular assemblies, either ecclesiastical or civil, are at once prepared to take an active part in the discussions. * * * It may be added, as deserving special notice, that there was, from the first, an important exercise introduced into these societies, which had not been introduced at Princeton, nor any of the eastern colleges. We refer to the Literary *Contest* between the two societies, in *composition, oratory,* and *debate.* This takes place once a year. Judges are appointed to decide on the merits of the performances. These exercises, though attended with some disadvantages, have had a most powerful influence in stimulating the students to aspire after excellence in these attainments. The *Contest,* first introduced at Canonsburg, was afterwards adopted in Washington College, and since, by a number of Seminaries in the West and South. The societies are secret, to some extent; their constitution, rules and proceedings, are kept secret. But they are not secret, *affiliated* societies, bound together by one common bond—subject to one superior power, to give laws to the subordinates; and thus, by an unseen, powerful influence, control the whole. Such societies are evidently of dangerous tendency—are odious to the great body of Christians, and have had a most unhappy influence in the church, and on the community at large. The literary societies in college are not, as stated, *affiliated,* but rival institutions. They cannot combine to effect evil purposes. Members of the Faculty are also members of these societies; and no plot or combination could occur without their knowledge. It is absurd to plead their example in justification of secret affiliated combinations, bound by solemn oaths and pledges, held by many of them as of higher obligation than the oath administered by civil authority. Within a few years past, some new orders of secret societies have been introduced into colleges, and have their connection in most of the literary institutions of the United States. Their tendency is most dangerous. Linked together by sacred badges and oaths, their influence has been, in many places, disastrous. It is to be deeply regretted that they have had influence to induce members of the church, and some beneficiaries to join them. It is to the honor of the Literary Societies of Jefferson College, that they have taken a noble stand against them—adopted resolutions to expel any who are known to adhere to them. Still, it has been found difficult to detect them, and their pernicious influence is still experienced to some extent. Unless these societies are put down, the consequence must be ruinous to all colleges in our country, as to morals, discipline, and substantial learning." Thus wrote the late venerable President of Jefferson College, whose wisdom and experience of college life gave him a right to speak "*ex-Cathedra.*" He does not speak too strongly, we apprehend, on this delicate subject. The Trustees of Princeton College have recently determined to root out these secret societies from their institution. We hope they have succeeded. And we hope the Trustees of Jefferson College will follow their example. Though the above extract is somewhat long, we thought it due to Dr. M. Brown to give him a full hearing on this subject. * The attention of the Presbyteries of Ohio,

* We are well aware that it will require no ordinary prudence, as well as energetic decision, on the part of Faculties and Boards of Colleges, to suppress these secret associations. Young men are apt to regard such measures as an unreasonable, tyrannical, and oppressive exercise of authority; and as an infringement of their rights. It is not easy to convince them that such societies are of a dangerous tendency; and that a larger experience will eventually satisfy them that here is a case in which their relinquishment of an apparently harmless practice is due to the general welfare of colleges, and to the judgment and wishes of older heads. The co-operation of enlightened public opinion, and especially of the great body of the Alumni of our colleges, now engaged in the active scenes of life, would, perhaps, be of essential service, in giving practical efficiency to the efforts of the officers of colleges, in rooting out secret clubs. In what way such co-operation could be secured, we leave for the consideration of others. With the co-operation of public opinion, and of those who have formerly been students in our colleges, the Faculties and Trustees could scarcely fail in effecting the extinction of secret societies. But *reason, kindness,* and *persuasion,* not harsh decrees and menaces of expulsion, should be used. As we design to give a more extended historical sketch of the two Literary Societies, together with a list of the questions discussed at their *Contests,* we shall not here extend our remarks.

and of Redstone, during the period under review in this chapter, was directed with renewed zeal, to the interests of this child of their adoption. In the course of 1797, we find on the minutes of Redstone Presbytery, no less than three notices about it—first at their meeting at Fairfield, April 18, 1797. "The Committee appointed, at our last meeting, to assist the Presbytery of Ohio in an examination of the students, and an inquiry into the state of the Academy at Canonsburg, brought in their report, which was read and adopted." Then at Dunlap's Creek, June 28, 1797. And also recommended contributions by their next meeting, "finding that the Academy at Canonsburg labors under very great difficulties, from want of some pecuniary aid." Again, at Rehoboth, October 18, 1797, they repeat the recommendation to raise contributions, and appoint an examining committee. Lastly, at Pigeon Creek, December 26, 1797, the Presbytery of Ohio reiterate the same call for aid to the funds of the Academy.

CHAPTER III.

THE ACADEMY BECOMING A COLLEGE.

Trustees and Officers—Another Petition to Legislature—*Judge Edgar*—Presbytery of Redstone—Old Mr. Patterson's account of Academy in 1798—Rules and Regulations—Colonel Canon's death and character—Legislative aid—New Movement to get College Charter—Act of Trustees, about conditions of preaching in Academy—Members added to the Societies—Change of Constitution in 1798—Names of Trustees—Charter of Jefferson College, in 1802—Why called after Mr. Jefferson—Good reasons for the name—New Trustees—New Rules—*Mr. Watson*, 1st President; his death and character—*Mr. Dunlap* elected President; his character.

We are now entering upon a period fraught with facts and incidents of no less interest, in their bearing upon the character and prospects of the rising Academy and future College than those of any previous period. The trustees, at their first meeting this year, in April, elected Judge M'Dowell, President, and Craig Ritchie, Esq., Clerk. The Board also appointed Dr. M'Millan, *President of the Academy*. This seems to have been merely an honorary office, at this time, and not requiring anything further than a general supervision of the institution. It may also be noted, that at the same meeting, they resolved they would, thenceforward, begin and close their sessions with prayer. This pious resolution, with all serious minds, will satisfactorily account for the eminent wisdom and judgment which guided most of their subsequent deliberations. They also fixed Professor Miller's salary, at this time, at £100; and as the income then was not sufficient to make up this sum, the trustees, themselves, pledged various amounts, from £10 to £3, as a loan, to be afterwards refunded.

Dr. M'Millan stands at the head of the list, for £10. Messrs. Patterson, Hughs, Moore, Marquis, and D. Smith for from £6 to £4; and Messrs. Allison, Edgar and Ritchie, £3 each. At their October meeting they appointed Messrs. Findley, Edgar and Ritchie, a committee to draught another petition and memorial to the State Legislature, for pecuniary assistance to the institution; which was afterwards reported and adopted, and being signed by the President, Judge M'Dowell, was committed to the Hon. William Findley, Judge M'Dowell, and John Wright, Esq., to be forwarded by them to the Legislature. This petition, differing materially from the former one in its object, contains some new items of interest, and some arguments very forcibly put, and will repay a perusal. It is as follows:

"*To the Senate and House of Representatives of the Commonwealth of Pennsylvania, in General Assembly met*:—The memorial and petition of the Academy and Library Company, of the town of Canonsburg, in the county of Washington, respectfully showeth—That the said Academy and Library was originated and carried on by the attention and at the expense, chiefly, of a few public spirited citizens, residing in the town and vicinity of Canonsburg, and that, owing to the convenience of accommodation, the low price of boarding, and the care that has been taken to provide suitable teachers, this institution has been very beneficial in promoting the education of youth. In the course of a few years past, twenty-one young men, who are now employed in the professions of divinity, law and medicine, received the rudiments of their education at this school; nine others have also completed their classical education, and are pursuing the studies requisite to qualify them for one or other of the learned professions. Thirty-two are at present employed in learning the languages, and acquiring the knowledge of the Mathematics and Natural Philosophy. One master, and assistant, are employed in teaching the learned languages, and another teacher, the other branches. Each of the masters has had a regular and extensive education; and they are men of fair character. The tuition money for teaching the languages, though the charge is moderate, is nearly sufficient to defray the expense of that part of instruction. But the profits arising from teaching the mathematics and natural philosophy, come far short of the expense, though the teaching of them is indispensable to the institution. We trust we are warranted in saying, that the said Academy has been more successful, notwithstanding the want of public aid, than any or all of the other institutions in the western counties of Pennsylvania. Permit us to add that there is a convenient house erected for the purpose, at the personal expense of the trustees, with the assistance of private contributions; but the Library is so small as to be wholly insufficient for the purpose. From this view of the situation of the Academy and Library, of which we are trustees, we hope that the Legislature will, in pursuance of the powers vested in them by the Constitution, be convinced of the propriety of granting such assistance to this institution, as they, in their wisdom, shall judge proper. They will, no doubt, think with us, that it will be a public injury to suffer it to perish, after having been productive of so much good, and having its character for usefulness so well established. We are also sufficiently warranted in saying, that no place in Pennsylvania affords cheaper accommodations for students, and that the situation is central to all the western counties, and very little exposed to public resort, or such amusements as have a tendency to corrupt the morals of young men, or divert them from their studies. We further assure the Legislature, that if public assistance is not given, the institution cannot be carried on to advantage, nor the library be rendered competent. We beg leave to state that petitions in behalf of this Institution, and a Bill, read the second time, for granting assistance to it, are on the files of a former Assembly. Hoping that the Legislature will enable the Trustees to support an Institution which has already been productive of so much good, at the charge of a few public spirited citizens, your petitioners, as in duty bound, will ever pray, &c.

"Signed,

"JOHN M'DOWELL, *President.*

"Attested by the Secretary."

The Trustees again advanced, on individual loan, various sums, as before, to secure the continued services of *Professor Miller.* They also elected *Judge Edgar* President of the Board, for the ensuing year, and adopted a variety of by-laws for their own benefit. Nothing further as to the doings of the Trustees seems to claim attention at this time. Mr. Patterson says, as to this period: "The Academy appears to flourish under the tuition of Messrs. Watson and Hughs." Again, October 24, 1798: "This morning I am setting out to attend the examination at Canonsburg. It is expected that Mr. Watson will continue at the Academy, where the power of God yet appears among the students." Again, the next day: "Canonsburg Institution here is truly useful." The *Philo Literary Society,* report as belonging to the year 1798, the following additional regular members: "The Rev. Reed Brecken, Pa., Rev. James Robinson, Rev. Robert M'Garragh, Rev. Alexander Boyd, Thos. Vincent, Caleb Baldwin, John Findley." The *Franklin Literary Society,* for the same period, the following: "The Rev. Messrs. Andrew M'Donald, Nicholas Pittinger, Smiley Hughs, Wm. Neil, D. D., Ex-President Dickinson College, Pa., Daniel Milliken, James Ramsey, D. D., Ex-Professor Hebrew, Jefferson College, and Messrs. Wm. Hartley, Thos. M'Giffen, Esq., Washington, Pa.; Hon. Geo. Torrence, Cincinnati, Ohio; George Paul, and Wm. Jones.

In the following year, the Trustees adopted some excellent regulations, in regard to the course of instruction. They prescribed a curriculum of studies, which they would require, in order to secure their final Latin certificate. They prescribed, as to the Latin course, besides the common introductory books, "the three first books of '*Selectae e profanis*,' six books of *Ovid*, the *Eclogues* and *Georgics* of Virgil, and the first six Aeneids; all *Horace*, and the *Orations of Cicero*. Then, in the Greek, the usual parts of the *Greek New Testament*. The first four Books of Xenophon's Cyropædia, and four Books of Homer's Iliad. In Mathematics, "the whole of Arithmetic." "The first six books of *Euclid's Elements*," "Simpson's Algebra" to the 50th problem, or the equivalent in some other author. "Trigonometry, Surveying, Martin's Natural Philosophy, Astronomy and Geography, comprising the use of the Globes." Also "Rhetoric, Logic, and Moral Philosophy." But they did not prescribe the authors to be studied in these branches. This course, thus prescribed, will give us some idea of the extent of educational training then attempted. Though very inferior, in some respects, and, indeed, altogether wanting in various branches of science, now considered essential to a thorough college course, it was nevertheless suited to those times, and certainly laid a good foundation of scholarship, which, in many cases, was afterward matured to a degree of attainment, in no respect inferior to the liberal education attainable anywhere in our country, at that period. We believe there were as large a proportion of respectable scholars prepared and trained in this way, *then* as *now*. The Latin certificate ran in this form:

"Præses et Curatores Academiae Canonsburgiensis, omnibus et singulis, literas lecturis, Salutem in Domino. Notum sit, A. B , artibus liberalibus, in hac Academia, datis operam dedisse, et harum ejus peritiam examine accurato esse approbatam, cujus nomina nostra huic membranæ, subscripta sint testimonium.

"Datum Academiae Canon.	"Nomina Presidis,
"Octavo Kalendarum Nov.	"et
"Anno Domini—"	"Curatorum.

The Trustees resolved also to mention publicly the names of such students as were remarkable for their industry and accuracy; and also those who should be marked for their indolence and deficiency, at every public examination. And at every Fall Examination they determined to designate *four* students, whom they shall think most deserving, as accurate diligent scholars, two of them being of the Mathematical School, the other two of the Languages; which students, in the order in which they shall be mentioned by the Trustees, as meritorious, shall have the privilege of choosing their places of speaking, on the day of public exhibition, and of wearing honorary badges; which privileges shall be granted to no other students at that time. These regulations, no doubt, exerted a salutary influence in those early days of the Academy. At a meeting of the Trustees, April 23, 1799, the Board proceeded to the choice of a Trustee, in the place of *Col. John Canon*, deceased; and the Rev John M'Millan was duly elected. It is thus we incidentally learn the fact of the recent death of that early friend and patron of the Academy, whose name should stand high on the roll of its venerable founders. He lived to see that school, to which he was so much attached, and to the interests of which he devoted so much of his care and time and money, fairly on the way in its glorious career. * Immediately following the above minute, it is added: "On motion, adopted as a rule that any person who receives a salary from this Academy, shall not be a trustee." This was entered, no doubt, to show

* "*Col. Canon*, the founder of Canonsburg, was an active, intelligent, and gentlemanly man. He died when but little past the meridian of life; leaving a widow and several children. Mrs. Canon was regarded as the lady of the place, and deservedly; for she was eminently pious, friendly, and generous. Her house was the seat of hospitality, the favorite resort of Christian ministers, and serious students. She and all her children are dead, except Mrs. Patterson, widow of the late Rev. R. Patterson, a lady of quiet worth, and attractive social qualities."—*Dr. Neill in Pres. Mag. Feb.* 1857, *page* 87.

that Dr. M'Millan's election, though nominally Principal of the Academy, yet, as he received no salary, was unexceptionable; and could not, therefore, be made a precedent for a a similar election of a member of the Faculty, unless he was merely an honorary member.

The ensuing year, 1800, was signalized in the history of the Institution, by a Legislative grant of $1,000; which, no doubt, though long deferred, was most seasonable; and for awhile relieved the Academy from pressing embarrassments. Besides discharging several debts, it enabled the Trustees to make repairs and alterations of their house, and to purchase a small supply of Philosophical Apparatus. It is worthy of notice, also, that the trustees, with scarcely an exception, threw up their claims for the several sums they had loaned the Institution. Though they were almost all of them in very moderate circumstances, they were a noble, public-spirited set of men, who willingly made great sacrifices for the Academy. Their names should be had in everlasting remembrance. A movement was now made (in October, 1800) to get the Academy converted into a College. The appropriation which they had received from the Legislature, encouraged them to make the effort. They accordingly appointed Messrs. M'Millan, Allison, Cook, and Ritchie to draft a petition for this purpose. Their memorial is not on record; but we can well conceive, from their former petitions, what was its general drift. It was not, however, granted the ensuing winter. Not till January 15, 1802, did the General Assembly pass that important act. In the meantime, though little of importance occurred in the history of the Academy, during its short remaining existence, we may note a few things. One item that now appears rather amusing, is that, in October, 1800, the Trustees passed an order, "That no minister be permitted to preach in the Academy, except those of the Presbyterian or Seceding denominations; and the latter only upon their paying one dollar for each day they are permitted to use it." At this distant period, we should not be hasty in forming our judgments of the character of this measure. Such a rule, were it now adopted, would bring down upon the Board the charge of being intolerant bigots. Yet, without any want of Christian liberality, these good men of those days might have found it necessary to protect the Academy from Sectarian attempts at forward and impudent intrusion, to the great annoyance of the place, and interruption of the regular exercises of the school. We know, from the earlier history of many sects, which are now not generally characterized by extravagant irregularities, that the most brazen-faced impudence was sometimes practiced. We have no doubt the rule of the trustees was, for those times, wise and seasonable, and sustained by the good sense and general approbation of the community. Old Mr. Patterson jotted down in his Diary, for this period, "Elisha Macurdy writes, 'our school is in a much better situation than formerly.'" During the last three years of the Academy, namely, 1799, 1800, 1801, there was a class of young men in attendance, that, in respect to their solid worth, and future distinguished usefulness and influence in various walks of life, were not exceeded by any similar number from any other college in the United States. The *Franklin Society* enrolled, during these years, the Rev. Messrs. Clement Valandingham, James Gilleland, James R. Wilson, D. D., Cincinnati, Ohio, and Gilbert M'Master, D. D., Cincinnati, Ohio; and Messrs. Ethan Baldwin, Esq., George Bird, Esq., Bedford, Pa.; Nathaniel Giffin, Esq., John White, M. D., Abraham Carmichael, John M'Donald, Esq., Pittsburgh; Joseph Patterson, Esq., Washington Parkinson, Daniel Heisler, Esq., John Bell, John St. Clair, Anthony Rollins, David Young, Andrew Shannon, David Allerater, Samuel Jenkins, Eliezer Jenkins, Matthew Williams, and Joseph Dunlap. The *Philo Society*, during the same time, claimed the following list: The Rev. Messrs. Thos. Marquis, Cyrus Riggs, John Harshe, James Boyd, James Scott, Moses Allen, John

Rea, D. D., and Abraham Scott; and Messrs. John Cameron, James Taylor, Marcus Haglin, Charles Moorland, Isaac Cowden, John Purviance, James Blackstone, David Drennan, Crawford White, Robert Gordon, James Wilson, Benjamin Boyd, James Cunningham, James Hoge, James Carr, Peter Ross, Joseph Colwell, James Walker, Rev. Thomas Hunt, John Creaton, Benjamin Woods, A. Thompson, John Vandyke, James Veset, William M'Millan, Jr., Rev. Messrs. Alexander Murray, and James Culbertson, D. D., Jared Smith, and Josiah Scott. These names have not always the proper designation attached to them. For instance, Andrew Shannon, James Cunningham, and James Hoge, we think were ministers of the gospel; the last, the Rev. James Hoge, D. D., of Columbus, Ohio, the Presbyterian Apostle of Ohio, who, though he did not graduate at Canonsburg, but perhaps at Hampden Sidney College, in Virginia, was a student, for some time, at Jefferson College. Several of the above named persons became eminent, in various professional and civil stations. Jefferson College, in her palmiest days in after years, need never be ashamed of her Academical history. We have thought the introduction of these names of students of the *old Academy* would be interesting to many, especially as but few of them occur in the College catalogue, (which will be found in our Appendix,) as that catalogue begins with the date of the Institution when it became a College.

We have now reached a very important era in the history of this Institution. It was about to emerge from its crysalis state. It was about to assume the loftier name, and more commanding position of a College. It had, indeed, passed through an important change in 1798. Amendments to its constitution, affecting considerable changes, were secured by a new charter. The trustees were no longer, under the new charter, elected annually, but for life; and when vacancies occurred by death or otherwise, the corporate trustees elected others to supply the vacancy. In other words, it became a close corporation. The number of trustees then amounted to twenty-one. Of these we find that thirteen were clergymen, and eight, laymen, although there was no provision in the constitution designating the proportion, as was afterwards the case in the College charter.* An application, it will be remembered, had been made by the Trustees to the Legislature, in 1796, that if they were about to establish a college west of the mountains, as they, the trustees, understood such a law was in forwardness, the previous year, for that purpose, they, the Legislature, would have due regard to the claims of Canonsburg, as a convenient place, and possessing other local advantages, &c. But it has been seen that this movement failed. They now resumed under better auspices, their efforts with the Legislature, to get a charter for a college. Accordingly, an Act was passed, January 15, 1802, establishing a college at Canonsburg, to be called *Jefferson College*. Who had given it this name, whether the Trustees, in their petition, or whether the Legislature, as some have supposed, is not clearly ascertained. The memorial to the Legislature is not on record. Nor have we access to the Journal and papers on file, of the Legislature at Harrisburg.† But it is immaterial. It may have been deemed a highly politic measure to secure the success of the petition, with that Democratic Assembly, and also to render their college popular throughout the West. No name was more respected by the great body of the people in Western Pennsylvania, than the name of Mr. Jefferson.

---

* The following are the names of those venerable men who were Trustees of the Academy from 1798 to 1802: The Rev. Messrs. James Power, James Dunlap, John M'Pherrin, David Smith, William Swan, John Smith, John Riddle, Joseph Patterson, Thos. Marquis, James Hughs, Boyd Mercer, Thos. Moor, Samuel Ralston, Wm. Findley, Esq., John Wright, Esq., Robert Galbraith, Esq., James Edgar, John M'Dowell, James Allison, John Canon, and Craig Ritchie.

† An unavailing search on this point has been made at Harrisburg.

He had been inducted into the office of President of the United States, in March, 1801. His administration, for some time, was like a continued ovation. The party who had triumphantly borne him forward to this high station, were in the utmost state of exultation. To call this first college in the West, this first seat of science in the Valley of the Mississippi, after this idol of the people, would be thought, on all sides, most felicitous. It might have been sincerely thought by the Trustees a compliment to Mr. Jefferson, which he deserved. Possibly William Findley, Esq., who then represented a large portion of Western Pennsylvania in Congress, a Trustee of the Academy, and a warm political partizan of Mr. Jefferson, may have led the Trustees to adopt this name; and may have suggested that a *douceur* might be given by Mr. Jefferson for the compliment, or he might help them by testamentary provision. Gen. Washington had, only a year or two before, left by his will a noble bequest, in James River stocks, to Washington Academy, in Virginia, that very institution that had sprung from the action of the Synod of Virginia, when the Synod took measures to found two seminaries, one in Rockbridge county, Virginia, and the other in Washington county, Pennsylvania. What so proper, in every way, as that the Institution which had, in a great measure, owed its earlier life to the action of the Synod, should become *Jefferson College,* now that the other school of the Synod had taken the name of *Washington?* When we take into view all the circumstances we have now mentioned, we are not surprised that this old Presbyterian Institution should take the name of the man who, to the day of his death, disliked *Virginia* Presbyterians, and apprehended their opposition to his *Virginia University,* (the child and the glory of his old age,) more than all other sources of annoyance, to his plans of building up a great seat of science, where Christianity should be ignored. This apprehension from Presbyterian opposition to his schemes he acknowledged to his infidel friend, Dr.

Cooper, of South Carolina.* Dr. Brown, in his unpublished "Life of Dr. M'Millan," thus remarks about the name of our college: "It has been a matter of surprise and regret, that an institution, founded in piety and prayer, and professedly designed to be devoted to religion, should bear the name

---

*But even if Mr. Jefferson's religious views were objectionable, his services to his country, unsurpassed by any other, except Washington, his authorship of the "Declaration of Independence," and of the Virginia "Bill of Rights," his efforts in the cause of unrestricted toleration, his persevering efforts to overthrow every vestige of religious establishments, his sympathy for suffering humanity, his contempt for, and internecine war against all privileged orders and aristocratical distinctions of society, and especially his opposition to the unrighteous excise laws of the General Government, which had produced so much misery and disaster in Western Pennsylvania, seemed really to entitle him to the compliment of having the first college in the Valley of the Mississippi called by his name. Again, if he was the author and originator of the Ordinance of 1787, establishing the North-Western Territory, as has been affirmed, even *for this one service* to his country, and especially to the West, he deserved to have his name stamped indelibly on the first seat of science west of the mountains. The following statement will be found in the New York Observer, June 28, 1855, headed

DID JEFFERSON DIE AN INFIDEL?

"Your last issue calls attention to the fact that the Congress of '54, distributed three hundred copies of the works of Thomas Jefferson, among several colleges and other literary institutions; and that these works contain infidel sentiments. It is much to be regretted that the author of the Declaration of Independence should have ever entertained or published '*infidel sentiments.*' We cannot deny the fact. He so identified himself with infidelity, while he held exalted positions—and his expressed opinions to the world were such, as to leave no doubt of the fact, that the Patriot, Scholar, and Statesman, was at one time an avowed infidel. But there is one little circumstance in the history of Jefferson, which I do not think is generally known. It is this:—In his old age, when he had retired to the quiet scenes of Monticello, he visited one Sabbath, a country church; it happened to be communion day, and when the invitation was given to the communicants to come forward and partake of the sacred elements, this man, who had given the influence of his high name towards extinguishing the light of Christianity, and obliterating the hope of the world;—this man came humbly forward, and meekly kneeling at the altar, received those precious remem-

of one, who, though distinguished and honored justly, as a philosopher and statesman, an advocate of the principles of liberty, yet must be acknowledged to have been an infidel, a deist, if not an atheist, and a bitter opposer of the Christian religion. It must, however, be recollected that the principles of Mr. Jefferson, at that time, were not fully developed, as afterwards. Occasional rumors, respecting his opposition to religion, were disbelieved and denied. It cannot otherwise be supposed that these Trustees and conductors of the Institution would have consented to such a name." But it is a matter of small account. "*De minimis non curat lex.*" "A rose, by any other name, would smell as sweet." One

---

brances of the death of Christ, which afford so much comfort to believers. It is something wrested from the powers of darkness to know that a man of Jefferson's mind and firmness of character, should respond to an invitation like the following:

"'Ye that do truly and earnestly repent of your sins, and are in love and charity with your neighbors, and intend to lead a new life, following the commandments of God, and walking from henceforth in his holy ways; draw near with *faith*, and take this holy sacrament to your comfort; and make *your humble confession to Almighty God,* meekly kneeling upon your knees.'

"I have this fact from a minister of the Methodist Episcopal Church, now over three-score years of age, who was born, raised, and spent the greater portion of his life in Virginia. If my recollection of our interview is correct, he received the account from the servant of Christ who administered the sacrament.

"Some of Jefferson's old manuscripts were published, I believe, after his decease, by an infidel relative. Is there not some reason to believe that he would have retracted them publicly, had he lived a little longer?

"J. W. K.

"*Hackensack, N. J., June* 16, 1855."

We have no confidence in this whole story; and are very sure it would not only be discredited in *Charlottesville,* but would be regarded as reflecting no honor upon the character of Mr. Jefferson, who, however much he admired *Voltaire,* and had his bust in full view of his dying eyes, would not have imitated him in receiving the sacrament. But we give the account for what it is worth, unwilling to withhold anything that may be alleged in Mr. Jefferson's behalf.

of the names of *Hampden Sidney* College, a thorough Presbyterian school, is the name of an infidel, if we may rely on the testimony of Bishop Burnet. One of our Western colleges is called after Franklin, and he was hardly a Christian, though we would not call him an infidel.

The Board of Trustees that were recognized in the charter of the College consisted of the following persons: The Rev. Messrs. John M'Millan, Joseph Patterson, Thos. Marquis, Samuel Ralston, John Black, James Power, James Dunlap, John M'Pherrin; and Messrs. James Edgar, John M'Daniel, James Allison, William Findley, Craig Ritchie, John Hamilton, Joseph Vance, Robert Mahon, James Kerr, Aaron Leyle, Alexander Cook, John Mercer, and William Hughes. In the original charter eleven constituted a quorum; afterwards the number was reduced to seven. A large majority of them met on the 27th of April, 1802, and continued in session, with the usual adjournments, for three days. Before they entered upon business, they took the oath prescribed by the Act; which is in the following form: "You and each of you do solemnly swear, that you will support the Constitution of the United States of America, and of this State, and that you will, with fidelity, perform the duties of a trustee of Jefferson College." * Judge Edgar, being one of the judges of the court for Washington county, administered the oath to the trustees, who were present, and then Judge Vance administered the oath to him. Dr. M'Millan was chosen President of the Board, and Craig Ritchie, Esq., Clerk. Messrs. Dunlap, M'Pherrin, and Ralston, were appointed a committee to arrange the number of classes which should be in the College, and the studies proper for each class; and to report the following day. Accordingly, their report was received, and, after debate, and some alterations, was adopted.

* No Old Side Covenanter or Reformed Presbyterian could take that oath, though the students of that body have generally gone to this college.

The following is the substance of it: "The Faculty shall consist of 1st., a President or Principal, who is also to be Professor of Moral Philosophy, Rhetoric, Logic, &c. 2d. A Professor of Divinity. 3d. A Professor of Mathematics and Natural Philosophy. 4th. That the Languages shall be taught, as hitherto, by the Professor. 5th. That the Mathematics be taught, till the Fall, in the manner hitherto, in the Academy, by the Professor. 6th. That the Professor of Moral Philosophy, teach all who would wish to apply to it, Logic, Rhetoric, Geography, &c. 7th. That, in the Fall, all who, by attending through the session on the Institution, shall sustain an examination on the Languages, Geography, Mathematics, Natural and Moral Philosophy, Rhetoric, Logic, Metaphysics, Roman and Greek Antiquities, and History, shall receive a degree. 8th. That the Rules and Regulations hitherto adopted for the good conduct of the students in the Academy, shall be continued in force till Fall. 9th. That each student shall pay his tuition a quarter in advance." The Trustees further agreed that they would now mention what classes they designed to constitute, and the studies of each; so that the students may, through the Summer, be making preparation for the class into which they design to enter. They also determined to support a Grammar School, or Preparatory Department, in which the usual elementary books in the Languages were to be used; and also Arithmetic, Composition, English Grammar, and speaking Orations were to be attended to. They prohibited the use of translations of the Classics. They adopted a general plan of three classes. The *first class* were to read Horace, Cicero's Orations, Xenophon, Homer, Longinus, together with the study of Greek, and Roman Antiquities, Geography, and some parts of Algebra. The *second class*, to be styled the Mathematical Class, were to finish Algebra, and study Euclid's Elements, Practical Geometry, Natural Philosophy, Rhetoric and Lectures on History. The *third class*, to be styled the Philosophical Class, were to study Logic, Moral Philosophy, and Metaphysics, and a careful Review of the Languages, and of the aforementioned arts and sciences. A strict attention to Composition and to speaking Orations was to be given by the students, in all the classes. Two years' connection with the College, and a sustained examination on all the above studies, were made the condition of a Diploma.

The Board then elected by ballot, the *Rev. John Watson* as Principal, and Professor of Moral Philosophy; *Dr. M'Millan*, as Professor of Divinity, and *Mr. Samuel Miller*, Professor of Mathematics, Natural Philosophy, and Geography.

As Dr. M'Millan could not remain a trustee, and at the same time become a member of the faculty, he resigned his seat in the Board, and *Judge Edgar* was chosen President of the Board in his place. President Watson was also appointed Professor of Languages, and he and Judge M'Dowell were appointed to prepare a system of laws and regulations for the College, and report them at the next meeting. The Board ordered a *College seal* to be prepared, with a device of "a figure of a Principal presenting a Diploma to a student, Jefferson College in Latin, round the bottom, and this motto, '*Deo juvante omnia possumus*,' round the top;" to be ready by next commencement.

The Rev. Dr. M'Millan was appointed Principal during the absence of Mr. Watson. Mr. Watson's salary was fixed at £150, he to provide his Tutors at his own expense. Professor Miller's salary was £100. The Rev. Thos. Moore was elected a trustee in place of Dr. M'Millan.

The College now commenced its new and brilliant career. Great expectations were excited, especially under the anticipated administration of that extraordinary son of genius, the Rev. John Watson. But these anticipations were soon to meet with a sad disappointment, occasioned by the early death of that gifted man. He did not live more than three or four months after he regularly entered upon his work. His death occurred November 30th, 1802. This mournful event threw a sombre hue over the rising prospects of Jefferson College. It was a heavy affliction to the students, the trustees, and the citizens, and especially to his venerable father-in-law, Dr. M'Millan. *

"Quis strepitus circa comitum!
Sed nox atra caput tristi circumvolat umbra.
Ostendunt terris hunc tantum fata, neque ultra
Esse sinent."

---

* The *Rev. John Watson* was a native of Western Pennsylvania, descended from poor, but respectable parents, both of whom died when he was about nine years of age, leaving him a helpless and dependent orphan. A friend of his father's, who kept a tavern and a retail store, received him into his family, and with a view to make him useful to him in his business, instructed him in writing and arithmetic. He early discovered a fondness for reading, and sought to indulge his tastes by a perusal of every book within his reach. As the lady of the house was a novel reader, and had many of this sort of books, she was obliged to keep her book case locked to prevent his access to them. When he was about eleven or twelve years of age, a copy of the Spectator fell into his hands, which he read with great delight. The Latin sentences prefixed to the various numbers gave him much trouble, and excited within him an earnest desire to become acquainted with that language. The only means within his reach of attaining his object, was a copy of Horace, and an old mutilated Latin Dictionary. With these, however, he went to work, and by dint of application, and without a teacher or a grammar, he acquired considerable knowledge of that difficult author. Many of the hours which others gave to sleep, he devoted to study. One night, the late Judge Addison, who lodged at the same hotel, upon returning to his lodgings at a late hour, after the family had retired to rest, found young Watson diligently engaged in reading Horace, by the light of the fire. Being much pleased and interested with the lad, Addison promised him that, on his return, at the next term of the court, he would furnish him with more suitable books for the attainment of a knowledge of the Latin. This promise was not forgotten by the Judge, but at the time fixed upon, he carried with him the books, and delivered them into the hands of his young acquaintance, who had been looking for them with much impatience. His pleasure on receiving them was very great. "Never," said he, "did I experience a more joyful moment." His studies being now greatly facilitated, he made rapid progress. Although he continued his labors at the counter and in the bar-room,

Yet the College, during its first session, in 1802, made a very auspicious beginning of its future glorious course. The students were, with few exceptions, young men of great promise, who, in after life, were eminently useful and successful men. There were some who were alumni, during the previous year, and part of the present year, though they did not graduate * at Jefferson College. Among these may be mentioned the *Rev. John Johnston*, of Newburg, New York, a man of great worth and eminent usefulness, who has long occupied a high place among his brethren of that State. Also the *Rev. Dr. James Hoge*, of Columbus, Ohio, the Apostle

---

he employed every leisure moment in the study of the classics, and finally became an accomplished Latin and Greek scholar. When nineteen years of age, through the influence of Dr. M'Millan, who had become acquainted with him, he was appointed Tutor in Canonsburg Academy, in which situation he remained about eighteen months. At the expiration of that period, he entered the College of New Jersey, where he was sustained in part by Dr. M'Millan, and where he was graduated, A. D. 1797. He studied theology with Dr. M'Millan, and was licensed by the Presbytery of Ohio, at Cross Creek, October 17, 1798, and ordained at Miller's Run, June 26, 1800. He was elected President of Jefferson College, August 29, 1802, and was the first President under the charter. He died November 30th, 1802, only three months after his accession to the Presidency. He was married to Margaret, the second daughter of Dr. M'Millan. By a remarkable coincidence, he and the Rev. Wm. Moorehead were married to sisters, by their father-in-law, on the same day, took sick on the same day, died on the same day, and were buried in the same grave, in the burying ground belonging to the congregation of Chartiers. Mr. Watson was a man of unusual endowments. The Rev. Dr. John Rea, one of his pupils, to whom we are indebted for most of these facts, says: "He possessed a mind pure, vigorous, and enlightened. He could unfold his ideas to others in language simple, clear, forcible, and not unfrequently eloquent. He was amiable in his disposition, conciliatory in his manners, of unblemished morals, and real, unaffected piety. He was esteemed by all who knew him, and beloved by all his students, by many of whom he will be cherished in remembrance as long as memory remains."—*Dr. Elliott's Life of Macurdy, App. p.* 281. *See also Chapter* 8, *of this book, for Dr. Brown's Sketch of Mr. Watson.*

* This mode of expression, and not "was graduated," we find now adopted by the Foreign Reviews, and good writers in our own country.

of Presbyterianism in that State—a man of giant intellect and ardent piety, whose services in the cause of religion and humanity, have rendered his name familiar in every part of our land. At the Fall Commencement, *Wm. M'Millan*, (afterwards the Rev. Wm. M'Millan, D. D., Ex-President of Jefferson College, and afterwards of Franklin College, Ohio,) *Israel Pickens*, (afterwards a distinguished lawyer and member of Congress, in the South, and Governor of Alabama,) *Johnson Eaton*, (afterwards the Rev. Johnson Eaton, one of the pioneers of Presbyterianism in North-Western Pennsylvania,) *John Rea*, an eminent minister of the gospel in Ohio, in after life, and Rev. Bracken, afterwards, through a long life, a useful Presbyterian minister, graduated, receiving their diplomas of A. B.

The Board, at their Fall meeting, elected the Rev. Samuel Porter, and James Allison, Esq., as trustees, in place of the *Rev. John Black*, deceased, and Mr. A. Cooke, resigned. No other record is made of the death of the *Rev. Mr. Black*, but simply this incidental mention of Mr. Porter, as elected to supply his place. As he was the *first Trustee of the College* that died, and as he was a man every way worthy of some notice, we will refer the reader to some further account of him in the Appendix to Dr. Elliott's Life of Macurdy.*

---

* "The *Rev. John Black* was a native of South Carolina, and was graduated at the College of New Jersey, in September, 1771, having entered the Junior Class half-advanced in May of the preceding year. He was licensed to preach the gospel by the Presbytery of Donegal, October 14th, 1773, and on the 22d of June, 1774, a call was presented to Presbytery for his ministerial labors, from the congregation of Upper Marsh Creek, in York county. The next Fall, a call was prepared for him by the united congregations of Shearman's Valley, which he subsequently declined, when presented. Having accepted the call from Upper Marsh Creek, he was ordained and installed the pastor of that church, August 15, 1775. In 1786, he was set off, with others, to form the Presbytery of Carlisle.

"Some difficulties having arisen in his congregation, he applied to the Presbytery, on the 10th of April, 1792, to have the pastoral relation dissolved.

The Trustees proceeded to draw up and adopt a set of rules and regulations for the government of the College. But as they are not materially different from those usually in force in public Institutions, we will not here transcribe them. We observe, under the chapter "of Dress," it is recommended to the students to be plain in their dress, but it is required of them always to appear neat, and cleanly; and for any gross deficiency in this respect, it was made the duty of the College officers to admonish them. It was also recommended to every student of the college to possess a "Black Gown," agreeably

---

The Presbytery, after taking the necessary steps to have the congregation before them at their next meeting, adjourned to meet at Upper Marsh Creek on the 6th day of June following. At that meeting, the parties were present, and after some conference between them, Mr. Black informed the Presbytery that 'he had obtained such satisfaction as induced him to ask permission to withdraw his application for leave to resign his pastoral charge.' This request, the Presbytery 'most cordially granted.' On the 5th of December, 1793, however, he renewed his application to be released from his pastoral charge, which was granted at a subsequent meeting of the Presbytery, on the 10th of April, 1794.

"From the time of his dismission from his pastoral charge, until the year 1800, he exercised his ministry chiefly in a congregation of the Dutch Reformed Church, near to Hunterstown, in Adams county. His labors to them were very acceptable and useful, and he has been heard to say, that among that plain people, he experienced more pleasure, as a pastor, than in any former part of his ministry. He there found a docility—freedom of spiritual communion, and confiding attachment, by which they were greatly endeared to him. With the reasons which induced him to leave them and remove to the West, we are not acquainted. But on the 9th of October, 1800, he obtained a dismission from Carlisle Presbytery to connect himself with that of Redstone. With this latter Presbytery he was present as a corresponding member on the 21st of that same month, and upon the application of commissioners from the congregations of Unity and Greensburg, in which the Rev. William Speer afterwards settled, was appointed a stated supply to these congregations. He was, moreover, received as a member of the Presbytery of Redstone on the 24th of December, and continued as a stated supply to the congregations above named, until April 22d, 1802; when he declined serving them any longer, and obtained leave to travel without the bounds of the Presbytery. It was but a short time, however, until he

to a fashion prescribed by the faculty; and to make his appearance no where under two miles distant from the college without his gown. We have never heard whether this recommendation was attended to or not. We know, if it was, it fell early into entire neglect, and has, we believe, never been revived. The rules requiring and enforcing morals, and attendance upon religious worship, were strict, and were, no doubt, enforced. The punishments were wholly of a moral kind, addressed to the sense of duty, and the principles of honor and shame. There were stringent rules also against wearing women's clothes. How the modern fashion of shawls, now worn by many gentlemen, would have fared at Jefferson College, in those days, may be conjectured. The laws were severe also against secret clubs and combinations, &c., and against any annoyance to the people of the town, either as to their persons or their property.

In the Spring of 1803, the Board elected the *Rev. James Dunlap* as Principal of the College, and successor of Mr. Watson, promising him £140 per annum, finding him also a house and garden, and he finding his own Tutors. And as *Mr. Dunlap* was thus removed from the Board to the Faculty, the Rev. Mr. Riddle, of the Associate Reformed church, was elected a trustee in his place.

---

was called to his final reward. He died, August 16, 1802, in the triumphant exercise of faith in the Lord Jesus Christ. On his death-bed, he requested his friends to sing the 17th Psalm, long metre, in Watts' version, 'Lord, I am thine,' &c. While they were engaged in this exercise, he united with them in a manner which showed how fully his feelings were in harmony with the sentiments contained in this beautiful psalm.

"He was a man of a high order of talent, an able disputant, and fond of metaphysical disquisitions. He published a discourse in favor of a New Testament Psalmody and in reply to the Rev. Dr. Anderson, of the Associate Church, which is said to have been written with much ability.

"The Rev. John Black, D. D., deceased, late pastor of the Fifth Presbyterian Church, (N. S.) Pittsburgh, who died in Allegheny city, February 13, 1847, was his grandson."—*Appendix to Elliott's Life of Macurdy, p.* 266.

At their Fall meeting, in 1803, the Board passed an order "That any Trustee, upon his request, shall have any subscription paper, upon which he has collected money, inserted upon the Minutes of the Board, the names and sums collected." This seems to us to have been wise and right; but we are sorry to add that it was not of any avail. Had it been duly attended to, it would have been useful, in affording us much curious and entertaining information. Almost all the Trustees were more or less engaged, for many years after, in collecting funds for the college much on the same plan with that adopted by old Mr. Patterson.

The graduates, that Fall, were *Andrew M'Donald, Cyrus Riggs,* and *Alexander Monteith,* who all afterwards became ministers of the gospel. The Board also took measures to provide the Faculty with *Black Gowns.* Whether they provided a dressing room, or wardrobe, we know not. Perhaps these black gowns were perquisites, which each member of the Faculty claimed as his own, and carried off in triumph upon resigning, or retiring from office. Had the gowns remained for successors, awkward fits in garments would have sometimes occurred; as when Dr. Muir, of Alexandria, a small man, made Dr. Speece, a tall man of six feet, before he entered his pulpit, assume his silk gown, which fitted him somewhat like a hunting shirt. Students also were forbidden at this time to board at taverns, without express permission.

The *Franklin Society* enrolled, for this year, (1803,) the Rev. James Patterson, Washington Robinson, John Marshall, George Crookham, Stephen Dod, Wm. Dunlap, John Canon, Hon. Jonathan Jennings, Angus Henderson, James Parkinson, and Jonathan Cox. And the *Philo Society* report for this year, Samuel Culbertson, Rev. George Vaneman, William Ritchie, James Kerr, Isaac Vandyke, John Phillips, Wm. Donaldson, Rev. Daniel Stephens, Rev. Samuel Porter, James Galloway, Rev. John Reed, Rev. James Dinsmore, and Simkins Harriman. In these two lists there were several more ministers than those designated, and several eminent physicians and lawyers. Indeed, both catalogues need many amendments throughout, to designate the future callings of their respective members.

The new President, *Dr. Dunlap,* of whom some account will be found in the "Life of Macurdy" and "Old Redstone," entered upon his important station with much to encourage him, in the prospects of the College. He had been long settled as a pastor in Dunlap's Creek congregation, Fayette county, to which place he had removed from the bounds of the New Castle Presbytery, in 1782. He was a graduate of Princeton College, and had likewise been employed as Tutor, for a short time, in that Institution. He also gave instruction to a few young men, principally such as had the ministry in view, after his settlement at Dunlap's Creek. His acquaintance with the classics was unusually accurate and extensive, and as a teacher of languages he excelled. He was about sixty years of age when he came to Canonsburg. He continued to exercise his ministry at Miller's Run, five or six miles from the College, of which church he became pastor. He was somewhat recluse in his habits, of an amiable, cheerful spirit, but inclined to despondency. His person was small, his features pleasing, and his manners popular. His health was not very robust; but his conscientious diligence in the discharge of his duties, secured him the respect and affection of the Trustees and students. We may have occasion to give some further account of him hereafter. A very large portion of the students, at that time, were pious, exemplary youths. A very extensive revival of religion, which had begun the previous year, prevailed throughout Western Pennsylvania, and many of the students shared in its blessed influence. They were accustomed to go in considerable numbers, with the consent of the Faculty, to various places where communions were held, sometimes to the distance of ten and even twenty miles. There was much warmth of piety among them. These excursions, in order to attend at "Sacraments," (as such meetings, where the Lord's Supper was usually administered, were then commonly called,) the pious and serious young men performed on foot. Religious conversation, and sometimes singing of hymns, beguiled the way. Many and delightful were the reminiscences of these young brethren, through all their after lives, of those seasons of Christian fellowship and spiritual enjoyment.

CHAPTER IV.

HISTORY OF JEFFERSON COLLEGE FROM 1804.

Graduates of 1804—*Ross' Latin Grammar*—Account of *Ross*—*Book-case* for the Societies; reminiscences about it—Graduates of 1805 and 1806—Presbyterian and Associate Presbyteries successfully appealed to for aid—Gen. Hamilton's success at Congress—Injunction of the Board upon Drs. M'Millan and Dunlap—Graduates of 1808—First communication from Board of Washington College; result—Dr. Ralston chosen President of Board—Dr. Murdock's Report about conference with Washington Committee—Graduates of 1809—State of Finances—Death and Character of *Judge M'Dowell*—Trustees' rule for order of procession at commencement—Description of an "*Exhibition,*" or College Commencement, in "old times."

There is little of any special interest to relate, in regard to the history of the College during this and the following year. The Trustees gave to President Dunlap the use and benefit of the lot connected with the old stone edifice, and ten pounds, in addition to his salary, in lieu of the house rent and garden, and passed an order again, that no student should board at a tavern; and another that no student shall continue at college who is two quarters in arrears. Judge M'Dowell was elected President of the Board. The graduates, in the Fall of 1804, were *Daniel Stephens*, who afterwards became an Episcopal minister, was for a few years a neighbor of the writer, in Staunton, Virginia, whence he removed to the West; a man of quiet, blameless life, and much esteemed by his people; *John M'Donald*, afterwards a member of the Pittsburgh bar; *John White*, and *Clement Valandingham*, a minister of the gospel, who lived and labored many years in New Lisbon, Ohio, where he died, greatly beloved and regreted by a people, among whom his ministerial labors had been eminently successful. The Board also elected the Rev. James Hughes, and the Rev. William Swann, trustees in the place of the Rev. Messrs. Power and M'Pherrin, resigned. The price of tuition, at this time, was fixed at six pounds per annum. About this period, Ross' *Latin Grammar* was introduced. *James Kerr, Esq.*, a trustee, who was also a representative of Washington county in the State Legislature, had brought out with him four dozen of these Grammars, then but recently published; and the Trustees took them off his hands, to be sold to the students. It was then, and for many years after, considered the best Grammar extant, greatly in advance of all its predecessors, as a useful manual for boys, beginning the study of the Latin language. Brooke's edition of it, we believe, is still in use. The author, *James Ross*, was a graduate of Princeton College, in the Fall of 1766—was a good classical scholar. His talents lay all in that direction, and he became a prodigy of pedagogical learning, though his knowledge of Mathematics and the moral and metaphysical sciences was but slender. Like the celebrated Rosseau, he never could clearly comprehend some of the simplest propositions in Euclid, and it was with some difficulty he succeeded in obtaining a degree of A. B., though he was, in after life, honored with the title of LL. D. He was a classmate of the Rev. Dr. Power, from whom we had the above account. He became an eminent teacher of the dead languages, * and in this vocation he continued till he was advanced in years, and old age disqualified him for his useful profession. But though of an obtuse mind for other branches of learning, he was pre-eminent as a linguist. We remember to have seen him when he was probably eighty years of age, at the first church in Philadelphia, of which Dr. Wilson was then pastor.

* He was, for many years, a Professor in the University of Philadelphia.

His seat was in the gallery; and before him he had fixed, on a little shelf, attached to the parapet or breastwork of the gallery, nearly a dozen of books—a Greek Testament, a Hebrew Bible, Concordance, Lexicons, &c. When the Doctor announced his text, which happened to be, "Come unto me all ye that labor," &c., Mr. Ross immediately took his Greek Testament, turned to the passage, and seemed for some time to be earnestly studying it. Such was the man who wrote the Latin Grammar that was long used at Jefferson College. In the Spring of 1805, the Trustees fixed the length of the *vacations* at three weeks in the Spring, and four in the Fall. They also ordered that the Principal or Professor of Divinity, at every Commencement, should hereafter deliver an address to the graduates, or procure a clergyman to do it. Dr. M'Millan was then elected Vice-Principal of the College. Messrs. Marquis and Macurdy were authorized to procure donations for the Institution. Dr. Samuel Murdock was elected a trustee, in place of the Hon. Wm. Findley, resigned; and the *Rev. John Anderson,* in place of the Rev. Mr. Riddle. Dr. Dunlap's salary was raised *to two hundred* pounds, he still finding and paying his assistant. And, if we may note so small a matter, eighteen Windsor chairs were procured for the use of the Board and Faculty. Probably stout benches, with straddling legs, served their turn up to this date. The *Literary Societies,* at the Fall meeting, (1805,) petitioned the Board for charters, and a place in the College building for their libraries and book-cases. Whereupon it was ordered, "That the said societies, viz: *Franklin* and *Philo,* be recognized as such, and that their respective Constitutions, as they now exist, shall be the Constitutions of said societies; and that a majority of either of said societies, adhering to their constitutions, shall retain the original name of the respective society; and that the Libraries of said societies are hereby taken under the care and patronage of the Board." The Board also appointed a committee to procure a double book-case for these societies, to be placed in one end of the upper apartment of the College. Well do we remember that *old Book Case*, and what we then regarded its inexhaustible treasures of wisdom and learning. At this day it would cut rather a ridiculous figure beside many a country minister's library, not to speak of the widely expanded and groaning shelves of the libraries of these societies now.

The graduates of the Fall of 1805 were *James Wilson*, afterwards the Rev. James Wilson, D. D., a very eminent minister of the Reformed Presbyterian body; *John Trevor*, *James Wills*, *James Patterson*, afterwards an eminent and successful Presbyterian minister in the Northern Liberties of Philadelphia—a man of great worth and usefulness; *Daniel Hayden*, *James Scott*, *Moses Allen*, afterwards an excellent and useful minister, settled first at Muddy Creek, Green county, then at Raccoon, and during the last years of his life, at Crabapple, Ohio,—son-in-law of Dr. M'Millan; *Carlos A. Norton*, *James Galloway*, *James M'Connell*, and *James Cunningham*, a Presbyterian minister, who died a few years ago in Ohio. The Trustees appointed Messrs. Ritchie and Murdock to prepare and forward to the Legislature a petition for the purpose of obtaining assistance in lands and money; and also to transmit to Gen. Hamilton, then in Congress, an account of the state of the College, for the purpose of aiding him in soliciting donations. The degree of Master of Arts was conferred on the Rev. Messrs. John M'Millan, Samuel Ralston, and James Ramsey, and on Dr. Samuel Murdock, and Prof. Samuel Miller. The petition to the Legislature proved successful. A donation of *three thousand* dollars to the College was the result. The Trustees met, March 27, 1806, in order to dispose of this pecuniary aid to their funds, and passed an order to lend the money to individuals, in sums not less than $200, nor more than $600, to any one person, and appointed Messrs. Allison, Ritchie and Murdock, a committee for this purpose. At their April meeting, Judge M'Dowell was again elected President of the Board, Dr. Samuel Murdock, Secretary, Craig Ritchie, Esq., Treasurer. Mr. Miller's salary was fixed permanently at $400, and Mr. Dunlap's salary advanced. At their September meeting, they conferred the degree of A. B. upon *Mr. James Scott*, of New York, and on Messrs. *Reed*, *Leslie*, and *Hunt*. The two last afterwards became ministers of the gospel, the last a Presbyterian minister, for several years pastor of the Second Presbyterian Church, Pittsburgh, and, after his removal to Ohio, he was pastor, for many years, of the congregation of *Two-Ridges*, Jefferson county. Here he ended, a few years ago, his long and useful life—*George Vaneman*, also, afterwards a Presbyterian minister, and believed to be still living in Ohio.

We now enter upon the sixth year of this first College of the West. The whole western country began now to be dotted over with her alumni. They were found in all the learned professions, and in Agricultural and Commercial life; in Courts of Justice, and in Legislative Halls. But her useful career was only just begun. When the Trustees met in April, 1807, the same officers of the Board were re-elected. The first matter of inquiry was in regard to an order of the Board, made last year, respecting an application for pecuniary assistance to the Presbyteries of Redstone, Ohio, and Chartiers. This last was the name of the Presbytery of the Associate body, or Seceders. It appeared that the application was favorably entertained, and strongly recommended by these Presbyteries to the congregations under their care. Gen. Hamilton also reported the success of an address sent to Washington City for pecuniary aid; and paid into the treasury two hundred and ten dollars, which, although given for the purpose of building a college, could, in the meantime, be appropriated to defray the current expenses of the College. Mr. Dunlap was, on his application, permitted to retain $100, which he had borrowed, a while longer, without interest, on condition that he would continue as Principal. His application for increase of salary failed, no doubt from the financial embarrassments of the College. A committee was appointed to explain to him the situation of the funds, &c., and strive to convince him of the necessity the Board was under to refuse his request; and also to require from him an explicit answer, whether, and how long, he will serve as Principal of the College, with the present salary.

The Principal and Professor of Divinity were required in teaching, each, in their respective classes, to cause their students, as they proceeded in their studies, to write dissertations "on the most striking things immediately connected with their subjects." Here was certainly something rather singular, so far as the Professor of Divinity, Dr. M'Millan, was concerned. It is true, he had been appointed by the Trustees of the College, as their Professor. And that itself seems to us, in these days, queer. That a Board, though consisting partly of ministers—always a minority, however—a Board appointed and incorporated by the Legislature—a secular body, a close corporation, under no ecclesiastical control, should dictate and prescribe to a man who was engaged in the discharge of one of the highest and most solemn ecclesiastical functions, the way in which they would require him to fulfill the duties of his office, sounds very strangely in our ears. Dr. M'Millan was also, at this time, in some sense, a quasi-Professor of Divinity, by the appointment of the Synod of Virginia, and by the recognition of the Presbyteries of Ohio and Redstone.*

* Even so late as October 5, 1821, the Synod of Pittsburgh recognized Dr. M'Millan as Professor of Theology in Jefferson College, and took measures to enlarge the Theological Library under his care, as appears by the following minute, on page 178 of Printed Minutes:

"Whereas, it appears to this Synod that a number of promising young men, who are setting their faces towards the gospel ministry, are not in circumstances to attend the Theological Seminary at Princeton—Therefore *Resolved,* that this Synod take measures for procuring a library for the benefit of such, to be under the control and direction of this Synod. That

But such strange things were not without precedents, in those times. The Trustees of Princeton College had, long before, appointed a Professor of Divinity as one of their Faculty. And so to this day do the Trustees of Harvard University and of Yale College. And if trustees may appoint such Professors, they may rightfully claim to instruct them in their duties. But we suspect there are few Presbyterians of this day, who would tolerate such an arrangement. Perhaps, however, in the case under consideration, the real object was to get the Principal of the College to attend to this matter; and then to take off the repulsive feature of their order, by requiring the same thing of Dr. M'Millan. Dr. Dunlap would not take offence by their approaching him in this way. He was a very sensitive man, easily wounded, and apt to take offence, as will hereafter appear; though a devotedly pious and eminently learned man.

Mr. Dunlap declared, as the committee reported, he had no design of leaving the College.

Messrs. Ralston, Hughes and Murdock, were appointed a committee to prepare an Address to the Public, concerning the present state of the College, and the views of the Board, in regard to the erection of a new and more capacious edifice. They had, during the preceding year, discussed the subject; and it was mainly with a view to this they had communicated with the ecclesiastical bodies around them, and had even pledged themselves to each other to raise money by subscription; having determined, as soon as funds could be secured, to raise at least the new shell of a college, large enough to contain one hundred students. But no considerable progress had yet been made, though something had been done; and

---

it be recommended to every member to solicit books or moneys, for this important purpose, and that this library be located at present in the edifice of Jefferson College, Canonsburg, and placed under the care of the Rev. John M'Millan, D. D., Professor of Theology in that Seminary."

perhaps they felt, from what they had ascertained respecting the feelings and wishes of the public on the subject, encouraged and assured of ultimate success. The committee above mentioned were instructed to address the public through the newspapers. At this time, also, they took upon themselves to provide assistant teachers, and to pay them, both of which things they had heretofore devolved upon the Principal.

In September, the following persons were admitted to the degree of A. B., viz.: *James Culbertson*, afterwards a distinguished Presbyterian minister, who was one of the pioneers of the gospel in Ohio, who labored for many years in Zanesville, Ohio, where, a few years ago, he died, greatly lamented; *Joseph Stevenson*, who also became a very efficient and successful minister, a son-in-law of the Rev. Thos. Marquis, and settled, for many years, near Springfield, Ohio; *John Matthews*, a minister of the gospel also, we believe, settled, at one time, in the bounds of the Presbytery of Erie, and afterwards, somewhere in the West; and *Wm. Dunlap*, of Virginia. This last person was probably a son of the President of the College, who, as a minister of the gospel, was settled at Abingdon, near Philadelphia, where he died, comparatively young. At his house, his father died, a few years before him. The Rev. Messrs. Swan and James Hughes were also admitted to the degree of A. M.

At this meeting, a matter was introduced to the attention of the Board, which, at various intervals, employed and agitated them for more than ten years afterwards, the effects of which are felt to this day. For a communication was received from the Washington College Board, intimating that they had appointed a committee to confer with a committee from the Jefferson College Board, if such a committee should be appointed, for the purpose of devising a plan for the union of the two Institutions. Messrs. Ralston, M'Dowell, Hamilton, and Murdock, were accordingly appointed a Committee to meet the Committee from Washington, and make report a the next meeting of the Board. Any two of the committee were authorized to act, in the absence of the others. An application was directed to be made by a committee, appointed for that purpose, to the next Legislature, praying that an alteration be made in the charter of the College, making *nine* instead of *eleven* members, a quorum. A committee was also appointed to make and enforce regulations for keeping the College clean, and to have it washed out, at least twice a year, defraying the expenses out of College funds. Another address to the public was ordered in behalf of the Institution; and Messrs. Ralston, Ramsey and Murdock were appointed a committee for that purpose. Perhaps this was merely a renewal of an order passed at their Spring meeting, which had not yet been attended to. It is manifest that neither at this time, nor in after years, did they suffer communications from Washington to interrupt their efforts for enlarging their College and extending their building accommodations.

During the next meeting, in April, 1808, Dr. Ralston was chosen President of the Board, an office to which he was afterwards annually elected for nearly forty years! Gen. Morgan, also, who had been previously elected, was now duly qualified, and took his seat as a trustee. Dr. M'Millan was appointed Treasurer, to receive and lend out any money bequeathed to the College for the purpose of educating poor and pious youth.

Dr. Murdock, from the committee appointed to meet the committee from Washington College, to confer about a union of the two Institutions, reported—

"That upon meeting with the Washington committee, a desultory conversation took place upon the business in question, which finally resulted in the following specific propositions:

"1st. It was proposed by the gentlemen from Washington, that the whole number of members from each Board should meet, and by a joint vote should determine on the seat of the United Institution. This was objected to by your committee, because a number of the Trustees of Washington College lived contiguous to their present seat, and were locally interested in retaining it there, whereas the number of members in this situation, with respect to Jefferson College, was very small in comparison.

"2d. It was proposed by your committee that all the mem bers belonging to the respective Boards, whom it be supposed from the places where they lived, were locally interested, should be set aside, and the remaining members, by a joint vote, fix upon the future seat of the Institution. This was objected to.

"3d. It was proposed by the gentlemen from Washington to exclude all their members actually residing in the town of Washington, whose number amounted to at least seven or eight, and exclude an equal number from this Board. But they alone must be the judges whom of our number to exclude. This was objected to by your committee, chiefly on this ground; because a number of members belonging to this Board agreed with them as to the future seat of the Institution, and was disposed to fix it at Washington. If this were a fact, it was injustice to give such an advantage. And, indeed, whether it was so or not, your committee thought it unreasonable that our opponents should be the exclusive judges who of our number should vote and who not, on this important question. Finally, your committee thought it reasonable to propose that all the members constituting the Boards of both Institutions should agree to set aside any of their number who were locally interested as to their dwelling places; and if a greater number of one Board were thus excluded, the members of the other Board were alone to judge who of their members to exclude, so as to make the number of both who were to vote on the question, equal. This proposal, without any reasons satisfactory to your committee, was also rejected."

Thus the conference ended. The Board approved of the conduct of their committee, and at the same time expressed their regret that the object for which the committee was appointed was not obtained, recording, however, their willingness, at all times, to express their hearty desire that a union of the Institutions should be effected, if it can be done on liberal and equitable principles.

In the fall, the Rev. John Anderson resigned his seat as a trustee, and the Rev. Wm. M'Millan was elected in his place. The students admitted to the degree of A. B. were *Stephen Boyer*, afterwards a Presbyterian minister, settled at Little York, where he died some years ago; *Joseph S. Hughes*, afterwards an eloquent and useful minister, settled at *Delaware*, Ohio. He was the son of the *Rev. James Hughes*, and grandson of the *Rev. Joseph Smith*, of Buffalo; *James Smith*, and *Ira Condit*, afterwards ministers. The degree of D. D. was conferred on the Rev. *James Power*, of Westmoreland county, Pa., and the *Rev. John Anderson*, of Beaver county, Pa., (Seceder.) Dr. Dunlap, the Principal, asked for the appointment of another Professor. But the Board, deeming it inconvenient, no doubt from the state of the finances of the College, to comply with this request, appointed a committee to assist in arranging the classes and studies, in such a manner as to lighten the burden of the Tutors. Drs. M'Millan and Dunlap, and Messrs. Ramsey, Ritchie and Murdock, were appointed a committee to receive any poor and pious youth, and admit them to the benefit of the funds placed in the hands of the Trustees for that purpose.

At a regular meeting of the Trustees, in April, 1809, it was found that the funds of the College, at the disposal of the trustees, consisted—

1st. Of a donation of the State, at interest, - -	$3,000
2d. The price of land bequeathed by the Rev. Mr. Clarke,	1,600
3d. Money in the hands of Mr. Snowden, of Philadelphia, at interest, - - - - - - -	1,300
4th. Money at interest in the country, - - -	1,290
Making in all the sum of - - - - - -	$7,190

Dr. M'Millan, Judge Allison, Craig Ritchie, and Dr. Murdock, were appointed a committee to lend out the money arising from Mr. and Mrs. Clarke's estate. A complaint was entered that too much time was allowed the students for recreation, &c., and it was ordered that in future, besides the usual time of vacation between the sessions, there shall not, for any purpose, be allowed by the Professors more than ten days in the year; for example, one day in each month. It is left with the faculty to fix the particular days.

A communication was received, at the Fall meeting of the Board, from Isaac Kerr, Register, intimating that John M'Dowell, Esq., in his last will and testament, had bequeathed fifty dollars to the Institution, payable at Mrs. M'Dowell's death.* The Rev. Mr. Porter was authorized to call on the

---

* There is no particular minute made in the Records of the Board, when the seat of this great and good man was vacated by death. *Judge John M'Dowell* left few men superior to him, when he was called to his rest. He is believed to have been born in York county, Pa., about 1737. He probably removed to the West, near the beginning of the American Revolution, and settled in the bounds of Chartiers Congregation, Washington county, of which he became a ruling elder; and was eminent for his piety and active efforts in the cause of Christ. His strong mind and great integrity of character secured to him, at an early period, the appointment of Associate Judge, in Washington county. He was one of the most efficient men in getting up the Academy at Canonsburg, and was one of the trustees from the first. After the College obtained a charter, he succeeded Judge Edgar as President of the Board, to which office he was chosen April 27, 1803, and thenceforward for four successive years. He died August 12, 1809, in the 73d year of his age. On his tombstone are the following lines:

"Sleep, sacred earth; but thou shalt soon arise!
Dust turns to dust; but virtue never dies;
M'Dowell lives; blest in immortal youth,
Who lived while here, the advocate of truth.
Firm in the cause of God, he held to view
A character sublime, yet humble, too;
God's word his guide, he bent his eagle flight
On faith's strong pinions, to the realms of light.
'O! death, where is thy sting;
O! grave, where is thy victory.'"

executors of John Baird, Esq., of Westmoreland county, and obtain any money left by him for the use of the College. The persons admitted to the degree of Bachelor of Arts were—*Joseph Scroggs*, who afterwards became a minister in the Secession church, and is now pastor of a church in Ligonier Valley, Westmoreland county; *James Milligan*, (who became, we believe, a minister in the Reformed Presbyterian body,) and *Christopher Rankin*. The degree of D. D. was conferred on the *Rev. Joseph Clarke*, of New Brunswick; and the degree of A. M., on the Rev. Messrs. *Samuel Porter*, *Wm. Dunlap*, *Alexander Monteith*, and *Jonathan Leslie*. *Mr. Thos. Briceland* was elected a trustee to fill the vacancy, by the death of Judge M'Dowell. At this time, it was deemed expedient by the Board to settle the order of procession on commencement day; and they adopted the following, viz: "That the Trustees and Faculty meet at the house of Craig Ritchie, Esq., (now owned and occupied by James M'Cullough, Esq.,) that the students shall assemble in front of the same house, and that they walk two and two, according to their respective classes, after the Trustees and Faculty, in the following order: The President of the Board in front, then the Secretary and Treasurer, clergy, and other members of the Board, two and two; then the Faculty, and the procession to be brought up by the tutor or tutors." This arrangement continued in force for many years. Those Commencement days were great events in College life; and that procession, with Dr. Ralston at its head, and Dr. Murdock and Craig Ritchie, Esq., just behind him,—all three very portly gentlemen—and then brought up by the trustees, faculty and students—the students generally powdered, and sporting flaunting blue or white ribbons on their arms or coat breasts—appeared to the young students awfully sublime. The slow and solemn tread of the procession, away up the middle of the street, if the walking was good, surrounded by an immense assembly of the people, who had been for hours before pouring in from the surrounding country, the sound of the violin at the taverns which were passed, the neighing of horses, far and near, the hum of the human voice in all directions, the merry laugh, and the loud giggle, all combined to throw upon the scene an exciting interest, and to make many a young heart delirious with joy and gladness. The younger students, the Freshmen especially, thought that day and place the most delightful and attractive in all the world. It was a full compensation for wearisome hours of study, and for the dull, jog-trot pace of ordinary college life. On went the procession, up street, past Dr. Murdock's and Neil's corners, and past the crowds about Wistby's and Emory's taverns, and past Mrs. Canon's beautiful yard, and old Mr. Robert's store and post office,* till it reached the gate, in front of the old stone College, then wheeled to the left, at right angles, through the gate, and on through the yard, and up the outside steps, on the upper side of the old building, and landed, and disbanded, in the second story; the Trustees and Faculty scrambling through a front window, from which the sash had been removed, on to the stage. Over that window, however, and extending over the lower end of the stage, was a tent, of white sheets, making a small room of about ten feet square. From this room was the entrance, or rather the exit, on to the other part of the stage. This stage or platform was about twelve or fifteen feet wide, and extended the whole length of the college building, in front, and about eight feet from the ground, covered with a substantial rag carpet. Here were the Trustees and Faculty seated, with their backs to the college wall, and their faces to the gathering throng that was fast filling the front yard of the college, back to the gate, through which the procession had just passed. After all the Board were seated, the President of the Board rose, and said, in a loud and distinct voice,

---

* We purposely mention old names and places, as they will serve to renew pleasant reminiscences in the minds of old people.

"Let us pray." All rose, and great silence and order prevailed, while the short but appropriate prayer was made. Then began the business of the day. At this moment, we believe, it was customary to announce the names of those on whom they had conferred the degree of A. B., and of those who received the first and second honors; and then was mentioned the order of their speaking. Programmes had not yet come into use. Then the exercises of the graduates began. These sometimes took up the first part of the day; sometimes, only an hour or two. Then followed the speeches and dialogues of the under-graduates. There was often much fun and amusement in these exercises. Various *dramatis personæ*—soldiers, clowns, sailors, drunkards, pedlars, negroes, &c., &c., were introduced in their appropriate costumes. Sometimes an Act or two from Shakspeare's "Merchant of Venice" or "Julius Cæsar," or Addison's "Cato," would be exhibited. These dialogues were interspersed with single speeches; some serious, and some ludicrous. The people would roar with laughter, and even the old trustees would unbend themselves to many a hearty and healthy laugh. About one-third of the audience would be seated. The rest were standing. If the day was fine, it was full of mirth and enjoyment to the young people of all the country round. There was not much refinement of manners in those times. The whole affair was adapted to the state of society; and, for a period in the history of the college, was really of much advantage to its interests. It made the College popular. It awakened a desire, in many a lad, to go to college. And though such a feeling was rather of a low birth, it led to better things. Let us not, in these times of greater improvement and refinement, despise these old-fashioned times and ways. The first *Exhibition*, as it was then called, we ever witnessed, was in the fall of 1812. It was a glorious day. Every thing above and around conspired to make the scene joyous and exciting. Yet it is a solemn thought that few who witnessed and enjoyed that day, are now among us. Not a single Trustee or member of the Faculty is now living. Those throngs of gay young ladies and young country farmers are now in the silent grave, or are frosted with advancing age. Their children and grand-children now fill their places, and crowd Providence Hall on Commencement days—soon to yield their places to another generation, who will, perhaps, enjoy many a jest, at the expense of the old fashioned ways of the present race. Indeed, there is one feature of our present Commencement days, that the writer is, perhaps, such an inveterate old fogy, as to disrelish. We refer to the brass-band accompaniment. We would much prefer the music of a piano, or of a bass-viol, violin and German flute, with vocal music, if it could be secured—as more in unison with the exercises of the day, and with the refinement and dignity of a Literary Institution. The brass-band is too loud and military in its character; and, in our view, throws a coarse, vulgar element into the whole scene.

CHAPTER V.

NEW PRESIDENTS AND "COLLEGE WAR."

Dr. Dunlap and the Board—Graduates of 1810—Dr. Dunlap resigns—Graduates of 1811 and 1812—*Dr. Wylie* elected Principal—About Ezekiel Hannah's will—Graduates of 1813, 1814 and 1815—New negotiations with the Board of Washington College—Various conferences—Final failure in attempt to unite the colleges—Much sharp shooting, on both sides, but none killed, and few wounded—Reflections on the whole case—*Rev. R. Johnston,* a trustee for seventeen years—Sketch of his life—Dr. Wylie resigns—Dr. Wm. M'Millan succeeds him—Dr. Matthew Brown—Remarkable circumstances connected with his election.

When the Board met in April, 1810, the same officers were continued, viz: Dr. Ralston, President; Dr. Murdock, Secretary; and Craig Ritchie, Esq., Treasurer. A letter was received from Dr. Dunlap, intimating his determination to resign his office as Principal of the College, at the next fall sessions of the Board. In this communication it was stated that if reasons were required, they would be given. Being called upon by the Board to state them, his answer was that, though weighty, he was not then altogether prepared to give them, but designed to communicate them along with his resignation in the fall. However, being urged to mention them now, as it might be too late to be of any service in the fall, he consented, and said that there ought either to be a new house, or the old one kept in better repair; that the Board generally, and some trustees particularly, had found fault with him for not attending closely enough to the business of the College; that the Board had insulted him, some time ago, by taking the power of employing an under teacher of the languages out of his hands, and reserving it to themselves; and finally, that his salary was too small. A committee was appointed to confer with him, and to strive to remove his difficulties. Messrs. Moore, Hamilton and Allison, the committee appointed for this purpose, reported that they had a free conversation with the Principal, and that all his difficulties were in a great measure removed, except that of salary, and they conceived that some arrangement might be made as to this point. Dr. M'Millan was added to the committee, and they were sent back to lay before Dr. Dunlap a statement of the finances, and remove his misconceptions concerning them. But their report was that the Doctor peremptorily refused to continue longer, unless his salary was increased. This the Board decided to be inexpedient under the present circumstances of the College. An extra-meeting in June was appointed to take into consideration the securing of a successor to Mr. Dunlap. And the Clerk was directed to notify absent members of this meeting. When this meeting took place, a letter was received from Dr. Dunlap, reiterating his design of resigning his charge, and asking for the loan of some money. They agreed to lend him $600, to be refunded by three annual installments, with interest. The Board being informed that, besides the reasons which Dr. Dunlap had given, at the last meeting, for his intention of resigning, a rule passed September, 1807, by the Board, requiring the Principal and Professor of Divinity to observe a certain mode in teaching their respective classes, aggrieved him much, refused, nevertheless, to repeal their former action on this subject. Upon its being intimated that Dr. Dunlap would be content to continue, if another teacher of languages were employed to assist him, they voted, however, that this was inexpedient and unnecessary, at this time. A committee consisting of Messrs. Hughes, Marquis, Ramsey and Swan, was appointed to wait on Dr. Dunlap, and after stating to him the above resolutions, to request of him to give his final determination as to his resignation. Upon their interview with him, he declared that he had not understood the rule respecting the mode of teaching, above referred to, and was sorry for it; and that he was now satisfied with the action of the Board, and recalled his notice of resignation.* At the fall meeting, the following persons were admitted to the degree of A. B., viz: *Andrew Wylie,* afterwards a minister of the gospel, and successively President of Jefferson and Washington Colleges, and Indiana University; *James Kerr,* afterwards an eminent physician, residing for many years in Claysville, now in Jefferson or Clarion county, Pa.; *John Reed,* afterwards a minister of the gospel, settled at Indiana, Pa., where he died; *James Hervey,* afterwards the Rev. James Hervey, D. D., an able and distinguished minister of the gospel, settled near Wheeling; *William Hendricks,* a distinguished lawyer and United States Senator; *Wm. Johnston,* afterwards a very useful minister, settled at Dunlap's Creek, Pa.; *John Canon,* and *Robert Lusk,* ministers of the Reformed Presbyterian church; and *Jonathan Gill.* Several matters of minor interest were transacted by the Board, but nothing of special concern, bearing upon the general character of the College.

At the meeting of the Board, April 25, 1811, the same officers were re-elected. Dr. Dunlap insisting upon the

---

* Let it not be supposed that the above account reflects unfavorably upon Dr. Dunlap. We must remember that this account is *ex parte*—taken from the Records of the Trustees. Again, there is no doubt that Dr. Dunlap's circumstances were those of almost pinching poverty. He had come to the rescue of the college during a period when it was almost threatened with extinction. He had stood by it through the most trying period of its history. He had nobly discharged his duty, and aided most efficiently, in bearing the college onward in its course; while, all this time, he was receiving a very inadequate support. He had also a small but very pious congregation, that loved him, and urged him not to leave them. Several of the trustees, including Dr. M'Millan, were anxious that he would not now withdraw from their service. But old age was advancing apace, and he felt, that after all his past sacrifices, he had a right to have some of his difficulties removed, and his support increased. Without a knowledge of all these things, the reader of the above account might be liable to form a wrong judgment about that worthy old servant of God.

appointment of another teacher, and increase of his own salary, both of which being refused, *tendered his resignation*, which was accepted. Dr. M'Millan, the Vice-Principal, was entrusted with the administration and empowered to employ teachers, and $226 67 were appropriated out of the College funds to meet his expenses, in securing the necessary assistance during the Summer session. They also appointed a meeting in June, to take into consideration the choice of a Principal. *James Mountain, Esq.*, who had been elected in place of Mr. Vance, at the last meeting, was present, and being duly sworn, took his seat as a Trustee. At the June meeting, a petition was received from Miller's Run Congregation, praying the Board to re-appoint Dr. Dunlap as Principal of the College. A motion was then made, and carried, to postpone the choice of a Principal till the fall meeting.

At the fall meeting, September 24th, the committee who had been appointed to examine the graduates, reported in favor of conferring the degree of A. B. on *James Wright*, afterwards a Presbyterian minister; *George M' Cook*, afterwards a distinguished physician, now residing in Pittsburgh; and *James Mitchell*. Their report was accepted and adopted. Dr. M'Millan was again instructed to contract for teachers, as he had done last session, until a Principal should be chosen; and he was empowered to draw $450 out of the College funds to defray expenses. The *Rev. Wm. Wylie* was elected trustee, in place of Mr. Porter, resigned. A committee was also appointed to draft an Address to the State Legislature, praying for a donation to the College.

At the April meeting, in 1812, Dr. Andrew Wylie *was elected Principal* of the College by the Board, having eleven votes from the fifteen members present. Mr. Wylie was sent for, and being notified of his election, declared his acceptance of the office. Dr. Wylie's salary was fixed at the same amount that Dr. Dunlap received, which was $533 33, he paying his teachers out of it. In September, the committee that had been appointed to examine the graduates, reported in favor of the following, viz: *Wells Andrews,* afterwards a Presbyterian minister, first settled in Alexandria, Va., and afterwards in the West; *Joseph M'Elroy,* afterwards Rev. Joseph M'Elroy, D. D., of New York; and *James Coe,* a highly esteemed Presbyterian minister in Ohio, lately deceased. They were accordingly admitted to the degree of A. B.

Whereas it appeared that the late Rev. John Brice had left sundry legacies for the use of Jefferson College, the Trustees, considering the peculiar circumstances of the case, unanimously relinquished them for the sole benefit and use of said testator's widow and children, their heirs and assigns. The degree of A. M. was conferred on the Rev. Joseph S. Hughes.

In the Spring of 1813, the Board, at their April meeting, conferred the degree of A. B. upon *George Miller,* formerly of this College. He was a son of Professor Miller; and as he was appointed, or about to be appointed, an Army or Naval Surgeon, it is probable that this circumstance accounts for the irregularity of the time when he graduated. A classical book, called "Collectanea Græca Minora," was ordered to be introduced and read in the College; and "Lucian's Dialogues" dispensed with. It was left optional with the Principal to continue or dispense with "Xenophon's Cyropædia." Professor Miller was requested to instruct his class in the *principles of Chemistry.* The examining committee, in September, reported in favor of *John Monteith,* afterwards a Presbyterian minister in New York and Ohio; *Archibald Johnston,* afterwards a Covenanter minister of *extraordinary oratorical powers,* who lived but a short time; *James Rowland,* a Presbyterian minister, settled at Mansfield, Ohio; *Jeremiah Wilcox,* and *George Junkin,* afterwards Rev. George Junkin, D. D., a man of great energy, talents and usefulness, President, successively, of La Fayette College, Pa., Miami University, Ohio, and now of Washington College, Lexington, Va.

When the Board met in 1814, it was found that there had

not been a full quorum at the previous September meeting. But they now sanctioned their proceedings, and gave full validity to their action in regard to the graduating class. It was ascertained, at this meeting, that *Ezekiel Hannah*, of Indiana county, Pa., lately deceased, had bequeathed his property, to a large amount, for the use of the College; but that the friends and heirs of the deceased would contest the validity of the will. It was necessary that the Trustees should have the will proven, and take the proper steps for defending the suit. The Secretary of the Board had obtained satisfactory information from the witnesses of the will, and others, leading the trustees to determine to sustain the suit in court. Some of the adverse party came over to Canonsburg, seeking an interview with the Board, and bringing with them various depositions, tending to show that the testator was not of a sound and disposing mind, when he made the will, and wishing the trustees to give up all claim to the property, or leave it to the decision of some persons in Indiana and Westmoreland counties. The trustees, however, deemed it expedient to appoint *Dr. Murdock* and *James Kerr, Esq.*, a committee, for the purpose of taking the necessary measures for carrying on the suit. The price of tuition was now fixed at $18 per annum; but it was understood that the Board would be at the expense of providing fuel for the College, making of fires, keeping it clean, &c. *John M'Donald, Esq.*, of Pittsburgh, was elected Trustee in place of *James Mountain, Esq.*, deceased. And the *Rev. Elisha M'Curdy* was elected in place of the *Rev. Thos. Moore*, resigned. The Rev. Messrs. *Ralston* and *Marquis* were appointed a committee to prepare and present a petition to the *Synod of Pittsburgh*, at their next meeting, praying that measures might be taken for erecting and maintaining a *Divinity Hall*,, to be connected with the College.* In September, 1814, the Rev. James Hughes

* There is no notice of this in the printed Records of the Synod.

and John Mercer resigned their seats in the Board. The students petitioned, complaining of the difficulties they labor under, in being obliged to provide fuel for the College, keeping the College clean, stage expenses at the Fall Exhibition, and praying that the Trustees would take charge of all these matters; and that so much be added to the price of tuition as would defray all such expenses. Their prayer was granted, and the tuition raised to $20 per year. The *Rev. Moses Allen*, and *Abner Lacock, Esq.*, were elected to supply the two vacant seats in the Board. The committee on the subject of Mr. E. Hannah's will, reported that they had attended at Indiana, and had gotten the will proven, which, together with some other testimony, they had transmitted to Mr. Duncan, the Attorney in behalf of the College, at Carlisle. At the meeting of the Trustees, in 1815, it appeared that Mr. Duncan had not received the documents—that they had miscarried; (a suspicious circumstance,) and Dr. Ralston and James Kerr, Esq., were then appointed to go to Indiana and proceed, *de novo*. The Trustees, in view of the defective condition of the old stone college, resolved to proceed, forthwith, to make preparations for the erection of a new edifice; and that every Trustee should exert himself to procure subscriptions for that purpose. They then resolved to meet again in June, to see what had been the result, and to take measures accordingly. Upon their meeting at that time, they could not make a Board, but from the liberal subscriptions which were produced, they were encouraged to appoint another early meeting, and to notify the absent members. They accordingly adjourned to meet again August 3d. But it was again a failure, perhaps through disaffection to the object, or influence from another quarter, which may hereafter appear. Those who met, however, examined the subscriptions, and some plans for the new college, and then adjourned to the usual time in September. They now, without appointment from the Board, proceeded to examine the graduates, as no committee for this purpose had been appointed in the spring; and agreed to recommend to the Board, as entitled to the degree of A. B., *Joseph Smith*, (the writer of this history,) *Thos. Johnston*, (who died a few years after, near Mercersburg,) and *James Frasier*, (who died also shortly after.)

A letter was received from the Trustees of Washington College, at the meeting of the Jefferson College Board, September 26, 1815, informing them that a committee had been appointed to meet and confer with a committee from the Board of Jefferson College, should they appoint such committee, respecting *a union of the two Colleges*. Accordingly, Dr. M'Millan, and Messrs. Kerr, M'Donald, and Murdock, were appointed a committee on that business, to meet at Emory's tavern on the ensuing Friday. Information was received from the Rev. Mr. Pringle, that the suit respecting Mr. Hannah's will, had been tried by Arbitration, and that the decision was against the Board; but that an Appeal was entered against the decision; consequently it must take its course in Court. The Board approved and confirmed the course pursued by a part of the Board, in respect to the graduates above mentioned, and conferred on them the degree of A. B. The degree of A. M. was also conferred on the Rev. James Wilson, of Philadelphia; Andrew Wylie, Principal of the College; Stephen Boyer, of Lancaster county; Robert Lusk, of Cumberland county; and John M'Donald, Esq., of Pittsburgh; all alumni of the College. Another effort was made to obtain legislative aid towards the building of the new college, and Messrs. Murdock and Ritchie were appointed a committee for this purpose. Messrs. Ritchie, Morgan, Mahon, and Murdock, were also appointed a committee to procure materials for the building, which at that time it was determined should be erected on the lot of the old college.

The Trustees again assembled, October 25th, upon a notification of the committee appointed to confer with the Washington committee, to hear their report, and, if necessary, to act upon it. It will be remembered this committee consisted of *Dr. M'Millan, James Kerr, Esq.*, and *Dr. Murdock.* The Washington committee were the Rev. Messrs. *John Anderson* and *Wm. Spear*, and Messrs. *A. Murdock, Esq.*, and *Parker Campbell, Esq.* The Jefferson College committee stated they had called a meeting of the Board to lay before them the following statement, which seems to have been jointly agreed upon by the two committees, for it is dated, "Canonsburg, September 29, 1815," the time when the committees met: "A difficulty having arisen with regard to the *place* of union, which could not be obviated by the Conferees, it was proposed by the committee on behalf of Washington College, and agreed to by the committee on behalf of Jefferson College, that it be recommended by the different committees to their respective Boards of Trustees, to select and appoint three trustees from each Board, in manner following; that is to say: the Board of Trustees of Washington College to select and nominate three trustees from the Board of Jefferson College, and the Trustees of Jefferson College to select and nominate three trustees from the Board of Washington College, whose duty it shall be to meet and confer upon the subject and place of an union between the two colleges, at the tavern of Mr. Graham, on Thursday, the 26th of October, and at such other times and places as may be most convenient to them, until their duty is fulfilled; and further, to make report of their proceedings and determinations, or that of a majority of them, to their respective Boards of Trustees, for their approbation or rejection." After this paper was read, a difficulty arose in the minds of some of the members of the Board of Jefferson College, whether the Board had legally met. It no doubt occurred to them that their action on this report would be of serious consequence. And it was well to be sure whether they could now legally proceed, in either approving or rejecting the course suggested by the Conferees. It was carried in the affirmative, however, that it was a legally constituted Board. Then they agreed to the report, and appointed Messrs. Gwin, Allison, and Stephenson, trustees of Washington College Board, to meet with the committee which should be selected from their Board, for further conference. But they also *Resolved*, "That this Board is not prepared to remove the site of the college from Canonsburg, except the hand of Providence is clearly discernible in such a measure, either by casting lots, or leaving it to the decision of the Legislature." President Wylie's salary was now raised to $700 per annum; and Prof. Miller's to $500. Whilst the Board were still in session, they were informed that the Washington Board had selected the Rev. Messrs. *Marquis, Macurdy*, and *James Allison, Esq.*, of the Canonsburg Board, to meet those above mentioned of the Washington Board; and as that important joint committee were to meet the next day, the Board adjourned till then, to be ready to hear their report. Accordingly, on the following day, the Board received the following paper:

"*Graham's Tavern*, October 26, 1815.

"The Committees from the Boards, &c., met according to arrangements of these Boards, last evening; Judge Allison was chosen Chairman, and the Rev. Thos. Allison, Secretary of the meeting. After some conversation, in which the design of the Boards respecting the propriety of uniting the Colleges was expressed, it was agreed that the commissioners from the Board of Washington College should state the grounds upon which they proposed to form said union. The commissioners then stated that they were instructed to say that all the present funds of the college of Washington should be at the disposal of the United Board, together with five thousand dollars, to be obtained by the present Board of said College, upon condition that the permanent site of the united college shall be in the Borough of Washington, which condition is a *sine qua non*. The commissioners from the Board of Jefferson College stated that they were instructed to say that the site of the united college shall be determined by the mind of Providence, expressed either by lot, or a decision of the Legislature of this State. As it was evident that the two Boards could not agree, according to the above resolutions, the committees were of the mind that the object of uniting the colleges should still be pursued; and from a free conversation, it appeared practicable, by some further deliberations in said Boards; and agreed to recommend a reconsideration of the subject, and give further instructions to their respective committees.

"Signed

"JAMES ALLISON,
"THOS. ALLISON."

After some conversation on the report, the following resolution was moved: "*Resolved,* that provided the Board of Trustees of Washington College will not recede from their *sine qua non,* but will give five thousand dollars, in addition to their present funds, half of the Trustees and the casting vote in the choice of the Faculty, this Board will agree to give up the site to them, and will unite with them in petitioning the Legislature to effect the object in view." The consideration of this motion was, however, postponed, for the purpose of choosing a committee to confer with the Professors of Jefferson College on the subject. Messrs. Ramsey, Murdock, and M'Dowell, were appointed that committee; and after some time, brought in the following report, in writing, from President Wylie: "On condition that the Board of Jefferson College do not see proper to accede to the proposals that may be made from the Board of Washington College, and that there should be a unanimity of views, and a coincidence of exertions in supporting the interests of Jefferson College, I will agree to continue in my present office, till means may be put in operation for rendering this Institution respectable. If, however, the proposals from Washington will be such as to secure the preponderance and priority to the Board and Faculty of Jefferson College, my opinion would be that they ought to be acceded to, and my conduct shall be regulated accordingly. P. S.—Upon conversation with Mr. Miller, I believe he will agree with the views stated above." The original motion was then called up, when the vote was taken, "accept or not?" The votes, when counted, were found exactly equal, and the motion was lost of course. "The President having declined voting, made the equality." When the Board met again on adjournment, January 4, 1816, it was moved and carried to make the last minute (above given) read thus, viz: after the word "equality," "the President was then called upon to vote; for some time he hesitated, but afterwards he did vote in the affirmative; no reflection upon the Secretary is hereby intended or designed." A petition of the students against the removal of the college was received and read. The report from the Committee upon a union of the Colleges was again read. Then the following resolution was adopted; "That the diligence and fidelity of the committee be approved; but that *from a change of circumstances*, since the last meeting of the Board, the union recommended cannot be confirmed and ratified." This was approved without any dissent, and gave the final quietus to the whole business. But it did not release them from further trouble on this subject. For at their following Spring meeting, in April, they received another communication from Washington, insisting that the Board of Jefferson College, having committed themselves to certain conditions of a union, which had been agreed upon, through their committees, in accordance with alleged instructions, were now bound in good faith to carry out their action. A majority of the Trustees of Jefferson College thought otherwise, and claimed still to have reserved to themselves the right of confirming or receding from the terms proposed by the committees. It was a delicate and difficult point in diplomacy. Some of the very same questions involved in the case, have often been discussed in the Senate of the United States, with immense ingenuity and argument, whenever the subject of confirming and ratifying treaties has been before them. If any body, on either side of this subject, thinks it a very plain case, we would advise him to read over the arguments, *pro* and *con*, on the subject of Jay's celebrated treaty; and he will not, perhaps, think it is so easy a question to decide. Perhaps the Jefferson Board would have yielded the point to the Washington Board, had they not been disturbed by other influences, especially the discovery, as they, perhaps erroneously, thought, that some of the Washington Board had been tampering with their *President*, and *some members of their Board*. However this may be, they returned a spirited but respectful answer to their brethren in Washington. These papers are on file, but we think it unnecessary to burden our narrative with them.

The Board, now released from this troublesome affair, went on, with renewed spirit, in their enterprise of erecting a new college—purchased from Mrs. Canon her lot, the most eligible in the town for the site, directed a committee to sell the old college and lot, and pledged themselves to the amount of $200 additional, if that amount should be necessary, after the proceeds of the sale of the old property, and the collections of the extra subscriptions should be gathered in, to pay Mrs. Canon. When the Board met in September, 1816, they received and confirmed the report of the Examining Committee, recommending that the degree of A. B. be conferred on *Hugh Dickey*, *Wm. Graham*, and *Wm. Wallace;* who all, we believe, afterwards became ministers of the gospel in the Presbyterian church. James Kerr, Esq., was appointed to attend at Carlisle, employ counsel, and manage the suit respecting E. Hannah's Will, in behalf of the Trustees. September 24th, 1817, the Rev. Andrew Wylie, D. D., having resigned his office, the Rev. Wm. M'Millan was chosen in his place. The Rev. Francis Herron, D. D., and the Rev. Michael Law, together with Richard Johnson, Benjamin Williams, Andrew

Munro, and John Reed, Jr., were elected Trustees to fill the places of the Rev. Thos. Marquis, Rev. Wm. M'Millan, John Morgan, Dr. Samuel Murdock, James Allison, and Abner Lacock, resigned. Another meeting was appointed in December, and in the meantime, each member was to use his "best endeavors" to collect money to defray the expenses of the new college. The Examining Committee reported in favor of the following persons: *Abraham Anderson*, (afterwards A. Anderson, D. D., a distinguished minister and Professor of Theology in the Secession Church, recently deceased,) *Daniel M'Intosh*, (a Presbyterian minister of great promise, from the Scotch Settlement, in Ohio, who went to the South for his health, and died in Georgia or Florida,) and *Andrew Todd*, who were admitted to the degree of A. B. Another effort was made to obtain legislative aid. The thanks of the Board were voted to the *ladies* of Canonsburg and vicinity, and the students, who had contributed for the purpose of painting the walls of the college edifice, and purchasing a new bell for Jefferson College; and the Secretary was directed to publish it in the newspapers. This is the first record of thanks we have met with, to the ladies, for their kind offices in behalf of the College. But it ought never to be forgotten that the zealous and efficient co-operation of the ladies was afforded from the earliest period in the history of this Institution. Many of our pious mothers and grandmothers offered up their prayers, and devoted a part of the labor of their own hands, for the support and prosperity of Jefferson College. Our readers will not forget what facts old Mr. Patterson's subscription papers prove, about the early efforts of our mothers, seventy years ago, when they lived in log cabins, and were not yet free from exposure to the incursions of the Red Men of the Woods.

Another communication was received from the Trustees of Washington College, informing them that Messrs. Campbell, Murdock and M'Giffin, were appointed a committee for the purpose of renewing the negotiation for the union of the Colleges, and to report whether it be practicable to effect such union. To which the Board of Jefferson College returned the following rather caustic answer: "On motion, *Resolved*, That as it is the duty of those to whom the education of youth is committed, to inculcate, both by precept and example, the virtues of candor, honor, justice and truth; this Board, therefore, cannot, consistent with the duty they owe to the public, to the youth committed to their care, and to the respect they owe to themselves, open a correspondence with the Board of Washington College, until they explain their conduct, respecting the agreement they made with Mr. Wylie, the late Principal of Jefferson College, while in our employ." They then adjourned till December 3d, 1817. In the meantime, the Board of Washington College, upon receiving this answer to their overture, drew up and published a long and able paper, vindicating themselves from the charge insinuated by the Board of Jefferson College, and hurling back, with much severity, but in very polished style, various charges against the Board of Jefferson College. To this paper, the Trustees, at their second December meeting, replied in a *memorable answer*, that produced a deep sensation in the public mind at the time. The paper was reported by the Rev. Messrs. Ramsey and M'Millan, who had been appointed a committee (December 3d) for that purpose. We have heard that much of it was written by Dr. Ralston. But of that we are not certain. This long and able paper was assailed with the utmost severity from various quarters; and not without partial success. For it had its weak and assailable points, especially in relation to the origin of the movement against Dr. M. Brown, in Washington congregation; also in relation to an alleged secret contract with Dr. Wylie, and in reference to the charge of disingenuousness on his part. An able defence was also made of the alleged conduct of those Trustees of Jefferson College, to whom Mr. Wylie had made known his purpose of resigning his office at Canonsburg. All about the midnight plotting to destroy Jefferson College was set in a very different light, by the answers which appeared through the press at the time. It may suffice to satisfy our readers that there were two sides to almost every matter in discussion, when they learn that such men as the Rev. John Anderson, D. D., the Rev. Thos. Marquis, and the Rev. Elisha Macurdy, differed, almost *in toto*, from most of the statements and arguments advanced in this powerful paper of the Jefferson Board. Those who wrote it, and almost all the members of those two Boards, are now in the grave. There were earnest and eminently pious men enlisted on each side of that exciting subject. They are now at perfect peace; and even long before they left the world, every root of bitterness had been drawn from their hearts. We had thought, at one time, of placing in the Appendix some of the able papers published by these Boards and their friends, simply as "Curiosities of Literature;" but lest old fires might again be kindled, we have concluded to withhold them.

In April, 1818, a valuable accession was secured to the Board of Trustees, by the election of the *Rev. Robert Johnston,* who had been a pupil during the times of the old Academy; and who continued a trustee for *seventeen years.** In

* Few men in the Synod of Pittsburgh, for the last half century, took a more prominent part in its counsels, or exerted a more beneficial influence, than the subject of this notice. And Jefferson College had few more valuable and substantial friends. "*Robert Johnston* was born in Perry county, (then a part of Cumberland county,) on the banks of the Juniata, in August, 1774, where he spent the first years of his life. Little is known of his youth, and his first religious exercises of mind. It seems probable that about the beginning of this century, he was a student of Canonsburg Academy, with a view of preparing himself for the gospel ministry. For, from the records of the Presbytery of Ohio, it appears that he was licensed to preach the gospel, on the 23d of April, 1802. It is believed his theological studies were under the direction of Dr. M'Millan. He obtained from the Presbytery, at its next meeting, June 30th, 1802, liberty to itinerate in the bounds of the Presbytery of Erie until the first of August, and was also appointed to supply

the fall of 1818, the following students received the degree of A. B.: *Wm. Blair*, *Robert Baird*, (afterwards the Rev. Dr. Baird, of New York, the distinguished European Traveler and Lecturer, and at the head of the Evangelical Protestant

---

statedly at Buckskin and Mount Pleasant, Ohio, for two months. The Presbytery of Erie, October 5th, 1803, reported to the Synod that they had received Mr. Johnston, a licentiate from the Presbytery of Ohio, 'who accepted a call from the united congregations of Scrubgrass and Bear Creek;' and at the next meeting of Synod, they reported 'that they had ordained and installed him.' After laboring with eminent usefulness and success in this field, where the spirit of God was poured out in a remarkable degree, during a considerable part of the seven years of his ministry, he was then, at his own request, dismissed, January 2d, 1811. He then entered a new and important field, in Crawford county; and on the 15th of October ensuing, he was installed pastor of the united congregations of Meadville, Sugar Creek, and Conneaut Lake. Here, for six years, and during a portion of the prime of his life, he was engaged in that laborious and scattered charge. Thence, at his request, he was dismissed, April 2d, 1817. During the following year, he removed into Westmoreland county, and became a member of the Presbytery of Redstone, having accepted a call to the united congregations of Rehoboth and Roundhill. He was installed pastor of these churches, June 18th, 1818. Here, for thirteen or fourteen years, he was laboriously engaged in his Master's work, and many were given to him as seals of his ministry. From the congregation of Roundhill, he was, at his own request, dismissed, December 14, 1831; and, in the following year, from Rehoboth. Some time in 1833, we believe, he removed into the bounds of the Presbytery of Blairsville, and took charge of the congregation of Bethel or Blacklick, an old and most respectable congregation, whose history dates far back in the last century. Here Mr. Johnston continued in his ministerial work for a number of years. Upon retiring from this field, and now becoming infirm through years of laborious and self-sacrificing toil, he removed to the town of Indiana, where he resided, without a pastoral charge, with his son, *James Johnston, Esq.* Upon the removal of his son, a distinguished lawyer, to New Castle, the county seat of the new county of Lawrence, he and his aged wife accompanied him, to this their last encampment on their way to the Heavenly Canaan. Mrs. Johnston did not long survive this removal, but died in the faith about two years afterwards, leaving her bereaved husband to follow her, after a further trial of his faith and patience. He is now waiting at a very advanced age for his dismission. Mr. Johnston was an able instructor and faithful preacher of the word. He was a bold and fearless man in the discharge of his duty; devoid of all fear of man, either in or out of the

Alliance,) *Samuel Evans*, *Salmon Cowles*, (now a venerable Presbyterian minister in Iowa,) *Thos. Hannah*, (the Rev. Thos. Hannah, D. D., a minister of the Associate Church in Washington, Pa.,) *Joshua Moore*, (a Presbyterian minister in Lewistown, Pa., lately deceased,) *Wm. M'Clure*, *Alexander Williamson*, *Wm. Jeffery, D. D.*, and *Jas. P. Miller*. Principal M'Millan's salary was $600 per annum. *Mr. Abraham Anderson* (late Dr. Anderson) was chosen Professor of Languages. In the spring of 1819, Principal M'Millan was commissioned to spend two months to solicit contributions for the College—especially to defray expenses for building the new College. In September, the graduate class consisted of David

---

pulpit, an excellent pastor, a wise and judicious Presbyter, a valuable Trustee of Jefferson College, and a faithful champion for Old School theology, and strict church discipline. He had a cast of manners and a mode of social intercourse that led many to consider him as overbearing and tyrannical; but it was altogether his manner, arising, perhaps, from a constitutional temperament. For a more kind-hearted man, and a warmer friend, could not easily be found. The period of his ministerial and pastoral labors in *Scrubgrass*, *Meadville*, *Roundhill*, and *Bethel*, should be long remembered as one of much spiritual prosperity in those churches. Mr. Johnston did much among his people in promoting the cause of religious benevolence. Nor was his usefulness in this respect confined to any one field. He was the ardent and efficient friend of domestic and foreign missions, of our then infant Theological Seminary, and of the cause of education. As a member of Presbytery, and of the Synod of Pittsburgh, from the latter of which he was not absent a single meeting for more than forty years, his services in these respects were invaluable. More than once, important agencies were entrusted to him.

"During the great struggle of the church from 1832 to 1838, against the alarming revolutionary movements of the New School party, Mr. Johnston stood a firm, unyielding, and efficient friend and advocate of the doctrines and the ecclesiastical policy of the church of our fathers. May he yet be spared just so long as his Divine Master has anything yet for him to do or suffer for his cause, and may his *nunc demittis* find him filled with faith and hope and love!"

The foregoing notice is taken from the Appendix to a sermon, entitled "The fear of God, woman's true praise;" preached at Roundhill in 1855, and published by request. A more extended memoir of Mr. Johnston is in preparation, with a view to insertion in a second volume of "Old Redstone."

Carson, Adam Coon, Alexander M'Candless, Jno. M'Kinney, Wm. Smith, and Joseph Trimble. We find here the name of A. M'Candless, long known and highly esteemed pastor of Long Run Congregation. He afterwards removed to New Jersey, where he died some years ago. Also the Rev. Wm. Smith, D. D., who has been for more than thirty-five years a Professor of Languages in Jefferson College, and pastor of Miller's Run Congregation. If long and faithful services, both as professor and pastor, entitle any man to distinction, Dr. Smith has won for himself lasting honor, and his name will stand high among the friends and benefactors of Jefferson College. The Rev. Joseph M'Elroy, D. D., (then of Pittsburgh,) was chosen a trustee. A renewed movement for Legislative aid, was also made at this time. The Rev. Messrs. Ralston, Ramsey, and Johnston, were appointed a Committee to select and recommend a system of *Metaphysics*, for the use of the College. What was the result is no where recorded. We believe that the old scholastic systems of *Metaphysics* were never much in vogue. A manuscript Epitome was in use in Dr. Dunlap's time—perhaps brought by him from Princeton. Dr. Wylie introduced Reid and Stuart on Mental Philosophy, in lieu of the old metaphysics. The metaphysics of the olden time is now entirely neglected, and its entities and quiddities nearly forgotten. *Requiescat in pace.*

In April, 1820, the Board conferred the degree of A. B. on *Wm. Nesbitt, John Peebles, Wm. S. Roberts, Chas. E. Gilletts,* and *John Kennedy.* And at their fall meeting, in September, on Alexander Campbell, Alexander Sharp, Thos. Williamson, M'Knight Williamson, and Robt. Crooks. The *Rev. Elisha P. Swift, D. D.,* was elected trustee in place of the Rev. Elisha Macurdy, resigned.

The committee appointed to settle with Dr. M'Millan and C. Ritchie, executors of the last will and testament of Mrs. Margaret Clark, deceased, reported that they had examined the papers and vouchers in the hands of the executors and found them correct, and that there now remained in the hands of Dr. M'Millan, and at his disposal, $4,685.10. Of this sum there belonged to the poor fund, $2,573.50, and to the Trustees, $2,111.60. This report was received and approved. In April, 1821, Mr. A. Anderson's salary was increased $50. The Legislature had passed an Act, making an appropriation of $1,000 to aid the funds of the College, and at this meeting, C. Ritchie, Esq., was authorized to draw on the State Treasurer for that amount. Messrs. *Geo. Buchanan, Wm. Johnston, John Pinkerton,* and *Levin Rogers,* received the degree of A. B.

In September, *Joseph B. Adams, Lewis W. Andrews, Richard Campbell, Meredith Helm, John Hunter, Wm. M'Connell, David M'Kinney, Samuel Reed,* and *Aaron Torrence,* were admitted to the degree of A. B.*

Mr. Anderson having resigned his office as Professor of

* We find on the printed Records of the Synod of Pittsburgh, October 6th, 1820, this minute: "The following resolutions, relating to the establishment of a Theological Seminary in the bounds of this Synod, were brought before Synod, viz:

"1st. *Resolved,* That it is expedient for this Synod, to take measures to establish a Theological Seminary within their bounds.

"2d. *Resolved,* That the said Seminary shall be located in the borough of Washington, Pennsylvania, upon the following conditions: 1st. That the Boards of Trustees of the Colleges of Washington and Jefferson, shall enter into an agreement to unite the said Colleges, with a stipulation, that the united literary institution shall be established at Canonsburg. 2d. That the united College shall agree to appropriate the College premises and buildings thereon erected in Washington, and also the funds, or a proportion thereof, for the use of a Theological Seminary, a Professorship or Professorships, to be therein established, with the concurrence of this Synod. 3d. That an act of the Legislature of Pennsylvania be obtained, should the same be found necessary, to sanction the measures aforesaid. 4th. That these resolutions be submitted to the Boards of Washington and Jefferson Colleges, and, provided the respective Boards concur therein, that commissioners be appointed to take measures to prepare the contemplated plan for the consideration of the next Synod.

"*Resolved,* That the motion to adopt these resolutions be postponed, in order to introduce a substitute, viz: That the first two resolutions, with the

Languages, Mr. Wm. Smith (now the *Rev. Dr. Smith*) was elected in his place. Upon his signifying his acceptance, the usual oath of office was administered to him. In April, 1822, the Board recorded that Thos. Byers, one of the executors of the last will and testament of John M'Pherrin, deceased, had paid to the Treasurer, $2,033.25, the original sum bequeathed to the Trustees of Jefferson College, the interest of which is to be applied to the education of poor and pious youth for the gospel ministry; together with $125, of interest arisen therefrom. This money, Messrs. Ritchie and Monroe were appointed to lend out on sufficient security. *Miss Mary Armitage* presented a *gold watch*, valued at $50, to aid the funds of the College, and $10 of which were returned to her, with the thanks of the Board for her valuable gift.

Vacancies in the Board were filled: but as we have now reached a period when this item of history can possess little interest, we will not further notice it.

Mr. Ritchie reported the receipt of the State donation. Messrs. *J. Claybaugh, Adam Gilliland, John Pitkin* and *Benj. Spillman*, were admitted to the degree of A. B. The Board also agreed to confer the same degree on John Closkey,

---

conditions annexed to the second, be referred to the Boards of the Trustees of the Colleges of Washington and Jefferson for their consideration.

"On motion, *Resolved*, That the Rev. Messrs. Thos. Marquis, Thos. Hoge, James Harvey, and Wm. Johnston, with James Hare, elder, be a Committee to confer with the Boards of Jefferson and Washington Colleges on these resolutions, and report at the next meeting of Synod; and that the stated clerk furnish a copy thereof to each Board of Trustees, and that it be recommended to this Committee to endeavor to effect a meeting with said Boards on the subject, in April next, or sooner, if found practicable."

There is no evidence that this paper ever came before the Board of Trustees of Jefferson College. They have taken no notice of it on their records. It would, apparently, have been an admirable scheme, could it have been carried out. Why it was altogether dropped or neglected, we are at a loss to explain. The Committee made no report at the next meeting, "but by information received from a member of the committee, it does not appear probable that such a union can now be effected." The committee were discharged, and that was an end of the whole matter.

James Johnston, John M'Cluskey, Ebenezer Monroe, and John Smart.

It was also determined at this meeting, in regard to the two societies, the *Philo* and *Franklin*, that should they, at any time, violate their own laws and regulations, to the aggrievance of any member or members, they shall have a right to appeal to the Faculty, and the Faculty shall be governed in their investigation of such appeals by the laws and regulations of the societies—an appeal still allowed to the Board.

In August of that year, the Board was called together to hear and investigate charges brought by the Faculty against several students, for being the authors and promoters of mutiny, sedition, and rebellion in college; and as having circulated calumny and slander against the character and reputation of the Principal, *Mr. Wm. M'Millan.* Upon a full investigation, the charges were not sustained. But the students were severely censured for their rash and precipitate conduct, especially in their treatment of the Principal. One student had published in the *Washington Reporter*, a publication which, in appearance, burlesqued praying societies and associations for sustaining pious youth; and upon his disclaiming any evil intention, and making proper satisfaction, and promising to state the matter in a true light, in the same paper, the Board accepted his explanation and promise, and let him escape any further action of the Board. Whereupon, the Rev. Principal M'Millan publicly declared his resignation, which was accepted: and the Rev. Wm. Smith was appointed to take charge of the College, in the room of Mr. M'Millan, until the next meeting of the Board; and was further authorized, in conjunction with Messrs. Ramsey and Ritchie, to employ a teacher of languages until that time. At the September meeting, Messrs. Morrow, Livingston, Martin, Frazier, Shellady, and Brown, were admitted to the degree of A. B. At this meeting, the *Rev. Matthew Brown, D. D.*, was duly elected Principal of the College, with a salary of $800. This was one of the most important events that ever occurred in the history of Jefferson College. But we must begin a new chapter in further proof and explanation of this remark. Dr. Smith received $50 for his extra labors, and his salary was thenceforward raised to $300 per annum. What he then received from Miller's Run congregation for his faithful ministerial and pastoral services, we have not learned. In the mean time, before we close this chapter, we deem this the proper place to state how it came about that Jefferson College obtained the distinguished services of Dr. Brown—a man who, but a few years before, was President of Washington College. This singular circumstance is so well explained by a writer in the *Presbyterian Advocate*, January 4, 1854, believed to be James Veech, Esq., of the Uniontown bar, that we shall not hesitate to adopt his statement, which is as follows: "The College War of 1816–1818 had ended. Dr. Brown's first wife had died. The conflict had made him enemies who seemed to have triumphed. His usefulness, as pastor of the Presbyterian church, had seemed to have been impeded. Strife and affliction had sunk his spirits and marred his happiness. He began seriously, though with much reluctance, to think of a new field of labor. In this state of mind, the late eminent and estimable Dr. Griffin, who had been invited to the Presidency of Danville College, on his return from the West, spent a night with Dr. Brown, at Washington, and communicated to him the conclusion he had come to, not to accept; and thereupon suggested the station to his friend, Dr. Brown. The suggestion was favorably received and entertained. Dr. Griffin thereupon wrote to the Centre College Trustees, recommending Dr. Brown to them in strong terms. In this he was zealously and efficiently seconded by the late Rev. Andrew Todd, who was a student of Washington College at the time of the disruption, and a devoted adherent of the Ex-President. In due time, the Danville Board offered to Dr. Brown the Presidency of Centre College. He thereupon went to the West, to Kentucky, to Danville; and looked into the prospects and position of the new College—favorably. This was in 1821 or 1822. He did not, however, then give a definitive answer to the offer, further than to say to the Board that he would duly consider the matter, and if the way was clear, and God and duty pointed him to it, he would go, if his Presbytery would dismiss him from his church at Washington, for that purpose. Soon after his return home, he informed the Danville Board that he accepted the offered Presidency, subject to the condition last above named. In this state of things, and preparatory to his removal, Dr. Brown procured a special meeting of his Presbytery, to be called to meet in the latter part of the summer of 1822, to dismiss him from his charge. And in confident anticipation of the desired dismissal being voted for, he, during that summer, visited the eastern part of Pennsylvania, to see old friends, and settle some secular business. On his return, he stayed all night in the 'forks' neighborhood, and then, for the first, heard of what was called 'the Rebellion,' in Jefferson College, and the resignation of the President, Rev. Wm. M'Millan. On his further progress homeward, he stopped to dine with his ancient and trusty friend, the late Rev. Dr. Samuel Ralston,* then, and for many years before and after, President of the Board of Trustees of Jefferson College. The exciting proceedings which had lately transpired at Canonsburg, were of course spoken of during the brief visit. But nothing was said about the Presidency, directly or indirectly, until just as Dr. Brown was about to mount his horse for home. Dr. Ralston, who knew of the *pro re nata* meeting, and its object, significantly inquired, 'Are you pledged to go to Danville?' Dr. B. replied that

---

* Whoever has read Dr. Ralston's "Philologus," on the College War, will be at no loss to discover the Irish strength and fervency of his friendship to Dr. Brown.

he was, if his Presbytery would dismiss him from his church. 'Very well, sir,' said Dr. R., 'good bye; I will see you at Presbytery, God willing.' The meeting of Presbytery came. Dr. Ralston was there. The request for dismissal was regularly presented. But when the motion to bring about decision came to be made, instead of being 'that the request be granted,' the latter word was, to the surprise of Dr. Brown, preceded by a 'not.' The Rev. Thos. Hoge, then of Washington, Pa., was, I think, named as the mover. The request was, however, persisted in, and urged by such reasons as were pertinent and proper. But the Presbytery was inexorable. The request was flatly though kindly denied; and thus the door was shut against Dr. Brown becoming President of Centre College, Danville, Kentucky, which, but for this unusual action of his Presbytery, he would doubtless have soon become.

The Presbytery having adjourned, the secret, or unavowed reasons, were explained to Dr. B. by his friends; which were in substance that he could not be released until after the Board of Trustees of Jefferson College should have met to elect a President; which would be in a few weeks thereafter—the last Wednesday of September, 1822, and if he were not chosen, then he might be let go. The Jefferson Board met at the appointed time. On the night of that day Dr. Brown was elected President of that College—a committee was dispatched for him in the night, who, before breakfast the next morning, (Commencement day,) returned with the President elect; who, before nine o'clock, took the oath of office, and on that day, within eighteen hours of his election, conferred degrees, and made a brief impromptu Baccalaureate address, as President of the Faculty of Jefferson College. 'In all this,' said the Doctor, in his relation of it, 'events crowded upon me so fast and so heavy, that I had no time to reflect and deliberate. Had time been given me I might have declined. But I thought I saw in it the finger of Providence, and I became passive in his arms.' The event was one of

10

great joy and gladness to the eighty students then at Jefferson College, and to the friends of that time-honored Institution. It was hailed as an omen of prosperity, and a triumph of retributive justice. It was an event from which untold benefits and blessings have resulted, not only to that College and its hundreds of students, but to thousands of the human race, to whom, through them, Dr. Brown became, under God, by his pre-eminent capacities for government and instruction, and by his piety and prayers, a benefactor of the highest order to which humanity can attain."

CHAPTER VI.

DR. M. BROWN'S PRESIDENCY.

A new era in the state and prospects of Jefferson College—Dr. Brown's extraordinary character and qualifications—Connection of Jefferson College with Jefferson Medical College in Philadelphia—*Jacob Green, Esq.*—Literary Societies in difficulties—Theological Seminary of the Associate Presbyterian Church established at Canonsburg—New College building in 1829–32. Crisis in the life Dr. M'Millan; Death of his old friends, *Prof. Miller* and *C. Ritchie, Esq.*; their lives and character—Agricultural labor provided for students by a College farm; its ultimate failure; reflections about it—Recent movement by Synod of Pittsburgh for *Ecclesiastical supervision*—Its failure; reasons—Aids to be sought in investigating that whole subject—General winding up of the whole subject.

We are now entering on a new era in the history of this Institution. Under the administration of Dr. M. Brown, which extended over the long period of twenty-two years, the College rapidly advanced in its glorious career. Never was there, perhaps, a more popular, or a more successful President. He was peculiarly gifted with qualities of head and heart that secured to him the affection and respect of the students, both while under his watchful care, and through after life, however long they might be separated from him, and in whatever walks of life they might be found. The pious students were generally ardently attached to him; and the wildest and most reckless respected and venerated him; and, in many instances, would speak of him, years after their residence in distant parts of the country, with a degree of affection that was often surprising. Yet he was constitutionally of a hasty, passionate spirit, and would often rebuke the students in the most unmerciful manner. Yet, somehow, he always had the art of making up his quarrels with them, without losing their respect, or his authority. He was certainly the most remarkable man of our day, for the possession of qualities apparently the most incompatible, but strangely and happily balancing each other. Into many a scrape, his impetuous feelings would hurry him; and yet he hardly ever failed to recover himself with grace and manliness. He had an admirable talent for governing a college. The success of his long presidential career was a complete proof of this. But his peculiar talent for canvassing and electioneering, among the people of all classes, in favor of the College, was not less remarkable. In this respect, he did more for Jefferson College than all others put together. He was, in fact, an eccentric man; and yet never was eccentricity more completely governed by good sense and sound judgment. His very oddities and personal mental peculiarities contributed to his usefulness, and to the success of the Institution over which he so long and so efficiently presided. It was an auspicious day, when, on the 24th of September, 1822, Dr. Brown was elected Principal of Jefferson College.

In April, 1823, the Board granted the degree of A. B. to James Arbuthnot, Wells Bushnell, John Cunningham, Boyd Emory, Sen., Boyd Emory, Jr., James C. Hall, Robt. Henry, Samuel Jennings, John Lee, George Lyon, Robt. Moody, Alex. Macklin, James Nourse, Wm. Pollock, Moses Roney, Josiah Scott, Andrew Wilson, and Benjamin Yoe. Many of these will be recognized as living ministers of the gospel, in various ecclesiastical connections, or as respectable members of other professions. We have now reached a period when we think it expedient to close the further mention of the graduates, as they are mostly still among the living, and our cotemporaries. We shall, however, give their names in an appendix. In the fall, the Board took Mr. M'Millan's house off his hands, at $1,000, and took back the old lot, exonerating him from $550, which he was to have paid for it. At this time the degree of D. D. was conferred on the Rev. Messrs. *F. Herron* and *Robt. Bruce*, of Pittsburgh.

In 1824, the Board was called together in June, to deliberate upon an extraordinary communication just received from Philadelphia, which led speedily to a new feature in the history of the College, and, for a while, to a new element in her prosperity. We refer to the establishment of the *Jefferson Medical College* in Philadelphia, under the wing and charter of our College. The following letter was laid before the Board:

"*Gentlemen*:—The undersigned, believing, upon mature consideration, that the establishment of a second medical school in the city of Philadelphia will be advantageous to the public, not less than to themselves, have formed themselves into a Medical Faculty, with the intention of establishing such a school, and they hereby offer to the Trustees of Jefferson College to become connected with that Institution, on the conditions herewith submitted; subject to such modifications, as on a full and free explanation, shall be found satisfactory to the parties severally concerned. The undersigned beg leave to submit herewith, the plan which they have devised, for forming the Faculty contemplated, and for conducting the concerns of the same—open to amendments and alterations in the manner already proposed.

"Signed by order of the Faculty,

"Joseph Klapp, M. D.,
"George M'Clelland, M. D.,
"John Eberle, M. D.,
"Jacob Green, Esq.

"Philadelphia, June 2, 1824."

After some discussion and due deliberation, the Board adopted the following resolutions, viz: "1st. That it is expedient to establish in the city of Philadelphia a Medical Faculty, as a constituent part of Jefferson College, to be styled the 'Jefferson Medical College.' 2d. That the Faculty of the Medical College shall consist of the following professorships: 1st—a professorship of Anatomy; 2d—of Surgery; 3d—of the Theory and Practice of Medicine; 4th—of Materia Medica, Botany and the Institutes; 5th—of Chemistry, Mineralogy, and Pharmacy; 6th—of Midwifery, and the diseases of women and children. 3d. That whenever a vacancy shall occur by death, resignation, or otherwise, it shall be filled by a gentleman who shall be nominated by the remaining Professors, or a majority of them, and appointed by the Trustees of the College. 4th. That a Professor may be removed by the Board of Trustees, with the consent of a majority of the other medical Professors, after a fair and full investigation of the alleged causes for the removal; but in no other way. 5th. That the Medical School shall have no claims whatever on the funds of Jefferson College. 6th. That the medical Professors shall make arrangements among themselves for the time and place of lecturing, for examinations, and for the general benefit of the school: the time for conferring medical degrees shall be determined by the Trustees, on the representation of the medical Faculty. The same fee shall be paid to the President of the College by the graduates for a degree, as for a degree in the arts. 7th. That this College shall use a suitable influence to send medical pupils to the medical school connected with it in Philadelphia; and the medical Faculty shall promote in every way the interest and prosperity of the College. 8th. That the young men who have attended one course of lectures, in any respectable medical Institution, shall be admitted to a standing, in all respects, equal to the one they had left. 9th. That ten indigent young men of talents, who shall bring to the medical Faculty satisfactory testimonials and certificates, shall be annually received into the medical school, receive its medical instructions, and be entitled to its honors, without any charge. 10th. That the following persons, duly elected, be and they are hereby appointed to the following professorships, viz: *Doctor George M'Clelland*, Professor of Surgery; *Doctor Joseph Klapp*, Professor of Theory and Practice of Medicine; *Doctor John Eberle*, Professor of Materia Medica; *Jacob Green, Esq.*, Professor of Chemistry, Mineralogy and Pharmacy. 11th. That the President of the Board be, and he hereby is appointed to forward these resolutions to the Professors elect, and to hold any necessary correspondence with them on the subject until the next meeting of the Board."

Toward the close of the following year, the Trustees applied to the Legislature, and obtained an enlargement of their charter, authorizing them to appoint ten trustees in the city of Philadelphia—not more than four of whom to be ministers of the gospel—and authorizing any Judge of the Supreme or District Courts to administer the oath of office to the Professors and Trustees: and then, in 1826, the Trustees, at a June meeting, elected the following Trustees, in Philadelphia, for the superintendence of their Medical Department, viz: Rev. Ashbel Green, D. D., Rev. Jacob J. Janeway, D. D., and the Rev. Ezra Styles Ely, D. D., together with Edward Ingersoll, Joel B. Sutherland, Samuel Badger, Wm. Duncan, and James Broom; and they were directed, as soon as qualified and organized, to inquire into the state of the Institution, and report to the Board at Canonsburg. They also created another Professorship of the Institutes of Medicine and Medical Jurisprudence, and elected Dr. Wm. C. P. Barton to fill that chair. Two months after, in August, the Board elected Messrs. Edward King, Samuel Humphreys, and Charles C. Cox, additional Trustees for the Medical College, and six of the whole Board was to form a quorum. Dr. Green also was appointed chairman. In 1828, the Board surrendered more entirely the whole concern to the Philadelphia Board, and agreed that their decisions, in all cases, should take effect without waiting for the confirmation of the same at Canonsburg; and only retaining the right of reversing their proceedings, if, in their judgments, the interests of the Institution required it. One important result, which grew out of this matter, was, that an arrangement was made in 1828, to secure the services of one of the Professors of the Medical College, *Jacob Green, Esq.*, to come out to Canonsburg and deliver a series of lectures on Chemistry, Mineralogy, &c., during a part of the summer sessions. And certain perquisites, arising principally from matriculation fees at the Medical College of Philadelphia, were appropriated as a compensation for his services. The interest of the last appropriation from the State, was also employed to purchase chemical and philosophical apparatus, and enlarge the College Libraries. And $500 also from the funds of the Board, were employed for the same purpose. In 1833, the Board appropriated $100 for the payment of Prof. Green's services, as Professor of Chemistry, &c. Thus, through successive years, was this arrangement continued. The Chemical Laboratory and Apparatus were enlarged from time to time, and much advantage to the College and to the interests of science was the result.

But to return. The Board, at their meeting, April, 1825 provided that the students should be allowed to occupy the vacant rooms of the new College edifice, as lodging rooms; that the education funds should be appropriated for the accommodation of their Beneficiaries, in this way; and that Benjamin Williams and John Philips should be a committee, in connection with the Faculty, to arrange these matters.

It appears that up to the year 1826, the decisions at the contests, held by the two Literary societies, were made by the Trustees. The Philo Society asked, by petition, at this time, that the Board should hereafter discontinue this usage. The Board advised the Philo Society to invite the Franklin Society to a friendly conference by committees, and get the whole matter adjusted in whatever way they should mutually determine upon, in regard to this point. In January, 1827, the two societies applied to the Board to settle this difficulty, and establish some order or rule about the matter. The Board informed them that they had never, by any formal act of the Board, heretofore acted in the case, and suggested to the societies that hereafter it would best comport with the harmony of the College, and the peculiar nature of these literary exhibitions, that the comparative merits of the respective performers should rest upon the impartial decision of the spectators generally. Whether the societies adopted the course suggested, and how long, we are not informed. They soon agreed upon the plan of selecting judges of the Contest, each society choosing a certain number, and they, perhaps, choosing an umpire. And on this plan the thing is managed to this day.

In 1827, the State Legislature granted another appropriation of $1,000, and the same amount for each of two or three successive years. There is also a notice on their Records, March 27, 1833, of $2,000, "as an installment due from the Legislature on the first of the ensuing May." It would seem that the Legislature had passed an act, some years before, granting an appropriation, by yearly installments. The whole amount we do not know.

In 1828, the Rev. Robt. Baird, D. D., was appointed Professor of Languages, and Dr. Smith was transferred to the Mathematical chair. But as Dr. Baird declined the appointment, Dr. Smith was continued in his former chair. In 1829, the Associate Body, or the Seceders, as they are commonly called, located their *Theological Seminary* at Canonsburg; and as they had not, for some time, the requisite buildings, the Trustees resolved "that the two rooms on the north-west corner of the College be appropriated to the use of the Associate Church of North America, for their Library and Theological Hall, until they shall have time to provide other buildings; and that public ground be afforded them, if they wish to build in this place." This body, however, did not avail themselves of this last proposal—judging wisely that the Theological Seminary should be, on many accounts, removed to some distance from the College buildings. They chose an eligible site on the left side of the Washington road, near a quarter of a mile from the borough; and there the Seminary has long flourished. They have recently removed the Institution to Xenia, Ohio. The above arrangement, afforded to them for their temporary accommodation, was not only for the interest of the College, but was justly due to a church whose members had always been the staunch friends of Jefferson College from its earliest days. Old Mr. Henderson, we have already seen, was actively concerned in fixing the Academy at Canonsburg, and in watching over its interests in the days of its childhood. The Chartiers Presbytery of that body likewise united with the Presbyteries of Ohio and Redstone, in vigorous efforts to sustain the Institution, when, but for their united efforts, it must, in all probability, have gone down to rise no more. Dr. Ramsey, also, the successor of Mr. Henderson, in the pastoral charge of that large and respectable Seceder congregation, in the vicinity of Canonsburg, was, through a long life, a most devoted friend and patron of Jefferson College—always an active member of the Board, whilst in it, and for many years the Hebrew Professor in College. Jefferson College owes much to Dr. Ramsey and the respectable body of Christians of which he was a greatly honored and respectable minister. He was also one of the first Professors in their Theological Seminary. In the Appendix will be found some further notice of him from the pen of Dr. Bevridge.

In 1829, the Board took measures to erect a new building, so as to afford a spacious hall, and also a sufficient number of rooms for recitation, library, apparatus, &c., and having the basement story so constructed as to furnish accommodation for a refectory and dining room. Measures were also adopted to raise the necessary funds. Dr. Brown was appointed agent for this purpose, and his salary increased. The Board determined that $1,000 should be the endowment, for a perpetual scholarship, for the education of a poor student, designed for the gospel ministry. This arrangement was adopted, perhaps, with a view, in part, to invite contributions towards the new building contemplated. The tuition, also, was raised this year to $25 per annum. In the fall of this year, having received an encouraging account of Dr. Brown's success in raising funds, and having appointed the whole Faculty as agents for further efforts, authorizing them to appoint sub-agents, with subscription papers, the Trustees now felt themselves warranted to appoint a building committee, (Messrs. *Williams*, *Philips*, *Monroe* and *Allen*,) to examine as to the site and dimensions of the building, the propriety of purchasing additional ground, the expense of erection, &c., &c., and to receive proposals. Early in the following year, the Board received their report, and proceeded forthwith in this important enterprise. In the course of less than two years, this building was ready for use. The Trustees held their first meeting in it, March 27, 1833, and called it, at the suggestion of the Rev. Moses Allen, *Providence Hall*. This is a spacious edifice—sixty feet by ninety in size—furnishing a magnificent hall, where now Commencements and Contests are held, and where public worship is also conducted every Sabbath; and it serves as a house of worship for the Presbyterian congregation of Canonsburg. Whether Dr. M'Millan ever preached in Providence Hall, we are not informed. His death occurred November 16, 1833. He had lived, however, to see this building finished and occupied. It does not appear that he was present at the meetings of the Board for the last few years of his life. He had been Secretary and Treasurer for ten years, from 1817 to 1827. There is no record of his having resigned his seat as a Trustee, and it is probable he did not resign. But his age and growing infirmities, perhaps, prevented his attendance at the meetings of the Trustees for some time before his death. But he lived to see this last edifice completed. And now, when from his home in the country he would visit Canonsburg, how contrasted the view of the College buildings and the town, with that scene which he first beheld when descending the hill east of Chartiers creek in 1775, or 1776. Then a single log cabin occupied the site of Canonsburg, with, perhaps, a few acres of cleared ground around it. Now his aged eyes rested upon that thriving village, and its home of science and literature. How often had his heart throbbed with anxiety for its interests, and even for its continued existence, more than once in imminent peril. And when he remembered how many had been trained already there, who were now preaching the everlasting gospel, far and wide over the West, and how some who, in poverty and in russet garb, had once been there, and had struggled on through many difficulties, till they were prepared to go forth as heralds of the Cross—had early sunk to the grave, and been called home to their rest; when he remembered how God had blessed with complete success, the efforts and struggles of himself and his fellow-laborers, in the cause of that College, he would, perhaps, exclaim, "what hath the Lord wrought!" The remembrance of these early associates in this noble enterprise, would perhaps bring before his mind the names and persons of many of those that were sleeping in their graves, before Providence Hall was built. He would recollect Henderson and Canon, and M'Dowell and Anderson, and Allison and Brecken, of those earlier times. His early friend and step-brother, *Prof. Samuel Miller*, had but recently been dismissed to his heavenly home, in a good old age, beloved and respected by all classes, and almost idolized by all the students that had ever been at Jefferson College. One of the first records of that *first meeting* of the Board in Providence Hall, reads thus: "On motion, *Resolved*, That the Treasurer be authorized to pay C. Ritchie six dollars, for the College expenses on the funeral of Prof. Miller, deceased." *

---

* "Mr. Miller's course through life was like that of the rivulet, winding its gentle and noiseless and healthful way among the spreading elms which line its margin, and serve in part to hide its surface from the vulgar gaze. it was very rarely that his own history formed the subject of his conversation with others; and the only record which now remains is that inscribed in the hearts, which once greeted his presence and profited by his instructions." "*Samuel Miller* was born on the 4th of March, 1757, at Barrow Water, in the county of Derry, Ireland. His great-grandfather emigrated from Scotland during the persecutions under Charles II, at which time his estate was confiscated, on account of his attachment to the principles of civil and religious liberty, and bestowed on a younger and more pliable member of the family. The subject of this memoir came to America when he was eleven years of age, in company with his widowed mother, two sisters, and a brother-in-law. Until his sixteenth year, he resided with his mother, in Chester county, Pa., prosecuting his education in the academy of a Mr. Law, of whom he always spoke in a tender and respectful manner. At sixteen, he began to teach in Chester county, and for fifty-seven years, with but two short intervals, he was employed in giving instruction. His first temporary abandonment of his post had in it something of the romantic. He had been occupied in teaching about two years. An old acquaintance appeared at his school-house, commissioned as a recruiting officer. Our teacher, and every pupil of a suitable age, were induced to enlist as common soldiers for one year. Mr. Miller remained in the service during eighteen months. He formed one of the 'Pennsylvania Line,' in the regiment of Col. (afterwards Gen.) Wayne, and breasted the shock of war at Brandywine, Germantown, and in several less important engagements. It is believed that Mr. Miller might have obtained a pension for his revolutionary services, but he never saw fit to apply for one. On retiring from the army, he had recourse to his old employment. At the close of the Revolutionary war, he revisited his native country. The estate which now fell into his hands induced him to think of a less laborious mode of life. On his return, he married into the family of Mr. John Nesbit, a ruling elder in the Presbyterian church of York, Pa. He soon after embarked in mercantile pursuits at Carlisle. His speculations, however, proved disastrous. Our merchant was constrained to resume his former employment, and was doubtless much more useful, and probably more happy, than would have been possible in the line of life previously contemplated. The mathematical chair being at that time vacant in Dickinson College, Mr. Miller was persuaded to be a candidate for the situation. His application was unsuccessful, but he expressed himself to be fully satisfied with the decision, and uniformly spoke of his successful rival (Mr.

M'Cormick,) in respectful and affectionate terms. This professorship was in his offer at an after period, but was then declined by him, Providence having given him an allottment elsewhere, with which, though less inviting in some respects, he was very well satisfied. In 1791, he came to the West, and taught an English school in the neighborhood of Canonsburg. He was appointed Professor of Mathematics in the Academy, in 1792; and this appointment was renewed in 1802, after the College charter had been obtained. From this time, until his resignation, in the autumn of 1830, his history is identified with that of Jefferson College. He was its friend in times of trial, and contributed a full share to its prosperity. In grateful remembrance of his fidelity, he was appointed honorary Professor for life, after he had become unable longer to discharge the active duties of the station. From the time when he ceased to officiate in the College, his physical and mental faculties were visibly on the wane; and on the 8th of June, 1832, he departed without a struggle, aged 75 years, 3 months and 4 days. In token of respect to his memory, the ordinary duties in College were suspended. The trustees, faculty and students, walked in procession to the grave; and on the evening following, an address suited to the occasion was delivered by the President, in the College Hall. Some portrait will be expected of the person and character of our deceased friend. To begin with the less important, we will give our views of him *as a man.* His personal appearance and address were prepossessing, notwithstanding the disadvantage of a stature a little below the ordinary size. His features were prominent and expressive; his eye lively, and always lighted with the smile of benignity; his health, as the result of strict temperance and regular exercise, was remarkably vigorous, until he resigned his professorship. His manners were obviously the spontaneous effusions of a spirit which breathed good will to all around. An intelligent lady made the remark, that she was never in his society without a lively impression of the beauty and utility of courteousness. He was naturally a gentleman, and his manners, originally amiable, were still further softened and sanctified by kindly and Christian principle. No one was ever heard to speak disrespectfully of Mr. Miller; and while this may be ascribed in part to his seclusion, it was no doubt owing mainly to his suavity of temper and manners. In Mr. Miller, as a *Professor,* we find talents of a very high order. He attained to considerable eminence without the advantages of a thorough academic or collegiate education. His attainments in mental, moral and theological science, were creditable; but the exact and physical sciences were those best suited to the original bias of his mind, and those to which his studies were chiefly directed. His acquisitions in this department, were not so extensive as those of learned Mathematicians of Europe, or perhaps of some few in our own country; but as regards aptness and accuracy, he was second, we think, to no one. There was one faculty he possessed, which generally occasioned no little surprise to his pupils. We refer, if the mental analyst permit, to his capacity of attending to several exercises simultaneously. Pupils not unfrequently came to the Professor for instruction on some point, while he was occupied in solving some difficult problem; and for fear of distracting his attention, would be disposed to defer their inquiries. Mr. Miller would apprise them very pleasantly that he had *two;* and without in the least degree turning off his eye, or at all lessening the rapidity of his other calculations, could hear and answer every question that might be propounded. This faculty, though not often necessary to professors, was of the greatest advantage to the then condition of the College, on account of the number of branches in the department, and the injudicious multiplication of classes. His acquaintance with what are termed Natural Sciences, was equally accurate, during the vigor of life, although it is not likely that his knowledge, during the last ten years of his life, kept pace with the improvements in some of these branches, particularly chemistry. His mode of communicating instruction was peculiarly happy, and his explanations of abstruse points remarkably lucid and satisfactory. He never read lectures, but his extempore remarks and illustrations, were always entertaining, and sometimes highly valuable. Original theories, in explanation of natural phenomena, were not unfrequently suggested, and insurmountable difficulties presented to the adoption of existing theories. Many of these are safely deposited in the memories of his pupils; but as some of them might have led to valuable practical results, it is much to be regretted that his extreme diffidence prevented him from communicating them in a less perishable form. His manners in class were not less decorous and winning than in private life. His punctuality was proverbial. During the thirty years he was Professor, he spent, on an average, about five hours daily in the recitation room; and though he resided about a mile from College, he was never known to disappoint a class, until within two years of the time when he resigned his charge. Mr. Miller's failing, as a Professor, was an undue lenity to delinquents. The diligent student had every facility for improvement, and, as a consequence, made rapid progress in science; but those of an opposite character were ferreted out of their lurking places, and goaded with too sparing a hand. Faculty meetings, at which unpleasant business was to be transacted, were the only meetings at which Mr. Miller's seat was ever vacant; but this was perhaps the infirmity of age, rather than the defect of the man; for our animadversion is to be understood of the decline of life and not of its meridian.

"Finally, we refer to Mr. Miller as a *Christian.* The commencement of his Christian course is dated about the time of his arrival in the western country. Of his early religious exercises, the writer knows nothing; but the genuineness of these may be safely inferred from the after fruits of holy living. At the *fireside,* in the *recitation room,* and in the *sanctuary,* the Christian was pre-eminent over the man, and the scholar. His religious character partook of the defect already alluded to. He was over timid, and therefore less prominent, and, in some respects, less useful, than many of not

The second meeting of the Board, but a few months after, (September 25, 1833,) tells another memorable incident. "The Board proceeded to elect a member in the room of *Craig Ritchie, Esq.*, deceased." * Thus, within a few months

---

half his moral worth. He sought first the kingdom of God and his righteousness, under the healthful conviction that all things else which are necessary will be added therewith. This was a principal reason of his attachment to the College which he served for so many years. He always regarded that Institution as eminently the offspring of faith and prayer. His salary, during a great part of his life, was exceedingly small, and he is known to have declined several professorships when the emoluments were far greater than those he actually enjoyed.

"Our deceased friend's Christianity was the result of *intelligent*, as well as heart-felt conviction. His accurate mind weighed soberly the arguments in favor of the divine origin of Christianity. The evidence he saw to be equally fair and irresistible, though of a different nature, as that in support of any proposition in Geometry. The system, if true, he perceived to be infinitely momentous, laying claim to the homage of his heart and the service of his life; and these were accordingly yielded to its influence. He was attached to the Presbyterian church, and for many years a ruling elder: a Calvinist in doctrine, exemplary in the discharge of every duty, and yet, when all was done, deeply sensible that he was but 'an unprofitable servant.' The benevolent operations of the day received his cordial support, and though a strictly temperate man, he readily gave his pledge and his heart to the blessed reform now in progress in our land.

"He conversed about his decease calmly, expressed his deep sense of his own sinfulness, and his exclusive reliance for pardon and salvation on the atonement of his Divine Saviour. Shortly before his decease, he experienced a 'fiery trial,' from an apprehension that he would be 'a castaway.' This lasted for nearly two days. He subsequently enjoyed great tranquillity, and finally fell asleep in Jesus, without a struggle, trusting in the mighty Saviour's name. 'Blessed are the dead who die in the Lord, for they rest from their labors, and their works do follow them.'"—*The Rev. John H. Kennedy.*

* *Craig Ritchie, Esq.*, was born in Glasgow, December 29, 1758. When only fourteen years of age he emigrated to this country, in 1772. He early evinced extraordinary talents for business, and soon succeeded in working his way to the position of a successful merchant, in Canonsburg. At the age of thirty, he secured to himself the possession of a most estimable and valuable wife, by marrying Miss Mary Price. This excellent lady, who became the mother of a la[illegible]e family, pre-eminently adorned her station, and greatly

of each other, immediately after the erection of this last fine building, were called away from earth, Prof. Samuel Miller, Craig Ritchie, Esq., and Dr. John M'Millan. They had been closely united for more than forty years, in their efforts to conduct Jefferson College up from feeble infancy to sturdy manhood. When Providence Hall was finished and occupied,

---

contributed to Mr. Ritchie's happiness and success in life. She sympathized with him in his toils and struggles to sustain Jefferson College, through its earlier history; and her name ought ever to stand with those of Mrs. Canon, Mrs. M'Millan, and other noble women who labored and prayed, and made such sacrifices for this Institution.

Mr. Ritchie's energy of character, business habits, integrity of principle, and general intelligence, secured to him a widely extended reputation. He was early elected to the Legislature, and served his country for some years in this capacity. During the "Whisky Insurrection," he took a decided stand on the side of law and order; and rendered himself so unpopular with some of the leaders of that unhappy affair, that he was in danger of their vengeance. Indeed, nothing but his absence, in attendance at the General Assembly of the State, saved his property from the torch of the incendiaries, at the time that Gen. Neville's house was burned to the ground; as some of the party told the family. He enjoyed the confidence and special friendship of Gen. Washington, who often visited him, and corresponded with him, and availed himself of Mr. Ritchie's aid, in the management of his landed interest, so far as Washington county was concerned. He not only lodged with Mr. Ritchie, and often dined with him, but took many a walk with him along the banks of Chartiers, conferring with him, not only about his own private interests, but the public concerns of the country. He also enjoyed the friendship and confidence of Dr. M'Millan, who made Mr. Ritchie's house his home, whenever he was in Canonsburg. For more than forty years, there was an unbroken intimacy between these good men.

It would be hard to say how much Jefferson College is indebted to Mr. Ritchie for its successful struggles in its most perilous times. He was one of its first Trustees, and the Secretary of the Board for a long time. He also was appointed Treasurer, at various times, and managed the financial affairs of the College with great judgment and success, often paying large sums in advance, from his own pocket. He was by far the most business man they had, and did more in devising ways and means to sustain the College, than perhaps all the other Trustees together, even including Dr. M'Millan himself. He gave a large portion of his time and personal attention in superintending the progress of the new building, and providing from his own resources, whatever might be temporarily wanted by the workmen. And

they might well consider their work on earth as done. And the remarkable Providence of God so ordered it that *these three men* should all successively die immediately after the completion of this work. It was a circumstance of almost as striking a character as the deaths of Adams and Jefferson, the one the author, the other the eloquent advocate of the Declaration of Independence, just fifty years after that national birthday, on the 4th of July, 1826. But we return to notice one or two matters that ought not to be passed over in silence; and which belong to the few years which precede the last dates we have been giving. We have often had occasion to notice the generous benefactions which poured from time to time into the College Treasury, to aid poor and pious youth in preparing for the gospel ministry. Indeed, it is believed the guardians of the Institution never turned away a worthy young man, destitute of means, who sought their doors, whether he was a professor of religion or not. It had long

---

when, in 1817, every other Trustee seemed to despair of the further existence of Jefferson College, Mr. Ritchie was unmoved and immovable, and took such energetic steps as reanimated the friends of the Institution, and secured its continuance.

He died, June 13th, 1833. He was a gentleman of the old school. His dignified and somewhat aristocratic manners, and his fine personal appearance, commanded respect wherever he might be found. For honesty of principle, goodness and charity, and for self-sacrificing efforts in behalf of Jefferson College, the church of his choice, and the country of his adoption, Mr. Ritchie had no superior in our Western country. To have so long enjoyed the confidence and esteem of Gen. Washington and Dr. M'Millan, is a high honor to which few, living or dead, can lay claim. He left behind him a large and well educated family, of uncommon intelligence and refinement. Their offspring are scattered over the land, from Baltimore to New Orleans. The *Rev. Dr. Andrew Wylie*, President, first of Jefferson College, then of Washington College, and lastly of Indiana University, married his oldest daughter. *Rev. Samuel F. Leake*, also married a daughter. The *Rev. Joseph T. Smith, D. D.*, of Baltimore, is married to his grand-daughter. His oldest living son, *John Ritchie, Esq.*, resides in New Orleans. The *Hon. David Ritchie*, of Pittsburgh, is perhaps his third son. His youngest son, *Craig Ritchie, Esq.*, is a merchant in Canonsburg.

been a subject of serious conference amongst the members of the Board, Faculty, and other patrons of the Institution, whether a better system could not be devised to aid poor, but talented and promising young men, through a college course. The plan of a self-sustaining Institution had not then been much heard of. But in some parts of the country, attempts had been made to unite the manual labor system with schools and academies. The scheme was becoming popular, and exciting much attention in the public mind. Some had read about what Pestalozzi and Fellenberg were doing in the old world. Could something like this be done, in whole or in part, at Canonsburg? If half the glowing declamation that was beginning to fill the public press on the subject was founded in truth, it was worth the trial. Surely Jefferson College, that had been sustained, through its earlier life, by the hard earned and humble offerings of the comparatively poor, all over Western Pennsylvania, as we have already seen, was now, in her better and more prosperous days, peculiarly bound not to forget "the rock whence she was hewn and the hole of the pit whence she was digged"—was bound not to forget the poor. It was worth the trial, at any rate, to see whether facilities offered for agricultural labor, could be secured to young men who were willing to work their way to a diploma, by the toil of their hands. Accordingly, at a meeting of the Board, September 30, 1830, the following preamble and resolutions were adopted:

"Whereas, it has pleased the Great Head of the church, eminently to own and bless the instrumentality of this College, in preparing men for usefulness in the gospel harvest, as well as in other professional and public stations, and whereas the Board cherish the hope that his kind and benignant Providence may still continue to watch over it for good, and to increase the amount of its usefulness to the cause, and the kingdom of Christ, and the public welfare; and whereas they feel it incumbent on them to use every measure in their power to facilitate the acquisition of classical education on the part of indigent and promising young men of our country; therefore,

"*Resolved*, That in order the more fully to attain the objects above adverted to, it is expedient to connect with the College premises, *a farm* of such location and size as may give to all such students as may be disposed, an opportunity to employ a part of their time in mechanical, horticultural and agricultural pursuits, with a view to the decrease of their expenses, and for other purposes, on such plan and under such regulations as may hereafter be adopted by the Board."

Messrs. Williams, Johnston, and Logan, were appointed a committee to take measures to obtain the requisite funds for the purchase of a farm, and were authorized to select and purchase the same, whenever the requisite funds shall have been subscribed or guaranteed. In April, 1831, the committee made a report, unfavorable to the purchasing of a farm at that time. But while the subject was under consideration, Messrs. Allen and Williams stated to the Board that they had made a purchase of a farm, adjacent to the town, for the sum of $3,000, which they would tender to the Board, if they would accept of it, on the terms purchased. The Board agreed to the terms—these gentlemen pledging themselves, at the end of one year, to take back the farm, provided the Board should be disposed to give it up, and that they would, in that case, refund the money now advanced by the Board, without interest. We find but little subsequently recorded about this farm. It is stated that on September 28th, 1831, "A request was laid before the Board, by Mr. L. Streit, a student of the College, for a lease of three or four acres of ground, on the College farm, with the privilege of erecting a house and making certain improvements thereon. His request was granted, and Messrs. Moses Allen and Benjamin Williams were appointed a committee to contract with Mr. Streit, and make such arrangements with other students desirous of residing on the farm, as shall appear expedient. We know but little more of this enterprise. We believe, however, that after the trial and experience of a few years, it was deemed expedient to abandon it, not having fulfilled the expectations of those who were at first very sanguine in its success. A similar fate has attended such schemes almost everywhere else. And we hear but little now of manual labor Colleges and Academies. A real agricultural school, however, is a different affair. Our State Agricultural Society is about to make the experiment of such an institution. But though we should rejoice in its success, if conducted on right principles, we fear it will be a failure. For how shall moral and religious instruction be provided that will be worth any thing, and at the same time be acceptable to all the parties interested? If it be entirely left out—if an open Protestant Bible and scripture lessons be excluded, what guarantee can we have for its moral influence, and even for its successful management? But this is aside from our present purpose. We cannot yet think that a plan of manual labor in mechanical departments, in connection with Jefferson College, would be necessarily a failure, if some of the faculty, or some suitable person employed by them, could take the direction of it. Most students would labor with more advantage in rooms or shops, than on farms, often exposed to scorching suns, or drenching rains; for these could not always be avoided. And young men or boys, reeking with perspiration or discomforted with soiled clothes, feel little taste or fitness for study, or the lecture room. This has been our experience, and that of those with whom we have conversed. If, indeed, a professor of agricultural chemistry could be sustained, and a sufficient amount of land could be secured to afford an opportunity of illustrating the various scientific improvements in the cultivation of different soils, in sub-soil plowing and spading, and in the preparation of manures, it might be rendered a valuable acquisition to Jefferson College, and to Western Pennsylvania. Perhaps, after all, the great difficulty is to provide, in the *same institution*, for those who are *willing to work*, and also for those who have *no need*, or are not *inclined* to work. Those who being poor, are willing to work their way to a diploma, or even to acquire a part of a college education, by the labor of their hands, will perhaps always prefer to perform that labor elsewhere, or to resort to such institutions as require all, without distinction, to work certain hours of the day. Work, to a certain amount, must be made the rule for all alike, perhaps, in order to secure complete success, whether it be mechanical or agricultural labor.

We have now brought down our history to a period sufficiently near our times to justify a winding up of our narrative, by a very summary statement of what belongs to the remaining period. Dr. Brown, after a long and prosperous career in his office, resigned, in 1845. He had been, during the greater part of his residence in Canonsburg, also engaged in pastoral and ministerial labors, in connection with Dr. M'Millan. And when, in 1830, the church in Canonsburg was organized, he became its stated Supply. That church, along with the College, was favored with many refreshing seasons of divine influence. No college in our country has, perhaps, been more highly favored in this respect. There were especially two very *remarkable revivals*, both in the College and in the town, during his presidency; and before he died, he had the happiness of knowing several scores of ministers laboring through the wide land, and some who had gone to heathen lands, that first, as they believed, drew the breath of spiritual life while at College in Canonsburg.

The *Rev. R. J. Breckenridge, D. D.*, was his successor. He continued in office, however, only till June, 1847—not long enough to fulfill the great expectations that were raised by his eminent abilities—but long enough to give a new impulse to the interests of the College. He was succeeded by the Rev. A. B. Brown, D. D., son of Dr. Matthew Brown. He had been a member of the Faculty some time before, and stated supply or pastor of Chartiers congregation. This charge he of course surrendered, upon accepting the Presidency of the College. For he was about the same time unanimously called to the pastorate of the church in Canonsburg. After his entrance on this new and arduous field of labor, he soon evinced eminent and peculiar talents for his station. The College continued to flourish under his administration, assisted as he has been, by an able and efficient Faculty. Though it was thought the loss of *Prof. Samuel Williams*, and the *Rev. H. Snyder*, both eminent in their departments, could not be easily repaired, the Trustees were fortunate in securing the services of *Prof. Jones* and *Prof. Frazer*—one from the Emerald Isle, the other a North Briton—both well educated and experienced men. Still further, they have now also the faithful services of the *Rev. A. Williams, D. D.*, whose long experience as a Professor in Athens University, had fully prepared him for his present office and labor. He is also co-pastor with Dr. Brown, of the church. It was hoped this arrangement would afford such relief to Dr. Brown as his feeble health required. But he has found the labor and confinement too oppressive for him. This, together with the feeble health of part of his family, has led to his removal to the country, and to his resignation of the Presidency, much to the regret of the Board, and of all the friends of Jefferson College. The Board, however, on the 7th of January of the present year, (1857,) have unanimously elected the *Rev. Dr. Alden*, late Professor at La Fayette College, Easton, Pa. And he has recently entered, with great acceptance, upon the duties of his responsible office. The Institution is now in a state of great prosperity. The number of students is as great as at any former period. The plan of raising by scholarships $60,000, for a permanent endowment fund, has succeeded. The effort to raise another endowment of a Greek Professorship, is in progress, and it is hoped will be completely successful. There is still much need of an enlargement of the College Library, of a more extended Chemical and Philosophical Apparatus, of an improved Natural History department, and, above all, of a good Astronomical Observatory, with a full supply of Optical Instruments. The honor is yet reserved for some generous friends of science to afford the requisite funds.

There is one other matter connected with the more recent history of our College, that may be briefly stated. A movement was made in the Synod of Wheeling, a few years ago, with a view of getting up an Institution under ecclesiastical supervision; and a committee was appointed to confer with a similar committee, to be appointed by the Synod of Pittsburgh, with the hope that a plan might be devised by which they might act conjointly in this measure. Nothing, however, resulted from this, so far as the Synod of Pittsburgh was concerned. In the course of another year, a negotiation was opened between the Trustees of Washington College and the Synod of Wheeling, which resulted in the transfer of that College to the control and supervision of that Synod. Believing that many ministers and churches in the bounds of the Synod of Pittsburgh, would be glad to lend their co-operation in favor of this Synodical College, that Synod sent delegates to her sister Synod to invite such action and friendly response, in regard to this enterprise, as might be deemed proper. Many members of the Synod, though declining any synodical relation to the Institution, expressed their hearty good will in the cause, and their willingness that agents in behalf of Washington College should visit such of their churches as were favorable to the enterprise of the Synod of Wheeling, and invite such aid to endowment funds as could be obtained. When the Synod of Pittsburgh met in 1853, it was moved by the late lamented and eloquent young brother, the Rev. Mr. Cook, and seconded, we believe, by the Rev. L. M'Aboy, that a committee be appointed to confer with the Trustees of Jefferson College, in order to ascertain whether that Institution could be placed in a relation to the Synod of Pittsburgh, similar to that of Washington College with the Synod of Wheeling, and to report to the Synod at its next meeting. Their report was as follows:

"O tober 20th, 1854. The committee appointed to correspond with the Trustees of Jefferson College, as to the expediency and conditions of its being placed under the ecclesiastical supervision of this Synod, or in case the General Assembly divide it, the joint supervision of the two Synods report, That in accordance with their instructions, they diligently and faithfully attended to the duty enjoined, and were respectfully and cordially received; but, for reasons assigned by those who were entrusted with the management and control of the Institution, your committee failed to accomplish the object contemplated in their appointment."

David Kirkpatrick,
L. R. M'Aboy,
T. H. Neven.

No further action has been subsequently taken by the Synod of Pittsburgh, in reference to this matter. Even on the supposition that those who moved in this affair expected the result which occurred, we suppose their desire was that it might be seen that they, as well as a majority of the Synod, were not hostile to ecclesiastical supervision; and that the churches and the world might see that the position of Jefferson College was such as to render it impracticable, or, at least, altogether unadvisable that any nearer relation with the Synod of Pittsburgh should be effected than such as already existed, and that, notwithstanding this, the present status and historical antecedents of the College, entitled it to the undiminished confidence and patronage of the whole Presbyterian church. From this report of the committee to the Synod, it does not appear what the reasons were that led the Trustees of Jeffer-

12

son College to take such ground, as led the committee to report the failure of the object of their appointment. The Board, however, took care to publish to the world, in the *Presbyterian Advocate*, and several other papers, during the month of April, 1854, their action in relation to the proposals of the Synod of Pittsburgh, which was as follows:

"After maturely considering the important communication of the Synod of Pittsburgh, the Board feel constrained most respectfully to decline the proposed ecclesiastical connection with the Synod, for the following, among other reasons, viz: 1st. Fidelity to the commonwealth of Pennsylvania, from which we hold our charter, and from which considerable donations in money have, from time to time, been received, precludes us from the right to transfer to other hands, and for other purposes than those originally contemplated, a trust so important, and assumed under the solemnities of an oath. The very terms of our charter would be violated, in their spirit at least, by surrendering the exclusive control of the Institution to any one religious denomination. 2d. The interests of other religious denominations, especially of those which have, from the beginning, been largely concerned in the patronage and control of this College, forbid the transfer of its management and supervision to any single denomination. It is true that the Institution has always been predominantly Presbyterian in its character, from the fact that it was originally planted in the midst of a population almost exclusively Presbyterian, and has always been dependent chiefly on Presbyterian patronage. This character it is expected still to maintain. Its Presbyterianism, however, has never been exclusive or sectarian. At least three branches of the great Presbyterian family, all holding 'the like precious faith,' have always been united in its support. For one of these denominations, largely in the majority, to usurp the exclusive control of an institution in which the others are alike interested, in proportion to their numbers, would be a gross violation of good faith and Christian courtesy. 3d. The past and present prosperity of the College, on its existing basis, satisfies us that the proposed change is not called for. God has been graciously pleased to bless the Institution with the smiles of his Providence, and the frequent effusions of his spirit, so that it has been enabled to send forth an unusually large number of laborers into the spiritual harvest field in our country, and in foreign lands; and to furnish hundreds of men for posts of distinguished honor and usefulness, both in Church and State. We have, therefore, no inducement to abandon our old foundations, and especially to have recourse, in the midst of prosperity, to a measure which we could not, in good faith, adopt under any circumstances. 4th. We see no necessity for the proposed change, on the alleged ground of a demand for 'a more sanctified education;' or for the greater security, as to the faithful and unperverted use of our funds, in future years. There has always been as large an infusion of the religious element into the educational appliances of this College, as we think is proper or practicable, in a literary Institution. It would be obviously improper and unwise for us to subvert the very foundations of the Institution, in order to secure for it an advantage which it already enjoys, in as high a degree as any Ecclesiastical College in the land. And whatever may be the apparent necessity for adopting the principle of ecclesiastical supervision in the founding of new institutions, in those parts of our country where all other denominations are pursuing the same course, we believe that in our case there is no such necessity. We are happy, moreover, to be able to afford an example of harmonious Christian union and co-operation on common ground, at a time when the Providence of God seems to call so loudly upon all the true friends of Christ to combine their efforts in opposition to common enemies. In regard to the security of funds from future perversion, we believe that the peculiar constitution of this Board, as consisting of members belonging to four different Presbyterian denominations, affords a more ample guarantee for the safety of funds, than if they were under the exclusive control of any one of these denominations. The history of endowments proves that they are as liable to perversion in ecclesiastical as in other hands. But while we do not feel at liberty, for the reasons already stated, to place the Institution under the direct control of the Synod, yet, in order to satisfy those who think that the church is the safest depository for funds, we are perfectly willing, and would propose, that any funds which the Synod may see proper to raise for the endowment of a Professorship, or for scholarships in this Institution, shall be held under the care and control of the Synod, and be subject to withdrawal, whenever applied in a way that does not meet the approbation of that body. We are likewise willing to enter into a similar arrangement with the other ecclesiastical bodies represented in this Board.

"In thus declining the proposals of the Synod, we wish it to be distinctly understood that we do not undervalue the patronage and the maternal care of that venerable body. We trust that the reasons we have assigned for our course will commend themselves to the approbation of all the friends of the College, and to the Christian public generally; and we feel assured that the Synod of Pittsburgh will not withdraw its confidence and favor hitherto enjoyed, from the Institution under our care, so long as we adhere to the principles and policy by which we have hitherto conducted it, and to which the Synod itself has recently given the strongest and most unqualified approbation. We should deprecate, above all things else, the withdrawment from us of the sympathies and prayers of the people of God. We shall still be dependent, in a measure, on their pecuniary patronage, but much more upon their prayers, for a continuance of the prosperity which we have heretofore enjoyed. Trusting that God and our friends will not desert us, we decide to go forward, on the old basis, on which the fathers of this Institution placed it. Adopted unanimously at a meeting of the Board, held March 29, 1854.

"JAMES M'CULLOUGH, *Sec'y.*"

The reading of this paper was not called for when the synodical committee made their report, as it had been previously published, and was doubtless read by most of the members of the Synod.

It is not out of place here to state, simply as a historian, that the minds of the friends and advocates of the old system of government were about this time enlightened, or mystified, by an elaborate paper that appeared in the *Southern Presbyterian Review*, on the subject of denominational education. It is said to be from the pen of the Rev. R. J. Breckenridge, D. D., and was published in a separate pamphlet, and put into the hands of some of the Trustees of Jefferson College. Those who wish to examine the whole question about ecclesiastical supervision, should read the very able Annual Reports of the Secretary of the General Assembly's Board of Education, for the last few years, and also this paper of Dr. Breckenridge, together with several able articles published by the Rev. Drs. Thornwell, Dabney and Hope, and also an excellent paper from the pen of the Rev. Mr. Vaughan, of Virginia. Those written by Thornwell and Vaughan, are considered as strong on that side of the question as any that have been written. But we hasten to close this chapter, with but a few remarks.

It is not easy to state with any precision what Jefferson College has done for the cause of literature and science throughout this country. There are some facts, however, that are interesting to every man who loves his country and his race. She has had the honor of training *twenty-four* Presidents of Colleges,* in ten different States. More than *fifty* Professors in Colleges were once sitting at her feet. A large number of Professors in Theological Seminaries, and in Academies and Female Seminaries and Institutes, are amongst her alumni. About *six hundred* ministers of the gospel received their literary training, in whole or in part, at this seat of science. The number of lawyers, physicians, judges, governors of states, legislators, and public men, cannot be told with any certainty. We will not venture our conjectures. The whole number, however, is vast. When Messrs. *Henderson*, *M'Millan* and *Smith* stood in the shade of the sassafras bushes, in July, 1791, to inaugurate the Institution in its humble form of academical life, how little did they dream of the glorious career that awaited their humble protege! May successive generations witness a still brighter halo of glory gathering around the brow of Jefferson College, until its brightness shall mingle and blend and melt away with the glories of the millennial morn!

---

* The present Principal of Washington College, now under the care of the Synod of Wheeling, the *Rev. J. W. Scott, D. D.*, graduated at Jefferson College, in 1827; and the President of Washington College, Lexington, Va., that Institution which owed its origin to the same action of the Synod of Virginia, in 1791, that helped forward the Canonsburg Academy, (*"par nobile fratrum,"*) the *Rev. George Junkin, D. D.*, graduated also at Jefferson College, in 1813.

CHAPTER VII.

SOME ACCOUNT OF THE LITERARY SOCIETIES OF JEFFERSON COLLEGE.

History of Philo Literary Society—And of the Franklin Literary Society.

Our work would be incomplete without some notice of two important institutions that have been connected with the fortunes of the College, for about sixty years. We begin with

The Philo Literary Society.

This Society is a few months older than its rival sister, being founded August 23d, 1797.

Its founders were the Rev. John Watson, first President of the College, Rev. Samuel Tate, Rev. Robert Johnston, Rev. James Satterfield, Rev. John M'Lain, Rev. Elisha Macurdy, Wm. Fowler, Rev. John Boggs, Rev. Robert Lee, Rev. Wm. Moorehead, Rev. Wm. M'Millan, D. D., and Joseph Smith. Of these, only Messrs. Johnston and Satterfield still survive. Most of them were eminently useful men in their day; and some of them will long be remembered in Western Pennsylvania.

The object of the Society was the cultivation and promotion of science and literature, and of friendship and morality among its members. The first meeting was held in the garret of the old stone edifice, where they continued to assemble for several subsequent years. They labored under every inconvenience. Their seats were benches; their great coats were used for window blinds; and their table was but a stool. Yet, with a laudable ambition, they surmounted every obstacle, and laid the foundations of an institution that has passed through the trying scenes of sixty years.

The government was substantially the same with that of the rival Society; and both resembled those of the literary societies of Princeton College, and of other Institutions. Indeed, their constitutions were, to some extent, copied from those of the Whig and Cliosophic Societies of Nassau Hall. The details will not be expected in our brief narrative. Suffice it to say, they were well suited to secure the objects in view—their mental and moral improvement, mutual friendship, and habits of system and good order in their exercises, deliberations, and business transactions. They met weekly, during the sessions of College,—the Philo Society, generally on Friday evening. In earlier days, their exercises were *spelling, speaking select orations, debating,* and *reading compositions.* The *first* of these was, after some time, laid aside: whether wisely or not, is not, perhaps, so clear. Though it might seem rather humiliating and undignified, such an exercise could not fail to be profitable, through all future life. Strange as it may appear, graduates of colleges are not always good spellers, or thoroughly grounded in orthography. Perhaps the end might be attained, in such societies, without adopting a school-boy method of drilling. The Society was opened and closed with prayer. The presiding officer was required, upon his induction into office, to read an original composition. The members were divided into three classes, which alternately engaged in debating, select speaking, compositions, recitations on history, and reading and spelling. Four debaters were chosen by the presiding officer, from the class that read and spelled, for the debate of the ensuing evening or meeting. One of these had choice of sides as to the question, another, choice of assistant. Translations were sometimes allowed from some one of the classics, in lieu of select orations. This was considered of great advantage to the younger members, to promote their accurate acquaintance with the classical writers. But this was during the earlier history of the Society. If a student failed to perform his proper exercise, he was required to do it at the next meeting, in addition to what was then tasked. One of the earliest items recorded is a resolution of March 30th, 1798, requiring two persons to be appointed to speak orations before the Trustees, at the following examination. Again, on the evening of March 18th, 1799, it was resolved that *three* persons should be elected to speak orations, two of which were to be delivered before the Trustees, and one "on the last night of the singing school!" These were the first public exercises of which there is any record.

On September 5th, 1799, a proposition was received from the Franklin Society, to contest with the Philo Society, before the Trustees, at the following examination, in *select speaking, composition,* and *debating;* which proposition was agreed to. Thence originated those *Contests* which have so long been annually sustained by these literary societies, at the close of each Spring session. It is unnecessary to enlarge upon the influence of this remarkable feature of Jefferson College history, upon the improvement of the members, and upon the development and cultivation of the talents of the students.

The first question discussed was, "Whether the mathematics, or the languages—Latin and Greek—be more necessary?" The question is sufficiently vague to allow of a wide range in its discussion; and perhaps, for that reason, was better adapted for the purpose. The next question discussed was, in substance, "Whether the immediate emancipation of the slaves would be right?" But as we purpose to give a list of the questions, down to the present time, we shall not further notice them here. For the first *four* years, they had no library. They then began by purchasing a *pronouncing dictionary.* This was their first book, and is still retained in their library, as a venerable piece of antiquity. It was their only book for *four* years more; when some member happily hit upon the idea of a subscription by the members, and patrons of literature in the town and country around, to raise a fund, with which they might begin a library. *Twenty-four* volumes were thus secured. About $60 were raised in this way. In 1806, with their *two dozen* of books, and a treasury containing $29.18¾, and an outstanding subscription for $120, they also required of each member, on dismission, $1, to be devoted exclusively to the purchase of books. They also petitioned the Trustees for a suitable repository for their books. In those early days, they adhered to the old style of reckoning, by pounds, shillings and pence.

The questions discussed in the Society in those early days were adapted to their circumstances. Having no library of any account, they did not often venture on discussions that required much book research; preferring such as were of a *practical nature*, and about which they had some experience, or could gather opinions that were floating in the community around them, in those days. A few specimens may be given: "Is it right to inoculate for the small-pox?" Decided in the negative. "Is the farmer or the student the more happy?" "Whether is it naturally immoral to have more wives than one?" "Is it right for a student to marry while at learning?" Decided in the negative. "Whether is it right, in public worship, to give out more lines than one?" "Or to give out two lines of a Psalm at once, in this congregation?" Decided in the negative. "Whether would the State of Pennsylvania be better with, or without lawyers?" "Is it as proper for young ladies to make proposals of marriage to young gentlemen, as for young gentlemen to make proposals to young ladies?" "Have we any good reason to say that a black skin, flat nose, and curly hair, are uglier than the color, noses, and hair, we have among us?" "Whether is activity, joined with sharpness of speech and temper; or good humor, joined with indolence, to be preferred in the character of a young lady?" "Is it right to drink whisky in a tavern?" Decided that it is right in certain cases. "Should a married couple continue to cohabit, when they become odious to each other, and desire to separate?" "Does marriage weaken the powers of the mind?" To debate this question, two single persons were appointed upon the affirmative, and two married upon the negative; but the latter, having the advantage of experience, found little difficulty in sustaining the negative, before a body who little regarded all theoretical views, when they could receive the evidence of practical men. Indeed, to account for several questions above stated, it must be remembered that in those days, there were always several married students at College, and the others found amusement in teasing and roasting them by such discussions. "The above questions," says the Philo historian, "were all, doubtless, debated with that gravity and dignity which their importance demanded." Even so late as 1823, the following question was discussed: "Suppose a young man, bred a farmer, but without any fortune, has it in his power to marry either of two women; the one, a girl of large fortune, but neither handsome in person nor agreeable in conversation, and can manage the household affairs well enough; the other, a girl every way agreeable in person, conversation and behavior, but without any fortune; which of the two should he choose?" From the minutes of the next meeting, it appears that the decision was in favor of the girl without fortune. From the ludicrous length of the question, one might think that the proposer of it had been recently reading "Pike and Haward's Cases of Conscience."

Of the founders of the Philo Society, Dr. M. Brown, who was requested to furnish some reminiscences to a committee, in 1837, gave the following brief account: "Of *John Boggs*, I am not certain; but believe he is the same who was, for some time, pastor or stated supply, in the Second church,

Pittsburgh; and teacher of a female academy—being a respectable scholar and preacher, and a man of piety, taste and eloquence. Of *Wm. Fowler*, I know nothing. *Robert Johnston* is well known as a distinguished preacher, and very useful man. He was for some time pastor of the Presbyterian church in Meadville. Afterwards settled in the Forks of Yough—several years a member of the Board of Trustees of Jefferson College—a punctual and useful member, who has ever taken a deep interest in the concerns of the College. He is now (1837) pastor of a church in Indiana county, Pa. He received the best education this Institution could afford, while an Academy. He left before it received a charter for a College; and of course is not numbered among our graduates. *Robert Lee* became a preacher, and was settled in Westmoreland county, Pa. Of his history, I know nothing. *John M'Lain* was a preacher of high standing for a considerable time; was settled at Montour's, near Pittsburgh—a man of talents; but was charged with intemperance, and silenced. He afterwards practiced medicine. *Elisha Macurdy*, well known as one of the most respectable laborers and useful ministers in this country. He was settled at Cross-Roads, when first licensed, where he remained until infirmity of age admonished him to resign. He will be remembered especially for his missionary spirit, and the friend of the poor Indians, having done more in that cause than any other man in our region. Macurdy's education was very limited, having been advanced in years before he commenced. *Wm. M'Millan*, formerly President of the College—a man of solid, rather than splendid talents; a substantial, rather than polished scholar. He was nephew to Rev. Dr. Millan—succeeded Mr. Wylie. Unhappy differences having occurred, he resigned the office of President—was afterwards President of the College of New Athens, Ohio, where he died. *Wm. Moorehead* was the same whose name is associated with Watson. He graduated, as I believe, at Princeton, at the same time with Watson—licensed to preach the same day. They were married to two sisters, (daughters of Dr. M'Millan,) at the same time, died on the same day, and were buried in the same grave. This singular coincidence is engraved on their tombstone, on the hill, (Chartiers graveyard,) as most of the students may have seen. *James Satterfield.*—He was a respectable clergyman; still living—one of the first pioneers west of the Allegheny river. He was located somewhere in Mercer county, Pa., or Trumbull county, Ohio. *Samuel Tate,* a pioneer, very early settled in the town of Mercer, where he has been greatly useful: known over all that region as an excellent man, whose labors have been blessed extensively. He is still living, (1837,) and honored as a father. *John Watson.*—His history is very remarkable and interesting. He was a poor lad, employed as a clerk or bar-keeper, to a Mr. Purviance, who kept a public house in Washington. He possessed an uncommon eagerness to acquire knowledge. He began to read the "Spectator," and finding so many Latin sentences as mottoes, he was determined to understand them, and somehow to learn Latin. He procured a grammar and dictionary, and without any teacher, commenced the process. He was brought to notice by the celebrated Judge Addison, an admirable scholar himself, and patron of learning. Addison, being at Washington, at court, returned to his lodging in the tavern, late at night, after all had gone to bed except Watson. Him he found at his books. He had a Horace, and was laboring at it. Addison, surprised and delighted, furnished him useful books. And, after some time, he was brought to the knowledge of some benevolent persons, who agreed to send him to the Canonsburg Academy. He became truly pious; as was exhibited by his Christian life and happy death. His talents were of the highest order. He was sent to Princeton College, where he sustained himself by teaching a class, as tutor; and prosecuted his studies with such success, that no one pretended to rival him for the *first honor*. Yet he, for various reasons, modestly declined it. He was the *Kirke White* of Nassau Hall. The Hon. Charles F. Mercer, of Virginia, was his classmate; and in the address which he delivered, a few years since, to the Societies in Princeton, he spoke of Watson in language of the strongest eulogy. Modest and retiring, yet clear in intellect as a sunbeam, he was sent to Princeton, with a view to preparing him for the Presidency of this College. After his return, he was licensed to preach the gospel, and chosen President, August, 1802, the *first* President after the College received its charter. He died, November 30th, 1802, about three months after his appointment. His constitution was radically effected by study, and a laborious sedentary life before he left Princeton. I had the pleasure of seeing him and hearing him preach but once. It may be observed that none of the above list except Wm M'Millan, are among the list of graduates. The reason is that they completed their education in the Academy, and before the first regular Commencement. Watson and Moorehead graduated at Princeton."

Thus far Dr. Brown, whose account we preferred to give just as he wrote it, being a valuable paper, which he designed simply as brief notes, to aid an historical committee. Had Dr. Brown lived to write the history of Jefferson College, as he designed, he would doubtless have given a much fuller and more accurate account of these founders of the *Philo Literary Society*. We throw it into our brief narrative, as worthy of preservation, coming from his pen.

Of the subsequent fortunes of the Society, its various times and scenes of excitement, its internal reforms and revolutions, its ups and downs of prosperity and adversity, we shall not attempt a tedious recital. Like their sister Society, they were more than once on the brink of dissolution from internal factions. Indeed, it appears that something like extinction of the old Society did occur in 1808. For, during that year, so terribly did faction and division reign among them, that the friends of order actually re-organized themselves under the name of the "Reformed Philo Society;" adopted an amended constitution, and set out on a fresh career, receiving members, *de novo* and ignoring the former organization altogether; thus, like a Phœnix, rising from the ashes of the old one, plumed its pinions for a fresh flight. Thus the elements of faction were eliminated from the body; and the society thenceforward held on its noble pathway to honor and renown. After some time, we believe the new name was quietly dropped. In subsequent years, as the College became more prosperous, under the long and successful administration of Dr. Matthew Brown, this Society continued to flourish in every way. With a spirit of almost lavishing liberality, they provided for themselves a magnificent Hall, and a splendid library, of many thousand volumes. Indeed, the halls and libraries of the two Societies are an honor to Jefferson College, and reflect great credit upon the liberal and generous impulses of their members. A stranger would be struck with astonishment, after winding his way up through the rather gloomy and dingy passages and stairways of the old College, to find himself suddenly ushered into either of the rooms of the Societies, and would be apt to recall Sir Walter Scott's description of the luxurious splendor of some of the inner apartments, in the shabby and repulsive-looking houses of the Jews in the middle ages. He would remember Rebecca's home, described in Ivanhoe. As their library increased, and their means of investigating truth on all subjects were enlarged, the questions discussed became more philosophical and metaphysical—such as, "Is emulation commendable?" "Is there any such thing in human nature as disinterested benevolence?" "Do we sin in dreaming?" "Is it an abridgement of the liberties of freemen to pay license for marriage?" It is no longer necessary to discuss *this* question in Pennsylvania. But it would be worthy of attention in several of the States, where the license system prevails, especially in *Maryland*, where the tax is enormous, and really oppressive to the poor.

The *Contests* between the Societies underwent some changes in process of time. The "original oration" was introduced without dropping the "select." The decision about the "original oration," must often perplex the judges, if they must decide both upon the *merits* of the speech and of its *delivery*. As "composition" is still retained, where the question turns exclusively upon the intrinsic merits of the pieces, we cannot perceive the wisdom of retaining the "original oration." The debates were allowed to occupy a longer time. The Trustees were no longer the judges, as was the case at first. After some trouble and various conferences, it was at length settled to adopt the plan of each Society selecting two judges, and these an umpire.

One of the historians of the *Philo Literary Society* has given the following account of the first *ten* years of the Society: "In taking a view of the state of Society, during the first decade, we find several things in addition to what has already been stated, worthy of special observation. And first with regard to the *number of members*. The chief difficulty under which the Society labored, for a number of years after its formation, was the fewness of its members. It commenced its operations with *twelve*; and for several years, this number increased but very little. If, therefore, very many of the members were absent, through sickness or otherwise, it was felt by the Society. And we find the epoch in the first report ever presented to the Society, mourning over the fact that several of the members were prevented by sickness from attending to their duties. In May, 1798, Society adjourned, on account of two members being absent. And on April 4th, of the same year, the members convened, but did not proceed to business, on account of the greatest number of them being sick with the mumps. In July, 1708, Society adjourned two weeks during harvest. During the year 1799, we also find Society on the decline, from the fewness of members. The office of Orthographists was, at that time, combined with that of Eparch and Clerk, in order that there might be two more performing members. This, however, was only to continue in force until the necessity would be removed by an increase of members. In 1801, Society was in a more prosperous condition. The number of members had increased to *twenty-seven;* and consequently the exercises were attended upon with more regularity, and with more profit. From this period until the close of the first ten years of the Society's existence, the number of members seems to have varied but little."

A historian of a later period, mentions the fact that, for a considerable time, they refused to receive any more new members, in order that the other Society might be recruited, and brought up to something like an equality with them, in point of numbers. A similar course we believe was pursued by the Franklin Society, in later years. Our former historian proceeds: "At the formation of the Society, £1 2s. 6d. was contributed by the members; which amount, it appears from the report of the Eparch, was expended for the immediate wants of the Society, except one shilling and one half penny. For several years the pecuniary fund never exceeded one pound at any one time. In 1801, (being about the time they commenced calculating in dollars and cents,) there was in the treasury three dollars and seventy-one cents. The treasury, however, did not remain long empty; yet at no time did the funds amount to five dollars, until an effort was made to establish a library. Closely connected with the funds of the society, is the subject of fines. All breaches of order, at the present time, were punished in this manner; though it appears, much to the honor of Society, that the officers were seldom called upon to impose fines upon the members. We find the Eparch repeatedly congratulating Society upon the fact that no fines had been assessed during his term of office. When such happened to be the case, Society was considered to be in a good state. And we think, justly. The first fine ever assessed was one sixteenth of a dollar, upon Mr. M'Millan, for not obtaining permission to speak an oration"

The highest importance was attached to the observance of *secrecy*. Society was not esteemed in a prosperous condition if members were in the habit of revealing secrets, through carelessness, or otherwise. In May, 1798, on account of some of the transactions of Society having been divulged, a committee of five persons were appointed to investigate the matter; and on the next meeting, make such a report as their evidence would justify, and the real good of Society demanded. This committee could not obtain evidence enough to convict any member. Yet the motion to appoint such a committee stands as a memento of the desire of the Society to keep all their transactions from being known to any except Philos. This feature of Society was very objectionable to the good people who inhabited Canonsburg at the time Society sprung into existence. One of its founders, (Mr. Tate,) in a letter which was written in answer to some inquiries, remarks on this point: "There was much excitement in town, and even in the country, because we kept the doors shut against all but Philos, and would not tell what we were doing: and to keep our doings secret, we made window blinds of our great coats, (we had no cloaks,) at the time. These proceedings gave alarm; and some supposed that we held a Free-Mason lodge, and others that there was about to be a resuscitation of witchcraft," &c.

"At this day, perhaps, it is impossible," the historian continues, "to form an entirely correct opinion on the state of feeling between the two Societies; as we have nothing but the records of the Society to guide our judgment. It is very evident, from the reports of the several Eparchs, that a spirit of rivalship generally existed between the two Societies; and, perhaps, it was sometimes accompanied by rather bitter feelings. In the report of June, 1802, the members of the Franklin Society are spoken of as competitors, and charged with 'having vainly and falsely boasted that the Philo Society had lost its dignity and honor.' On another occasion, the Eparch urges the members to persevere in the discharge of their duties, stating that 'thereby they would be able to withstand the most powerful attacks of their rivals!'" This spirit of rivalship owed its origin, no doubt, to the institution of *Contests;* as we find but little reference to any thing of the kind, by the Eparchs, previous to their existence. We suppose that, at the present day, no one will be disposed to deny that such a spirit of emulation had a tendency to advance the welfare of society. The members esteemed it a privilege to belong to the Society. "To us," says this judicious writer, "surrounded as we are with so many advantages which were denied to them, the benefits to be derived from our Society, during its earlier days, may appear small indeed. But such was not the opinion of the primitive Philos. They thought they were highly favored, indeed, in being permitted to enjoy the advantages of such an institution. One of the Eparchs, in his own peculiar style, remarks: 'We ought, no doubt, to muse upon the kindness of our Heavenly Benefactor, in giving us a seat in such a Society, where we may have our minds, which are deeply immersed in ignorance, cultivated and prepared, in some measure, to answer the great end of our creation.' This opinion, of course, had a very beneficial tendency. It made the members more attentive to the exercises of Society, and assisted in forming that attachment for it which never leaves the breast of a true Philo." "It was esteemed an indispensable part of the duty of each member to use every exertion to advance the dignity of Society. It was supposed not sufficient, merely to adhere strictly to those laws which related to the exercises of Society; but that those which had a reference to the *conduct* of members, both in and out of Society, should be observed with great strictness. Especially were the members urged to have a particular regard to their conduct out of Society; knowing that, if it was becoming, it would reflect honor upon Society. They were frequently advised to pay strict attention to the duties of the Academy, as, in that way, the character of the Society might be greatly advanced. Neatness of dress and suavity of manners, were considered requisite in Philos. One of the Eparchs, in alluding to these particulars, remarks: 'The students of this place have often been remarked for their rusticity. Let this never be remarked of Philos. As rusticity is neither virtuous nor honorable, let each one endeavor to excel in the elegance of his manners.'

"Such is an imperfect picture of the Philo Society during the first ten years of its existence. When we reflect upon the circumstances under which it was formed, and the difficulties which it had to encounter in its progress, we cannot but admire the wisdom and perseverance of its founders. In the laws which were formed for its government, we discern the traces of no inferior minds; and in overcoming the obstacles which retarded its advancement, we see a zeal which an ardent thirst of learning, and the hope of being useful, could alone have inspired. Besides these motives, we can conceive of but few others which would have induced persons to attach themselves to Society. For it was not in a hall hung with gaudy tapestry, and spread with the richest carpet; it had no forty-dollar chair in which the Archon might sit at ease. The members had no other seats but long sawed planks, with stool feet; no desks, no plastered walls, nor ceiling over their heads. The love of literature, and a desire of being useful, therefore, was the stimulus which enabled them to overcome every obstacle, and to found the Philo Literary Society—a Society to which many have since been proud to belong."

The writer of the above sketch, as found in the historical records of the Philo Society, is the Rev. William Eaton, now pastor of the Presbyterian church in Morgantown, Virginia.

We have little more to add. In 1831, the Societies got their new and beautiful halls. The Philo Society seems to have spared no pains nor expense in adorning and beautifying their room. After a costly outfit of chairs, desks, rich tapestry, candelabras, &c., they took formal possession on the 23d of June, 1832. The amusing style in which they record their defeats and triumphs, at the Contests, during those times, is the last thing we shall notice. In 1829, when the Franklin Society obtained most of the honors in the Contest, the Philo historian remarks: "At this Contest, our defeat was almost as the last. Our champions went forth, armed with mail and spear, only to be borne back, wounded, upon their own shields. The *Composition* was taken by the Franks: the *Debate* and *Oration* were divided. These disastrous consequences were, doubtless, to be traced to the spirit of indolence and misrule, to which the minutes of last year bear lamentable evidence. Success was impossible, and our household gods were left to the mercy of the Goths!" But when, in 1832, they could record their *triumphs*, the style is equally amusing: "The spirit of the Philo Society was on the ascendant. Victory perched upon her banners, not again to take its flight till the noble sons of the Philo Literary Society had swept the entire field, and struck astonishment and dismay into the ranks of our rivals. Mr. R., our Composer, and Mr. R., our Debater, were crowned as victors, while the Franklins took only their *favorite*, the honor in *select speaking*." This style is really rich and amusing, and reminds us of many a passage in Weem's Life of *Washington* and of *Marion*. The insinuation about the *favorite* of the Franklin Society, is highly diverting, in view of signal triumphs of that Society in the other exercises, during some of the previous years, which the Philos were obliged to record. But who would begrudge them their chuckle, when their historian read this passage?

We now proceed to give the history of

The Franklin Literary Society.

From an Address of the Rev. W. A. Passavant, delivered before that Society, at its Semi-Centennial Anniversary, November 14, 1847.

The origin of the *Franklin Society* may be recorded in a few words. The *place*—the Canonsburg Academy; *the time*—November 14th, 1797; *the hour*—seven o'clock in the evening—Sunday evening last, fifty years ago; the *founders*—nine students—*James Carnahan, Cephas Dodd, James Galbraith, Thomas Hughes, David Imbrie, Jacob Lindly, Stephen Lindly, William Wood,* and *William Wick.* Of this first meeting, it has been truly remarked—"Many a larger assembly has had a less lasting influence!'"

The early laws and regulations of the Society are unfortunately lost. Some Solon, zealous in the collection of institutes, has probably abstracted them from the minute-book. The original constitution, however, did not materially differ from the present one, and the objects which convened the first assembly—"*Scientia, Amicitia et Virtus,*" have weekly assembled its members for half a century.

It is a fact worthy of notice, that the first resolution ever passed by the Society was, that "The members be required to keep its business a profound secret." So fearful were they of any violation of this, that members were not permitted to read an essay in the Academy, which had already been read in Society. Subsequently, when leakages were discovered in certain quarters, married students were not eligible to membership. The principle of secrecy then laid down, has ever since been sacredly recognized; and though its application has been occasionally carried to an excessive degree of strictness, the wisdom of this regulation must be apparent to all.

Of the nine members who founded the Society, *five* were officers—a Chairman, Clerk, Inspector, and two Correctors.

The duties of the Inspector answered to those of Vice President, but it was made his duty "in *particular*, to watch over the morals of the members, and their diligence and attention to the business of the Academy." Judging by the number of citations on the minutes, this duty was faithfully performed. It was one of the duties of the Correctors, "to see that the minutes were well written, and to give out the words for the members *to spell*." The Society was divided into three classes, and these performances are thus recorded on the minutes—"One class offered compositions and translations; another spoke select speeches; and a third read and spelled." Every one was required to read his essay carefully over before attempting it in Society, and if found to have neglected this, he was fined. Members from the lower classes of the Academy were allowed to present translations from some Latin author, in lieu of a composition of their own. Those who debated were not exempt from the performances of their class—a fact which indicates the low estimate in which this exercise was then held. This order continued until 1810, when important changes were made in the constitution and by-laws. In 1817, the constitution was again revised and amended; and from that period the minutes wear a more modern dress. The subjects of the essays are no longer transcribed—the Chairman becomes a President, the Inspector a Vice President, the Clerk a Secretary, and the Correctors were dignified as Reviewers. At that time, too, a distinction was first made between the merits of an argument and those of the question. Debate was made the exclusive performance of one class, so that as many as eight members would participate in the discussion. After this year, the exercise of spelling is no longer mentioned, and the "spelling class" was remembered only with a smile at the simplicity of early times.

And here we pause and direct your attention to the character of these exercises. Would that the power were given us, to wake again the long silent echoes of former years.

But the breathing energy, the living voice is gone, and its earnest tones have passed away with those who gave them utterance. The glow of impassioned eloquence hath left no traces of its power; and the flashes of wit, like the drops of morning dew, cannot be gathered again. The grace, the sparkle, and the form are gone! To them, as to us who succeeded them in later years, the Society was a world in miniature. Its circle bounded the sphere in which they moved. It had its chiefs and subordinates—its parties and divisions—its objects of ambition and objects of jealousy—its ardent friendships and bitter animosities—its noble strifes for intellectual mastery, and its topics of deep and all-absorbing interest. To them, as to us who occupied their places, the observance of its laws and the performance of its duties, seemed as vitally important as though the destiny of an empire depended on the issue; and, like us, they entered into its exciting life with the whole ardor and enthusiasm of youth. We cannot pronounce on the merits of these early performances, or institute a comparison between them and those of the present day. The age and manners of the people were widely different from ours; and these often gave character to the exercises of Society. But, while we at times involuntarily exclaim—*O sancta simplicitas!* oftener can we discover, in the subject of an essay, or the wording of a question, the presence of a secret power, which, in after years, made itself felt in the councils of the nation, or the churches of God.

In perusing the annals of the Society, in the first years of its existence, we are struck with the tone and character of its decisions on some of the great questions which now agitate the frame-work of American society. To select one instance only, from many—as early as 1798, the question—"Would it be politic in the Southern States to abolish Negro Slavery?" was discussed and decided in the affirmative! A vigorous writer, of the last century, in speaking of the Universities of Europe, remarks, "Colleges have always been the cradles of liberal principles." The truth of the observation is strikingly confirmed in the history of this Institution. The atmosphere of freedom floated over and around it—inspiring its sons with a quenchless love of liberty, and impelled them to write upon the monstrous system of human slavery, "*delenda est!*" They fervently sympathized with the manly utterance of Thomas Jefferson, on this subject, and in the hopefulness of truthful hearts, anticipated the hour

"When Heaven upon our ransomed race
Her bounteous gifts shall shower;
And every land and every sea
Proclaims the blissful Jubilee—
All bonds are broke, all men are free!"

On other moral subjects, some of their decisions are strangely at variance with the common verdict of society at the present day. Thus, the question, "Would it not be more advantageous to cease the distillation of rye and raise more wheat?" was unanimously decided in favor of "the Rye!" Some time after this decision, a similar question was discussed—"Is not the use of spirituous liquors more injurious than beneficial to a country?" This, also, was decided "in favor of spirituous liquors!" These decisions throw a strong light on the popular sentiment of that day, and may be accounted for without difficulty. The business of distilling was considered as respectable in that day as making flour, and the use of whisky was as universal as coffee or tea at the present time. No one was "Sessioned," whether Minister, Elder or Member, for taking as much as could be comfortably carried about their persons—though drunkenness was universally discountenanced and denounced!

A rich vein of humor often ran through the early performances of the Society. A wider latitude, in this respect, was given to the members, than at present; and if we may judge from the subjects of debate and composition recorded on the minutes, they made good use of their liberty. Thus, for instance, one member read a dialogue between "A Student and a Tailor," while another presented a dialogue between "A Spider and a Fly." A youth who had, doubtless, tasted sweeter dews than those of Castalia, edified Society with an eloquent essay on "Kissing." *Brunot* graphically described "the pleasure of having a clean pocket handkerchief." *White* convulsed the Society with laughter by a "description of a Country Singing School." Like the individual commended in the English Bards and Scotch Reviewers, for his happy selection of a subject suited to his capacities—a stupid fellow read, as an essay, "a description of an Ass." *Black* enlightened Society "on his own weakness," while *Wills* feelingly described "the Itch."

If we may judge from the same records, the days of Chivalry were not yet over. There was a remnant of the old spirit which kindled into enthusiasm at woman's name, and fervently knelt at the shrine of her beauty, or broke a lance in defence of her charms. Thus the question—"Is female modesty natural or artificial?" being debated at one of the first meetings of the Society, it was decided, by acclamation, to be natural. The question "ought a man to whip his wife on any occasion?" was gallantly decided in the negative. The interesting question, "Is it proper that ladies should be deprived of courting, of which they are deprived by custom in this country?" was discussed "with much warmth," as the faithful Secretary informs us, and this custom of our country was strongly condemned! It has been hinted that if ladies would only take the invitation given by Franklins of tried and sterling worth, the rooms of Collegians would undergo an entire transformation. The gloomy old cloisters would smile and brighten, to enclose such angelic visitants. The chivalry of '96, in the very face of the constitution, politely decided "that the fair sex of Canonsburg should be admitted into the Franklin Society," while her ungallant sons of 1847 show no mercy to the poor unfortunate who has launched his bark on the sea of matrimony—and, for this one offence, debar him from membership!

The subjects of many of the essays, read in Society at this early day, strongly bring out the same sentiment. Thus, it is recorded, that *Mitchell* gave "a description of a beautiful damsel;" *M'Donald*, "an argument to prove that the female sex is the life of society;" *Jennings* wrote "on the romance of a lady;" *Bates* "on preserving a medium in visiting the fair sex;" *Roberts* "on female efficacy;" *Chaplain* "on the choice of a wife;" *Sturgeon* "on the felicity of the married state;" while *Clayton* brought the whole Society to the highest pitch of indignation by "a love-letter," purporting to have been written by an injured and broken-hearted fair one! A solitary individual, *Caldwell*, had the fortitude to stem the popular current of opinion, and chose for the subject of his essay, "the horrid practice of dancing with the girls!"

We resume the thread of our history. In this age of gold-dust and dollars, when Mammon rules most imperiously over the thoughts, feelings, and conduct of men, it will not be uninteresting to state a few facts concerning the financial history of the Society. Of this, little can be said, so badly has the business been managed, and so disordered are the old accounts. Students have never received much credit for business habits, and are far more worthy of a diploma for their spending, than their saving propensities—as the good people of these parts are duly aware! Like the country apprentice, just opening a shop of his own, the Society, at first, "kept no books;" and, in the reports of the Inspectors, no mention is made of expenses. Each member, in turn, furnished candles, brought water, and kept the door, at the meetings of Society. "Lifting a collection," was the usual method resorted to, when funds were needed. Six years after the organization of Society, the rule was adopted requiring entrance moneys. The first initiation fee was only twenty-five cents! From 1811 to 1823, it was one dollar; in the latter year it was raised to two dollars, and in 1832, a further addition of several dollars was made. What it now is, those who have paid it know already; while those who are curious, on this point, are invited to make the discovery as the speaker did.

It has been truly remarked, that the doctrine of *fining* has always been kept alive, with religious fervor, in the Franklin Society. Some of the early punishments, and the ludicrous manner in which they are recorded on the old minutes, will serve to illustrate the manners of the primitive Franklins. The following are selected, as specimens, from many. Sinclair and Wilson were fined *one cent* each, "for laughing and talking without permission." Henderson was fined five cents, for "a ridiculous composition," and two cents additional, "for frequently changing his own seat without permission." Moore was excused from performance "because he had no ink to write his composition." Graham was punished with a fine for "a continuation of cachinations." Knott was find six cents, for "offering a nocturnal sacrifice to Somnus;" and Wallace the same sum "for holding the poker in his hand while debating." Among the delinquents, at a later day, the name of the *Rev. Dr. Wm. Smith* occurs, whose book-worm propensities, even at that early period, led him into the temptation of keeping books out of the Library beyond the constitutional time!

The jurisdiction of the Society extended over the conduct of its members, not only while in session, but also during the intervals. The early minutes contain many curious records in proof of this fact. Members were tried for profanity, playing cards, and becoming intoxicated—and, on conviction, were fined, suspended, or expelled, according to the aggravation of their offence. One member was found guilty of "acting disorderly in the streets of Canonsburg," and fined accordingly. The no-punishment doctrine, so popular at the present day with a certain class of self-styled Reformers, was utterly eschewed by the original Franklins. All deviations from *law*, both in and out of Society, were dealt with according to their just deserts. The Society soon became a terror to evil doers, and a praise to those who did well. Its moral influence over the students, was, in the highest degree, salutary, and often drew from the Faculty and Trustees of the College, a public acknowledgment of its worth.

An interesting page in the history of the Society, contains the account of its judicial proceedings. The strictness of the early regulations, savor rather strongly of the celebrated Blue-laws, and the zeal with which they were enforced, reminds one of the activity displayed by the good people of New England, in burning witches and banishing Quakers, and other heretics, out of their coasts.

Three lists were kept of the members. One contained the names of the regular members; a second, the honorary; and the third, called "The Black List," the names of those who were under the censure of Society. The first case of suspension occurred some months after the organization of the Society, and was for "long continued neglect of the duties of a member." The next trial was that of M'Giffin, "for having left Society in a disorderly manner." When his trial came on, "he acknowledged his fault, and, on account of his youth and inexperience, was restored, with no other punishment than reproof." Such instances of leniency were not rare. A few weeks after the above, another M'Giffin was cited by the Inspector to answer the charges of "disrespect of Society, gambling for money, and violating the Sabbath day." Each of these crimes he confessed, but, on appearing sorrowful, was continued a member, as usual. In spite of sorrow and forgiveness, however, these M'Giffins again wandered from Franklin rectitude. One was punished with expulsion from Society "for absenting himself"—and the other "for profanity," was deprived of "acting the Dialogue at the Contest!"

The next trial of consequence, was on the impeachment of James Lytle. The impeachment itself, is an amusing instance of legal precision. Several charges were made. 1st. That he, the said James, being a member of said Society, on the 16th of February, A. D. 1803, *vi et armis*—did beat, and in other respects evilly entreat Joseph Henderson, of said Society, without resistance being made, or actual assault given by said Joseph. 2d. Also, that the said James, notwithstanding he was honored with the office of Clerk of said Society, did, some subsequent time to said 16th of February, willfully drink spirituous liquors, by which he, the said James, was very much intoxicated, and being so intoxicated, did not conceal himself from public view, but did act in a very disorderly manner." The third charge was for betting for liquors—"to wit, whisky and cider." The fourth charged him with "acting riotously at *Morrow's Tavern*, and bantering James Smith to fight, either in a lot or even in the streets of Canonsburg!" The fifth charge was for neglect of his duties as a student and as a member of Society. On this multifarious impeachment, Lytle was tried and found guilty. For the four first crimes, he was fined heavily—and for the fifth, received an admonition before Society. He was, also, required to confess sorrow for his past conduct, and to promise reformation for the future.

The minutes, about this period, are crowded with such cases, and citation and impeachment appear to have been the order of the day! In 1808, the Chairman was impeached for not opening and closing Society with prayer. A member was admonished, before Society, for saying "*by Ned!*" Fulton, who reported Morgan to the proper authority, for profanity, was himself convicted of profanity, saying "*by George!*" This appears to have been a profane period in our history. Several were fined for swearing, while some were suspended, according to the aggravation of the crime. Two members were found guilty of "card-playing and dice-casting," for which they were suspended four weeks. Hunter was tried on the charge of "having himself shaved on the Sabbath day, in his room, at the house of Joshua Emery." Of this he was acquitted, but another member convicted of the same offence was suspended!

The darkest page in the history of the Society occurs about this time. An unhappy spirit of dissension had found its way into the brotherhood, and the fine feelings of friendship were turned into the bitterest hatred. Accusations were signed by the members against each other, and few, if any of the officers escaped impeachment. A member, named Wills, who had previously been convicted of profanity, and severely punished, was again cited to answer the charge of a similar offence. With this accusation, opened the stormiest period in the history of the Society! Having been found guilty of the crime alleged, a punishment was annexed by the officers, not only unnecessarily severe, but in the highest degree arbitrary. The Society, however, sanctioned the decision of its officers, and refused to entertain a motion to reconsider the whole matter. Wills refusing to submit to the punishment imposed, was expelled on the following evening, immediately after the opening of Society. Smarting under this treatment, and evidently wishing to create a disturbance, he sought re-admission into the Society; but his request was refused. His perseverance, however, overcame all obstacles; and two weeks later, having again asked for admission, his request was granted. The question then arose, whether he should be re-admitted without taking the promise to obey the constitution, usually administered at the entrance of new members. Owing to the difference of opinion on this point among the members, a motion was made that the Rev. Mr. Dunlap, then President of the College, should have a vote in the settlement of this question. This proposal excited the indignation of a portion of the members to such a degree, that when the motion was put to vote, *it instantly occasioned the disruption of the Society!* The Secretary of that meeting, in recording these disgraceful proceedings, mentions that "the vote was carried;" but a "Nota Bene" is here inserted by the President, in these words—"Here is a positive falsehood, for a vote was refused to Mr. Dunlap, in the case of Wills, and upon this refusal, the supporters of order and morality withdrew." "But when it was determined," continues the Secretary, "that Mr. Wills should be admitted without taking the usual promise, the Society, after having spent the whole evening in warm debates, *dissolved*, sixteen declaring themselves to be no more members." This occurred in December, 1803. To the minutes of this meeting the name of the Secretary is not attached; but the Chairman gives the reason why the above N. B. was added—"To give a true idea of matters to future readers."

A week passed by, and the difficulty remained unsettled. The usual evening of meeting arrived, but no Society convened. In reality, it no longer existed; and members considered themselves free from all obligations to obey the constitution. At length the Faculty of the College took the matter into consideration, and a reconciliation was effected between the two parties. A meeting was held, two weeks after its dismemberment, and through their intervention the Society was again re-organized. Of this meeting, however, two distinct and contradictory statements are contained in the minutes. One of these asserts, that it was the unanimous opinion of the Faculty, that the Society should not be dissolved, but should continue to meet as usual, some amendments being made in its constitution. The other account states, that "the proceedings of the former Franklin Society, having been for some time disorderly and immoral, a number of the members, deeming the end for which it was instituted defeated, protested against the proceedings and withdrew." After this an entire cessation of business took place. The Faculty of the College took the state of the Society into consideration, and agreed that it should be dissolved, and a new one instituted by such of the old members as they should nominate. Some of these having been called together, agreed to obey the constitution, with various amendments, and to constitute a new Society, bearing the name of the former. None who were members of the old Society were made acquainted with the business of the new, previous to their becoming members of it; and it was resolved, that the new members should not have access to the minutes of the old Society. "It was also resolved, that the minutes also be written from that time, without any reference to the past."* With these distinct and contradictory accounts to perplex and embarrass the mind of the Franklin historian, it becomes a matter of no small difficulty to date the origin of the Society. As, however, the new Association was composed of a majority of the old members, met for the same purpose, and governed by the same constitution, in the main, we shall not hesitate to trace back our origin, as we have always done, to November 14th, 1797. Few of the present members know anything of this unfortunate dismemberment. So strong is the golden chain of friendship, which now binds all hearts together, none would have imagined that it had been rudely broken!

During the first years of its existence the Society was without a library. The want of books does not seem to have been seriously felt, and no efforts were made to procure them. It is a singular historical fact, that the present library originated in the want of a standard of appeal, by which the merits of the class in spelling might be tested. To remedy this, a propoposal was made on the 10th of September, 1799, "that a collection be lifted for the purpose of purchasing such a Dictionary as may be thought necessary for the Society." This proposal, after lying on the minutes for one week, was duly considered and adopted the succeeding evening. Walker's Dictionary was selected as the standard, and for many years was used by

---

* We are indebted for the above account to the manuscript history of the Franklin Literary Society, already referred to.

the officers as the final arbiter, "when the class came out to spell!" This was the first work purchased by the Society, and the first volume in the library. Around this nucleus the fine collection of books, which now adorns the hall of the Society, gradually clustered.

As early as 1813, the members imposed upon themselves the payment of a certain sum each session, towards the purchase of useful books and the increase of the library. Since then, it has been almost exclusively from the contributions of the regular members. The present library numbers nearly 3,000 volumes, and comprises many of the most valuable standard works in the English language, in History, Poetry, Philosophy, Theology and the Natural Sciences. The admirable order in which they are kept, and the fine appearance they present, never fail to call forth the commendation of strangers who visit the College; while the literary treasures they contain, and the advantages they afford, can be appreciated only by those who enjoy them.

At first, the duties of the present Librarian were attended to by the Secretary. The Library was opened every third week on the evening of Society. This order continued as late as 1829, when it was resolved to open it one hour every Saturday afternoon. Owing to the increase of members, and the taste for reading among the students, it is now opened several times a week.

For many years the two Societies had their book-case in common. In 1821, the share of the Franklin Society was transferred to the Philos, after much financiering on both sides, and the appointment of numerous committees to settle this important transaction. The Society then procured a "standing library case, made of pine, and painted green, having the words *The Franklin Library* painted in a right line along the door." This elegant piece of furniture continued in use until the erection of the new College, and as it could not be sold, was gratuitously presented to the Faculty!

The custom of appointing Library Committees every session, has existed ever since there was a library. A report of such a committee, in 1832, of which Washington M'Cartney, Esq., was Chairman, still remains. This report is particularly interesting for the information it contains, concerning the library, and the facetious style in which it is written. The number of volumes in the library, at that time, was 676; and no less than 300 are reported as having been lost. The committee deprecate in the strongest terms the habit of lending books to the ladies—to which custom they ungallantly attribute the loss of many of the volumes! This caveat did not, however, produce the desired reformation, and through the gallantry of the members, the library opened its treasures, as before, to the fair readers of Canonsburg and vicinity.

As contests between Literary Societies were formerly peculiar to Jefferson College, it becomes a matter of interest to inquire into the origin of this custom, which has been introduced into the principal institutions of learning in the South and West. From the minutes of August, 1799, it appears that a proposal was brought forward by *W. Neile*,—"That a challenge be given to the Philo Literary Society for four members to be chosen out of each Society, for the purpose of reading compositions, speaking select orations, and debating at the Fall Examination, before the Trustees, and that they publicly give their opinion which Society has gained the victory."

Neile's proposition was received with enthusiasm by the chivalrous Franklins, and a challenge to a Literary Contest was forthwith sent to the Philo Society, who at once accepted it. Such is the origin of Literary Contests in the United States! The honor of their suggestion belongs to a member of this Society; and the honor of their introduction, to the Society itself! It may well be asked, "What results may not be traced to that simple proposal on an obscure page of our Minutes?" Who that has breathed the inspiring atmosphere which this custom has infused into College life, but will acknowledge its commanding influence on the minds of young men. Doubtless, it has blasted many ambitious hopes, and occasioned the bitterest disappointments. Its victories, too, have sometimes been more fatal to character than defeat. But these are not necessary evils, and, at most, are confined to few, while its advantages are enjoyed by all. They elevate the standard of literary excellence—discover and develop latent talent—exercise the judgment—correct the taste, and furnish the mind with proper incentives to exertion. We hesitate not to make the assertion—and its truthfulness will be confirmed by those who are acquainted with the facts—that in the Contest performances of these Societies, there are specimens of as rare and classical beauty, as can be found in the pages of the Spectator, the orations of Burke, or the debates of Pitt, Sheridan, and Fox!

The Contest had not, at first, precisely the same features as at present. One composer, one select orator, and two debaters were annually chosen. We are not informed how the debate was managed, whether the honor was conferred on an individual contester for superiority, or on two of them for their Society—as would appear from the wording of the proposal. At the third Contest, a composer and orator were elected, and two members from each Society, "to act a dialogue," while at the next Contest, two were selected to speak, one to read a composition, and one to take part in a dialogue. The following year, the order of exercises was again changed, and the dialogue gave place to debate. At the suggestion of the Trustees, the Societies, in 1814, made further alterations in the Contest. The debate was limited to two persons—one from each Society, who were allowed to occupy twenty-five minutes. This arrangement, excepting, perhaps, the limitation in the time of performance, continued until 1832, when the original oration was added to the other exercises. It would appear, that the honor of composition was, at first, considered the highest. This is probable, from the fact that one member having resigned on composition, another who had been elected debater, was chosen to fill his place, and a re-election held for debate. The old minutes contain the questions discussed at these Contests. Some of these would puzzle older and wiser heads than young shoulders usually carry. Such, for instance, is the question debated at the contest of 1810: "Is the soul created immediately at the time of its infusion into the body?"

The primitive manner in which the Contests were conducted, may be conjectured from various amusing details recorded on the minutes. So late as 1817, a committee was appointed "to build the stage, hold the candles, snuff them, carry water, and do all the little drudgeries implied in the nature of their office!" Their successors—the honorable "Committee of Arrangements," who now do the honors of Society to Judges, and fare sumptuously with these dignitaries, at its expense, may congratulate themselves on this evidence of progress. Offices half a century ago, were no sinecures, and "the little drudgeries" of the above resolution, would now be considered too formidable an affair for any committee to undertake. It was then, however, an honor "to hold the candles, snuff them, and carry the water," which was conferred only on members of the more advanced classes!

The collection and transcription of the Contest performances is of comparatively recent origin, and it is to be regretted that many of these are irrecoverably lost. No decisions have been preserved further back than the Contest of 1809. In the thirty-one years which elapsed between that time and 1840, (since which we have not the decisions,) our sister Society has gained four more debates and even one more select speech than we; while the Franklins have borne away the palm nine times more for composition, and once more for original oration. We take it for granted, that there has been no falling off since then, and the old Franklin is still *excelsior!*

The history of the Contest would be incomplete, unless

reference were made to the Articles of Convention between the two Societies. In 1818, at the suggestion of the Franklin Society, the first articles were formed. These were very incomplete, and had little resemblance to those in force at a later period. The correspondence of the Societies previous to this, was marked by little of the high and honorable bearing which now characterizes their mutual intercourse. They regarded each other not as friends, engaged in a generous rivalry, but as almost enemies, in conquering whom, it was lawful to employ any species and means of warfare. This unhappy jealousy often led to mutual recrimination, and, sometimes, even resulted in open ruptures between the Societies. It is amusing to read the series of terrific resolutions forwarded from one Society to the other; which at the time, smoked with wrath, but now lie before us like spent thunderbolts! Happy as has been the influence of these conventional Articles upon the Societies, it must be confessed, that there has not been always calm and sunshine. Difficulties connected with the Contest, and other subjects, have sometimes thrown their dark shadows over our sky. One of these, occurring in 1827, remained unsettled until 1830, when the Articles of Agreement were annulled by our sister Society. The annual Contest was held as usual, but, owing to this difficulty, no decisions were made. Other Articles were afterwards agreed upon, and these again, in the memory of some now present, became in turn, "a bone of contention." But kindness, and the spirit of mutual concession, finally removed every difficulty, and *Friendship* has bound her golden chain more closely and firmly around these Brother bands!

We now come to a period in our history when old things passed away, and all things became new! The erection of the new College, and the dedication of the present hall, was the advent of our Augustan age. We have seen the Society in its infancy and youth, we now behold it entering upon its manhood. The name and features remain the same, but how great the change which hath passed upon its spirit! It hath put away childish things. Its step is firm and steady, its voice, the voice of a man, and its deliberations, though warmed by the fervor of youth, are tempered by the wisdom of riper years.

Both the literary Societies of this Institution delight to refer back to this interesting period. Never was there a brighter era in our common history. The enthusiasm of the members was raised to the highest pitch. To furnish and adorn the new hall, in a style worthy of the object to which it was devoted, was the great ambition of the members. Committee after committee was appointed, and resolutions upon resolutions were passed, with reference to this matter. No expense was to be spared in its decoration. It was resolved that the floor be covered with the best imported carpets; that the room be furnished with settees and sociables; that the walls be painted a light blue, with an appropriate border; that the name of the Society be inscribed, in gilt letters, above the door; that the windows, together with the stage and rostrum, be hung with handsome drapery; and the hall and library room be heated by suitable stoves. These, with a variety of minor arrangements, indicate the feelings of Society. The expenses of these numerous outlays, were nobly borne by the members, who vied with each other in their devotion to the Society. It has been beautifully and appropriately said: "They seemed to bend every thought and purpose to adorn the Nuptial Hall, where they were to wed Literature; as the young bride will visit often the destined chamber, disposing and arranging its furniture; smoothing the pillow till it is free from wrinkle as her own brow, and as she leaves, still lingers and blushes at the strange flutterings of her heart."

The spirit of activity, which was called into life at this period, did not confine itself to the decoration of the new hall. The minutes, and other papers of Society, were collected and arranged; the Legislature was applied to for an Act of Incorporation, (which was *almost* obtained,) and the whole internal frame-work of the Society was new-modeled. The struggle of Greece for liberty from the grievous thraldom of the Turk, at that time, called forth an enthusiastic address from the Society, and resolutions were adopted to aid the revival of Literature on its classic soil, and the establishment of a College at Athens!

On the 22d of June, 1832, the new hall of the Society was dedicated. The record of this event on the minutes, is as follows: "The Literary Societies of the College convened on the banks of the Chartiers, and, accompanied by the Faculty and a few Honorary members, walked in procession, to excellent music, through the streets of Canonsburg, and entered their respective halls." The Dedicatory Address before the Franklin Society was delivered by *Washington M'Cartney, Esq.*, after which the beautiful hall was devoted to the sacred purposes of *Literature, Friendship* and *Virtue*, with appropriate ceremonies.

The history of the Society, since this interesting period, has been one of constant and increasing prosperity. Within a twelve-month after the dedication of the new hall, the roll of regular members numbered eighty. With each succeeding year, the proportion of members from the higher classes in College increased; and thus the Society grew with the growth and strength of our Alma Mater. There was also a corresponding improvement in the character of the exercises. The standard of literary excellence was greatly elevated, and a higher tone and character imparted to it, by the scholarship and talent of numerous gifted minds. The influence of the Society on the literary tastes and habits of its members became more marked and decided. It dignified and made honorable the pursuits of knowledge, and all who sat under its refreshing shade felt the magic of its power. From this period, too, the Society seems to have directed its energies to the cultivation of Science and Literature. as its proper objects, leaving to other institutions the correction of moral delinquency and the reformation of moral character. And finally, since the same period, the spirit of partyism and narrow clannish feeling has gradually become weaker and fainter in both Societies. The time is forever past, when we stood like

> "Heights—whose mining depths so intervened
> That they could meet no more."

The recollection of that day is fast fading from memory, and *we* would not renew it. Perish the hand which would again throw the apple of discord among brethren of *Friendship's* firm-knit family!

Our work is done. The history of the Society in later days, and its present flourishing condition, are as familiar to many of this audience, as household words. We have only to regret the incompleteness of our information, and the imperfection of our own labor. If, occasionally, we have indulged in digression, so has Homer, in his veracious narrative of the adventures of Ulysses. If we have been prosy, so at times is Herodotus, the Father of History, whom we have endeavored to imitate, in being the faithful chronicler of the times.

On a soiled and almost illegible page of the old Minutes, the following prophetic passage occurs. It bears the date of January, 1798, and concludes the report of *James Carnahan*, one of the first Inspectors. "The Franklin Society promises to exceed our highest expectations: we trust it will be an honor to the members, a benefit to the Academy, and will extend its happy influence throughout America!" The venerable President of the College of New Jersey has lived to see his prophecy fulfilled!

Go where we may, throughout America, we meet with students of Jefferson College, and the members of this Society. The graves of our departed brethren cover the land;

> "Their spirits wrap our dusky mountains,
> Their memory sparkles o'er our fountains."

Many, also, have gone to the Missions beyond the seas. Consecrating themselves to the work of the Apostolate, they have fallen with their armor on, in the holy conflict for souls. The Indian, the Ethiopian, the Scythian, the Persian, the Chinaman, have heard and obeyed their word. Christianity and Civilization, with the blessings of Science, Virtue, and the holy influences of Friendship, have followed their steps. And in those lands of darkness, an unknown force of moral regeneration has appeared, which will develop and perpetuate itself in all coming time, and live indestructible in the midst of revolution and ruin. But *they* have died. And now, after life's fitful fever, they sleep well!

Our *living* brethren, and their name is legion, are every where. They fill all offices, and are found in every department and situation of life. They occupy the bench of the Judiciary; the halls of the Legislature; the seats of Congress and the Senate; the high places of Government, and the higher places of the Church. They are Instructors, Pastors, Professors and Presidents of Institutions of Learning, in *three* Continents. They are Ambassadors at Foreign Courts, and Members of the Learned Societies of Europe and America. They seem to be possessed of the power of ubiquity. Though eight years have elapsed since we left these sacred walls, we have never taken a journey, either long or short, without meeting the face of some brother Franklin! In the stage coach, on the steam boat, in the rail road car, on ship board, in the French "diligence," in the German "eilwagen," every where, and under every variety of circumstances, we have met and recognized the members of this Society. How sweet to meet in later life the companions of our youth. Tender recollections are awakened by looking again upon well known features. But few recollections are more sacred than those called up by meeting with some companion of College hours. A mysterious brotherhood unites the sons of the same Institution. And should that companion be a class-mate, the connection is still closer. The hours spent in the same pursuits, over the same volume, in the same company, and at the same recitation, are dear to the remembrance. They were once thought tiresome, but we ever recur to such friendships, as green spots in the journey of life. But should this companion and that classmate be a Franklin, the mutual satisfaction would be complete. To meet with such a one, would be—

"To grasp the hand
Of brother in a foreign land!"

Distance could not remove such remembrances, nor time efface the impression which such a meeting would renew. The frosts of age would melt from round the heart, and the affections flow again, in the long forgotten channels of early years! *

How gladly would I linger among the labyrinths of memory, and impress upon your minds the lessons of wisdom which it teaches! But the lateness of the hour forbids any lengthened remarks. The topics which have been suggested by the record of the past, are too numerous to refer to, and too intimately connected with our internal history to enlarge upon. But if the voice of the past, speaking to us through the history of this Society and College, has given utterance to one fact more certain and prominent than all others, it is, *that the truth of God is the appointed instrumentality for the regeneration and civilization of the world.* That truth, which God has revealed in his word, and written in living characters over the broad face of nature—two volumes, but one book—constitute the stone and the sling, to smite with death the gigantic forms of wrong, under which the whole creation groaneth and travaileth in pain until now. Simple weapons, yet how effective! None other is needed. The truth, in its illustrious simplicity, in its harmonious proportions, in the strength of its native energy, in the sublime consciousness of its own rectitude, is omnipotent. It must and will prevail!

---

*MS. History of Franklin Society.

To the study and advocacy of that truth—which is mighty and which maketh free—consecrate the years and energies of your whole life. It will lead you to its great Author, and standing in His presence, you will look forth over the broad field of the world, with the holy resolution, to live, labor, suffer, do and die in the service of humanity, and to stamp upon society the impress of truth, in characters which shall remain when sun and moon are no more!

We have met on this occasion to renew the recollections of the past, and to exchange the signs and words of friendship—like ships on the ocean, which exchange signals and then pursue their different courses upon the pathless deep. But ere we part, and "mingle with the universe," from which we have escaped to participate in the solemnities of this night, let us again unite the Student's song, and, with heart and soul, give a "*vivat*" to our Alma Mater! Then—

Gaudeamus igitur
Juvenes dum sumus,
Post jucundam juventutem,
Post molestam senectutem,
Nos habebit humus!
    Vivat Academia,
    Vivant Professores,
    Vivat membrum quodlibet,
    Vivant membra quælibet,
    Semper sint in Flore!
Vivat et respublica,
Et qui illam regit,
Vivat nostra civitas,
Maecenatum caritas,
Quæ nos hic proteget.

QUESTIONS DEBATED IN CONTESTS.

It will doubtless afford interest and amusement to see a list of the *Questions* which were debated at the Contests, since they began. They are as follows:

1799. Whether the Mathematics or the Languages, Latin and Greek, be more necessary?

1802. Whether is luxury or war most ruinous to Nations?

1804. Should a Governor, when elected into office, under our present form of government, fill all the offices under his jurisdiction with men of the same political sentiments with himself?

1805. Are the natural talents of men superior to those of women?

1806. Would it be policy in the United States immediately to emancipate their slaves?

1807. Can the immortality of the soul be discovered by the light of nature?

1808. Would it be policy for the Americans to join in alliance with France, should a war take place between America and Great Britain?

1809. Are animals, inferior to man in the order of creation, possessed of immortal souls?

1810. Is the soul created immediately at the time of its infusion into the body?

1811. Should a system of religion, which is contrary to the Holy Scriptures, be tolerated by civil governments?

1812. Should capital punishment be inflicted in a well-regulated government?

1813. Should conscience be the ultimate rule of duty?

1814. Is the Deity discoverable by the light of nature?

1815. Is the human understanding naturally right?

1816. Does the belief of moral truth necessarily incite to the fulfilling of moral obligations?

1817. Is a high degree of refinement favorable to the Christian religion?

1818. Is war naturally lawful?

1819. Is there any such thing in human nature as disinterested benevolence?

1820. Suitable provision being made for the comfortable settlement of the blacks of this country in Africa, and for transporting them thither, would the Government of the United States, at any time of peace and common prosperity, be justifiable in passing a law, compelling them to colonize?

1821. Is a high degree of sensibility conducive to our present happiness?

1822. Is language a human invention?

1825. Would a community of goods contribute to the happiness of a people?

1829. Should Ecclesiastics have a vote in National Councils?

1830. Is utility the rule of moral action?

1831. Should a Republican government support a standing army in time of peace?

1832. Does a paucity of laws, as among the American Savages, subject man to greater evils than a superabundance of laws, as among the civilized Europeans?

1833. Should the power of pardoning those who commit offences against the laws (the military excepted) exist in a republican government?

1834. Should capital punishment be inflicted by civil governments?

1836. Should the Government of the United States discourage, by powerful restrictions, immigrations from Europe —not including that of paupers?

1839. Should provision be made by law for the maintenance of the poor?

1840. Should emulation be encouraged as a stimulus in education?

1841. Is our present Constitution more likely to terminate by the encroachment of the State Governments on the powers of the Federal Government, than by the consolidation of the powers of the States in the Federal Government?

1846. Is the human mind always active?

1855. Should our judicial officers be chosen by the people directly?

1856. Is there in the human mind a principle of disinterested benevolence?

1857. Should emulation be encouraged in common schools, as a stimulus to education?

N. B. For the years omitted, the questions could not be obtained; and in some instances, there was no Contest.

BIOGRAPHICAL SKETCH

OF THE LATE

REV. MATTHEW BROWN, D. D.

The former President of Washington and Jefferson Colleges.

BY REV. DAVID ELLIOTT, D. D.

The words "the memory of the just is blessed," express an aphorism sanctioned by the spirit of inspiration. Accordingly, the Jews, whenever they named an eminently just man who was deceased, were in the habit of adding, "let his memory be blessed." This practice of preserving the memory of good men, seems to fall within the scope and teachings of God's word on the subject: "The righteous shall be had in everlasting remembrance." "The elders, by faith, obtained a good report." And of the woman who poured the precious ointment upon the head of the Saviour, he himself declared that "Wheresoever this gospel shall be preached in the whole world, there shall also this that this woman hath done, *be told for a memorial of her.*" By thus recording and preserving the memory of good men—their sayings and their actions—they are made to live over again, and to furnish lessons to surviving generations. "He being dead yet speaketh," is an affirmation of the spirit of God, respecting Abel. And so it may be said of any other good man, on whom the grave has closed, and whose memory has been preserved. His good deeds live in history, and what he said and did while living, re said and done by him, in the records of his life. The demands of duty, therefore, as well as the promptings of friendship, require that there be some recorded memorial of a venerable and distinguished man, well known throughout the Church, who has lately been removed to the eternal world. The *Rev. Matthew Brown, D. D.*, has closed his earthly labors, and gone where neither the applause nor the censure of mortals can reach him. He was a man of strongly marked character. With certain inequalities of physical temperament, he was distinguished by many high attributes of a religious, intellectual, and social kind. Occupying as he did, during a large portion of his life, posts of public observation and influence, which brought him into contact with various classes of men, and in conflict often with their passions and prejudices, it is not surprising that he sometimes incurred their censure, and was subjected to harsher judgments, than a calm and dispassionate review of his whole life will accord to him. And we doubt not but that when his defects and eccentricities shall have been forgotten, or remembered only to be excused, the high moral attributes of his character will remain deeply embalmed in many a Christian heart.

Dr. Brown was descended from pious and respectable ancestors. His paternal grandfather, John Brown, was a native of Ireland, but of Scottish descent. He emigrated to this country about the year 1720. Not long after his arrival in Pennsylvania, he died, leaving five sons, all of whom were distinguished for their religious character. His son *Matthew*, the father of Dr. Brown, was born in 1732. He resided some years on Conodoquinnet creek, in the vicinity of Carlisle, Pennsylvania. From thence he removed to White Deer Valley, Northumberland county, of which place he was one of the early settlers. He was a ruling elder in the Reformed Presbyterian Church, to which the family of Brown belonged. He is reported to have been a man of talents, and of great sprightliness and wit. He took an active part in the early stages of the Revolutionary struggle for independence, and was a member of what was called the "Flying camp." In this service he contracted a fever, of which he died, in 1778, at the age of forty-six. He left eight children, of whom *Matthew*, the subject of the present notice, was the youngest. He (Matthew) was born in the year 1776, two years before his father's death. Upon the demise of his father, young Matthew and his brother Thomas were adopted by William Brown, his father's brother, who had no children of his own. This William Brown resided in Dauphin county, near to Harrisburg, and, as Commissioner of that county, assisted in laying out the town which is now the seat of government of the State of Pennsylvania. He was much in public life, and being a man of reading, as well as public spirit, he was frequently called upon to serve his fellow citizens in posts of honor and trust. He was repeatedly in the Legislature of Pennsylvania, and, as a member of that body, in 1776, it is said that he was the first who proposed the gradual emancipation of the slaves within the Commonwealth; a measure which, though not favorably received at the time, was afterwards adopted. He was, moreover, a member of the Convention which formed the Constitution of the State in 1790. His name appears among the signers to that instrument. He was also sent at one time as a Commissioner to Ireland and Scotland, on behalf of the Covenanters, to procure for them a supply of ministers. In this mission he was successful, and on his return brought with him Messrs. *Lind* and *Dobbin*, the former of whom was settled and preached for some time in a church erected on Mr. Brown's farm. We have other particulars of an interesting nature, respecting this gentleman, but which are reserved for the present. They may appear in connection with a more extended notice of Dr. Brown, at some future day.

It was with this uncle that the subject of this notice was placed after the death of his father. There, in a school in the neighborhood, he received his elementary education, preparatory to his being sent to college. In due time he entered Dickinson College, at Carlisle, where he was graduated on the 5th of May, 1794, during the Presidency of Dr. Nisbet, for whom he always entertained the very highest regard. Among his classmates were the Rev. Drs. Herron and Laird, of Western Pennsylvania, and the Hon. Alexander Nisbet, of Baltimore, son of Dr. Nisbet, President of the College. After his graduation, he was engaged in teaching a classical school in Northumberland county, near the place of his nativity, where he became intimately acquainted with the celebrated Dr. Priestley, and other distinguished men in that region. This was probably before he commenced the study of theology —when he made a public profession of religion, we are not at present able to state; nor are we informed at what time he commenced his theological studies. It was probably about the year 1796, as he was licensed October 3d, 1799; and the Presbytery of Carlisle, by which he was licensed, are known, for a long period, to have exacted a three years course of study of their candidates before licensure. His theological studies were pursued in part with Dr. Nisbet, and in part with Dr. King, both of whom were learned and able men, and sound theologians. Two years after he was licensed, he accepted a call from the united congregations of Mifflin and Lost Creek, within the bounds of the Presbytery of Huntingdon, and on the 6th of October, 1801, he took his dismission to that Presbytery, and was by them ordained, and installed in due time as the pastor of the above named Churches. Here he labored faithfully for several years, in the midst of a good deal of reproach and opposition, on the part of a few disaffected persons, who were connected as pew-holders with the congregation of Mifflin. Finding his situation uncomfortable, and having a call from the congregation of Washington, Pennsylvania, and an invitation from the Board of Trustees of Washington Academy, he accepted these offers, and having obtained a dismission from his pastoral charge, he removed to Washington in the spring of 1805. There he labored in the double capacity of pastor and principal of the Academy, having an assistant to aid him in the business of giving instruction. During the spring of 1806, the Academy of which he was the principal became merged in Washington College, a charter for that purpose having been procured from the Legislature of Pennsylvania. It was eminently through his influence, and that of one or two others, that this charter was obtained. Of the new College, Dr. Brown was elected President, on the 13th of December, 1806, retaining, at the same time, his pastoral connection with the congregation. This imposed upon him duties of a very arduous kind; and to meet the responsibilities of his situation, he was obliged to labor with unceasing assiduity. Nor did he labor in vain. The results of his efforts were soon rendered visible, in the growing prosperity of the Church, and in the healthful and extended reputation of the College. It is true that, owing to the proximity of Jefferson College, which was only seven miles distant, and which was then, as now, extensively patronized, the number of students at Washington increased rather slowly, and the number of graduates, during his administration, was not very large. But among those who were graduated, during the ten years of his incumbency, there were many who have since risen to stations of eminence in the different learned professions, and a few who have acquired considerable distinction in the political world. During the progress of events, and from causes which, in a sketch of this kind, need not be investigated, some dissatisfaction arose in the minds of some who were intimately connected with the College, against Dr. Brown. This led to the adoption of measures in the Board, having for their object the separation of the duties of the College from those of the congregation. After various conferences on the subject, and some conflict of opinion and of feeling, Dr. Brown, on the 16th of December,

1816, tendered to the Board his resignation of the Presidency of the College, preferring to retain his pastoral charge of the Church, to which he was bound by many solemn and tender ties.

The reputation which Dr. Brown acquired, as the President of Washington College, attracted attention to him abroad, and in different directions. The Trustees of Centre College, at Danville, Kentucky, tendered to him the Presidency of that Institution. This he declined. And we know that at one time, though at a later period, his name was prominently before the Board of Dickinson College, for the same station. In 1822, however, he was elected to the Presidency of Jefferson College, at Canonsburg, which he accepted, and shortly afterwards entered upon the duties of his office. By his accession, new vigor was infused into that Institution, and during the whole of his administration, a period of twenty-three years, it continued to enjoy a high degree of prosperity. As evidence of this, it may be noted that the aggregate number of those who were graduated under his Presidency was seven hundred and seventy, making an average number per annum of fully thirty-three. This fact truly attests the skill and vigor with which the College was conducted. And it is worthy of special observation, that of this large number of graduates, not less than three hundred and fifty became ministers of the Gospel, the greater portion of them in the Presbyterian Church. It is due also to truth to state that of the ministers now in the Presbyterian Church, (Old School,) there are more who have been graduated at Jefferson College than at any other single College in the United States. During Dr. Brown's incumbency, also, the College shared frequently and largely in the renewing influences of the Spirit of God, which were poured out upon it from time to time. This is to be attributed to a great degree, under God, to his faithful labors, and those of his colleagues, not only in the pulpit, but in visiting the students in their rooms, and conversing and praying with them in private. Few Presidents of a College have been more faithful or assiduous in this department of labor than he was, and few Colleges have been more largely blessed in the visible fruits of such labor than that of Jefferson. For several years after Dr. Brown removed to Canonsburg, he preached by invitation a part of each Sabbath in conjunction with Dr. M'Millan, at Chartiers, of which Dr. M'Millan was the pastor. After some time, a separate organization was effected in the town of Canonsburg, in connection with the College, and Dr. Brown became their regular pastor, and continued to serve them in that capacity until he resigned the Presidency of the College, when the pastoral relation ceased. For a number of years before his retirement, it had become evident to his friends that his physical strength was giving way, and that the labors of the College and of the congregation were becoming oppressive to him. He himself felt it, and often referred to it. And he would have doubtless retired much sooner than he did, but from the apprehension that if he ceased from active labor he would be in danger of sinking into a state of imbecility. At length, however, he was constrained by his rapidly increasing infirmities, to seek repose from his too arduous labors, and in the year 1845 he tendered to the Board his resignation. In accepting it the Board evinced their appreciation of his long and faithful services, by conferring on him the honorary degree of Doctor of Laws, (that of Doctor of Divinity having been conferred on him by Princeton many years before,) and by the adoption of resolutions expressive of their deep feeling of regret at the necessity which led to a dissolution of the ties which had bound them so long and so happily together. The people of Washington were not insensible to the loss they had sustained by the removal of Dr. Brown to Canonsburg. Occurrences, also, connected with the history of the College in Washington, subsequent to his resignation of the Presidency of that Institution, had convinced the Board that they could not better subserve its interests, than by recalling him. Accordingly, some six or seven years after he had left Washington, he received a united call from the congregation and College to return to his former position. This occasioned him great perplexity. His attachment to his old congregation, among whom he had labored seventeen years, was very strong. The College, too, which had sprung into existence under his hand, and whose early growth had been the object of his watchful care, made a strong appeal to his sympathy and regard. But while his feelings led him strongly in that direction, he finally, after full deliberation, and consultation with friends, decided to remain at Canonsburg, much to the gratification of the people of that place, and the friends of Jefferson College. With what untiring devotion to the interests of that Institution he continued to labor for her prosperity until, through infirmity, he was constrained to retire, is well known and amply attested by the facts already recited, and by the whole current of her history. From the time that Dr. Brown retired from the Presidency of the College and the pastorate of the Church in Canonsburg, he embraced every opportunity of preaching the Gospel to his dying fellow-men. In this work he took great delight. He never appeared more in his element than when proclaiming the riches of God's grace to lost sinners; and, notwithstanding the decline of his bodily powers, it was surprising to observe the vigor with which he continued to preach till near the end of life. It is due to the memory of Dr. Brown to state that, for a few years before his death, he suffered much from morbid bodily excitement. This acted unfavorably on his mental perception, and induced, in many cases, an eccentric and anomalous form of action, which subjected him to unfriendly remarks by those who were unacquainted with the cause. Those who were familiar with his true condition, knew how to make allowance for these peculiar forms of opinion and of action by which some portion of the latter part of his life was marked. In the midst of all his infirmities, however, he evinced the same strong and unwavering attachment to evangelical truth, and the same deep sensibility in relation to the prosperity of the Redeemer's kingdom, which distinguished his more favored years of health, and of bodily and mental vigor. Some weeks before his death, alarming symptoms of disease made their appearance. Of these his physicians informed him, intimating at the same time that he might die very suddenly. In communicating this report of the physicians to the writer, in a brief note, he added, in this laconic manner, "The story is soon told—may go off in a few days. But my trust is in God: He will not forsake me in the trying hour." He was not taken away, however, for some time; but he continued gradually and slowly to decline until death did its work. On the Monday preceding his death, his disease (gangrene of the right limb) so changed its character as to mitigate and almost entirely remove that singular irritabiilty of his physical frame which had so painfully characterized his latter years, and the previous stages of his illness. From that time he appeared to be a different man, and like to what he was in his former and better days. He was himself again. His affections once more went forth with full flow towards his children and relatives; from whom, through the disturbing influence of his nervous complaints, they appeared at times to be almost withdrawn. Having summoned his son and daughter to his bedside, he reminded them of the dying scene of their dear departed mother—how she had committed them to the faithful care of a covenant-keeping God, and expressed her confident hope of meeting them in heaven. He desired now, he said, to do the same thing. He exhorted them to "love one another"—to be kind to each other; and then referring to his absent daughter, he added: "And oh that my dear absent child were here also, that we might altogether renew our mutual pledges of meeting in heaven." Then clasping his son in his arms, he said, "I have sometimes dealt roughly with you, my son, but let all be forgotten and forgiven now." With much calmness, he spoke of the disposition he had made of his property, and expressed a hope and belief that it would be entirely satisfactory. He referred, also, with great composure, to his approaching dissolution, saying, "Death to me has no terrors: I have long looked him in the face." He desired his friends to conduct his funeral as quietly as possible—"no parade;" he indicated the spot where he wished to be buried—"in the graveyard at Washington, between my two wives"—"a place reserved for my poor body; I have long looked at it—a pleasant spot." When asked about an inscription, his reply was, "Ah, take care! There I am afraid of you; pride come in—in the fewest possible words—'a sinner saved by grace.'" Howard's motto was suggested: "*Christus mea spes.*" "Yes," he replied, "that would do; it would honor learning, to which my life has been devoted—'*multum in parvo*'—what you please." After drinking some water which was given him, he exclaimed, with inexpressible pathos and energy—"Water! I shall soon be drinking of the pure river of water of life." His heart seemed to be full of love and kindness to all around him. When he received any refreshment, or when his bed was smoothed, or his pillow adjusted, he frequently said in a most winning and affectionate manner: "That will do;" "very well;" "all right." These were the genuine expressions of a Christian temper, now that the irritability and restlessness, superinduced by complicated disease, had been removed. In conversation with a ministerial brother, two days before his death, he made the following emphatic observation in reference to himself: "I have one evidence; yes! one thing, the devil himself cannot persuade me out of it: I have been a friend of revivals. I have always loved to see sinners converted. I would die happy if ministers and Churches were baptized with the Holy Spirit." When asked by his son-in-law if he thought the Presbyterian Church would be again united, "Yes, certainly," he replied, "God can do it; he will do it. I shall not see it; but you will." He fully realized the approach of death; and to his son-in-law, on one occasion, he said with great solemnity: "And this is death! death!" But in death itself, when it came, there was no apparent pain, no convulsive action or groan; but peacefully as a child, he fell asleep in Jesus. His children, though watching round his pillow, knew not the precise moment of his departure, and could scarcely realize that it was death. He died on the 29th of July, 1853, at the house of his son-in-law, Rev. Dr. Riddle, in Pittsburgh. The night after his decease, his body was conveyed to Canonsburg. The next morning it was placed in Providence Hall, which was clad in mourning; and where a funeral discourse was pronounced by the Rev. Dr. Swift, of Allegheny. This service was touching and solemn. The population of the village were largely present. The shops were closed. Many a face was wet with tears. The citizens seemed to feel that Canonsburg and Jefferson College had lost their best friend, and the poor their benefactor. At the close of the religious services, the funeral cortege passed through the ranks of students, as it proceeded on its way to Washington. There it was met by a procession of the faculty, trustees, and students of Washington College, and many citizens. The members of the old session of the Washington church requested the privilege of bearing the corpse of their former pastor and friend to the grave, which was cheerfully granted. In this particular, his closing scene was like that of Stephen—"Devout men carried him to his burial, and made great lamentation over him." The Rev. Mr. Brownson, the present pastor of the Washington church, offered prayer at the grave; and the crowd slowly retired, leaving his cold remains in the tomb, there to sleep until the morning of the resurrection. Dr. Brown was twice married. By his first wife he had two children, one of whom, the Rev. Alexander B. Brown, D. D., is now the President of Jeffer son College, and the other, Elizabeth, is the wife of the Rev. Dr. Riddle, of Pittsburgh. By his second wife he had one daughter, Susan Mary, now the wife of Henry Alexander, Esq., of New York.

In the foregoing brief narrative, the reader will doubtless have obtained some glimpses of the character of Dr. Brown. It was intended by the writer to have attempted a more formal delineation of his character, in its various forms of development. But further reflection has induced him to defer it, for the present, from a conviction that, when the records of his personal and public history shall have been more fully written, such a delineation being sustained by incontrovertible facts, will be received with more favor, and will better vindicate his claims to a place in the affectionate remembrance of the friends of learning and of religion.

BIOGRAPHICAL SKETCH

OF THE

REV. SAMUEL RALSTON, D. D.

President of the Board of Trustees of Jefferson College.

The Rev. Samuel Ralston, D. D., was born in the county of Donegal, Ireland, A. D. 1756. His family were of the most substantial and respectable yeomanry of that part of Ireland. Some of them were engaged in agricultural pursuits, and others in trade and merchandise. Judging from the letters he received from various relations, after his arrival in this country, we infer that there could have been few more thrifty or influential people in the northern part of the province of Ulster, than the Ralstons. Probably of Scottish descent originally, they were all thorough Presbyterians. His religious education, and his early training in catechetical instruction, were carefully attended to. It is probable that the rudiments of a classical education were afforded him, in the neighborhood of his birth; and, like the Irish Presbyterian schools of that day generally, his must have been thorough in its pedagogical drilling, if we may judge from his accurate and extensive classical attainments, for which he was afterwards distinguished. As some of his father's family were business men, engaged in trade and commerce, he was probably, at an early period, employed occasionally in their service. His careful, methodical habits, in reference to his financial concerns, through afterlife, seem to have been formed in this way. There is evidence from his papers that he would have become a thorough business man, had Divine Providence given this direction to his life. But his mind, which, from his boyhood, seems to have been thoughtful and serious, received, through divine grace, a decidedly religious tone; and his thoughts were early turned to the Gospel ministry. In order to become qualified for this important work, so far as human instrumentality was concerned, he was sent to the University of Glasgow, in Scotland. After completing an extensive collegiate course, he entered upon his more immediate preparation for preaching the Gospel, and was in due time licensed by his Presbytery. He at once attained to a very respectable standing among his countrymen, as an able and instructive preacher. He was engaged for several years at Donaughmore, and adjoining places, either as a regular stated supply or assistant preacher. But his mind having early received a strong bias towards the new Western World, he seems to have declined all thoughts of settling, as a pastor, in his native land. Dark political clouds, portentous of future troubles and disasters, were then beginning to gather over Ireland. The American Revolution, which had been brought to a successful issue a few years before, was soon followed by the terrible Revolution in France. Many in Ireland, both of Protestants and Catholics, fondly conceived that the day of their country's release from British thralldom was at hand. Many young and ardent minds among the Presbyterian ministry, caught the patriotic infection, and were full of zeal for their country's freedom. Though young Ralston was a warm patriot, and earnestly longed to see his country free, he was too wise to commit himself to rash measures. But he began to foresee that the country would soon be convulsed by the coming struggle. He had consecrated himself to the Gospel of Peace. He saw little prospect of pursuing his Master's work much longer in Ireland, without compromising his conscience or his safety. He determined to withdraw, and to seek a field of labor in the New World, across the Atlantic. Accordingly, he emigrated to the United States early in 1794. Soon afterwards, he put himself under the care of the Presbytery of New Castle; and under the direction of that fruitful mother of our early Western ministers, he labored for about eighteen months, in portions of Eastern Pennsylvania, Delaware and Maryland. This period of his life, no doubt, was spent with much advantage to himself, as well as benefit to others. It was the very kind of life adapted to acclimate him, both physically, intellectually, and morally. And no better region could have been selected, perhaps, in order to trim up a young Scotch-Irishman, prune off his excrescences, and refine, or at least Americanize his manners. And Mr. Ralston would not be wanting, on his part, to avail himself of the advantages afforded him. He had been early accustomed, in his own family circle, to a manly and refined tone of society. His vigorous mind, and his quick penetration of men and of society in all their various phases, would facilitate his progress in this new school of life. His intelligence, wit and conversational powers, would give him a welcome passport to every social circle. And his dignity and commanding personal presence would always command respect. He has left no journal of this period of his life. We remember but one incident which he related, connected with it. He was itinerating on the Eastern Shore of Maryland. On a warm summer day, a congregation were seated in an unfinished log meeting-house, the floor not entirely laid—some of them sitting on the sleepers, and their feet on the ground, listening to the young Irish missionary. All at once, a row of ladies, sitting next the wall, rose, in apparent agitation, and pressed forward from their places, some of them casting their glances up the wall just above their seat. There was quite a sensation through the whole house, though not a syllable was uttered. It was all a mystery to young Ralston. He paused for a moment, but he was soon relieved. A gentleman, armed with a large horsewhip, advanced to the wall, and struck up against it with his whip several times, most vigorously. Ralston yet saw nothing. At length, by a successful stroke, a large snake, more than a yard long, was dislodged, and came tumbling down, and was instantly killed and carried out of the house. It was the first snake he had ever seen in his life. For every body knows there are no snakes in Ireland—St. Patrick, according to a popish legend, having, many centuries ago, driven both snakes and toads out of the island into the sea.* Mr. Ralston and his congregation soon recovered their composure, and there was no further interruption to the services of the day.

In the fall of 1795, Mr. Ralston crossed the mountains into Western Pennsylvania, and spent some time, perhaps two months, preaching in several vacant congregations, in the Presbyteries of Redstone and Ohio. He then returned and spent the winter in the bounds of New Castle Presbytery. Thither calls were sent to him, through that Presbytery, from Bethel and Ebenezer, now in the bounds of Blairsville Presbytery, and also from Mingo and Horse-shoe Bottom, in the Presbytery of Ohio. Early in the spring of 1796 he returned to the West, and attended a meeting of the Presbytery of Redstone, at Laurel Hill, April 19th, of that year. He was received as a licentiate, upon his certificate of dismission from the Presbytery of New Castle. The call which he had received from Bethel and Ebenezer, he informed the Presbytery he was not yet prepared to accept. He, moreover, requested and obtained leave to spend some part of the summer in the bounds of the Presbytery of Ohio. There were several supplies assigned him, however, through the wide-spread territory of the old Presbytery of Redstone. He was

* The writer has seen a fine engraving in the house of a Catholic friend, representing snakes and toads in great numbers, retreating and plunging in terror into the sea, before the advancing Saint, armed with his crozier.

sent to Glade Run, Bethel, and Ebenezer on Blacklick, Ebenezer on Puckety, Tyrone, Morgantown, Clarksburg, and Crab-Orchard. Whether he traveled over this whole field, indicated by these places, we know not. It appears that he visited, at least, some of those in Virginia. For it is a tradition yet remembered, that once, when near Morgantown, he was at a house-raising, lending his powerful frame in that laborious operation. He was up on the top of the building, which had reached a considerable height, when a man, newly arrived amongst the throng below, was indulging in excessive cursing and swearing. Ralston, though aloft, heard and rebuked him. The man became enraged, threatened vengeance, and dared him to come down. Mr. Ralston hastened down and advanced. But when the profane fellow saw what a herculean, six-foot, brawny Irishman he had challenged, his wrath forsook him in a moment—he became as humble as a lamb, begged pardon of his reverence, and sounded a masterly retreat. An uproarious laugh burst from the whole company, and re-echoed "over the hills and far away."

In the course of the week next ensuing after the meeting of the Redstone Presbytery, above mentioned, he had repaired, before entering on the above appointments, to a meeting of the Presbytery of Ohio, April 26, 1796; and obtained from that Presbytery leave to visit some of their vacancies, especially Mingo Creek and Horse-shoe Bottom. Whether he visited these places before or after the appointments given him by the Redstone Presbytery, we are not informed. We only know that, by the fall meeting of that Presbytery, he informed them that he had concluded to decline the call to Ebenezer and Bethel, and to accept that of Mingo and Horse-shoe Bottom; and as these were in the bounds of Ohio Presbytery, he was dismissed to that Presbytery, and was duly received, October 26, 1796. Measures were immediately adopted with reference to his ordination and installation at Mingo. An adjourned meeting was held at that place. The Presbytery was opened with a sermon from Mr. Ralston, on a subject previously assigned, as a part of trials. On the following day, November 30, 1796, he was ordained and installed, Mr. Patterson preaching the ordination sermon, on 1 Thess. 5: 12, and Mr. M'Millan presiding and giving the charge. As we have no record of any subsequent installation at Horse-shoe Bottom, it is probable that this service at Mingo was intended and appointed for both congregations; the people of the other congregation being present in part, either by commissioners or representatives, or by the session, or part of the congregation. Horse-shoe Bottom was situated some miles up the Monongahela river, and included a "settlement," extending for some distance up and down the river, and wide out from it, having taken the name from the figure made by the curve of the river around the "settlement." These places, constituting the joint pastoral charge of Mr. Ralston, extending along the west side of the Monongahela, and ten or twelve miles off from it, all within the limits of Washington county, formed the wide and laborious field of Mr. Ralston's labors, through a large portion of his protracted life. He entered at once with vigor and unsparing diligence on his work. The pastoral fields of all our first ministers were very extensive, and quite indefinite in some directions. Mr. Ralston's was one of the largest, and one of the roughest, at least as to its physical, if not its moral features. Let any one now, with all the advantages of modern improvements in roads and modes of conveyance, start at the western boundary of Mingo, traverse the hills and hollows, constantly occurring, as he crosses successively the Mingo and Pigeon creeks, and Pike run, and Maple creek, and persevere till he reaches the eastern limits of Horse-shoe Bottom congregation; and he will wonder that any one man could ever undertake such a wide-stretching scene of pastoral and ministerial labors. But Dr. Ralston not only undertook it, but held on to this entire field for thirty-five years. It is true that for some years, towards the close of that period, the Presbyterian population of the Horse-shoe Bottom "settlement," having become greatly reduced by emigration to the West, were brought into connection with the members in and around Williamsport; and that place became the principal field of that part of Dr. Ralston's labors which had formerly been devoted to the "settlement" farther up the river. We need hardly state that Williamsport has, for some years past, taken the more ambitious name of Monongahela City.

The subject of this memoir soon afterwards sought and obtained the hand of Miss Ferguson, of Pigeon Creek, who proved a valuable help-mate to her husband, sustaining and cheering him amidst his toilsome and exhausting labors.

Mr. Ralston had not yet become an American citizen, in due legal form. But next to the Church of Christ, he loved his adopted country. He was a thorough Republican in sentiment, and took a deep interest, all his life, in the cause of human liberty. In due time, he sought and obtained his legal rights of American citizenship, according to the form then required. The official document lies before us, and will, perhaps, by some, be read with interest. It is rather a curiosity to those who have not seen such a paper. It is as follows:

"I, Edward Burd, Prothonotary of the Supreme Court of the State of Pennsylvania, in the United States of America, hereby certify, that at a court of Nisi Prius, held at Washington, for the county of Washington, on the thirtieth day of May, in the year of our Lord one thousand seven hundred and ninety-nine, before the Honorable Jasper Yates and Thomas Smith, Esqs., two of the Justices of the Supreme Court of the said State, *Samuel Ralston*, a native of Ireland, but now of the Commonwealth of Pennsylvania, exhibited a petition, praying to be admitted to become a citizen of the said United States; and on his solemn oath on the Holy Evangels, did declare, in the said court, that he had resided, two years at least, within and under the jurisdiction of the United States, and one year, at least, within the State of Pennsylvania: that he was a resident within the limits, and under the jurisdiction of the United States, on the twenty-ninth day of January, in the year of our Lord one thousand seven hundred and ninety-five; that he had never borne any hereditary title, or been of any of the orders of nobility, in any country whatever, and did absolutely and entirely renounce and abjure all allegiance and fidelity to any foreign Prince, Potentate, State or Sovereignty whatever; and *particular to the King of Great Britain*, of whom he was heretofore a subject: and that he would support the Constitution of the United States. And the facts as aforesaid appearing to the satisfaction of the said Court, in full proof; and, moreover, that during the said term of two years, the said *Samuel Ralston* had behaved himself as a man of good moral character, attached to the Constitution of the said United States, and well disposed to the good and happiness of the same. The said court, thereupon, admitted the said *Samuel Rălston* to become a citizen of the said United States, and of the State of Pennsylvania aforesaid, and ordered all the said proceedings to be recorded by the Clerk of the said court, which record was made accordingly.

SEAL.

"In witness, I, the said Edward Burd, have hereunto set my hand and affixed the seal of the said Supreme Court, at Philadelphia, this twenty-third day of September, in the year of our Lord MDCCXCIX.

"EDW. BURD, *Prothon'y.*"

Dr. Ralston resided within a few miles of Mingo church, shortening, somewhat, the distance to his further place of preaching. After his settlement and marriage, his laborious but peaceful life wore pleasantly away, amidst much domestic happiness, and much to cheer him in his labors as a minister of

Christ. In process of time he had a lovely circle of children around him. He had, in all, three sons and six daughters. But two of these daughters, and two of his sons, he lived to see passing to the grave before him. One of the sons had just completed his preparatory studies for the ministry, with bright promise of distinguished usefulness, when he was removed by death. All these children gladdened their venerable father, by a seasonable and hopeful connection with the visible Church. In his long loneliness, after the death of his wife, whom he survived twenty-four years, his children, and especially one daughter, who remained unmarried, cherished his life and health with more than ordinary filial faithfulness and tender care.

His pastoral charges shared largely in those remarkable effusions of Divine influence which were witnessed and felt so extensively in our Western Zion, during the years 1802-3, and '4. The writer remembers, when quite a small boy, to have accompanied his parents (then residing in Rehoboth, Westmoreland county,) over to *Horse-shoe Bottom.* It was in May or June, 1802. There was a great assembly of people, for those times; and great religious excitement. Public meetings extended through much of several successive days. And, at night, many again collected at the meeting-house, and the services were continued to a late hour. It was a very solemn time. The writer's father was assisting Dr. Ralston; and he faintly remembers how they both preached, and prayed, and exhorted. This was nearly, if not quite, the beginning of the revival in Dr. Ralston's charge. It was believed that many were awakened and converted, at that sacramental meeting. There were similar meetings at Mingo, for several years, beginning about that time. Such a season, it is supposed, Dr. Ralston never witnessed before. But he was ready to welcome it, and to co-operate with his brethren, with all his might, in their now increased and abounding labors, during this spiritual harvest. Though Dr. Ralston had not the advantage of a smooth mellifluous voice, or of much natural pathos, he made all the amends in his power for these defects by his earnestness and plainness, and strong and faithful appeals to the reason and consciences of men. Though he could not be said to be a popular preacher, the people of God, and indeed all people of good sense, were always pleased to see his presence at the great revival meetings, and to hear his voice, amidst those scenes, when multitudes were inquiring for the way of salvation, overwhelmed with sharp conviction and deep distress, or melted into penitence and contrition at the foot of the cross. In those days, there was little of that critical and fastidious taste that now prevails. People seemed to hunger for the bread of life; and they did not turn away from it with indifference and contempt, if the voice that directed them to it did not always fall on their ears soft as the gentle murmurs of Siloah's brook: or if the poor earthen vessel, that bore to them the provisions of God's house, did not always remind them of "apples of gold in pictures of silver." Dr. Ralston was called to take his full share in assisting his brethren, especially Dr. M'Millan, on sacramental occasions. For many years, these were memorable seasons in the history of Western Presbyterianism. But as we have spoken of them somewhat at large in our former work, "Old Redstone," we will not here attempt further remarks. The great revival, to which we have referred, has been so well described by Dr. Elliott, in his "Life of Macurdy," that we will not attempt another account. We are sure that it would be no improvement upon his interesting narrative, though indeed many things might be told which he has omitted; and the materials are not wanting, or difficult of access, for this purpose. But we think it much better, on the whole, to refer our readers to the "Life of Macurdy." It is true, nothing may be found there about the great work in Mingo or Horse-shoe Bottom. But the reader has only to transfer, at least to some extent, what he will there find related of the several scenes in the pastoral charges of Messrs. Anderson and Marquis, and Macurdy and Patterson, and M'Millan. But Dr. Ralston was called to render a peculiar service to the cause of religious revivals, in those times. That remarkable work had not long progressed, before it excited dissatisfaction and opposition among some other denominations, and especially the *Seceders*. Many of their preachers, as early as 1802, began to warn their people against the work. They denounced it as fanatical, and of Satanic origin. Many of their people, however, could not be kept away from those solemn scenes. In some instances, they became subjects of the revival. In other cases, they knew not what to say; their mouths were stopped. The ministers of that body became more and more alarmed. At length, in 1804, they prepared and published a sort of pastoral Letter and Testimony, and sent it out, far and wide, over their Churches, and among their people; and even sought every opportunity to obtrude this publication into our houses and families. This was, however, perhaps, the course pursued only by some of the weaker, yet well-meaning brethren of that body. The sophistry and misrepresentations of the pamphlet were easily answered by our ministers, from the pulpit, and on other occasions. But something more formal and better suited for parrying the attack, and for silencing the enemy, seemed necessary, and loudly called for. Dr. Ralston undertook it. In 1805 there issued from the press, in the town of Washington, a pamphlet of sixty-one pages, with the anonymous signature of "A Presbyterian." But it was well known to be the production of Dr. Ralston; and was popularly called "*The Currycomb.*" How that name was given to it, we have never heard. The title-page is as follows: "*Letters addressed to the Rev. Messrs. John Cree, John Anderson, William Wilson, and Thomas Allison, members of the Associate Presbytery of Pennsylvania,* in answer to their pamphlet entitled 'Evils of the work now prevailing in the United States of America, under the name of a revival of religion.' Wherein their objections to this work are examined, and shown to be unfounded; and the work vindicated, as being agreeable to the Word of God. Prov. 17: 17, 'He that is first in his own cause seemeth just; but his neighbor cometh and searcheth him.'"

The first letter is dated November 1st, 1804, and begins thus:

"*Gentlemen*:—It may be a sufficient apology for addressing the following letters to you, that I believe the work now prevailing in the United States of America, under the name of a Revival of Religion, to be a gracious work of the Spirit of God; but which you, in a late pamphlet, to which you have affixed your names, style in your title-page, "an evil work," and elsewhere, "a work of delusion;" "a work of enthusiasm;" nay, "a work of the devil." My design in these letters is to examine your objections to this work, and the testimony on which these objections are founded; and then to assign the reasons which have induced me to believe, and attempt to defend it, as a work of the Spirit of God, for the conviction and conversion of sinners, and for building up believers in their most holy faith."

We shall not attempt an abstract of this able production. He takes up the several objections, or charges brought against the revival, as,—"that it is a work upon the bodies of men;"—"that it cannot be a work of the Spirit of God, because bodily affections are not means of grace;"—"that it tends to bring the subjects of it under such an influence of their imagination and feelings, as is inconsistent with a due regard to the word of God, as the only ground of faith and rule of duty;"—"that it savors of enthusiasm, because the subjects of the falling exercise are opposed to any medical applications;"—"that it tends to the burial of a faithful testimony for many of the precious truths of God's word, that are denied by various religious denominations at the present day;"—"that bodily exercises are rather to be deprecated, as a judgment, than prayed for as benefits;"—"a judgment," it is insinuated, rather than expressed, "for singing Watts' Psalms and Hymns;" and lastly, "the gross disorders of it." Dr. Ralston takes up these several charges, meets them fairly, and candidly makes many admissions, in perfect consistence with a full and conclusive refutation of the several grounds of objection. "The Currycomb" must be carefully read to be fully appreciated. We cannot withhold a passage towards the close of the discussion, that may serve as a sample of its power: "Having thus examined your pamphlet particularly—more particularly than I at first intended, or than it, perhaps, deserved—I will now leave it with the reader to decide whether your objections to this work are well founded or not. That they are not supported by the evidence and arguments you have produced for that purpose, I think I may say, without vanity, I have clearly shown; and, therefore, before you overthrow it, you must take some other ground than that you have taken. I will now, as I have promised, assign you a few of the reasons which have convinced me that it is a gracious work of the Holy Spirit. In the first place, this work was begun and carried on, in this country, (for I do not choose to take my testimony from mangled scraps of foreign letters, for which no person or persons are accountable but their authors,) under the preaching and influence of the following doctrines, viz: the doctrine of the infinite guilt and total depravity of the human race, by the first sin of our first parents, in consequence of being represented by them in the covenant of works: the doctrine of the election of part of the human race to eternal life, through sanctification of the Spirit and belief of the truth: the doctrine of justification through the imputed righteousness of the Lord Jesus; of regeneration by the almighty power of the Spirit of God alone; and of the certain perseverance of all believers, by virtue of the complete satisfaction of Christ, and the unchangeable promises of God; together with the other doctrines of grace, depending upon and connected with these leading doctrines. You cannot but know, gentlemen, that these doctrines are contained in the Confession of Faith of the Presbyterian Churches in the United States of America: and I can say, that they are preached by the ministers of this Church, in this country. It is not true, then, as you say, in the eleventh page of your pamphlet, 'That they insist perpetually upon the sanction of the law, to the exclusion of other doctrines no less necessary in their place;' and 'that they preach the terrors of the law to the people, as if they had nothing else to preach to them.' That you meant them in that paragraph, I believe; and I think you have so much candor left as to acknowledge it, if you were interrogated. You cannot say so, from your own personal knowledge; for your doctrine respecting 'occasional hearing' has prevented you. Your ground, then, for saying so, is taken from hearsay, or the reports of enemies; as was the case respecting the work we have been considering. No wonder, then, that you mistake and blunder, when you depend upon such vague and indefinite evidence. But not to insist upon this: Secondly, that this is a gracious work of the Spirit of God is apparent to me, from the effects it has produced. It has arrested the attention of the careless and unconcerned. It has aroused the stupid sinner to a sense of his danger, and induced him to cry out, 'what must I do to be saved?' It has discovered to the ignorant and self-righteous, that they are not only guilty before God, but also that 'their hearts are deceitful above all things, and desperately wicked;' and that they need the righteousness of Christ, in order to justification and acceptance with God. It has caused those who seldom or never bowed the knee to God, or attended on the ordinances of the gospel, to cry, 'God be merciful to me, a sinner;' and to attend diligently on the means of grace. It has reclaimed the wicked and the profligate, and transformed the lion into a lamb. It has brought professed deists to become professed Christians, and turned their cursings into blessings, and their blasphemies into praises. Many who could not relish any religious conversation, are now only delighted when talking about the plan of salvation, and the wonders of redeeming love; and many, very many, give evidence, by their life and conversation, that they are born of God. And to this I would add, that it has had this effect on many of all ranks, ages, sexes, and colors; the African as well as the European and American. And the combined hosts of deists, hypocrites and formalists are generally opposed to it. Some also have fallen away: but this is no objection, but rather an evidence that it is a work of the Spirit of God; for Christ informs us, in the parable of the Sower, (Matt. 13,) that the seed, or the Word of God, fell by 'the way-side,' upon 'stony places,' and 'among thorns,' as well as into 'good ground.'"

This able pamphlet was most seasonable and effective. It completely silenced the hostile party. Their pamphlet was written with great plausibility, and evinced pre-eminent talent. It was far from being a weak or scurrilous production. Indeed, the greater part of it is admirable; especially the first twelve or thirteen pages, in which the nature of the Holy Spirit's operations, in convincing and converting sinners, is described. This part of the Seceder pamphlet deserves to be republished, as a tract. Nothing that we have ever read, is better suited to warn the Church against fanatical errors. Being placed in the outset of the pamphlet, it is well suited to gain the confidence of the reader. No one can doubt the piety and deep experience of the writers. But all this rendered their attack on the revival so much the more mischievous. It reminds us of the plausible manner in which certain brethren would begin their speeches in the General Assembly, twenty years ago.

They were so pious and meek, and peace-loving, so earnest in deprecating strife and contention, &c., and then they would pour out the bitterest invectives and sarcasms, and pelt their brethren of the opposite party most unmercifully. But, in regard to these Seceder writers, we believe they were sincere and honest, and truly pious men. But they were misled by prejudice. They were misinformed. They relied too much, as Dr. Ralston told them, on hearsay. The giant among them was Dr. John Anderson, of King's Creek, a man of profound literary and theological attainments, and of eminent piety, but a perfect recluse in his habits, as ignorant of the world as a monk, or Goldsmith's parson in the Vicar of Wakefield; and easily misled by others, as to what was going on in the world around him.

Soon after the "Currycomb" was published, Dr. Ralston wrote to his countryman and ministerial brother, the *Rev. Samuel Porter*, and sent him a copy of his pamphlet, asking his remarks upon it. He received in due time the following highly characteristic and entertaining answer:

"*Westmoreland*, March 24, 1805.

"*Rev'd. Brother:*—I received your letter and pamphlet, and have taken up my pen to make observations, to which nothing could have excited me but the urgency of your request. Few clergymen can bear anything but flattery; and I despise the want of candor. Therefore, silence is generally best. Your piece is a good desultory defence and attack, and looks more like the fortunate opening of a campaign than the battle which terminates a war. You have, with propriety, made excursions into the territories of your enemies; and have treated them as they deserved, and with the very same kind of delicacy with which they have treated the Presbyterians; except that you have given them some fal, lal, about your friendship to their Church, and hopes of their reformation. You charge your antagonists with the crime of assigning particular causes for the judgments of God, and, although you use qualified language, yet you are, in fact, strongly guilty of the same practice. It will give you some trouble to defend your reasoning from Hebrew 12: 5.—'Strengthen the hands of Voltaire.' Voltaire is dead: what figure in rhetoric will support the expression? Pages 13, 14, you insinuate that it is not strange for those who have been educated in America, or in the backwoods, to be ignorant of logic and destitute of common sense. 'Sucked the breasts of the Universities,' is not, to my recollection, sanctioned by any of the English classical authors. Your criticism on the difference between 'suffer' and 'experience,' as applied to convulsive spasms, is ingenious, but it will probably be thought to belong to the wire-drawing system. 'Is the work in question a work of the Spirit of God, and can Anderson's theological pills prevent the Almighty Spirit from extending the work?' Page 37. Your reasoning respecting Peter's hearers is liable to criticism. I am not certain 'that the work has neither impaired the bodies nor the minds of any of the subjects of it, in the smallest degree.' Page 48. I do not see how the absurdity in question, nor any other absurdity of the Seceders, can afford a strong proof that the work is a work of the Spirit of God. 'Falling away' is not a very strong evidence of a work of the Spirit of God. You may be able to defend what you have advanced respecting a concert of prayer, but I could not. It is probable that the eye of criticism will discover, in several places, that your assertions are stronger than the evidence by which they are supported. On the whole, you are able to defend the main ground. And you will understand my idea of the piece generally, when I inform you that since I read it, I have determined that I will not deliver my sermon before the Synod, but will take some common-place subject, for the reason that I think the Seceders are in good hands, and they have got, and will get so much beating, that it would be unmanly and cruel for me to fall upon them too. Therefore

I shall transcribe my sermon, make some alterations and additions, and leave it among my papers for the use of my children, when I am gone. I am, &c.,

"SAM'L. PORTER.

"*Mr. Ralston.*

"P. S. On reading your pamphlet, I committed the above observations to paper, and intended to correct and enlarge them, and send them to you by post. But just as I had finished my outlines, Mr. M'Millan, Jr., came in; and I now send them in their original dress. I have read the piece a second time, and am more strongly convinced that your comment on Heb. 12 : 5, will not stand the test of sound criticism. Your criticism on the expression 'some ministers,' &c., page 32, may possibly be traced to the hair-splitting system. 'Ye,' instead of 'you,' has become in a great measure obsolete, with good writers. Your excursions to Noblestown, &c., &c., &c., are deservedly severe; but I am afraid that men who are not acquainted with the treatment we have received from the Western Seceders, will think that they were written in the old exploded polemic spirit. In a word, your pamphlet will please the majority of the friends of the work; and it will bring the coldest Seceder under heaven, who reads it, to experience warm, lively feelings. You are undoubtedly able to fight the Seceders, up and down, crooked or straight, rough or smooth, and with their own weapons, too.

"S. P."

On the back of the letter is written, "Send me two dozen copies of your Spirits of Vitriol." *

---

* It will be seen from this letter, that Mr. Porter twice refers to Mr. Ralston's inference from Heb. 12 : 5, "The Word of God is quick and powerful," &c. "Not only," says Dr. Ralston, "is it evident to me, from this passage, that the Word of God, in the hand of the Almighty Spirit, acts sometimes as instantaneously on the soul as an electric shock on the body, but that when applied with power, the body, or what the Apostle styles 'the joints and marrow,' is affected as instantaneously also, by virtue of its union with

Upon a review of the positions taken and the course pursued by the Seceders, in reference to the great Western revival, at this distant point of time, we are by no means certain that, after all, they did not exert a wholesome conservative influence during that period. We are not sure that but for them, there was not some real danger, in certain quarters, of the friends and subjects of the "falling work," as it was called, running into fanatical and pernicious excesses. Nor, on the other hand, were the Seceders cut off from all benefit of that mighty outpouring of the Spirit. For many years past, dating back nearly, if not quite, to that period, this section of the Presbyterian body has been growing into a more evangelical spirit, has been becoming increasingly active, in the various causes of Bible and Tract distribution, of Sunday-

---

the soul; and this passage satisfies me with respect to the bodily affections so prevalent in the present day, which seem to be a stumbling block to so many." Most readers will, perhaps, concur with Mr. Porter in doubting the soundness of this reasoning. Mr. Porter's remark that Dr. Ralston had insinuated that "it is not strange that those educated in the backwoods should be ignorant of logic and destitute of common sense," is altogether a mistake. Dr. Ralston's language is this: "That those of you who have been educated in America, or in the backwoods, where, *as I have been told, some of you say* there is little learning to be found, especially among the Presbyterian clergy, should reason in this manner, would perhaps not be strange; but that two of you, who have sucked the breasts of the most renowned Universities of Scotland, and one of you, the father of a whole volume, besides several pamphlets, should thus reason, is to me truly astonishing." It is plain that Mr. Porter's criticism is without foundation. He excepts also to the classical purity of the expression, "sucked the breasts of the Universities," forgetting the language in Isaiah, 60 : 16: "Thou shalt also suck the milk of the Gentiles, and shalt suck the breast of kings." We shall not, however, examine all Mr. Porter's remarks and criticisms. As in the foregoing specimens, some of them appear to be sound, and others of little force. We cannot concur with Mr. Porter in his remark that Ralston's pamphlet "seemed more like the fortunate opening of a campaign than the battle which terminates the war." Though it was doubtless open, in many places, to successful assault, yet as a whole it was the closing battle, as it certainly proved in fact.

schools, and of foreign and domestic missions. Their preaching, always instructive in *matter*, is, of late years, improving in *manner*. Their sermons, considered as exhibitions and vindications of "the faith once delivered to the saints," were generally superior to those of most of our ministers. But their preachers lacked animation, pathos, and unction. They seemed to eschew all natural eloquence. It was certainly right for them to cherish an abhorrence and contempt of all appearance of playing the orator, or making rhetorical flourishes in the sacred desk. But from some unaccountable cause, they seemed to run to the opposite extreme. We have heard many of them making able speeches in their judicatories, with natural tones of voice, in an easy, fluent and graceful manner. But when they entered the pulpit, they left all this behind them, and seemed to think it a sin to preach in the same easy, natural way in which they made their speeches. But we are satisfied that there is a great improvement, as we deem it, in all these respects, of late years. And we cannot but rejoice that this branch of the Presbyterian family, to whom the church at large is more indebted for its conservative influence than we have ever, perhaps, been willing to acknowledge, abounds with many of the most eloquent, as well as the most sound and orthodox ministers in our Western Zion.

For several yaers, Dr. Ralston pursued the even tenor of his course, as a diligent and faithful country pastor. Soon after his settlement at Mingo, he became a Trustee of the Academy at Canonsburg. His name first appears on the records of the Board, April 24th, 1798. When, in 1802, a charter for Jefferson College was obtained, his name is found in the Act of the Legislature, among the list of Trustees. He was chosen President of the Board, April 26th, 1808, and re-elected to that office every year for nearly *forty years!* His attendance at the semi-annual meetings of the Board was almost constant. Regularly in March and September, he would be found wending his way from his home, through all kinds of weather, fourteen miles, to Canonsburg. Over the interests of that rising institution he watched with parental solicitude and care. And richly was he rewarded by its growing prosperity and success, and especially by the great number of ministers of the Gospel that were conducted through their collegiate course, during his long administration as President of the Board. It may not be out of place, or uninteresting to some, to observe that as President of the Trustees he succeeded *Judge John M'Dowell,* who had been chosen April 27th, 1803, and re-elected four successive years, till his age and infirmities compelled him to resign. When, in 1802, the Academy was raised to a College, *Judge James Edgar* was chosen President. It is true Dr. M'Millan was chosen the first President of the Trustees of the College; but two days afterwards, when he was appointed Vice President of the College, and Professor of Divinity, his seat as a Trustee was necessarily vacated, and Judge Edgar was appointed President in his place, and another person was elected to fill the vacancy in the Board. Having already, in "Old Redstone," given some account of this very eminent man, we will add nothing further respecting him here. But the first President of the old Board of the Academy, whose name appears on their records in 1796, was another man, perhaps not much inferior to either of those above mentioned—*Judge James Allison,* who, like the others, was also a ruling elder in the Church. These three men were all very eminent for their piety and great influence in the Church. They were all of Scotch-Irish descent—all emigrated from Eastern Pennsylvania about the same time, and lived to exert a blessed influence on the cause of education and religion in the West. Dr. Ralston might well be gratified by having such a noble set of men as his predecessors in office.

It is a little out of chronological order to notice here a circumstance in the life of Dr. Ralston, which properly belongs to the summer of 1801 or 1802. He took an excursion to Ohio, and was engaged for some weeks in preaching the Gospel, visiting destitute "settlements" and organizing churches. Among the churches he organized were Mount Pleasant and Buckskin, not far from Cincinnati. In these churches, shortly after, began that mighty work of grace, the first revival of religion west of the Ohio. This was in the summer and fall of 1802. These, and several other churches in that region, had applied to the Presbytery of Ohio, at their April meeting, in Washington, for supplies: and the Rev. Robert Johnston, then but recently licensed, was sent out by the Presbytery to supply these churches for two months. While he was there, the revival, which had spread extensively during the previous year, through the southern and western part of Kentucky, seemed to cross the Ohio, and make its first beginning and gather its first fruits in those churches which Dr. Ralston had previously organized. We may well conceive how this circumstance would fill him with rejoicing and gratitude; and perhaps it greatly contributed to deepen his interest in that mighty work, which he was, three years afterwards, engaged in defending against the assaults of its enemies. For the greater part of the above statement we are indebted to the Rev. H. S. Fullerton, of South Salem, Ohio, and to the Rev. Dr. William Wylie.

We pass over a considerable period of Dr. Ralston's life, which, though filled up with arduous labor, and with many interesting incidents, in his various relations of pastor, presbyter and trustee, yet scarcely possess sufficient importance to find a place in our limited biographical sketch. We come next to notice his second debut, as an author, in 1824. A few years previous to this time, there appeared in Western Pennsylvania and Virginia, a young Scotch-Irishman, *Alexander Campbell*, accompanied by his father, the Rev. Thomas Campbell. The elder Campbell had been a preacher before he left his native land, and came out from Ireland some time before the son. He preached in one or two vacant Secession churches in Washington County, without leave or authority from the Presbytery. And when he subsequently sought admission into the Presbytery and was rejected, he still continued to preach in some of their vacant churches, to the serious, though temporary distraction and confusion of those churches. Upon the arrival of his son, they both sought ecclesiastical connection with the Associate Presbytery of Chartiers, and with the Presbytery of Ohio. But failing to attain the position they sought, they soon obtained notoriety by a new and bold path they made for themselves, in connection with the Baptist church.* It was but a short time, before the novelty of their principles, and the revolutionary tendency of their discourse, threw them out of fellowship with that body. But they drew after them an immense number of followers, principally from the Baptist persuasion. In respect to the ordinance of baptism, they were thorough Baptists, both as to the subjects and mode of that Christian rite. But they discarded the old doctrinal system of the Baptists, in almost every other respect. When they reached this point in their career, the younger Campbell became the great leader and champion. According to their new creed, to be immersed

---

* "They first appeared before the Redstone Association, in September, 1813, with one or two others, as delegates from a recently organized church on Brush creek, about twenty miles west of Washington; asking for themselves and the church which they represented, the fellowship of the Association. They had recently been baptized on a profession of their faith in Christ, by the Rev. Matthias Luce, pastor of a Baptist church on Ten-mile creek. The Messrs. Campbell, father and son, had recently come from Ireland, where they had been connected with the Secession church, of which the father had been a distinguished minister. They then maintained with firmness and ability the leading doctrines of the Calvinistic school, but refused to acknowledge any Confession of Faith; but at the same time agreed to submit to the most rigid examination of their doctrinal principles that the Association, or any of its members, might think proper to make. A careful examination was made and they were received into the fellowship of the Association."—"*Two Discourses*," *by Dr. Estep.*

was to perform the act of faith; and baptism, by immersion, secured the remission of sins. There was no need of a special agency of the Holy Spirit to regenerate the sinner. The doctrine of regeneration, as we, in common with orthodox Baptists, hold it, was utterly repudiated by Alexander Campbell. These, and a few other less important points, together with a furious assault upon all creeds and confessions, made up what is now extensively known by the name of "Campbellism." Mr. Campbell, Jr., eagerly sought public discussion, and challenged the clerical world to furnish a champion. The Rev. John Walker, of the Secession church, took up the gauntlet and met Mr. Campbell. They discussed the subject of baptism for several days. This debate Mr. Campbell soon after published; giving of course his own version of it, very much to his own advantage. He claimed a complete victory. He and his friends were active in giving a wide circulation to the pamphlet. The adroitness of Mr. Campbell was particularly displayed in making this debate turn mainly on the subject of baptism, its mode and proper subjects; and under covert of this pretended triumph, more successfully propagating his more vital doctrinal errors, and gaining proselytes, especially from the Baptists, to his party. This was, indeed, the result, beyond, perhaps, his most sanguine expectations. Great pains were taken to throw this pamphlet over the entire field of Dr. Ralston's labors. The Doctor found it necessary to buckle on his armor and prepare for battle. This he did in his pulpit. But in this way alone, he knew he could not fully reach the evil. He wrote and published in the *Presbyterian Magazine*, a series of letters, reviewing the debate. These letters he soon after published in a pamphlet of 300 pages. He had carefully revised and enlarged the letters, and added two more, addressed to Mr. Walker. The work is entitled "A Review of a Debate on Christian Baptism, between Mr. John Walker, a minister of the Secession, and Mr. Alexander Campbell, a Baptist minister, published by

Mr. Campbell—in a series of letters addressed and dedicated to the united congregations of Mingo creek and Williamsport: by their affectionate pastor, Samuel Ralston. To which is now added a reply to objections made by both Mr. Campbell and Mr. Walker." This little book was published in Washington, 1825. It is certainly a masterly performance. It carries us over the entire field usually occupied by the Baptist controversy. The reader will find every argument of essential importance fully and fairly brought forward, on both sides of the subject. It is a valuable storehouse, an excellent arsenal, where any one who may have occasion, will find all he wants, in discussing the subject of baptism. There is, however, one feature of this valuable work, which not a little mars it, in our estimation. He contends that the Abrahamic covenant, recorded in the 17th chapter of Genesis, is a mere ecclesiastical covenant—that as circumcision was its seal under the former dispensation, so baptism is now the seal merely of the external, visible church—that a profession of saving faith is not necessary to admission, through the ordinance of baptism; in other words, that an historical faith, a moral life, and professed subjection to the discipline of the church, are sufficient to entitle any one to admission into the visible church by baptism, and to bring with them also, of course, their children. Yet he would not, on these terms, receive them to the ordinance of the Lord's Supper. In order to admission to this seal of the covenant, satisfactory evidence of evangelical repentance and saving faith, should be required. In this way he would distinguish, in regard to the two ordinances of the Gospel. His views of the true construction of the commission "to disciple all nations," are of course modified by his positions, as to the qualifications requisite to admission, by baptism, into the visible church. He believed that not only infants, but others who are willing to place themselves under the culture of the church, are, by baptism, taken out of the visible kingdom of Satan, in which all are born, as the children of a degenerate parent, and planted in the vineyard, or church of God, *the usual birth-place of the children of grace;* and become entitled, by the divine promise, to what Christ calls, "digging about and dunging," or such instruction, by the Word and Spirit, through the instrumentality of their parents, and of the church, as is calculated to make them "trees of righteousness, the planting of the Lord, that he might be glorified." Through various portions of the work, Dr. Ralston maintains, with great ingenuity and force of argument, his peculiar views. He endeavors also to meet every objection. He is very far from defending any lax or latitudinarian system, as to the discipline of the church, or as to admission to the Lord's Table. He is no advocate for any mincing or softening down of the terms of the gospel, or the humbling truths of man's total depravity, and entire dependence on the sovereign grace of God, for a new heart and a right spirit. Yet we think he entirely breaks down, when he attempts to show a distinction between the conditions of the two seals of the covenant; or rather, to show that one is a seal of an ecclesiastical covenant, and the other the seal of the covenant of grace. And when he attempts to explain away the cases of Lydia, of the Jailor, and of the Eunuch, in every one of which it seems to us clear, that not a mere speculative or historical faith, but a true, saving faith was professed, we think there is what Mr. Porter calls much "wire-drawing." It is not our purpose, however, to discuss this subject. We must admit that Dr. Ralston has put forth the strength of a mighty mind in maintaining his ground. And we would advise any one who may ever meet with this work, to read over Turretine's "De fœdere gratiæ," especially his "Locus duodecimus," before he decides the question, which Dr. Ralston so ably discusses.

The progress of "Campbellism" in Western Pennsylvania, we have no doubt, was greatly checked by Dr. Ralston's work. That bold, eloquent, talented, but unscrupulous heresiarch, was shown up in his true colors, and his influence was crippled. Except in a few localities, where there was little opportunity to enlighten the people, his erroneous tenets gathered but few disciples. And so matters remain to this day. So far as we have been able to learn, that form of error is on the decline in Western Pennsylvania, and evangelical Christianity should honor the memory of Dr. Ralston.*

In 1842, Dr. Ralston published "A brief explication of the principal Prophecies of Daniel and John, as they regard the Church of God;" to which was added "An Appendix, containing an inquiry into the propriety of using an Evangelical Psalmody, in the worship of God." Of this work, though we have read it with great satisfaction, we prefer to let Dr. Magill speak: "Here, at the age of eighty-six, when retired from pastoral life to a quietude and seclusion from the world, which would have relaxed to second childhood many another man of sixty years, we have a display of power to observe, and generalize, and investigate profoundly, which very few, in the vigor of their prime can ever attain. Volumes of useful information are compressed in a duodecimo, of some one hundred and eighty pages. Faber, Newton, Croly, Scott, Keith, &c., dissected with a master's hand; their merits indicated, and their defects ascertained, with a brevity and fidelity which compel our admiration. Indeed, the student of philosophy can scarcely find a better history of criticism on this great

*Dr. Magill, in his beautiful obituary of Dr. Ralston, speaking of this work on baptism, says: "When Campbellism began to agitate the country, and the founder of the sect was glorying in his victory over Walker and others, whom he encountered in oral debate, Dr. Ralston published a book on baptism, comprising a review of the debate with Mr. Walker, and letters in reply to an attack of Mr. Campbell on this Review. This little work is one of remarkable force and erudition. No subsequent debate with Campbell, however triumphant and deservedly popular, has evinced greater skill or cogency in exposing his protean sophistry. Whatever diversity of opinion may exist among us respecting some positions taken by the author, all must concede that in originality and power, this book is one of surpassing merit."

subject, with any volume of moderate size. And as a key of interpretation, it is precisely such as was inevitable to a gigantic mind laboring without a library. Connected with this publication, and bound up in the same volume, is a pungent examination of a Mr. Reid's book, entitled "The Seven Last Plagues." The sixth vial of this book is poured out on all Christendom, excepting the sect to which the author belongs, with special aim to overwhelm the churches in which Christ is sung expressly, as having already come in the person of Jesus of Nazareth. His strictures on Mr. Reid brought Dr. Ralston into the Psalmody controversy, and occasioned the next and last publication from his pen, "A Defence of Evangelical Psalmody." Manly discussion, inflexible determination to keep his antagonist to the true point at issue, and a calm dignity of manner, which no misrepresentation or abuse could disturb, eminently characterize this last effort of his life to be useful through the press. It was made in the eighty-eighth year of his life. The whole history of modern polemics cannot produce a parallel instance, perhaps, of such fresh activity, quick perception, spirited reply, and powerful concentration, beyond the limits of four-score years. We heartily unite in this testimony. Though there are portions of this work that we think Dr. Ralston would not have written in the full vigor of his intellectual powers, there are other parts that we regard as admirable. Nothing that has been written, on this rather unprofitable controversy, is more to the point, in our judgment, than Dr. Ralston's "No. V., containing Scriptural precedents for an Evangelical Psalmody." The part of the volume which we regard as least interesting, and most assailable, is what he says about "Human Inventions," and "Human Composure." The writer, we think, is betrayed into a species of logomachy, of little importance to the issue of the case.

This last work of Dr. Ralston was well received and extensively circulated. It was perhaps more generally read than any thing which he had previously written. But his pilgrimage on earth was drawing to a close. He had, in 1836, given up the charge of Williamsport church; a few years after he resigned also that of Mingo. In his quiet residence on his farm, he waited with patience the coming of his master. He continued till near his last days to attend the services of God's house—though increasing deafness must have greatly diminished his enjoyment in the sanctuary. He generally attended the Presbyterial and Synodical meetings of his brethren. But he had witnessed the successive departure from this life of all his first fellow-laborers in the gospel ministry. In 1832, he had been called to preach a discourse at Chartiers, in reference to the death of Dr. M'Millan, his earliest and most intimate Western friend.* But his own sojourn was protracted far beyond the usual limit of human life. For not till September 25, 1851, did he receive his dismission. Then, in the bosom of his family, in great quietness and peace, he gently sunk into the arms of death, and fell asleep in Jesus.

We cannot better close this memoir, than by giving the concluding part of Dr. Magill's obituary notice of this aged servant of God: "It was a matter of regret to this venerable father, as he once said to the writer, with manifest emotion, that nearly all his writings were controversial; that he had been a man of war from his youth. It had been his duty. It was not his natural disposition: his temper was peculiarly bland, and genial and courteous. As a remarkable illustration of his pacific turn, as well as honorable and delicate sensibility, his successors in the pastoral charge always loved him, more than feared; and always found him scrupulously

*No one can read that discourse without feeling a deeper sentiment of veneration and respect for the character of Dr. M'Millan. It will also, perhaps, exalt the talents and piety of Dr. Ralston more than anything he has ever written, while it cannot fail to throw a new interest upon the past and future of Jefferson College. It deserves to be read "twice through without stopping."—J. S.

careful to hold up their hands, and strengthen them in the respect and affections of their people. It is rather a sad commentary on the frailties of retiring ministers, that we must hold up this trait of Dr. Ralston as anywise remarkable and singular. It is true, we have other beautiful illustrations of such magnanimity among us; but it is to be lamented greatly that some men contrive, without exactly designing it, to embroil the people they can no longer feed, and take a perverse care that no one succeed to the confidence and love in which they were once embosomed. This noble patriarch in our Zion lived only to cheer and bless the young brethren who followed him, in one branch of his charge, twenty years, and in the other fifteen years, after his retirement. 'He loved peace,' writes the pastor of Mingo Church, where Dr. Ralston continued to reside and worship, 'and the business of peace-making was his great delight.* And all his influence went to establish the pastor in the affections of the people. There was much that was truly generous and kind in the elements of his soul. His friendship was ardent and constant.' As a preacher, he was eminently didactic and distinctive; clear, copious and profound in the exposition and defence of saving truth. And yet, like every man of truly gifted mind, he was full of strong emotion; which led him to earnest and strong appeals of a practical kind. Perhaps his manner of treating subjects had too much of a controversial air: but with him there was no bitterness of spirit. He was the very opposite of that modern picture of Christian

---

*When asked once in Presbytery for his session-book, he replied, "We have had nothing to record." "Do you never have any judicial proceedings?" was asked. "We never had but one case, and that many years ago; and I was determined then that we would never have another. We get such matters settled without a judicial process!" And yet he did not neglect discipline.—J. S.

love which hates nothing so much as honesty and earnestness, in maintaining one's own conviction of truth and duty. What he stoutly claimed for himself, he heartily granted to others. He was therefore truly catholic in his feelings, and utterly remote from bigotry and rancor. He loved with broad and deep affection all that differed from him; just in proportion to the enlightened zeal with which he vindicated the distinctive tenets of his own profession. As an ecclesiastic, he was ever distinguished for punctuality and faithfulness in attending church courts. Always attentive and interested in the business of a judicatory, he acquired such a ready apprehension of matters usually transacted there, that even when he ceased to hear the ordinary tones of speech on the floor, he could discern what many others who had ears to hear, failed to perceive; and mingle the expressions of his own opinion with a pertinence which often excited the wonder of his juniors. Indeed, until he was over ninety years old, and his infirmities absolutely hindered him from travel, he was among the most regular, useful members of the Presbytery and the Synod. He possessed pre-eminently that triple element of Christian courage, which the Apostle describes as 'the spirit of power and of love and of a sound mind.' Ardent as were his feelings, constitutionally, and ready as they were to be zealously affected in every good thing, (as in the great revival, where bodily affections were strangely intermingled,) he was exceedingly discreet and sober, and well balanced in his estimation of a popular rage or fanatical excitement. Long before the General Assembly was brought to rebuke the technical Abolitionism of the day, and before the Princeton *Review*, or any other conservative journal, spoke out on the subject, Dr. Ralston was well known to inculcate the very same principles of scriptural truth and practical wisdom that now govern, with almost universal consent, our favored Church on the agitated subject of slavery. Resembling these solid attributes of his understanding, was the type of his personal piety. It was remarkably free from irregular impulse and distressing variation. Tender and humble, and self-abasing, it was yet almost uniformly serene and cheerful. Few men exhibited a more delicate and lively appreciation of God's favor, in the smallest mercies of his Providence or grace. Gratitude, then, fiducial gratitude, which will, under any circumstances, 'thank God and take courage,' which so beautifully distinguished the piety of David, and with which he ever imbues even the saddest song—'Because thou hast been my help, therefore in the shadow of thy wings will I rejoice'—was the prevailing characteristic of Dr. Ralston's personal piety. Upon this beautiful adornment of a calm and thankful spirit, he wore the gem of consistency, which no man could ever impeach. Temptation to swerve was not only repelled by the dignity of his peculiar character, but far more was vanquished by a conscientiousness, which a fitful and variable experience of personal religion lamentably wants. His powerful mind, active, unclouded and strong, till the very last, grappled with the last enemy, death, as it had been wont to do with sin and error, for almost a century of time. He was cheerful and happy in the prospect, girded and roused, yet tranquil, and even sublime, in the near approach. On the day of his death, he looked out once more on the visible militant Church, that he had loved so much, and watched with so great solicitude—reading with fresh interest a late number of the *Presbyterian*. Then as the struggle came on, he calmly felt his own pulse, found it sinking away, and exclaimed, without faltering or agitation: 'I am ready; I am a sinner saved by grace. Tell my brethren—tell the congregation that I die in the faith I have so long preached. I die relying upon the meritorious righteousness of the Lord Jesus Christ: What a blessing to have such a rock!'"

The congregation of Mingo and Monongahela City erected

a beautiful marble monument over his grave, in the Mingo creek burying ground, with the following inscription:

REV. SAMUEL RALSTON, D. D.,

BORN

IN IRELAND, 1756.

DIED

SEPTEMBER 25, 1851.

He was educated in the University of Glasgow, Scotland.
Emigrated to the United States, A. D. 1794.

Ordained pastor of the United Congregations of Mingo Creek and Monongahela City, 1796. On this field he sowed the good seed of the word, for nearly half a century. Distinguished as a scholar, a profound expositor of sacred truth, a faithful watchman on the walls of Zion, and a devoted servant of God, he was intimately identified with the advancement of literature, religion and religious liberty, in this Western country.

"And he, being dead, yet speaketh."
"The righteous shall be in everlasting remembrance."

The following discourse, delivered on the death of Dr. M'Millan, contains so much that is worthy to be read, that we cannot doubt its insertion here will be acceptable to many readers:

A FUNERAL SERMON

On the occasion of the death of the Rev. John M'Millan, D. D., late of Chartiers. By Samuel Ralston.

"My father, my father, the chariot of Israel, and the horsemen thereof."
2 KINGS, 2 : 12.

These words are the strong and fervid exclamation of the prophet Elisha, when he saw his spiritual father and beloved master ascending to heaven in a chariot of fire. To understand the full import, and feel the force of these words, it will be necessary to recollect that, in those days, the principal strength of a nation for defending themselves, and repelling their enemies, consisted in their chariots of war, and cavalry or horsemen. From the days of Abraham to the coming of Christ, the visible church, the usual birthplace of the children of grace, was confined to the descendants of that patriarch, in the line of Isaac and Jacob; who, on account of his prevalency with God, by prayer, was surnamed Israel. In the days of Elijah, true religion, which consists in the knowledge and sincere worship of Jehovah, the true and the living God, had experienced a woeful decline in the Jewish nation, especially in that portion of it comprehending the kingdom of Israel. We are told in the 19th chapter of the 1st Book of Kings, that in all that kingdom there were only seven thousand men, with the prophet Elijah, who had not bowed the knee to Baal, one of the idol gods of the surrounding idolatrous nations. Elisha was doubtless acquainted with this woeful degeneracy; and it was doubtless this circumstance, with other mournful considerations hereafter to be mentioned, that constrained him to exclaim, when his beloved master was removed from him, "My father, my father, the chariot of Israel, and the horsemen thereof:" It was as if he had said, "what will become of the church of the true and living God, when thou, my father, the unbending advocate of the truth and of true religion, the honest preacher of righteousness, and the undaunted reprover of error and immorality, even in kings, art taken from us. May we not expect still more degenerate days, unless Jehovah will, in mercy, raise up another, or others, who will vindicate the truth, and endeavor to put a stop to prevailing error and irreligion?" And the King and Head of the church did so, in the person of the mourning and almost distracted Elisha himself: he received a double portion of his master's spirit. The doctrine evidently deducible from this affecting incident is, that the death of good men, though to them unspeakable gain, is a most serious public loss, to both Church and State, but especially to the church; and ought to be deplored and improved by survivors, by being followers of them, wherein they followed Christ. "Be not slothful," saith the Apostle, "but followers of them, who, through faith and patience, inherit the promises." Our design, then, on the present occasion, is to show in what respects the death of good men is a public loss, especially to the church; with a special reference to the loss which we have experienced in the death of our father and friend, the late Dr. John M'Millan, whose decease we are assembled this day to deplore.

1st. All good men are lovers of the truth, especially of the truth as it is in Jesus. They love it not only for its own sake, but because they know that it is by the truth, and by the truth only, that man, immersed by sin in thick moral darkness, and the slave of vice, can be led to see his danger, and to feel his deep moral maladies, and be persuaded to accept of that remedy which God has provided in his Son, as a Redeemer from wrath and from sin, and who is able and willing to redeem all who will go unto him. Yes, it is by the mournful and Scriptural truth, that man is now a guilty, morally defiled, and morally helpless creature, that he can be convinced of his danger, and constrained to inquire, "what he shall do to be saved." It is also by the gracious and glorious truth, that God so loved the world, guilty and rebellious and wicked as it is, that he gave his only-begotten Son, that whosoever believeth on him, should not perish, but have everlasting life—that the awakened sinner is preserved from sinking into despair, and from rushing against the bosses of Jehovah's buckler, and to cry, "Lord, save me, I perish;" and who never suffered any to perish who have cried to him for salvation from wrath and from sin. And it is by the truth that there is an all-sufficiency of grace in Christ, that the humble and honest believer is supported and sanctified. "Sanctify them through thy truth: thy word is truth," is one of the last and gracious prayers that Christ offered up to his Heavenly Father in behalf of his church and people. Need I tell a single individual present how distinguished our father and friend, whose decease we are met to deplore, was in teaching and preaching these radical truths and fundamental doctrines of the religion of Jesus. Many of you remember how you felt, perhaps trembled, when that man of God, for the purpose of awakening you to a sense of your danger, and showing you your need of the Saviour, portrayed in his own peculiarly strong but scriptural terms, the indignation and wrath, tribulation and anguish, that await all who live and die without an interest in that blood that was shed for the remission of sins. As just now observed, this is a radical principle in the Christian system, and should be an indispensable element in every sermon; and in preaching it, our departed father and friend exceeded all men we have ever met with or heard preach. What avails it that a preacher unfolds to his audience in the clearest manner the character and offices of the Saviour whom God has provided, if at the same time he neglects, or but faintly points out the wretchedness and danger of the wicked, or of the thoughtless and unbelieving? They are not morally sick, but whole, in their own estimation. Therefore all that can be told them of the wisdom and grace of the plan of redemption, through Christ, is in the nature of things confined to the intellect, but can never pierce the conscience, nor affect the heart. Not so, however, was it with the late pastor of this congregation. Knowing the terrors of the Lord, and knowing also that Christ came into the world, not to call the righteous, or those who suppose they are righteous, but sinners, or those who feel they are sinners, to repentance, he spent his strength and life endeavoring to convince them that they were morally wretched and poor, and miserable, and blind and naked; for the purpose of persuading them to go to Christ, "for gold tried in the fire, that they might be enriched; for white raiment, that they might be clothed, and that the shame of their nakedness might not appear; and to anoint their eyes with eye salve of his grace, that they might see"—see at the same time their inveterate disease and gracious remedy. He did not tell you, as, alas! some preachers within even the pale of the Presbyterian church tell their hearers, that conversion is an easy work; as easy as to rise from their seats and walk out of their pews, and that they had sufficient ability so to do; but he told you, from the word of God, that you were without strength—that your ability and strength to turn from sin to holiness, was to be found in Christ, and Christ alone, through the agency of his Holy Spirit, given to all who honestly ask that gift in his name, or for his sake—that to obtain this strength you should cry unto him; and that while you were crying, you should endeavor to cast yourselves upon him, who is made of God, to all who do so, "wisdom and righteousnses and sanctification and redemption." He never told you, as some falsely charge those who hold that salvation is altogether of grace, as telling their hearers to wait God's own time to convert you; and if he converted you, well and good, and if not, you were not to blame; but he impressed upon you in the strongest manner, the obligation you were under to believe that record which God has given in his precious Word, respecting his Son, that in him, and in him alone, there is life; and exhorted you while you acknowledged and bewailed your deep moral imbecility to conceive even a good thought to plead his precious promises, "to take away the heart of stone and to give you an heart of flesh," or an humble, tender and believing heart to put his Spirit within you, and to cause you, "to walk in his statutes and keep his judgments and do them." And when you had ground to hope, that God had graciously heard your cry, you remember well, we trust, that in exhorting you to work out your salvation with fear and trembling, he told you that it is God who works in his children to will and to do of his good pleasure; and directed you at the same time to look unto and to depend on his all-sufficient grace.

And here let me further call up to your remembrance the glowing fervor with which he held up to your view the blessed Jesus, as the only city of refuge, where the sword of inflexible justice can neither reach nor punish. Do not many of you remember how your hearts burned within you, when he exhibited him in all his transcendent loveliness, as God-man-Mediator, the Brightness of the Father's glory, and the express image of his person, and in whom all the fullness of the Godhead substantially dwells? And when he depicted the love of Jesus in dying, the just for the unjust, and receiving the sword of inflexible justice into his own spotless bosom, to prevent its being sheathed in your guilty hearts, did not your trembling, and, at the same time, exulting souls, exclaim with the Apostle, "It is a faithful saying, or a saying worthy of all credit, and worthy of all acceptation, that Christ came into the world to save sinners, even the chiefest of them?" And have you not felt a willingness to be saved by this Jesus; to be washed in his blood from all your guilt, to be clothed upon with the spotless robe of his righteousness, to be sanctified by his Spirit, to be governed by his Word, and to be guided by his wisdom? With the Apostle Paul, this "Christ and him crucified" was the constant, and to himself, the delightful theme of all our departed father's ministrations; because he knew, from his own experience, and we trust that a number of you know from your experience also, that this theme, and this theme alone, is, in the hand of the Divine Spirit, the power of God, and the wisdom of God to the salvation of sinners. How jejune and empty and profitless are the abstruse speculations and metaphysical disquisitions of many of our published sermons in the present day, when compared with this apostolical theme, which ran and shone like a golden thread, in all the pulpit exhibitions of our departed father and friend, as all who have ever heard him can testify. The one is what the Apostle calls "philosophy falsely so called:" the other is the true philosophy sent down from Heaven, recorded in God's own book, and embodied in this heavenly theme, for the purpose of saving perishing sinners. The one is called by the Apostle James, "the wisdom that is earthly, sensual, and devilish;" or of human invention; calculated to please the blinded mind and depraved heart of man; and the invention of the father of lies and of error. But the other came down "from above," and "is pure, peaceable, gentle, easy to be entreated, full of mercies and good fruits, without partiality and without hypocrisy." And yet it was not merely to instruct the ignorant in the knowledge of the plan of redemption, through a crucified Christ, that he dwelt so much and so often on this, to him, delightful theme. He had another highly important object in view, to bring it to operate with its designed power and sanctifying influence on the heart. He knew he taught that man was at the same time a guilty and morally defiled creature, and that "without holiness no man can see the Lord." And he knew that nothing but the doctrines of the cross are in themselves calculated, and by God blessed, to subdue the proud heart of man to the obedience of faith, and to produce that repentance unto life, not to be repented of. Hence, then, as you can all testify, he inculcated, more or less, in every sermon, the indispensable necessity of experimental religion; or, as Christ expressed it, in his conference with Nicodemus, that unless a man is born again, or from above, he cannot see, he cannot enter the kingdom of glory hereafter. And in this, as well as for awakening the careless, thoughtless sinner to a sense of his danger, his sermons equaled, if not exceeded any I have ever read or heard on these subjects. You all remember how particular, close, clear, pungent and various were the questions for self-examination which he pressed upon you in every sermon on this highly important point. And here I would remark what I think many of you must have remarked, that scarcely a head of his discourses was dismissed without a particular application of the doctrine contained in that head to the hearts and consciences of his hearers. In this he had a peculiar talent and happy facility—that while the understanding of the hearer was admiring the wisdom, the mercy and the grace of God, in devising and executing the plan of redemption through a crucified Christ, he was constrained to ask himself, "am I in Christ and interested in this gracious and glorious plan? or am I yet in my sins; in the gall of bitterness and in the bonds of iniquity?" Under the divine blessing this, to myself, has, in a great measure, accounted for his *great success* in winning souls to Christ; for it is God's plan of redemption, and the way he requires that plan to be exhibited to sinners, that God blesses and ever will bless. And yet there is another and very important part of ministerial duty; in the discharge of which I have often admired the tact and talent of our departed father and friend, as much as in these which I have mentioned. This, in theological language, is termed *casuistry;* and consists in pointing out the specific difference between real and counterfeit graces, if graces the latter may be called, and also in pouring the balm of divine consolation into the perplexed and distressed heart. Experimentally acquainted himself with the devices of Satan, and with the influence which remaining corruption, in the hearts of God's people, has, in weakening their faith, lessening their love, and repressing their hope, he unraveled with a skillful hand all the snares and stratagems of the wicked one; held out in such captivating colors the many precious promises of needed grace, to all Christ's humble but fainting followers, as dispelled their doubts, strengthened their faith, expanded their love, and reanimated their hope, and disposed them to forget the things that are behind, to reach forth to those that are before, and in borrowed strength to press forward toward the mark for the prize of the high calling of God in Christ Jesus, the Lord. Frequently have I observed, under his preaching, many of the children of God hanging their heads like a bulrush; and if they lifted up their faces, they were covered with clouds and mental distress: but no sooner did he address himself to this delightful part of his public ministrations—no sooner did he begin to exhibit the grace of Christ in its exuberant riches, unbounded fullness, and unlimited freeness, than the accumulated clouds began to scatter before the rays of the sun of righteousness arising upon them with healing in his wings; and I thought I saw the resolution of Paul, when in similar circumstances, written on their countenances: "I will glory in my infirmities, that the power of Christ may rest upon me." Such was our departed father, as a man of God and minister of Christ, in handling the word of God, for doctrine, for reproof, for correction, and instruction in righteousness. And now, when we consider his soundness in the faith, and well-earned influence in this part of our Western Israel, on the church, when we consider that the enemy of truth and of righteousness is pouring a flood of error into our church, with a new set of means of grace, or "measures," as they call them, suited to these errors; and although we have reason to bless God that there are more than seven thousand men who have not bowed the knee to Baal, or adopted those errors with their corresponding measures, yet when we consider how great the loss of such a man is at such a period, have we not considerable reason to bewail it in the language of our text, and say, "Our father, our father, the chariot of Israel, and the horsemen thereof?"

2d. There is another point of light in which our departed father should be viewed, both to do full justice to his character, and that it may be profitable for our imitation. All good men, as good men, are necessarily possessed of a spirit of philanthropy, or a desire to do good unto others. And where they have been blessed with a liberal education, there is nothing which they desire more than to communicate its advantages to others. They know well that civil liberty, although obtained at a large expense of treasure and of blood, as was our own, can never be stable, nor perpetuated, but by the diffusion of useful knowledge among the people. Hence, then, they have ever been the supporters of schools and colleges, while demagogues and disorganizers discourage them, as far as they can do so, with safety to their own interests. Good men also know that as knowledge is indispensably necessary for the health and prosperity of the State, it is still more so for the health and welfare of the Church; while literature is cried down by errorists and heretics, that have, in every age, marred the beauty of the daughter of Zion. Now there are names enrolled in the different Encyclopedias, as benefactors of mankind, and patrons of useful arts and sciences, who, in their sphere, have not done as much for the support of useful literature as our lamented father has done. When he first came to this country, it was an awful moral waste. The country was filling up rapidly, and the settlements extending on every side. But himself and two others excepted, there were none to preach the everlasting gospel to them—the only means of salvation, and the only effectual barrier against the prevalency of vice and immorality. Well knowing that an ignorant ministry is as apt to do as much evil as good: "for if the blind lead the blind they must both fall into the ditch"—he did all that could be done. He built a small log house near his own; and as few men were better judges of others than he was, he there collected such men as Porter, Marquis, and M'Cready, whom some of you knew; and gratuitously instructed them so as to be useful in the ministry. And few were more useful in their day. And that little log academy was the germ of all the Academies and Colleges that adorn and fructify our country at present with the streams of science and useful literature. When the increasing demands of the church required an enlargement of this useful little academy, it was transferred to Canonsburg, then a young and rising village.* Through

* It appears that Dr. Ralston, in several particulars, has given an account respecting the Log-Cabin School, and its transfer to Canonsburg, in harmony with the current popular traditions about the whole matter. It will be remembered that Dr. Ralston came out to Western Pennsylvania in 1795, and could not have known personally anything about the movements of Messrs. Dodd and Smith, ten or twelve years before that time. It will not be forgotten also that he was not personally cognizant of what transpired in 1790 and 1791. The statements of Messrs. Robert Patterson and Darby, and the language of Dr. M'Millan himself, as quoted in "Old Redstone" and in the "History of Jefferson College," are slightly at variance with some of the above statements of Dr. Ralston. But we do not regard these statements as essentially derogating, in the least degree, from the just claims of honor and praise here given to Dr M'Millan.—J. S.

the influence of our lamented father, a house was erected suitable to the existing demands, teachers provided, among whom was the late amiable, modest, scientific, pious and lamented Professor Miller, and a charter of incorporation obtained from the Legislature of the State. I had then the honor of becoming connected with it as a Trustee; and well do I remember the difficulties with which we had to struggle in keeping it in operation. The greatest number of students were pious but not wealthy young men, and consequently unable to contribute that remuneration for their tuition that was necessary for the support of the professors. And here I should not omit to mention what may not be known to many here, or to the public at large, but is known to myself, and some who hear me, that our lamented father, whose liberality and philanthropy knew no bounds, when the interests of literature and of the church were concerned, for many years gave *ten pounds* yearly, out of a salary of one hundred pounds, Pennsylvania currency, for the support of the Academy. And there is no doubt but that he considered himself more than repaid, from the consideration and fact that in that Academy were taught most, if not all, those who have planted the churches beyond the Allegheny and Ohio rivers. In process of time, from causes not necessary to mention here, that Academy, then changed into a *College* by an act of the Legislature, suffered not only a great depression, but its very existence was jeopardized. Although I knew that it had been a child of prayer, and although I knew that many a fervent prayer for its success and stability were sent up daily from the family altars of the faithful around, yet I confess that my own faith for its continued existence failed; and I once thought that I saw it draw its last gasp. But not so was it with the faith of our deceased father. It was like that of Abraham when required to sacrifice his beloved son, Isaac, unflinching and unfailing; and he, like that distinguished Patriarch, "hoped even against hope." To continue its existence, a new and extensive College must be erected; and there was not a dollar in the treasury of the Trustees. At the suggestion of our father, a statement of our wants and an appeal was made to a generous public. It was not made in vain; and such generous donations flowed into our treasury from all quarters, as justified the Trustees to commence building a second College edifice. And I need scarcely say that the extensive influence of our father, and the veneration in which he was held abroad, had no small influence in procuring those donations. The foundation of the second building was laid deep and solid by our deceased father, by a fervent prayer of faith, and which, like every prayer of faith, is enrolled in the Archives of Heaven. Should Jefferson College, in the lapse of time, be brought to the same state of depression in which we have seen it, I think that there is neither fanaticism nor presumption in believing and saying, that the prevalency of that heaven-recorded prayer will prove the means of its resuscitation. The public donations for the erection of the second College edifice, though generous beyond expectation, were not sufficient to complete it, on account of its size and extensiveness; and a second appeal to the public was not judged prudent or expedient. In this dilemma, the public spirit and generosity of our venerated father, with that of the late *Craig Ritchie, Esq.*, of Canonsburg, were brought into action and came to our aid. Each of them advanced some hundreds of dollars; nor were their purses shut until the building was completed, and fitted for the reception of the students. And not only so, but both of them spent a considerable portion of their time in providing materials and superintending the work during its progress. These acts of generosity and public spirit are, perhaps, not known to many here; but are known to myself and to the Trustees of the College, some of whom are now under my eye. True, they were repaid the money which they advanced, after some years, out of a donation given to the College by the Legislature of the State; but it is as true that the prospect of their being repaid, when they advanced the money, was very doubtful. For the Legislature were not in the giving mood to colleges at that time, nor for some years after.

We have already observed that the Prophets of old were preachers of truth and righteousness, as well as predictors of future events. We are told that there were schools of the prophets in the days of the prophet Samuel, where the principles of the true religion were taught. We are also told that there were sons of the prophets, in the days of Elijah, and it is to be presumed that there were schools where they were taught; and that Elijah was a distinguished patron and supporter of those schools; and we think it a rational and fair inference that a consideration of the loss which those schools would sustain, by the removal of Elijah to Heaven, entered into and formed a principal element of Elisha's exclamation, "My father, my father, the chariot of Israel, and the horsemen thereof!" And now, when we reflect upon the many hundreds of men who have been educated in Jefferson College—that many of them have filled, and are now filling respectable and useful stations in the departments of law and medicine—when we also reflect upon the numbers who have gone forth from it, as preachers of Christ and of righteousness; (some of whom are respectable presidents of other colleges, and some are gone as missionaries of the cross, to announce pardon and peace through a crucified Christ—that delightful theme of our lamented father's ministrations—to those who are lying in the thickest shades of mental and moral darkness in Africa, in Hindostan, and in our own land,)—and when we reflect that our departed father was its sole founder, that he watched over its interests with paternal care for half a century—that he spent much of his precious time in promoting its interests—and that his purse was always open for the supply of its manifold wants—that next to the Church of Christ, it was the dearest object of his solicitude and supplications at a throne of grace—as I know from many conversations with him on the subject; and that the primary design of erecting Jefferson College, was to train young men for the gospel ministry—when, I say, we reflect upon these things, would it be a perversion of our text to substitute Jefferson College for Israel, and say, "Our father, our father, the chariot of Jefferson College, and the horsemen thereof." I risk nothing, nor will I offend a single individual of my brethren in the ministry, when I say that, for soundness in the faith, for unwavering love of the truth as it is in Jesus, and for opposition to the errors and innovations that have crept into our church—for an ardent love for the salvation of souls, and unwearied labors and endeavors in the support of literature, as the handmaid of true religion, our father has not left a superior, if an equal, behind him, in the Synod of Pittsburgh, perhaps in the General Assembly of the Presbyterian Church. Oh! when shall our church be blessed with another Dr. John M'Millan! But he has rested from his labors, and his works have followed him, as evidences of his love to Christ, and untiring labors amidst infirmities and the waste of old age, in promoting the interests of true and undefiled religion. And now, how shall we, whom he hath left behind, in this land of sorrows and valley of tears, profit by this afflicting dispensation of Providence? By being followers of him wherein he followed Christ. And those of us to whom the ministration of the gospel is committed, ought to improve this dispensation, by maintaining, like him, an unwavering love of the truth, as embodied in the standards of our church, whatever opposition we meet with in so doing; or whatever contempt may be thrown upon us by those who have swerved from the truth, or who are indifferent to the true interests of our church. Not many months ago, in this place, he raised his warning voice, and we might almost say his dying voice, to the watchmen on Zion's walls, directing them to the enemy, who has been coming in like a flood, and pointing out their duty in opposing that enemy of Christ, of truth, and of righteousness. Let us, then, as good soldiers of Jesus Christ, set our faces as flints against this enemy; and in reliance on the Divine Spirit, endeavor to keep the standard of Christ floating on the walls of our Zion, should we even perish in the attempt. Let us also, like him, be instant in season and out of season, in preaching Christ and him crucified, and in reproving, rebuking and exhorting, with all long-suffering and doctrine: and, like him, we will obtain a crown of life!

BIOGRAPHICAL SKETCH

OF THE

REV. MATTHEW HENDERSON,

First Pastor of the Associate congregation of Chartiers, Washington county, Pa., and one of the three ministers who united in the ceremony of inaugurating the Canonsburg Academy, in 1791, under the Sassafras bushes.

[*Abridged from the "Evangelical Repository."*]

The Rev. Matthew Henderson was one of the earliest missionaries of the Associate Church of Scotland to the United States, and was the pioneer of that church in what was then regarded as the western wilderness, embracing the western part of Pennsylvania and the unknown region beyond. As no account of his life has hitherto been written, and the few survivors who have any recollection of him were but children at the time of his decease, and are now far down in the vale of years, it is difficult to obtain a sketch of his life and character which will be either full or satisfactory. The following particulars have been gleaned partly from incidental notices of him in various publications, and partly from the recollections of some aged survivors of his family.

Mr. Henderson was born in Scotland, in the year 1735. His children suppose that his birth-place was Glasgow, and that his classical education was obtained at Edinburgh. He entered at a very early period of life upon the study of theology, under the Rev. Alexander Moncrieff, one of the four first Seceders; a man whose own theological course had been pursued under the celebrated John Mark, of Leyden, and who was himself eminent in his day for learning, piety, courage, and generosity. Mr. Moncrieff was called the lion among the fathers of the Secession; and his pupil, Mr. Henderson, appears in this respect to have imbibed the spirit of his preceptor. He was licensed at the early age of twenty-one, a thing very uncommon in Scotland, where the course of training both for mechanical and professional business is much more tedious, and, at least intended to be, much more thorough than with us. He was ordained two years afterwards, in the summer of 1758, by the Presbytery of Perth and Dunfermline, and was immediately sent across the Atlantic to strengthen the hands of the brethren who were laboring in Pennsylvania. He was the third permanent missionary sent by the Associate Church to these then British colonies; his predecessors being Messrs. Alexander Gellatly and James Proudfit. Mr. Andrew Arnot, of Midholm, was sent with Mr. Gellatly, but not obligated to remain except for one year, and accordingly, at the expiration of that time, returned to Scotland. Mr. Henderson's acceptance of this missionary appointment speaks highly in favor of his zeal and self-denial in the cause of Christ. At this time a missionary appointment to the wilds of America was regarded as nearly equivalent to a banishment to Botany Bay. It was with the utmost difficulty that one or two out of a large number appointed could be prevailed on to accept of such a mission. The most rigorous measures were frequently employed, and even deposition from the ministry threatened, yet all in vain. There is, however, no account of any reluctance on the part of Mr. Henderson, or any resort to coercive measures. He appears to have been willing for the work assigned him, and to have possessed the adventurous, fearless, and hardy spirit which fitted him so peculiarly for a pioneer of the gospel in the wilderness.—[M'Kerrow's History of the Secession, pp. 259, 274.]

Soon after his arrival in America, Mr. Henderson was settled at Oxford, Chester county, Pennsylvania, where he appears to have labored in the ministry for about twenty years. It is not improbable that he had the pastoral care of at least one other place; as several of his sermons written at this time are marked as preached at "*Pen*," but what place is intended by this contraction it is difficult to ascertain. About three years after his arrival, the Rev. Alexander Gellatly, the father of the Secession in the United States, died, in the forty-second year of his age, having exercised his ministry eight years in Middle Octorara, Lancaster county, not far from Oxford.* By this event, which took place in 1761, Mr. Henderson is said by Dr. M'Kerrow to have been left with only two associates in the ministry—Mr. James Proudfit, of Pequa, and Mr. Mason, father of the late Dr. John Mason, of New York. It is, however, probable, that about this time Mr. Annan had also arrived, and Mr. Smart, though the latter only remained for a short time in this country. These at this time constituted the Presbytery of Pennsylvania, the only court of the Associate Church in the United States.

Mr. Henderson appears to have continued in the pastoral charge of Oxford till the year 1781. During this time he was married to Miss Mary Faris, and became the father of several children. His name appears up till about this time in the minutes of the Presbytery, and of meetings held with a view to the union of the Associate and Reformed Presby-

---

* The Rev. J. P. Miller, in his "Sketches and Sermons," has fallen into some mistakes respecting Mr. Gellatly. He says that his arrival in the United States was in 1754, whereas it was in 1753. He mentions correctly that he died in 1761; but adds—"A little less than five years after his arrival," whereas, according to his own statements, it must have been seven. It was in reality eight. Mr. Miller is also mistaken in saying that Mr. Arnot's mission was for two years. It was only for one. He speaks of the mission of Messrs. Henderson and Mason as having been at the same time, and of Mr. Smart's as near the same time. Mr. Henderson was sent in 1758; and three years afterwards, (1761,) Messrs. John Mason, Robert Annan, and John Smart. [See Sketches, &c., pp. 11–14; compare M'Kerrow's History, pp. 259, 274.]

teries. In the measures adopted to effect this union, he took a decided part with Messrs. Marshall and Clarkson against what he considered the loose and ambiguous terms in which the union was at last consummated; and it is not unlikely that had he been present when the union was effected, he would have joined with these brethren in refusing to accede to it. But he had in the mean time been removed to a great distance, where he had not full opportunity of knowing the true state of things, and he and his people for a time acceded to the union. This union took place in 1782; and in 1789, having become dissatisfied with the newly-organized church, he made application to his former brethren of the Associate Presbytery of Pennsylvania, acknowledging his sin in having withdrawn from their fellowship, and was restored. The proceedings of the Presbytery on this occasion were published, together with a letter to Mr. Henderson, and another to the congregations of Chartiers, Mingo Creek, and Mill Creek. These proceedings evince a candid and ingenuous spirit on the part of Mr. Henderson, and a spirit of tenderness and faithfulness on the part of his brethren. This pamphlet of eight pages was republished in 1836, with some prefatory remarks by the Rev. J. P. Miller, in the Religious Monitor, vol. xiii., pp. 209–13.

Mr. Henderson was at this time pastor of the Associate congregations of Chartiers and Buffalo, Washington county, Pennsylvania. To these places he had removed, in compliance with a call in the year 1782. These places he had visited as early as 1779. In a manuscript volume of his sermons he marks some as preached at Chartiers and Buffalo, in April and May of that year. It appears, however, that on his way to the West with his family, the reports of disturbances caused by the Indians were so alarming that he left his family by the way at Canigocheague, and proceeded alone to his new charge. The family remained about a year at Canigocheague, and then followed him to Chartiers. Their situation, when left behind, was far from comfortable, as they had no better habitation than a rude cabin, or kind of shanty; nor was their situation greatly improved when they reached their journey's end. But the hardships of pioneer life are so well known that it is not necessary to reiterate the many descriptions given of them. Perhaps, however, in Western Pennsylvania these hardships were greater than in most other places. This region is separated from the Atlantic coast by vast ranges of mountains intersecting the country for upwards of a hundred miles. Salt, iron, and all kinds of merchandise had to be transported over these rugged mountains upon pack horses all the way from Chambersburg to Pittsburgh. There was at this time no railroad, canal, turnpike, or even carriage road, making but a rough and often precipitous path for horses. The products of the land were abundant, but there could hardly be said to be any market for the surplus. Money was of course exceedingly scarce, luxuries were out of the question, and even some of the necessaries of life only to be obtained with the greatest difficulty. The settlement of Mr. Henderson in Chartiers took place in the year 1782, and for some years he was the only minister of the Associate Church west of the mountains. In consequence of this, he had not only the care of his own widely-scattered flock, but of several vacancies in his neighborhood. Among these were Mingo and Mill Creek, to which congregations, as we have seen, letters were addressed by the Presbytery at the time of his restoration to their fellowship.

His life was evidently one of much labor, as well as hardship. He appears from some of his papers preserved by his children to have written his sermons regularly, though not altogether in full, and in a hand not easily legible. The inscription on his tombstone bears witness that he never for once disappointed his people on the Sabbath. He attended diligently to the duties of catechising and visiting from house to house. And as he abounded in labors, so an evident blessing attended his ministry. Mr. Daniel Houston, who took a very conspicuous part with Messrs. Marshall and Clarkson in opposition to the afore-mentioned union, received his first religious impressions under the preaching of Mr. Henderson when assisting Mr. Smith at the dispensation of the Supper. No doubt the case was the same with many others. The Presbytery, in receiving him back to fellowship, bear honorable testimony to the fruits of his ministry from the very commencement of his labors. They say:—"As your ministry was not without acceptance and usefulness at the time of your entering into the public service of the gospel, we pray God that it may be made more so now when the evening of your day draws nigh." [Proceedings, &c., pp. 5, 6.] Mr. Marshall, in defending him from an attack made upon his character by the Rev. Robert Annan, in consequence of his having withdrawn from the communion of the Associate Reformed Synod, observes:—"It might have been expected that Mr. Henderson's gray hairs in the service of Christ, his usefulness in the ministry, and his weakly and infirm state of health, would have gained better treatment than Mr. Annan has given him." Mr. Marshall proceeds to quote from letters, Mr. Henderson's answer to the charges made against him, and closes with Mr. Henderson's expression of his confidence—"That after all Mr. Annan's bluster, he hopes his character stands as fair in the eyes of the Christian world as Mr. Annan's." Such, too, was the general reputation of Mr. Henderson, that Mr. Annan's abuse of him was reprobated by his own brethren, notwithstanding his having withdrawn from their communion. [Marshall's Vindication, pp. 89, 90,] The generation which enjoyed his ministrations has chiefly passsed away; but the continued flourishing state of the congregations in which he finished his labors has no doubt been owing, in a great measure, to the character which his ministry had impressed upon them.

Mr. Henderson's voice was remarkable for distinctness and

power. In the summer season he usually preached in a tent at the foot of a hill now occupied as the grave-yard of the congregation of Chartiers. The place of the tent was near the grave of the late Jonathan Letherman, M. D. From the bottom to the top of the hill is about forty perches; and yet not only the sound of his voice, but his words, could all be heard distinctly at that distance. Neither in conversation nor in the pulpit, did he make any attempt to lay aside the broad vernacular of his country. His manner of addressing his people was also according to the custom of his country, plain and familiar. He called them all simply by their proper names, like a father addressing his children. His reproofs of vanity and ill-behavior, especially in the sanctuary, were sometimes exceedingly pointed and scathing, but not ill-tempered. It has been related, that on one occasion, when a young lady had made her appearance at the church in a new calico dress, which in those days was regarded as the height of female extravagance, and when she had frequently risen from her seat, and gone to different parts of the assembly, Mr. Henderson having noticed her movements, and observed her rising from her seat a fourth time, said to her very calmly—"That is the fourth time, my lass, that you have left your seat. You can sit down now, we have a' seen your braw new gown." The young lady, of course, did not wait for a second invitation to do as she was directed.

In appearance, Mr. Henderson was of a very swarthy complexion. He had very keen dark eyes, was of a large size, of an erect and majestic figure, and possessed uncommon muscular power. An anecdote has been related of him, and sometimes erroneously attributed to others, which illustrated his physical powers, and also the treatment to which even ministers of the gospel were exposed in those early times. On one occasion, when traveling over the mountains to meet with his brethren in Presbytery, he happened to lodge at a tavern where two men took the liberty of treating him with great rudeness. This he endured for some time with much patience. His patience, however, was mistaken for timidity, and only encouraged their impertinence, till at last nothing would do but he must fight. This, of course, he was disposed to decline; but, whether he would or not, they were determined upon an assault. Finding that he could not otherwise evade rough usage, he arose and deliberately stripping off his black coat, laid it aside, saying—"Lie there, the Rev. Mr. Henderson, and now Matthew defend yourself." So saying, he seized one of the ruffians, dashed him out through an open window, and was preparing to send the other by the same road to keep him company. But this one, seeing the kind of man they had to deal with, was in no hurry to put himself in the way of such rough usage. Mr. Henderson having thus taught them somewhat after the manner of Gideon's teaching the men of Succoth with the thorns and briars of the wilderness, passed the rest of the night in peace and quietness.

Another anecdote of a different character has frequently, though not correctly, been related of him. It has been said that he was very fond of tea; and, as it was seldom to be met with among the early settlers of the country, that he was accustomed to carry a paper of it with him in his travels. On one occasion, having brought it forth to be prepared by the lady of the house, when he sat down at the table, not seeing anything like his favorite beverage, he inquired what had been done with it. The lady directed his attention to a plate having the appearance of greens, nicely buttered and peppered. This was his dish of tea. "O madam," said he, "what have you done with the broth?" "Why," said she, "I threw that away." The individual whose tea was cooked for him in this manner was not, however, Mr. Henderson, but the Rev. Mr. Howlitson, an intimate friend of his who was of feeble health, and died in his youth. No mention is made of such a person in the account of the missions of the Associate Church in America. It is probable that he came to this country without any appointment; and little more is known of him than that he lies beside Mr. Henderson, but with no stone to mark the place of his grave.

Mr. Henderson was of a peculiarly affectionate disposition towards his family, and in all his intercourse with society. His numerous and scattered charge rendered it necessary for him to be often absent from home, and frequently for a week or more at a time. But he would surmount almost any difficulty rather than cause uneasiness to his family by an absence beyond the appointed time. He expected a like punctuality on their part; and if the return of any absent member were delayed, would ride a journey of ten miles or more to ascertain whether any accident had happened. The day before his death he had been disappointed by the continued absence of Mrs. Henderson and two of his daughters, who had been detained while on a visit to some friends at a distance. His daughter Elizabeth, however, returned during the day. He appeared to be much gratified at meeting her; and having walked out with her to the place where he was killed the next morning, he gave her repeated charges, in case of his death, to be kind to her mother. This, and some other occurrences, seemed almost to indicate a presentiment that his end was at hand.

At the age of sixty he had become somewhat infirm, but not to such a degree as to interfere with his labors. His infirmities were no doubt occasioned by the hardships to which he had been exposed, and from which he took but little pains to protect himself. An aged member of the church,* who heard him once in his youth preaching in a tent without any covering during a shower, recollects that when some one was so kind as to hold an umbrella over his head, he repectfully

* Mr. James Thom, of Pigeon Creek.

declined the proffered favor, and proceeded in the services regardless of the rain. But, though fearless of other evils, he had been much troubled with the fear of death,—not so much with the fear of leaving the world, as of the pains of dying; and it pleased a kind Providence, in taking him away, to exempt him from the evil which he so much feared. He was killed by the falling of a tree, upon the 2d of October, 1795, at the age of sixty, and in the thirty-seventh year of his ministry, reckoning from the time of his ordination.

The circumstances of his death, as related by the daughter who was with him at the time, are as follows:—On the evening of October 1st, he had expressed to his children a wish that they would fell a bee-tree which had been discovered on his farm, and preparations were accordingly made to proceed to it early in the morning. He had acquainted his daughter Elizabeth, then a child of ten years of age, with their purpose, and told her that if she could get up in the morning without awakening her younger sister Jane, she might go with him. Accordingly, the next morning he went quietly to her bed, and touched her gently to awake her without disturbing her sister. She was soon up; and having dressed herself for the expedition, hurried into her father's room, supposing him also to be ready. She found him on his knees engaged in secret prayer, and immediately withdrew. Soon after this she observed him going down to the spring with a basin and towel to wash himself, as was his custom in the morning. Some time after he had returned she again ventured into his room, and again found him engaged in prayer. Soon afterwards he came out, and taking her by the hand he led her to the place where his sons Ebenezer and Robert had been for some time engaged in felling the tree. The tree stood upon a bank, and it was supposed would fall down the side of it. Mr. Henderson and his daughter approached towards it on the higher ground, where it was thought there was no danger. Here they stood for a little time, at some distance from the tree, awaiting its fall. It proved to be decayed in the centre, and fell much sooner than had been anticipated, and also in an opposite direction from what had been calculated. Mr. Henderson, notwithstanding repeated cautions given him, would always, when a tree began to fall, run from it in a direction opposite to that in which he supposed it to be falling. On this occasion, as usual, he ran, but in the same direction with the falling of the tree. His daughter followed his example, but varied somewhat in her course, and escaped any injury. Her father had run to such a distance that it was only the branches which reached him, and his body was but little mutilated. Only a slight flesh wound was discovered on his head; yet he appeared to have died instantly, not having been observed to move or breathe by his sons, who were immediately beside him.

Mr. Henderson, and some of his brethren of other societies who first planted the gospel in the West, were anxious to promote the cause of literature in connection with religion, and from the first turned their attention to the establishment of literary institutions. The venerable Dr. M'Millan, who preceded him in his settlement a few years, appears to have led the way, but he found Mr. Henderson an earnest and efficient coadjutor. As early as the year 1780,* a "Latin school," as it was called, was taught in a small log cabin, erected by the Rev. Dr. M'Millan for his *study*. The teacher was Mr., afterwards the Hon. James Ross, of Pittsburgh. This log cabin, which may justly be considered the germ of Jefferson College, is still standing, and has been carefully preserved as a memorial of the past. Some years ago it was removed to a spot at a little distance from the original site, and its foundation

* The writer has adopted this date from the prevailing popular, but, as we think, erroneous tradition.—J. S.

renovated, so that it is supposed it may yet last a century. The number of classical scholars having increased, it was judged necessary to fix upon a permanent place, and erect a more spacious and suitable building. Previous to this important measure there was a solemn meeting for consultation by the Rev. Dr. M'Millan, the Rev. Mr. Henderson, and other venerable fathers, who spent a great part of the day in prayer. Canonsburg, so called from Col. Canon, on whose ground the town had been built, was selected as the site; and a tolerably comfortable stone building was soon erected, and ready to be occupied. The Canonsburg Academy was then organized, and respectable professors appointed in the various departments of literature. The following account of the commencement of this institution is chiefly extracted from a letter written by one of the first pupils of the institution to the late Rev. Matthew Brown, D. D., LL. D., for many years President of Jefferson College.

In July, 1791, a meeting was called to see the Canonsburg Academy opened, the site of the institution having been agreed upon the day previous. At 10 o'clock, Tuesday morning, many citizens were upon the ground to witness the opening of the first academy on the west side of the Allegheny mountains. Among them was the Rev. Matthew Henderson, of whom the writer gives the following account:—"Mr. Henderson was a Scotch Seceder clergyman, blessed with Scotch talents, Scotch education, Scotch theology, and Scotch piety. His memory is still highly cherished as a worthy contemporary of Messrs. M'Millan and Smith. These three ministers, with Mr. Johnson, (the teacher,) and two pupils, William Riddle and Robert Patterson, (the writer of the letter,) took their position in the shade of some sassafras bushes growing in (the corner of) a worm fence near the English school-house, which could not be vacated for a short time. And here, under the pleasant shade of the green bushes, protected from the rays of a July sun,—the two pupils were about to commence their recitation, when Mr. M'Millan, addressing his two brethren, remarked in substance as follows:

"This is an important day in our history, affecting deeply the interests of the church and country in the West,—affecting our own interests and welfare for time and eternity,—and the interests, it may be, of thousands and thousands yet unborn." Then turning to Mr. Henderson, he asked him to engage in prayer, seeking the blessing of God on the institution now to be opened. "And," continues the writer, "I must say, the broad vernacular pronunciation of the Scotch tongue never could be more delightful or impressive than it was while every thing proper to the occasion appeared to be remembered in prayer by this good man."

The Academy having commenced under these circumstances, was incorporated as a college in 1802, and is the oldest institution of the kind west of the mountains.

Mr. Henderson was blessed with a numerous family—in all, fourteen children. Of these, four died in their infancy. Five sons and five daughters lived to maturity. Matthew, his oldest son, was licensed during the time of his father's connection with the Associate Reformed Church, and remained in that society, of which he was a very respectable minister. He was for many years pastor of a congregation in the Forks of Yough, and died a few years ago at an advanced age. Ebenezer, his third son, was a minister of the Associate Church. He was settled for a short time at Pittsburgh, in connection with a small congregation in the country. From this place he was called to Philadelphia, and was about to be removed. Previous, however, to his settlement, he died at a public house while on a journey. He had given promise of much eminence in the ministry; and his death was much and long lamented by the congregation whose call he had accepted, and by the whole church. Robert, the fourth son, still survives, and has for many years been an elder of very respectable standing in his father's congregation. John, the second, and Joseph, the fifth son, have been dead for many years. One or more of the descendants of the former are at this time ministers of the Associate Church. Mary, the oldest daughter, became the wife of Mr. White, a member of her father's congregation. She died a few years ago, at a great age, leaving a numerous family of children, and children's children, to the third and fourth generation. Ellen, the second daughter, was married to the late Samuel Murdock, M. D., and died young, leaving but one child, Ellen, the wife of Joseph Templeton, M. D., of Washington, Pennsylvania. Ann, the third daughter, was married to the Rev. Thomas Allison, of Mount Hope, Washington county, Pennsylvania. She also died a few years ago, leaving several children. Elizabeth, the fourth daughter, was married to Alexander Murdock, Esq., of Washington, Pennsylvania. Jane, the youngest, was married to Mr. Clark, of Buffalo, Washington county, Pennsylvania. These last two both survive. The most of Mr. Henderson's children had numerous families; and these again have increased till it would be difficult, or perhaps impossible, to reckon up the number of his descendants. They are mostly, if not all, with the exception of Ebenezer's family, dispersed through the various regions of the West, though probably the larger part are in the region of their father's labors. In this case we see verified the promise that the generation of the just shall be blessed. Very few have left so many children, and children's children, who have so generally done worthily, and held such a respectable standing both in civil and religious society.

Mr. Henderson was among the first buried in the graveyard of Chartiers over whose remains a stone was erected. It has now for sixty years been exposed to the corroding tooth of time; and the inscription will soon, if not renewed, become illegible. The following is a copy of it. The poetry is not unexceptionable, yet is pretty well for those early times :—

"In memory of the Rev. MATTHEW HENDERSON, who departed this life October 2, 1795, aged 60 years, and in the 37th of his ministry.

"In heavenly toils, O Henderson, grown gray,
Thy earthly frame was hastening to decay.
Thy growing languor threatened to detain
Thee from thy loved employment, but in vain.
For in thy course no Sabbath failed t' attest
The love of souls which burned within thy breast;
Till by one transient stroke which gave release,
Thy Saviour bade thee enter into peace.
Great and (most) happy change from battered dust
Unto the glorious mansions of the just!
Let us prepare to measure that bright road,
The best of all our friends is there—our God."

T. B.

As the writer of the above article had not access to the minutes of the Associate Presbytery of Pennsylvania, we have, at his request, given them a cursory examination, as the result of which we present the following additional facts.

The name of the congregation over which Mr. Henderson was placed, in connection with Oxford, was Pencader, or Pen Calder. It is spelled both ways in the minutes. It seems to have been a place of little importance. We know not where it was located. It no longer exists as a congregation. The congregation of Oxford, however, still lives and flourishes. It was from this place that the first petition for preaching was sent to the Synod in Scotland, and we believe it is the place where the first Associate Presbyterian congregation in America was organized. It has for a long time been under the charge of Rev. Wm. Easton, in connection with Octorara and Muddy Run; but about two years ago he resigned that portion of his charge, and in February last it was placed under the care of Rev. J. H. Andrew, it present pastor.

We find that Mr. Henderson was very punctual in his attendance on the meetings of Presbytery; although in those days of magnificent distances and bad roads, this was no easy matter. Whoever was absent, the name of Mr. Henderson is at the commencement of the minutes of each meeting about as invariably as the date.

The statement in regard to the ministers who composed the Presbytery in 1761, after the death of Mr. Gellatly, is correct. Mr. Annan was ordained by Mr. Henderson and Mr. Proudfoot, on the 8th of June, 1763.

During all the time of Mr. Henderson's settlement in Eastern Pennsylvania, he, in common with his brethren, had to spend a great portion of his time away from home, traveling long, wearisome, and dangerous journeys, to supply the many places, in different parts of the country, which, at every meeting of Presbytery, were sending in urgent calls for divine ordinances. To give some idea of the state of things at that time, we give the following extract from a letter written by the Presbytery, in 1764, to the Synod in Scotland, asking for more missionaries:

"We hereby, in the most earnest manner, supplicate this Reverend Synod for more assistance in the weighty work among our hands; and if it be not sent us, the buddings of reformation work on this Continent of America will be in danger of being blasted, and the work mar altogether, and the constitutions of members of Presbytery worn out with the great fatigues they of necessity undergo, in watering, not only their own congregations, which are all divided into two, and some three parts, in this Province, but also are far distanced from one another; and this is not all; for they must go much abroad, and preach, and dispense the sacraments, in vacant congregations. One minister, with a probationer, frequently dispenses the sacrament of the Supper in congregations, sometimes two Sabbaths successively, in different places; and sometimes a minister has done this without any assistance at all. This has been done twice this last summer by one member; and two of our number have this year been in North Carolina, which is five hundred miles distant from this. So that our deplorable situation cannot miss to have a loud language in the ears of our dear brethren, for to influence them to send us more supply of probationers, and that speedily."

At the meeting of Presbytery at Oxford, November 17th, 1779, was read "a call for Mr. Henderson, and a petition containing reasons for the transportation, and craving his admission, from Chartiers and Buffalo." This call had been moderated at Chartiers, by Rev. John Murray, on the 18th of October. The members of session present at the moderation were James Scott, John White, Nicholas Little, and David Reed, of Chartiers, and John and James Brownlee, and Andrew Scott, of Buffalo. The result of the vote was for Mr. Henderson, thirty-four, and for Mr. Smith, then of Octorara, twenty-two. Seven of the latter signed the call. No action was taken in regard to it by the Presbytery, till their meeting at Muddy Creek, March 16th, 1780, when, in connection with this call and petition, was presented one from Oxford, containing answers to it, and praying for their minister's continuance. The matter was considered for some time, both privately in committee of the whole, and afterwards publicly in the Presbytery in their judicative capacity, and "nothing of disaffection to Mr. Henderson, in Oxford Church, nor the want of a support appearing to the Presbytery, they agreed to take the matter in this point of light, whether Mr. Henderson's continuance at Oxford, or his transportation to Chartiers, appears most for the ends of general edification in the church of Christ? Hereupon a long course of reasoning ensued on this subject." After prayer "for direction in this weighty business," the question was put, transport or not? On this the Presbytery was equally divided; "whereupon the Moderator, (Mr. Henderson himself,) with great tenderness, and assigning various reasons, gave his casting vote in favor of the transportation," &c. At the same meeting we find it recorded that "the Presbytery consider the relation between Mr. Henderson and the people in Chartiers and Buffalo, to commence from this day, and that his salary also now commence; and that these people should be at the expense of removing him, his family, and effects thither; and as they agreed to pay him one hundred pound hard money annually, or 400 bushels of wheat, the Presbytery agree he shall have it in his option to take either as it may best suit him," &c.

Some difficulty, the nature of which cannot be clearly ascertained, seems to have existed between Mr. Henderson, his congregation, and the Presbytery, in regard to his transportation. He seems to have been hurt at some things said on the floor of Presbytery in the course of the discussion in regard to his removal, in consequence of which he addressed a letter to the Presbytery (April 5th, 1781) which they characterize as "containing injurious reflections, &c.—with a vein of irony running through the whole," &c. He afterwards, (September 6th,) made acknowledgments for the offensive things contained in the letter, and the whole matter was satisfactorily adjusted.

Before Mr. Henderson's departure for the West, which took place in the latter part of the year 1781, several petitions were received from Canigocheague, desiring the Presbytery to send him there. And at the meeting, October 31st, 1781, their petition being called up, the Presbytery, "after much reasoning on the subject, agree that Mr. Henderson be recommended to prosecute his call to Chartiers—that these people be addressed in a letter by Mr. Murray, to make suitable provision for moving Mr. Henderson's family and effects thither in the spring, and remove every cause of just complaint of deficiency on their part—and that Mr. Henderson be appointed to supply some Sabbath at Canigocheague (pronounced *Canigojig*) before next meeting." From the circumstance that he was absent from the next meeting, which took place April 10th, 1782, we conclude that he had, in the mean time, removed to the West, his departure having been thus delayed in consequence of the Indian war, which also rendered it necessary, as stated in the preceding sketch, that he should leave his family at Canigocheague, where they remained for a year.

T. H. B.

BIOGRAPHICAL SKETCH

OF THE

REV. JAMES RAMSEY, D. D.

A Trustee of Jefferson College, and Professor of Hebrew.

BY REV. DR. THOMAS BEVERIDGE.

[*Abridged from the "Evangelical Repository."*]

The Rev. James Ramsey, D. D., was born March 23d, 1771, in Lancaster county, Pennsylvania. His parents, Robert and Mary Ramsey, belonged, at the time of his birth, to the Reformed Presbyterian Church, or Covenanters, and sustained throughout their lives a good reputation for intelligence and piety. Mr. Robert Ramsey, after his removal to the West, was for many years an elder of respectable standing in the Associate congregation of King's Creek, Beaver county, Pennsylvania, under the pastoral care of the venerable Dr. John Anderson. Both parents lived to an advanced age, and had the satisfaction of seeing their children, and many of their children's children settled around them, and generally following their footsteps in the ways of righteousness. James, the subject of this notice, was the first born of fifteen children, the larger number of whom he survived. About two years after his birth, his parents removed from Lancaster county to what was then known as the western wilderness, and resided about two years at Williamsport, on the Monongahela river. At this time (1773) the settlements in this region were few and scattered. The Indians were frequently troublesome, and rendered the protection of forts necessary. Mr. Ramsey pursued his labors in the vicinity of one of these forts. His custom was to take his gun with him into the corn field, and place it at the root of a tree or against a stump. He would then hoe around the place to the distance of fifteen or twenty yards. This done, another resting place for his gun was selected, and his labor around it performed in the same manner; thus keeping himself always ready for defence against any sudden attack. It was amidst these scenes of danger, and those of the revolution which immediately followed, and amidst the hardships and privations of a pioneer's life, that James first formed his acquaintance with the world; and these things no doubt contributed in giving to him that patience, that power of endurance, and that energy of character, for which he was afterwards distinguished.

At the end of two years, the family removed from Williamsport to Pigeon Creek, then within the bounds of the congregation of the venerable Dr. M'Millan, so distinguished in the history of the Presbyterian Church of the West, as one of its first and most eminent pioneers. With this church the parents connected themselves. Their son James was also admitted as a member at a very early period of life; and though afterwards connected with another branch of the Presbyterian Church, he always entertained a very great regard for his former brethren, and especially for Dr. M'Millan, whom he considered as his spiritual father.

When Mr. Ramsey became a member of Dr. M'Millan's church, he must have been under twenty-one years of age, as this was his age when he removed to another part of the country. Yet young as he was, he exerted himself actively and faithfully in the cause of Christ, both in relation to the interests of truth and of practical godliness. Many of the young people were very careless as to spiritual things, and indulged freely in promiscuous dancing, and other practices inconsistent with a religious profession. To promote a better spirit and put an end to these practices, he had the prudence and address to collect them into one or more societies for prayer and religious conference. In this way he exercised a happy influence upon the religious character of the congregation, and gave an early indication of that spirit which he manifested in his future life. During his connection with this congregation, a controversy arose among the people, in relation to what have been called the Marrow doctrines, *i. e.* certain doctrines taught in a book called the Marrow of Modern Divinity; such as that there is a gift or grant of Christ in the Gospel to sinners of mankind as such; that believers are delivered from the law as a covenant of works; and that holiness is not a federal means or condition of life. Mr. Ramsey and others of the congregation warmly advocated these doctrines. Dr. M'Millan at first appeared also to favor, but at last rather opposed them. This laid the foundation for Mr. Ramsey's ultimate separation from that church, and accounts for the zeal which he ever afterwards showed for these precious truths. According to the recollections of his nearest friends, it would however appear that he had not formally withdrawn from the communion of the Presbyterian Church till after his removal to Mill Creek.

At the age of twenty-one he made a joint purchase of a farm, two miles from the village of Frankfort, Beaver county, Pennsylvania, and removed to it with his brother William. This was within the bounds of the Presbyterian congregation of Mill Creek, and here, after some time, other circumstances occurred which issued in the change of his religious profession. About this time there was in the Presbyterian churches of the West a very general substitution of hymns of human composition in the room of the Psalms, which had hitherto been employed in the worship of God. Mr. Ramsey endeavored for some time to reconcile himself to the use of these hymns, and, in his own language, had "tried to sing them."

But this either was from the first, or soon came to be against his convictions of duty, and his conscience would not let him alone. However different the views of Christians may be on the merits of this question, none who knew him will have any doubt as to his conscientiousness in the decision to which he came to give the preference to the Psalms over all human productions. Indeed, few things in his life manifested more clearly the power of his convictions of duty, than the change which he felt constrained to make in his profession. He was at this time a young man somewhat ardent in his temperament, and much more likely to be seduced by the love of novelty than those advanced in years, who so often become the slaves of prejudice and habit. Being an excellent singer, and passionately fond of music, (which he occasionally taught,) he was the more liable to be captivated by the improvements in singing with which the introduction of the hymns was accompanied. But most of all, he was of a peculiarly affectionate disposition, and was in high esteem among the brethren with whom he was connected. Although a youth, and remarkable for modesty and diffidence, he had been taken into the society of ministers, elders, and such as were in the highest reputation for piety. He was treated by them as an equal, and enjoyed their confidence. He was accustomed to speak of the change of his religious profession under these circumstances as one of the sorest trials of his life; and has frankly owned to his intimate friends that when he left the Presbyterian Church he left his heart behind him. He always regarded that Society as very exemplary in their affectionate treatment of each other, and thought them, in this respect, commendable beyond many others, of whom equal, if not better things, might have been expected. As a proof of the high esteem in which Mr. Ramsey was held among his Presbyterian brethren may be mentioned the language employed by Dr. M'Millan to induce him to remain in their communion: "James," said he, "you will be a minister some of these days; yes, and you will be a bright star in the West."

The account which he was accustomed to give of his separation from that branch of the Presbyterian Church with which he had been connected was substantially this. Various expedients had been employed to reconcile him and others to the introduction of the hymns; such as employing them on more private occasions, and using them alternately with the Psalms in the public worship of the church. On the last sacramental occasion which he attended in that church the hymns were sung at tables occupied by those who preferred them, and the Psalms at one or more tables set for those who were opposed to the hymns. This, instead of satisfying, rather disgusted him, and he came to the resolution that he would use the hymns no more. During the occasion he lodged at the house of Mr. George M'Cullough, in company with a number of others, among whom were the Rev. Mr. Marquis and Mr. Jackson, an aged elder of the church. When the time for worship in the family arrived, Mr. Jackson was called upon to lead, and the Bible and hymn-book were laid down before him. Mr. Ramsey, who, as we have said, was extremely modest and diffident, was much perplexed. The elder was accustomed, when Mr. Ramsey was present, to call on him to lead in singing, and would no doubt do so now. But he had come to a fixed resolution that he would not use the hymns. Yet he was very unwilling to bring either himself or his scruples into notice before the company. He had watched with a keen eye and an anxious heart what was passing, and as soon as Mr. Jackson sat down at the table, he stepped up to him as quietly as possible, and whispered, that if he called on him to sing, he wished him to use the Psalms, as he did not feel at liberty to join in singing the hymns. However, the elder, much to the annoyance of the modest youth, spoke aloud of the difficulty, and observed that he believed there was no Bible with Psalms in the house. Mr. Ramsey immediately produced his own pocket Bible containing them, of which the elder made use. After worship, the Rev. Mr. Marquis observed that it was not a suitable time to enter into any controversy on the subject of the hymns. He would, however, make one remark for Mr. Ramsey's consideration. "Very many," said he, "who have had scruples at the first about singing the hymns, after having used them for awhile have overcome their scruples, and become quite satisfied." Mr. Ramsey, however, could not feel at liberty to venture on such an experiment for obtaining relief. He soon afterwards united with the Associate congregations of Service and King's Creek, then and for many years afterwards under the pastoral care of Dr. Anderson, professor of theology in the Associate Church. His change of ecclesiastical connexion, as it originated in no strife or ill temper, so it was attended with nothing of this kind. On the contrary, the most friendly feelings continued between him and his former associates. He was a man who could, both in his private life and public ministrations, be faithful to his convictions of duty without being ill tempered or censorious.

At what period of his life his thoughts were turned towards the ministry is not known, but before his connection with the Associate Church, he had been preparing the way for obtaining an education with a view to that office. He had sold his interest in the farm on which he had lived with his brother, to his father, who afterwards removed to it, and resided on it till his death. He also engaged in teaching schools of different kinds; and by these means obtained sufficient money to meet the expenses of his education, and had when licensed enough left to equip himself for traveling. It is thought probable that he commenced his classical studies under his minister, Dr. Anderson, about the twenty-fifth year of his age. He afterwards studied at the Jefferson Academy, since incorporated as Jefferson College. Soon after its incorporation as a college, he received from this institution the second degree in the arts. This was in the year 1805; and some time about the year 1824, he received, probably from Dickinson College, Carlisle, the honorary degree of doctor of divinity, a title which would be in higher repute if always as meritoriously conferred. After completing his classical studies, he pursued the study of theology under Dr. John Anderson; this must have been between the years 1800 and 1803. He was peculiarly beloved by his professor, and the warmest attachment continued between them, until the decease of Dr. Anderson, April, 1830.

Dr. Ramsey was licensed by the Presbytery of Chartiers at the same time with the late Rev. David Imbrie, December 14th, 1803, at the house of Mr. Ralston, in Buffalo. As he was at this time within a few months of completing his thirty-third year, and his preparatory course of study had not been hurried, but as thorough as the circumstances of the country would well admit, he entered on his ministerial labors with more maturity of mind, with more enlarged Christian experience, and better preparation, than are common to those beginning this work, and his ministry from the first proved every where highly acceptable to the intelligent and godly. He labored, during the months of December and January after his licensure, in the Presbytery of Chartiers, and then for the greater part of the remainder of the year 1804 in the Presbyteries of Cambridge and Philadelphia. At the close of this year he returned to Chartiers, and labored in the bounds of that Presbytery till his settlement. A unanimous and pressing call was given to him to take charge of the Associate congregation of Cambridge, New York, then left vacant by the removal of Dr. Banks; and the people were exceedingly grieved at their failure to obtain him as their pastor. For years afterwards they were accustomed to lament their disappointment, and they continued to cherish his memory with peculiar fondness. Shortly before his return to the

West, a petition from the congregation and Presbytery of Philadelphia, was laid before the Presbytery of Chartiers, earnestly soliciting that he might be continued in Philadelphia till the next meeting of the Synod, which request, however, the Presbytery, owing to the urgent demand upon them for supplies, found themselves unable to grant. At the meeting of this Presbytery, April 17th, 1805, four calls were presented to him, or rather three, and notice given of a fourth; one from the united congregations of Mount Pleasant and Burgettstown, one from Beaver and Brush Run, one from Cambridge, New York, and one from Chartiers. The last of these was accepted, although the worldly advantages connected with some of the other calls were much greater. He was ordained and settled as pastor of the Associate congregation of Chartiers on the fourth of the following September. The Rev. Thomas Allison preached on the occasion from 2 Cor. viii: 23,—"Our brethren—the messengers of the churches, and the glory of Christ." He also, as was the custom of the times, gave the charge to the pastor, elders, and members of the congregation. Dr. Anderson preached in the evening from Ps. cii: 16,—"When the Lord shall build up Zion he will appear in his glory."

When Dr. Ramsey commenced his pastoral labors in this congregation, not only the people but the Presbytery were in a very distracted state in consequence of dissensions which had arisen in Chartiers between the people and their former pastor, the Rev. John Smith, and also between the people of Buffalo and their pastor, the Rev. Robert Laing. These troubles had occasioned frequent and protracted meetings of the Presbytery, and some stormy debates. At the very time that Dr. Ramsey was licensed, the Presbytery continued four days in session, and such protracted meetings were not uncommon. These contentions had divided the people into parties, and the issue was the separation of some valuable members from both congregations. These and other things had also contributed to weaken, in those who remained, their attachment to their profession; so that the commencement of the Doctor's labors was in the midst of difficulties. But his prudence and faithfulness soon surmounted them, and in a little time he was established in the affections and confidence of the people, to an extent altogether uncommon. The hearts of the minister and people were so knit together that it seemed a thing impossible that they could ever be sundered. Soon after his settlement he was married to Miss Margaret Paxton, a lady in the neighborhood of Chambersburg, Pennsylvania. They became the parents of two children, the Rev. James P. Ramsey, pastor of the Associate congregation of Deer Creek, Lawrence county, Pennsylvania, and Maria, wife of the Rev. William M. M'Elwee, D. D., pastor of the Associate congregation of Frankfort, Beaver county, Pennsylvania. These, together with Mrs. Ramsey, still survive.

After Dr. Ramsey's settlement he applied himself diligently to the duties of his pastoral office, not only preaching regularly upon the Sabbath, and occasionally on other days of the week, but catechizing and visiting from house to house, which latter duties he attended to in the winter, in order to interfere as little as possible with the worldly business of his people. This, considering the size of the congregation, the inclemency of the season, and the almost impassable condition of the roads during much of the winter, rendered these duties exceedingly laborious. But he was not one of those who much regarded exposures of this kind. If it ever occurred at all, it must have been very rarely, that he was seen with an umbrella over his head to protect him either from heat or rain. Even when quite aged, he would rise long before day, and set out upon a journey, in the coldest weather, and very often without even taking the precaution to button his overcoat. He was particularly faithful in visiting the sick, and had many calls of this kind to attend to among his own people and others. Until quite disqualified by age, he was very punctual in his attendance upon the meetings of his Presbytery, and of the Synod; and in these courts his zeal in the cause of truth, tempered as it was by kindness, his readiness in forming a correct opinion upon the merits of questions, the clearness with which he was able to express himself, and his peculiar talent for exposing wrong doings, rendered him a most useful member. For more than forty years after his ordination, he never failed attending the meetings of Synod, whether near or remote, except once or at most twice, when providentially hindered. The last meeting he attended was at Allegheny, in 1852, and his infirmities at that time obliged him to return home before the close of the session. His salary was small, the journeys frequently tedious and expensive, but such was his interest in the cause of Christ, that he could not feel satisfied to neglect the meetings of the courts of his house, when it was at all practicable to attend.

In the sixteenth year of his ministry he was called to a post of increased responsibility. In 1819, Dr. Anderson, owing to the infirmities of age, felt the necessity of resigning the professorship of theology, which he had held for about twenty-five years. His resignation being accepted, the Synod at their next meeting, at Huntingdon, 1820, agreed to establish two seminaries, to be called the Eastern and Western. The Rev. John Banks, D. D., was unanimously elected professor of the Eastern Seminary, and the election of a professor of the Western was postponed till the next meeting at Pittsburgh, when the western members would be more generally present. At this meeting, 1821, though another candidate was named beside him, Dr. Ramsey was elected by a large majority; and in the ensuing winter entered upon the duties of his new office, being at this time fifty years of age. This post, in connection with his pastoral duties in a large congregation, no part of which he remitted, rendered his subsequent life very laborious. To his other offices was added the professorship of Hebrew in Jefferson College, which however did not occupy much of his time and attention. The Doctor at this time resided on a farm about a mile from Canonsburg, and read lectures to his students at his own house, and in consequence of his situation he was obliged to receive all or most of the students into his house as boarders. They had thus not only the advantage of his public instructions, but of his excellent example and instructive conversation in private, which was by no means inconsiderable. It is well known that his remarks in private, made in his own peculiar way, were highly entertaining and useful. In some instances they have been known to produce on the minds of young men impressions causing a happy change in their whole course of life. It was by one of these remarks, serious in import, but made in something of a jesting manner, that the late Rev. D. C. was cured of a tendency to excessive liberalism in his religious views; and the cure proved to be thorough and permanent. The conversation at the table among the young men, chiefly college students, had turned upon a late revival which had taken place at Baltimore. The Doctor, who had for some time been silent, at last inquired about the people who were the subjects of it. One of the young men, a Presbyterian by profession, replied that he believed they were chiefly Methodists. "Oh!" said the Doctor, "I am glad to hear of a revival, and especially among the Methodists; we know that some of their doctrines are erroneous, and no doubt, when a revival takes place among them, they will renounce their errors. I hope," added he, "they have all joined the Presbyterian Church." The young man, considerably confused, was obliged to admit that they had not. The Doctor pursued the conversation no further, but it at least led Mr. C. into a train of reflections which had an important influence upon his future course of life. The late Rev. Professor K. also attributed to Dr. Ramsey his first serious impressions. He had lived in the neglect of religion, and perhaps was somewhat more than commonly careless about spiritual things, till, while a student in the college, he became a boarder in the Doctor's family. Here the example, prayers, and conversation of the Doctor convinced him that there were a truth, power, and excellence in religion which he had not before perceived.

As the number of the students increased, the boarding of so many became oppressive to Mrs. Ramsey, and the Doctor removed from his farm into Canonsburg. He also added to the house which he had purchased an apartment built at his own expense for the use of the students. Still a number of them continued to board with him, but his situation now freed him from the necessity of taking more than suited the convenience of his family. After the death of Dr. Banks, in 1826, the Synod agreed, in 1828, to unite the two theological seminaries; in 1830 they fixed upon Canonsburg as the place, and the next year elected Dr. Ramsey professor in the united institution. At this time the Synod engaged in the erection of a suitable building for the seminary, which was completed about the year 1834. The site selected was a beautiful one, on a level tract of ground half a mile west of the village. The building was sufficiently large and substantial, but not well arranged, nor constructed with good taste. Soon after this the congregation found it necessary to erect a new church, instead of the old and delapidated stone building which had been occupied for about fifty years by the Doctor and his predecessors. This new church the Doctor and his congregation entered in the beginning of the year 1836. Some years before this the Synod agreed to establish a second professorship, which however was not actually filled till the winter of this year. As this professorship embraced branches of study not taught by the Doctor, it did not materially lessen his labors. he continued to attend to the duties of his professorship till the meeting of the Synod at Washington, 1841, when he gave notice of his intention to resign. This was in conformity with a resolution adopted by him long before. Having noticed that public men, when far advanced in years, and failed both in body and mind, would often cling with childish fondness to an office for which they had become totally unfit, he had formed and often expressed his resolution, that if he were spared in life, and retained in office till the age of seventy, he would then resign. He had made a kind of covenant with himself to pay no regard to his opinion on this subject at seventy, but to act according to his previous judgment and resolution. There was indeed no perceptible failure of his mind at this time, and but little for years afterwards. To the very close of his life, with occasional exceptions, caused by bodily debility, he retained in an uncommon degree his judgment, his memory, and the life and energy of his earlier years. Yet he considered it best to adhere to his resolution, and agreeably to the notice given at Washington, he presented the resignation of his office to the Synod at Xenia, 1842. His resignation was accepted, and the Synod testified by a resolution their "sense of the high obligations they were under to him for his long and faithful services as professor."

He still continued in his pastoral relation, and was able for several years more to attend to all his ministerial duties. Instead of any failure, it seemed as if his zeal and power in preaching the gospel increased with his years. Some of the sermons preached towards the last of his days were of uncommon excellence, and were delivered with great fervor of spirit. He felt himself, and made his hearers feel, that he was speaking as one upon the brink of the eternal world. In June, 1849, owing to his increasing infirmities, he felt it necessary to urge the acceptance of the resignation of his pastoral charge, which had been previously offered, but the consideration of which had been delayed by the Presbytery in compliance with a petition from the congregation. They had requested the continuance of the pastoral relation, and that arrangements might be made for the supply of his pulpit, so far as his declining health might render necessary. At the time referred to, he however urged the acceptance of his resignation, and was accordingly released from his charge. The congregation, in signifying their acquiescence, testified their high appreciation of his long and faithful services among them. He had been their pastor for something more than forty-four years. He had never spared himself in his labors among them. He had been with them as a sympathizing friend, a wise counselor, and an able comforter in all their troubles. The reputation of many of his people for intelligence and piety had long borne honorable testimony to the faithfulness of his instructions. The larger portion of them had been brought up under his ministry from their youth. He had buried their fathers. He had in many cases baptized and married parents and their children after them. He had been as a father among them, feeling any injurious reflections cast upon them, or any evil befalling them, as a parent would feel in like cases for a child. And, notwithstanding the occurrence of some things trying to his affections, he cherished to the last the liveliest interest in their welfare. It would be strange, and far from a favorable indication of the religious character of a people, if such a man should not be long held in the most honorable and grateful remembrance.

Some time after resigning his professorship the Doctor returned to the farm which he had left for the sake of the students, and continued to reside on it till about eighteen months before his death, when he and Mrs. Ramsey, becoming too frail to attend to their domestic affairs, removed to Frankfort, and resided with their son-in-law, Dr. M'Elwee, near the scenes of the Doctor's youth, the abodes of many of his relatives, and the grave of his father, beside whom, during the last years of his life, he had repeatedly expressed his desire to be interred. He still continued, though in his eighty-fourth year, to exercise his ministry occasionally in the pulpit of his son-in-law; and though feeble in body, was still cheerful and even lively in conversation. Three weeks before his death, he was taken with cholera morbus when about to lie down for the night. He was able to be up in the morning, but complained of headache, and appeared very dull and feeble. After a few days he recovered from this attack, but wasted away under an infirmity from which he had suffered for many years. On the last Sabbath of February, which proved to be a very severe day, he attended church, and in common with many others took a cold, which rendered him exceedingly hoarse. On Thursday morning he arose somewhat better, and Mr. Duncan, a gentleman from Pittsburgh, being a visitor in the family, he joined in conversation, and was quite lively and cheerful. But between nine and ten o'clock of that forenoon, he was seized with a chill followed by fever, which soon prostrated him both in body and mind, and occasioned some apprehensions of immediate death. On Saturday morning about the same time of day, he had another attack of the same kind, and became unable to speak intelligibly. He continued to sink rapidly till five o'clock Sabbath morning, when the family were called together to witness his death. It was thought he would not live till the hour of public worship, but about nine o'clock he revived, and appeared pretty clear in his mind, and more vigorous in body throughout the remainder of that day and the following night. On Monday morning he appeared more dull, and without any known cause, at nine or ten o'clock he became visibly worse, and, in despite of stimulants, continued to sink, till at five o'clock, Tuesday morning, March 6th, when he breathed his last. He lacked but a few days of having completed his eighty-fourth year. On the Sabbath morning immediately preceding his departure, he called for the reading of Isa. xlvi., in which that precious promise occurs, "And even to your old age I am He, and even to hoar hairs will I carry you," &c. The friend who has communicated these particulars of his last illness, has not related any thing of the exercise of Dr. Ramsey's mind in the immediate view of death; and it is very probable that owing to the feeble and wandering state of his mind, he was unfitted for much conversation. Besides, had it been otherwise, it would not be inconsistent with the Doctor's general character to suppose that he said but little on this subject. His modesty appeared in his religion as well as in every thing else. For several years he had been calmly awaiting his discharge, and spoke of it frequently and freely, and with the utmost quietude and contentment of mind, even as he would have spoken of a journey homewards; but he was so far from a spirit of boasting, that he even seemed to be altogether reserved in respect to his own religious experience. He had evidently made himself familiar with death, and was prepared to meet him, not as an enemy, but as a welcome messenger of Christ. His holy life was better evidence of preparation than any death-bed professions.

On the Thursday after his decease, his mortal part was laid in the grave-yard of the Associate congregation of Frankfort. Notice of the time of his funeral had not reached his late congregation in season; otherwise, no doubt, a large number of them, notwithstanding the distance, bad weather, and bad roads, would have attended.

The reader may easily infer from the preceding sketch of Dr. Ramsey's life, that he was a man of more than common excellence, and may also perceive what many of his particular excellencies were. Yet it is hoped that it will neither be without interest or profit, to exhibit some of the traits of his character more fully than could well be done in the mere detail of the events of his life.

Some of these traits of character were strikingly exhibited in his countenance and general appearance. He was quite tall and slender, and not altogether graceful in his movements, but it is rarely that a countenance meets our view in which are indicated, with such distinctness, and in such agreeable harmony, quickness of discernment, mildness of temper, affectionateness of disposition, and contentment of mind.

Few persons, even in their youth, have countenances so little marked with the lines of care, anxiety, and passion, as he had, even in extreme old age. Little children, of whom he was very fond, were attracted to him at once by the kindness and cheerfulness so apparent in the expression of his countenance, in his conversation and whole deportment. There were also blended with these indications, such seriousness and gravity, as ensured respect and gave force to his ministry.

The Doctor had a natural amiableness of disposition which had been much improved by grace. In some the chief work of grace appears to be to contend with corruptions, and its power and excellence appear in the victory gained over them. In him there seemed less for grace to effect in this way than in ordinary cases. His mind did not appear so much like a field grown over with thorns and briars, to be rooted out before the good seed could be sown, as like a field ready to receive at once the good seed and bring forth fruit. A singular remark once made by an acquaintance may be quoted here, as indicating the opinion entertained of the Doctor's natural disposition. In a company where his character had become the subject of conversation, and much was said in praise of his many excellencies, to the surprise of every one, a young man remarked that he did not think the Doctor had any virtue at all. When asked to explain himself, he observed that virtue was generally considered as consisting in the struggles of a man's better part against his corruptions. "Now," said he, "I don't believe that Dr. Ramsey has any corruptions to contend with." No doubt the Doctor had different thoughts of himself, and had grounds for them. But though depravity be inherent in all, it has different degrees of power, and in few did its natural power appear to be weaker than in him.

In his intercourse with society he always showed himself, as to all the substantial qualities of that character, to be a true gentleman. He was not, as has been admitted, distinguished for gracefulness in his movements. In this respect he appeared, both in the pulpit and in the parlor, to have no thought of his personal appearance. His mind was too much engaged about other things. Yet few could be compared to him in their talents for entertaining and instructive conversation. His mind was not only well stored with religious truth, but well informed on almost every subject of importance. He was not disposed to engross the conversation, or direct attention to himself, but in his own modest way, could express his mind freely and appropriately on all common topics. He was not rude, dogmatical, or overbearing, but remarkably affectionate, and ever ready to yield all due deference to others. While he abhorred duplicity and flattery, he was yet careful not causelessly to wound the feelings of any; but rather to say things which would be agreeable and useful. His friendships were warm, almost unbounded: and though he was capable of dislike, he knew how to treat even an enemy with decent courtesy. In a word, if the reader will turn to Rom. xii: 9–21, he will there find the truest and best rules of politeness ever penned; and few individuals ever lived up to these rules more faithfully than Dr. Ramsey. The consequence of this was, that he was always a most welcome guest in the houses of his acquaintances; he was usually the centre of attraction in the social circles with which he mingled, and his society was courted equally by young and old, rich and poor.

Perhaps no trait in his character was more prominent, more universally admitted and admired, than his strict unbending integrity. In this respect it would be hard to find his equal, and it is believed it would be impossible to find his superior. Such was his reputation for honesty and integrity, that not long before his death a gentleman of the highest standing in the county remarked, in reference to a question affecting his character for veracity, that if Dr. Ramsey were convicted of falsehood, he could never again believe himself. His honesty in his dealings was such that persons who could not comprehend his conscientiousness were ready to accuse him of simplicity. Few could be as watchful to take the advantage of others in a bargain as he was to avoid it. He has been often known at auctions to bid up articles where there was no competition, through an unwillingness to obtain them under their true value. A gentleman who had sold or traded away a horse for the Doctor, came to him and boasted that he had gained for him an advantage of ten dollars, supposing that this would be highly gratifying. The Doctor never signified whether he was pleased or not, but upon the first opportunity quietly handed over ten dollars to the person supposed to be the loser in the bargain. Not long before his death, finding himself unable to ride on horseback, an exercise of which he had always been particularly fond, he proposed his horse for sale. The animal was somewhat aged, but still sound, vigorous, and in good condition—(the Doctor's horses were always well kept.) A friend to whom he had intrusted this business being asked by a gentleman the price of the horse, replied, forty dollars. The horse was without any hesitation purchased for this sum. Soon afterwards the gentleman met the Doctor in the street and mentioned the purchase he had made. "Ah," says the Doctor, "you can't have the horse at that price." The purchaser, not a little surprised at the refusal, reminded the Doctor that this was all that had been demanded. "True," said the Doctor, "but I can't sell him for forty dollars; you may, however, have him, if you choose, for twenty-five." It is hoped the reader will excuse these anecdotes, as they serve better to illustrate the Doctor's character than whole pages of abstract description. Many others of the same kind might be repeated, exhibiting the same sterling honesty for which he was, throughout all his life and in all his transactions, so eminently distinguished.

In connection with this may be noticed his disregard of wealth; his indifference in this respect, if not indulged even to a fault in himself, was certainly in some cases the occasion of faults in others. It encouraged imposition. He was far from being ignorant of worldly things. He knew even better than the most of men what was just and proper in worldly transactions; he knew as well as others when he was defrauded, but would rather submit to injustice than contend; hence, unprincipled persons often took advantage of him in their dealings, presuming that it might be done with impunity. In a few, and but very few instances, his indignation against the meanness of individuals in their extortions, prompted a resistance to which the love of money could never have moved him. In the early part of his ministry, he had some difficulties to contend with in providing for his family, but the blessing annexed to liberality attended him, and for the remainder of his life, though not what would generally be regarded as a rich man, he had not only a competence, but an abundance. His salary was small, only a trifle over $300 per annum, a sum far from sufficient to support his family, but by the prudent management of Mrs. Ramsey, who proved in this as well as in other respects a help peculiarly meet for him; by means of what he inherited through her, by the increase in the value of the property which he had acquired, and by other means, Providence so favored him, that he had enough, and to spare; and he was ever ready to spare liberally of what the Lord had given him. When elected professor, he received an addition to his salary of $300 per annum from the Synod: a large portion of this, however, was expended in contributions to aid the Synod in the erection of a suitable building for the seminary, and in other public benefactions. He always, through an excess of modesty, opposed any movement of his congregation to increase his salary, although their ability so far exceeded what they paid, that some of them frankly acknowledged that they had felt for years as if guilty of stealing preaching, what they gave being so nearly nothing at all. At the time of his resigning his professorship in the seminary and the salary connected with it, he even opposed a small increase of his salary from the congregation, though in this instance his opposition was not successful. We may add the following illustration of the Doctor's indifference about the world, and of his generosity of disposition. About the year 1821, articles of produce were reduced to an exceedingly low value; wheat was only twenty-five cents a bushel, flour one dollar per barrel in Pittsburgh. To relieve the poor of his congregation, the Doctor announced, and to save the feelings of the poor announced without making any discrimination, that he would receive, at the mill in Canonsburg, wheat at fifty cents per bushel, in payment of salary. The consequence was that his granary was soon filled and overflowing. Several times when the congregation had fallen behind in their payments, he forgave their arrearages. These, however, they in a very honorable spirit, liquidated by a donation of equal value a few years before the resignation of his charge.

Dr. Ramsey was very celebrated for a peculiar kind of wit, which derived much of its power from his gravity, and was so far from detracting from his ministerial character and usefulness, that it rather added to both. His wit was altogether remote from levity; neither was he addicted to malicious and biting sarcasm; but he abounded in a species of wit of the most innocent and inoffensive character. His remarks were often so unexpected, uttered with so much apparent seriousness, and exhibited things in such a ridiculous light, that their power in provoking laughter was altogether irresistible. Something of his wit often appeared in the pulpit, but so restrained and connected with his seriousness, that it seldom if ever had any tendency to produce a smile, but often smote upon the conscience with great power. As an example of this may be mentioned a remark made in a sermon preached not many years before his decease. He had heard, as was thought, an unfavorable report respecting some young people whose parents were members of the church, and took occasion, without any allusion to individuals, to describe in a very striking manner their course of conduct, and its consequences. He closed by observing that such young persons were in the broad way that leadeth to destruction; "Yes," said he, "going to the pit as fast as their feet can carry them; unless," he added, as if correcting himself, "they take Judas's road." He often introduced observations of this kind in a manner so unexpected and yet so appropriate, that the hearers were at the same time agreeably surprised and powerfully impressed. He seldom preached without saying something which either in itself, or in the peculiar and pointed way in which he uttered it, was calculated to take a firm hold of the conscience, and excite serious reflections. To borrow one of his own expressions, sometimes used respecting the performances of others, "His sermons had teeth."

Something has been said already of the Doctor's conversational powers, which were much beyond the common standard. His power of discrimination and independence of mind, rendered his views of many things singularly just and original; and these he was accustomed to express in a brief and pointed way, often including in a single remark the substance of what others would have expanded into a long dissertation. For instance, the subject of conversation being ecclesiastical establishments, he observed, that though he had read many very plausible arguments in their favor, one thing had always appeared to him against them,—they had never worked well. In remarking upon a book relating to the proprieties of clerical manners, he observed that it was an excellent work, and calculated to be useful; "but," added he, "Thomas Boston would never have written it." He was of late years apprehensive that judgments were impending over our country, and having heard that one of the most pious members of his congregation was at the point of death, he inquired respecting him, and being told that he was recovering, "I am glad of it," said he, "I hope Methusalah will not be taken away yet," referring to the opinion that the flood was not to come till Methusalah's death. A student proposing himself for the study of theology, whose mind was too much occupied about matters of dress, having inquired of him what dress he thought most suitable for a student, he very gravely recommended to him the long jacket of humility. Another youth of a very different spirit, having asked him whether he thought it consistent in Christians to indulge in laughter, he replied, that he thought it about equally criminal with sneezing. This was said in a way so droll, that if laughter were sinful, the remark proved a sad stumbling block to the company. A lady in one of our eastern cities having observed to the Doctor that she had understood that our ministers in the West were not favorable to Sabbath Schools, he assured her that this was a great mistake. "We," said he, "endeavor to have a Sabbath School in every family of the congregation." Many remarks of this kind are still recollected by the Doctor's acquaintances, which, if they could be collected into a volume, would not compare unfavorably with other books of table talk which have found their way to the public.

As a preacher the Doctor would not be ranked among the most popular by a certain class, though by some of the best judges he was considered as one of the greatest orators. He undoubtedly possessed many and great excellencies. His general acceptability when commencing his ministry is evident not only from the number of the calls which he received, but from the respectable character of the congregations giving them. Three of these at least were at this time among the most numerous, intelligent, and pious congregations of the Associate Church. As he advanced in years, his application to study, and the increase of his religious experience rendered his ministerial labors still more valuable. The first impression with strangers was seldom favorable. He spoke slowly, though without any painful embarrassment. His style was plain, and his manner not altogether graceful. But after a little familiarity with his manner, the hearer not only became reconciled to it, but it seemed even to add to the effect of his preaching. It was obvious to every one that he had no thought of what he was doing with his hands or feet, or how he appeared in the eyes of the people—that his whole soul was engaged in his Master's work. Though slow, and not at all boisterous in speaking, he was always earnest, sometimes burning with zeal. The method of his sermons was clear and logical. His subjects remarkably appropriate to the occasion. His illustrations were scriptural, and often exceedingly pertinent and striking. He generally comprehended much in a few words, so that those who looked more to the thoughts than the volubility of the speaker, had no cause for weariness. He would weary intelligent people less by a sermon of an hour and a half than many rapid speakers would in half an hour. Looking merely at the thoughts, he would say more in a few minutes than many would say in a whole day, or perhaps in all their lifetime.

He had a just perception of things and a lively imagination, and hence excelled particularly in description. He made a frequent and unusually happy use of the figure called *Personification.* His example was once quoted by the Professor of Rhetoric in Jefferson College to illustrate this figure; with the observation that a distinguished member of Congress, who happened to hear him in passing through the village, had spoken of him as one of the few pulpit *orators* he had ever heard. Some of his descriptions, though they could not now be given in his own words or accompanied with his manner, will be long remembered by the hearers. Such, for instance, is his account of the descent of Moses from the mount, to which he on one occasion referred at the close of the dispensation of the Supper, expressing to the people his fear that, like Israel at that time, some of them would soon be found singing and dancing about the golden calf, applying his remarks to the sin of inordinately seeking after wealth.

He has been known to give a most life-like picture of worship as observed in some families at a late hour in the evening, making the hearers to imagine that they could almost see some of the children in bed, and the rest of the family ready to drop asleep, the father taking his seat by the Bible, and after yawning over it, looks out a psalm, singing a few verses, then hurrying through a chapter, and going to his knees to repeat over the same old prayer—the wife snoring in one corner and the children in another, and then as soon as the service was over all tumbling into bed without so much as a thought about what had been sung or read or prayed. On one occasion, when speaking of the approach of death, and warning people that it might be sudden, he observed that many lived in the confident anticipation that this approach would be gradual, so that there would be abundance of time to prepare; that death would come to them like a traveler who would just make his appearance at the end of the lane, and whom they would see riding up at a slow pace towards the house. After awhile they would see him alighting and fastening his horse; then making his way to the house, opening the gate, and coming through the yard; then again they would hear him knocking at the door, and knocking again and again before he would enter. In this way they thought he would come rather than as a thief in the night.

Among the last times that he preached at Chartiers, he introduced the services of the day with a few remarks on Ps. xviii; the hint leading to which he mentioned as borrowed from Rutherford, but the manner of exhibiting the truth was evidently his own. He observed, in substance, that it was with the children of God, as it was in our families when a child was sick. Everything in our houses must be regulated with a reference to the sick child till it is recovered. Business must be suspended, quiet must be observed, servants sent here and there, physicians must be called, nurses employed, some must be running up stairs, some down. Nothing else is regarded compared with the safety and comfort of that child. Just so, said he, it is in the case of God's children when any of them is in trouble. The earth is made to tremble, the foundations of the hills are moved, the heavens are bowed, the Lord himself comes down, the clouds are gathered and again dispersed, the thunders roar, the channels of the waters are seen, the foundations of the world discovered—all the elements are put in commotion, and all the proceedings of God in his kingdom are managed with a reference to the case of that child, till he is delivered. When he described the management of the house where there was a sick child, one could hardly avoid imagining himself in the midst of the scene, so strongly did it appear impressed on the mind of the speaker, and so vividly was it portrayed.

Another peculiarity in his preaching was the method which he often employed to gain and fix the attention of his hearers. He would, without any appearance of having studied this as an art, begin with some remarks, the particular object of which the hearers would not readily perceive. After he had excited their curiosity as to his design, fixed their attention, and prepared the way, he would make the application to the purpose intended so unexpectedly and so appropriately, that they were taken by surprise, and convinced almost before they were aware of it. He seemed in this to have copied the spirit without following the form of some of our Saviour's parables.

Upon a Sabbath which happened to be the first day of the year, the Doctor read for his text, John iii: 16, "For God so loved the world, that he gave his only-begotten Son," &c.; and after looking around for awhile upon the congregation, as his habit was, he commenced by observing that this was New Year's day, and then enlarged upon the practice of making it a time for giving gifts. After keeping the minds of the people for some time in suspense, as to the connexion of such remarks with the solemn work of the ministry, he added, that the text revealed to us the greatest and best of all gifts—God's gift of his only-begotten Son.

The subjects on which he delighted to dwell were those which constitute the substance and life of the gospel: the love of God in giving his Son, the all-sufficiency of Christ in his righteousness and grace, the gift of him to sinners as such in the gospel, the duty of appropriating faith, and the believer's deliverance from the law as a covenant. He seldom preached without introducing some of these topics; very often they were the main points discussed. The doctrine and duty of covenanting, both public and private, were also frequently brought into view. There was, however, nothing like a wearisome sameness in his sermons; even when he repeated them, as towards the close of his life he sometimes did, it was with many variations. The books which he delighted to read, and which gave character to his discourses, were those written by the Puritans of England, the Marrow men of Scotland, and others of a kindred spirit. Marshall on Sanctification was a particular favorite, and it was his regular custom to read this work once every year. Not that he confined himself to these writers and despised others of the present time. He often purchased and read with avidity modern productions, but generally came to the conclusion that the old wine was better. Some of his people imbibed so much of his love of books, and books of a like character, that not many ministers are furnished with libraries of equal value with those which they have collected.

All the Doctor's acquaintances agree in opinion that in no part of his ministerial duty did he excel more than in prayer. His manner in this duty, like that of his preaching, was slow and deliberate, almost hesitating; yet few could be compared to him for appropriateness, propriety and fervency. His theological students often remarked how apposite his prayers were to the subjects under discussion. The afflicted and dying appeared generally to regard one of Dr. Ramsey's prayers as the greatest of all services which could be rendered to them in this world. He seemed not only to have a peculiar power to carry his fellow worshipers with him to a throne of grace, but to bring away something for their profit and consolation. He was often sent for in cases of sickness, not only by the members of his congregation, but by strangers, and even by such as had previously professed but little regard for his ministry. There was no one whose conversation and prayers were more valued than his in cases of this kind.

Though noted for his strict adherence to his religious profession, he was far from being uncharitable towards those whose creeds differed from his. He loved the image of Christ wherever he could find any traces of it; he rejoiced in the prosperity of all parts of his kingdom, and spoke of the satisfaction which was sometimes manifested by the members of one denomination in hearing of some evil befalling another, as one of the surest indications of the want, or at least the weakness, of grace. In his private intercourse with his brethren of other churches, while faithful to his own profession, he was not forward to enter into controversy, or say offensive things; and in his public ministrations, when his subjects led him to speak of opinions and usages which he condemned, he did so in such a spirit that no reasonable person could be displeased. He was accustomed to inculcate upon students and young preachers a respectful treatment of such as differed from them, observing that there was little prospect of convincing men by causelessly wounding their feelings and insulting their judgments. As the consequence of this course of conduct, he secured the esteem and good will of all good men, and even the respect of bad men. No minister of the Associate Church had a better reputation either in it or out of it. Every one was ready to rise up in his defence, and to repel indignantly any attack made upon his character.

As a professor of theology his department was didactic theology and Hebrew. In teaching theology his custom was on alternate days to read a short lecture, and catechize the students on the subject of it. The latter of these exercises was what he chiefly depended on for informing their minds. He had no ambition to make to himself a name by an affectation of originality, or the introduction of novelties. With powers of judgment and discrimination, with an imagination and ingenuity sufficient to have raised him to a high rank among those having the reputation of original thinkers, he was content to travel in the old and safe way in which others had gone before him. He was firmly attached to the system of truth derived from the Bible by the first Reformers and their immediate successors. He was thoroughly familiar with it, and very capable of teaching it in a clear and comprehensive manner. In the Hebrew he was in a great measure self-taught, never having proceeded much if anything beyond the first principles of the language till his election as professor. But considering his age at this time, and the multiplicity of his labors, it was rather remarkable that he made such progress in this branch of business as he did. So far as known there were no complaints of his incompetency in teaching it. He excelled as a critic upon the performances of the students, having a quick discernment of any thing amiss in the doctrines advanced, the plans of their sermons, their style, and general character as speakers. Still he had not an eye merely for their faults, but could see and commend what was worthy of praise. In pointing out faults he was not usually severe, but sometimes could not refrain from the indulgence of his wit, and raising a laugh at the expense of the young men. Yet in doing this there was evidently no intention to give offence, and generally none was taken. The standing of those ministers who prosecuted their studies under him is generally such as to reflect no discredit upon their teacher.

There were many traits in the character of Dr. Ramsey which may easily be inferred from those mentioned; such as his affectionateness in his family and towards his friends, his hospitality to friends and strangers, his prudence and his uncomplaining spirit. Although he felt keenly, he had a wonderful control over himself, and would seem almost indifferent to troubles, by which his spirit was overwhelmed, and his eyes held waking in the night season. If some affairs brought before the Presbytery of Chartiers, a few weeks before his death, in which he and his family were deeply interested, did not hasten his end, they at least caused that his gray hairs were brought down with sorrow to the grave.

That which constituted his greatest excellence, and which is to him now, and will soon be found by us all in our own cases, to be the most important of attainments, was his sincere and ardent piety. No man was less disposed to make a parade of his religion; no man less needed to do it. His piety shone forth so clearly in his whole life, that it could not be hid; it was a piety not in word, but in deed and in truth. Like all members of the human family he had his infirmities, but they were neither numerous nor glaring. It has been said of some that even their faults lean to virtue's side. It might be said of Dr. Ramsey, that his chief faults consisted in the excess of his virtues. His modesty, his indifference to the world, his forbearance, and his friendships were sometimes carried to an extreme.

Such was his humble estimate of himself, that he never could be prevailed upon to become an author. It is not known that he ever penned any thing for publication beyond a short presbyterial report, or something of this kind; and even in these cases, he was only driven to it by necessity. His method of preparing sermons was to write an outline, pretty full so far as related to the ideas to be advanced, but as to the language, containing only hints, intelligible to himself, but not generally to others. It is not probable that he has left any thing in a state suitable for publication. But as his manner of speaking was very distinct and deliberate, some of his students and others of his friends occasionally took notes of his sermons; and it is possible that a volume, or at least some specimens of them, may yet be prepared for the press.

Although Dr. Ramsey was spared to a great age, gave very clear evidence of his preparation to leave the world, and was not called away till the days of his active usefulness were ended, the church in which he ministered, and the church at large, have reason to lament the loss of his example and his prayers. Such men still fill the office of Moses, who stood in the breach and turned away the anger of the Lord; and we may well mourn over their removal, and say, "Help, Lord, for the godly man ceaseth, and the faithful fail from among the children of men."

BIOGRAPHICAL SKETCH

OF THE

REV. ABRAHAM ANDERSON, D. D.

Professor of Didactic Theology in the Associate Seminary, at Canonsburg, Washington county, Pa.; also Professor of Languages in Jefferson College, from September, 1818, to September, 1821 and Professor Extra. of Hebrew in Jefferson College, from December, 1852, till his death, May, 1855.

BY REV. W. M. M'ELWEE.

[*Abridged from the "Evangelical Repository."*]

The parents of Dr. Anderson, (Abraham Anderson and Elizabeth Chesnutt,) were born in Ireland, but in what county is not known. They were united in marriage during the period of our Revolutionary struggle, and emigrated to America shortly after the renewal of amicable relations between the United States and the mother country. Having arrived in the United States about 1784, they took up their abode in Cumberland county, Pennsylvania, and there they continued to reside till 1805 or 1806. All, or nearly all, of their children, (five sons and three daughters,) were born in that county: Abraham, their second son and third child, was born in Newville, a small village of Cumberland county, on the 7th day of December, 1789.

As is generally the case with emigrants from the old world, Mr. Anderson, when he reached the United States, was in very limited circumstances, but by the blessing of the Lord upon his honest labors, his worldly condition improved from year to year. On removing from Cumberland county, in 1805 or 1806, to Washington county, in Western Pennsylvania, he was able to secure a small farm—that on which the Rev. Matthew Henderson spent his last days,—and on this tract, hallowed by the piety of his predecessor, he spent the remainder of his years, not in splendid affluence, but in plenty of all things.

To secure the stated dispensation of word and ordinances in their purity, so that his own soul might be continually edified and his family trained up in the nurture and admonition of the Lord, was Mr. Anderson's great object in removing to the West. The place to which he was directed in Providence, and on which he settled, was very suitable to the end he had in view, being but two and a half miles from the church of the Associate congregation of Chartiers, of which the late James Ramsey, D. D., was pastor at the time, and continued to be the pastor for several years after the death of Mr. Anderson. His object, so highly laudable, was fully gained. He enjoyed the plain, earnest ministrations of Dr. Ramsey during the residue of his days, and appeared to grow in knowledge, faith, and heavenly-mindedness. After a few years' connection with the congregation, he was advanced to the eldership, and all his children, yielding to the instructions of the word, written and preached, and to the force of their father's example, lived in sobriety and godliness; and as they reached maturity of life, professed the Christian faith, and sought communion with Christ and his people.

It is the desire of many parents to accumulate wealth for the benefit of their children. They persuade themselves that if they had thousands at their command, they could and would secure for their children the best teachers, have the brightest examples set before them, and give them all their time for improving their minds and their manners. But an humble condition, with piety, has its advantages, and they are greater than mere affluence can afford. These greater advantages were the lot in Divine Providence of the children of Mr. Anderson, and particularly of Abraham, the subject of the present sketch. He was taught from childhood to fear and reverence the God of Israel, to esteem and relish his word, to say, "Thou, God, seest me," and to make the will of God the rule and reason of his conduct. He was taught to pray, and taught how to pray; for though the elder Anderson was not one of the learned, yet he had a fine gift of prayer, and prayed in his own house morning and evening with a fullness and pathos not always attained, even by the public ministers of the gospel. He was taught to think and reason, to contrive and plan, to fix on an end and to pursue it laboriously, not regarding the clamors of the flesh for rest and ease. A good religious training is the best fortune which a young man can inherit, and those young men are in the fairest way to possess this inheritance whose parents are poor as to worldly things, but rich in faith and in the knowledge of the divine word.

It is no discredit to the son of Jesse, that he was taken from the sheep-fold, "from following the ewes, great with young, to feed his people Israel;" and it is no discredit to Dr. Anderson, if he was taken from the plough, to feed the people of Christ with the bread of life. The cares and toils of the farm were in fact his occupation, from the time that he was capable of helping in such affairs, till he was nearly twenty-three years of age. To persons of an upright spirit and sober mind, no business is more agreeable. Some of the greatest intellects have acknowledged and manifested a fondness for agricultural pursuits. Cincinnatus was taken from his plough to command the armies of the Roman republic, and our own Washington, as is well known, preferred the cares of his farm to the anxieties of the camp and of the court. No doubt Mr. Anderson took pleasure in the labors of the field, and it may be that he never would have been heard of as a teacher and leader in the Church of Christ, had he not been called from his paternal home and rural labors to other scenes, and labors of a more trying nature.

The second war with Great Britain, sometimes called the war for establishing our national independence, was declared by Congress on the 18th of June, 1812. Soldiers were needed to defend the eastern and northern boundaries of the Republic, and as a sufficient number could not be enlisted, the citizens were drafted to perform the duties of soldiers. Some were taken to the Atlantic coast to repel the enemy in that quarter, and others to the North and North-west to resist invasions from Canada, and to repress and chastise the atrocities of savage warfare, most of the Indian tribes having enlisted on the side of Britain. What portion of the yeomanry of the country was called to arms in the course of the war, is unknown. But so many husbandmen and artizans became soldiers, that there was scarcely a family in any part of our extended country, that was not made heavy in spirit by the draft or enlistment of one or more of its members.

In the autumn of 1812, a portion of the militia of Western Pennsylvania was called out by the War department, to defend the borders lying between Cleveland and Sandusky, against the British from Canada, and to repress and chastise the ferocity of the savage tribes in that region of Ohio. The joyfulness of many families was exchanged for heaviness and gloomy forebodings. The family of old Mr. Anderson was not exempted. Abraham, the beloved son and brother, was one of the draft, being at the time not quite twenty-three years of age. About the necessity and lawfulness of the war, the people of the United States were divided into two parties—equal to each other in numbers, or at least, very nearly equal. What were the private thoughts of young Mr. Anderson about these matters of public debate, the writer cannot state with absolute certainty. But he appears to have been with the democratic or war party, in judgment and in feeling. In compliance with the draft, he went out from his beloved home, and as a private went through all the hardships of a winter campaign in the North-west of Ohio, which it is presumed he would have found some means of avoiding, had he doubted of the lawfulness of the war, or had he not considered that the call of his country was also the call of Providence. Mr. Anderson, though at this time but a youth, had in some way acquired the habit of industry and forecast; the habit of turning every little portion of time to some good account; and in the intervals of military duty, he wrote a brief journal of the campaign in which he bore a part. The journal is preserved entire, and though the writer of it had to substitute his knee or a billet of wood for a table, the writing is easily read, excepting a small portion of it written with bad ink, and effaced, in a good measure, by the lapse of so many years. It appears from the journal that the regiment of which Mr. Anderson constituted a part, assembled in Pittsburgh, in the beginning of October, 1812, and from thence marched on the 19th of the month under the command of Major D. Nelson, to Beaver, Lisbon, Canton, Massillon, Wooster and Mansfield. At the latter place the band lay in camp from the 10th of November till the 12th of December, and strange as it may seem to those now living in that peaceful village, there were rumors of persons tomahawked and scalped in the neighborhood. Sentinels were placed with the utmost care, and scouting parties were sent out to discover, if possible, the lurking places of the foe. The rumors, however, were but rumors, and this being ascertained, the detachment marched to the plains of Sandusky, to Delawaretown, to Norton, to Franklinton, and Upper Sandusky. The band reached the latter place on the 31st of December, and lay there in camp till the 24th of January, when, in compliance with an express, they marched for Miami. Having to wade through mud and water, in many places to the knees, they made but eight miles in the day, and camping at Tiomocto, lay there from the 25th to the 29th, waiting for the waters to freeze up. While waiting, bad news was received, in consequence of which they had to march on the 29th, without their tents, and with three days' provisions in their knapsacks. On the 1st of February, the band reached Portage river, and on the following day came to the Rapids, where, says the journal, "We found a man killed by the Indians. He had been sent in company with two others to the British, and was killed. The other two not being found were supposed to have been taken as prisoners."

The band of soldiers being now in the midst of enemies distinguished by insidious cunning as well as by ferocious courage, cast up breast-works about the place of their encampment, and built a block house, to which was given the name of Fort Meigs. Spies were sent out to ascertain the position of the Indians, and on the 9th of February the spies returned and reported that they had found an encampment of about three hundred Indians, eighteen miles down the river, whereupon Major Nelson called for six hundred volunteers to go and attack them by night. The journal states that *twelve hundred volunteered*, and does not add that the writer was one of the twelve hundred. But such is the fact. It is distinctly recollected that Mr. Anderson stated in private conversation with friends, that he had volunteered to take part in the perils of that adventure; and this fact is implied in the journal, for it is added after the statement quoted above, "We commenced our march at 8 o'clock, P. M., and at 2 o'clock in the morning came to the Indian encampment, but they had all fled."

To follow the journal in all its details would be wearisome to most of our readers. It is judged, however, that the following extracts will be acceptable; and they will serve to evince us that Mr. Anderson, in the course of his campaign, went through great trials and hardships, though he was not engaged in any battle.

"On Friday, the 26th of February, a party of us set out for Lower Sandusky on a secret expedition. Reached Lower Sandusky on the 28th. Rested there till the 1st day of March. On the 2d, Captain Logan assembled the whole party, which numbered about two hundred men, and informed us that the object of the expedition was to burn the Queen Charlotte, lying at Malden, and requested all to retire to camp that did not choose to encounter the danger involved in the undertaking; or that could not be cool and deliberate under the yells of savages and the roar of cannon. No one of the whole party confessed the weakness of his nerves and prayed to be excused. But as the ice on the lake was broken up, the expedition failed to effect the object intended, and after much exposure and fatigue the company returned to the Rapids.

"On the 9th of March an alarm was given. Two or three of our men went down the river a few miles from the camp, who, on their return, reported that they were fired on by six Indians. No one of the little company was killed or wounded; but one of them had a bullet lodged in a Bible in his pocket.

"On the same day, a lieutenant in Major Nelson's battalion, of the name of Walker, went out of camp some distance, and on the 10th he was found, shot through, tomahawked, and scalped, and thrown into the river.

"On the 19th of March, a scouting party went out and returned with the loss of one man, supposed to be taken prisoner.

"On the 21st of March, another scouting party went out and found many signs of Indians. A large party went over the river to lie in wait that night. About ten o'clock at night we had an alarm by the firing of two platoons on that side of the river where our scouting party was. The party on returning, reported that they saw two or three Indians, and fired. No one was killed.

"On the 31st of March, our general collected us together

for the purpose of getting volunteers to stay fifteen days to keep the fort. Two hundred men turned out to stay."

The occasion of this call for volunteers was the fact that the time of service for which the militia had been called out was about to expire, and as yet the troops to supply their place had not arrived. It was important to the country and to the magnanimous regulars occupying the fort, that a considerable portion of the militia should stay beyond their time. But all naturally desired to be out of danger, and to enjoy the convivialities and comforts of home; and these desires prevailed with the greater part. On the 2d of April, between nine and ten hundred Pennsylvanians and Virginians took their departure. Only two hundred subjected the yearnings of their hearts to a sense of duty, and stayed to defend the fort and the lives of their brethren. Of this magnanimous little band, Mr. Anderson was one, and by his course on that occasion, he showed that high regard for duty which he often manifested in future life. He was very affectionate and tender-hearted, and no doubt desired to be at home as earnestly as those who returned home as soon as the strong hand of the law allowed them to do so. But asking his own conscience what is duty in the case? and receiving the answer, *stay*, he hesitated no longer—stay he would, and die.

The defence of the fort being greatly weakened, the enemy became more insolent, and the condition of the men holding the fort more perilous. On the 4th of April, two Indians killed and scalped a man within a hundred yards of the camp. They were pursued, but escaped. On the 8th, forty Indians attacked a fatigue party, while loading a wagon with wood. One of the party was killed, two taken prisoners; the rest were chased but escaped. Two bands went in pursuit of the Indians, one of which overtook and killed nine of them. Seven of the pursuing party were wounded, and two of them mortally.

The following paragraph is interesting, and bears witness to the humanity of the Commander-in-chief:

"On the 16th of April, a man having been condemned to be shot for desertion, an offence which he had repeated five times: the ring was formed in a hollow square; the criminal was brought forward by a guard, the band playing the 'Dead March;' he was set by on a bench, and a black handkerchief tied around his head. The charges against him were read with the sentence of the court. The handkerchief was then drawn over his face; the officer commanding the executioners ordered them to make ready. They did so, and at that instant General Harrison gave him his reprieve, and ordered him to the Provost Guard."

"On the 18th of April," the journal goes on to say, "We left Fort Meigs for home. Our number was ten, three of whom were not able to carry arms. It was twenty miles to Portage Block House. Five of our company gave out within two miles of Portage, where we lay during the night, without fire, after wading through mud and water to the knees as much as half the way. About ten o'clock, while I was on guard, a gun was fired three or four hundred yards off, which I suppose was done by an Indian, as no white men were near. There was also repeated yells of wolves, or rather of Indians affecting to be wolves. No other disturbance was observed till near break of day, when we were surprised by a savage yell, perhaps three hundred yards off. We were all awake and stood to arms waiting for an attack, till clear day. We then marched in order to Portage, expecting to be attacked by the way, but by the interposition of Providence, we escaped our enemies' hands. We took refreshment at Portage, and then continued our March through the Black Swamp, which was about three miles in breadth, and often three or four feet deep; and, indeed, our future march, at least as far as Sandusky, was through a continued swamp——"

The words of the last sentence are the close of the journal. It was not intended for public inspection, and was left incomplete. But though it was written for mere private use, without the ordinary conveniences for writing, and though it was written in a very trying and exciting time, when Mr. Anderson was but a youth, and had no education but such as he picked up in the common schools of the country, we confidently appeal to the performance as proof of a sound, vigorous mind, and a firm, manly spirit. As a dead fly causeth the ointment of the apothecary to send forth a stinking savor, so doth a little folly him that is in reputation for wisdom. But there are no signs of weakness in the journal—no whining about losses and hardships, no boasting of a heart proof against the sharp arrows of fear; nor of exploits done, or of exploits attempted, at the thought of which others blanched and drew back. There are no silly conceits, nor anything at all to make the writer blush, were he still living, and the whole spread before the world as the earliest production of his pen. We notice, however, a want which we did not expect to find,—the want of a religious sentiment and feeling. Mr. Anderson had professed the Christian religion some years before he was called to be a soldier, and had partaken of the Lord's Supper a number of times. Yet in his journal the Bible is mentioned but once, and in that instance it is mentioned incidentally. The interposition of Providence in behalf of himself and his companions, is mentioned but once. The Sabbath is not mentioned at all. There is no notice of any opportunity of attending public worship, and there are no lamentations about the want of such opportunities. How are we to account for these omissions? When Mr. Anderson repaired to the camp, did he leave his religion behind him? This supposition the testimony of his fellow soldiers forbids us to entertain. They report that he carried his Bible with him, and often employed his leisure moments in the perusal of it,—that he made an observable difference between the Lord's day and other days,—that when it fell to his lot to stand sentinel during the Sabbath evening, or to do any public duty on the Lord's day, he always avoided it, if it were in his power so to do,—that profane language was never heard from his lips,—that he was virtuous and honorable, and highly esteemed both by the officers and men.

It would not, therefore, be warrantable to infer from the want of pious expressions in the journal, that Mr. Anderson was at that time destitute of Christian faith and sentiment. It might, indeed, be inferred as well, that he was without natural feeling, for though he was at times in great peril, the journal says nothing of the anguish of fear; and though he was often in circumstances which all men everywhere regard as distressing, yet nothing is complained of in any part of the journal. Nothing is said of the pride and tyranny of officers,—nothing of the hard fare of the common soldier,—nothing of the painfulness of an alarm in the night; and even when he wades through water and mire all the day, and beds in the swamp at night, without fire, there is no expression to indicate that Mr. Anderson felt the discomforts of his situation. But surely he was not without natural feeling, and it is equally certain that he hoped and trusted in the living God, and was thankful to Him for His care and protection. But if he felt indeed, why did he not give utterance to his feelings? The proper solution of the difficulty appears to be simply this: having no accommodation for writing, and very little time for such business, he proposed not to write a complete history of his physical and spiritual experience during the campaign, but merely to write a memorandum of places, dates and incidents, for the help of his memory in thinking and speaking in after years of that trying season. How well his labor answered the design of it, is very evident from the extracts that have been exhibited.

Viewing, with the help of Mr. Anderson's journal, the trials and hardships of the North-western campaign, in the winter of 1812–'13, the considerate reader can hardly fail to reflect on the horrors of war. How unpleasant and painful is the whole business, and how great the havoc that attends it! The campaign over which we have glanced, was not signalized by any bloody engagement, but a number of persons were killed. All, at times, were disquieted with fear, though the journal does not tell us so, and all suffered greatly through exposure to piercing winds, and to water from above, and water on the surface of the earth. Though that was an age of greater vigor and hardihood than the present, yet many, by the severity of their trials, were brought down to the dust of death before the close of the campaign; and many others had the seeds of disease and death implanted in their systems. It is thought by a fellow-soldier that Mr. Anderson was never the same in respect of buoyant health that he had been before the campaign. If those who make wars had to fight them through to the bitter end, so many wars would not be proclaimed.

After leaving Portage, as stated in the journal, and touching at Sandusky, it is not known through what towns and villages Mr. Anderson passed. But he reached his paternal home in health and safety about the 1st of May, 1813. He was joyful and thankful, and no doubt his parents, now well on in years, rejoiced over him, and called their other children and their friends to rejoice with them, saying as the father in the parable, "This, our son was dead, and he is alive again; he was lost, and is found."

Though Mr. Anderson returned to his father's habitation, he did not return to his former employment. He had been seized with a desire to pursue studies in preparation for the gospel ministry, and had signified his desire to his parents, two or perhaps three years before he was called out to assist in defending the country. At that time his father opposed the project, alleging that his labors on the farm were very needful; and that the family could not dispense with his assistance, and at the same time bear the additonal burden that would be imposed by his college fees, and other incidental expenses. Mr. Anderson felt and acknowledged the force of the objection: he abandoned the project for the time, and it may be that he would never have taken it up again, had not the privilege which he had sought been freely accorded to him. This was done in a very engaging manner. When Mr. Anderson had told the family of the privations, perils and hardships of the campaign more particularly and fully than had been done in letters sent from the camp, his father reminded him of his former desire to enter on a course of study in preparation for the ministry, and how he himself had opposed the project at that time. "*But now,*" added the good old man, "*I will object no more, for the Lord hath showed* me, that if I will not spare your labors in the field for that purpose, he can, and perhaps will, deprive me of them in some other way."

Mr. Anderson's desire to engage in the work of the ministry was not extinguished by what he had seen and suffered in the camp. As he went out on that perilous tour, he had perhaps vowed a vow to this effect, that if God would be with him, and bring him again to his father's house in peace, then the Lord should be his God, and he would serve him in the gospel of his Son, if permitted to do so. Perhaps he had seen during the campaign, more clearly than before, that atheism, profaneness, irreligion, and all manner of wickedness, were pouring into the land like a flood, and that the Lord of Hosts, like the general at Fort Meigs, was calling for volunteers to go forth and stem the tide. But, however these things may have been, he accepted promptly and cordially of the privilege accorded to him by his beloved parent; and after a few days of relaxation and social enjoyment, he entered himself as a student of Jefferson College.

As the family were still in limited circumstances, he boarded with his parents, three and a half miles from Canonsburg, the site of the college, and then walked seven miles each day. The thought of having to travel so great a distance, would appall a young man of the present generation.

But, being accustomed to marches of fifteen, twenty, and thirty miles, Mr. A. made no account of the labor, and was not retarded by it. He committed to memory while walking to and from college; or if the weather was unsuitable for carrying an open book before his eyes, he reviewed in thought the subject of study, and made himself more familiar with it. It may be that his progress in learning was furthered by his long walks, and doubtless the considerable exercise made necessary by the place in which he boarded, was the means of maintaining his bodily health and vigor, notwithstanding his close application to study. But whether his boarding so far from the college was an advantage or disadvantage, his progress was rapid. He graduated in September, 1817, a little more than four years from the time of his entrance; and on the same day he was elected professor of languages in Jefferson College, a clear proof that the Faculty and Trustees of that Institution conferred upon him the first degree, *pro merito,* and not *pro gratia*—in consideration of his merits, and not in the way of favor. Mr. Anderson accepted the professorship, and discharged the duties of the office for four years. During this period he also studied Theology, being admitted to the study by the Associate Presbytery of Chartiers, shortly after his election to the professorship. The Theological Seminary of the Associate church was at that time under the care of the venerable John Anderson, D. D., and was located in Service congregation, Beaver County. The prescribed course of study occupied four sessions of five months each, the sessions commencing the 1st Monday of November, and closing on the 4th Wednesday of March. Mr. Anderson's full attendance at the Seminary was dispensed with, in consideration of the honorable and useful business in which he was engaged, and his ripeness in knowledge. He was at the Seminary two or three months only; but when not there, he prosecuted his Theological studies with diligence. It is natural to presume that his labors in the college hindered his advancement in Theology, and that his attention to Theology hindered his acceptance and usefulness in the college. But his trials were always heartily approved by the Presbytery: and in the college he was highly esteemed by his fellow professors and by the young men in attendance. Busy he must have been, and yet he found time to read a course of medicine with Dr. Jonathan Leatherman, of Canonsburg, by which he attained to considerable skill in medical practice, and qualified himself to be useful to his fellow men in sickness; as he was, in fact, wherever he went, giving counsel and medicine to good purpose and without charge. It is astonishing that a man should go through so many labors and accomplish so much in so short a time. But in this case our astonishment may be somewhat diminished by calling to mind that Mr. A. had been a student of Theology, under his minister and parents, for more than twenty years, before he was formally admitted to the *study*, by the Associate Presbytery. After the usual trials before the Presbytery, he was licensed to preach the everlasting gospel, in July or August of 1821; and as that was the work to which he had dedicated himself, he resigned his professorship at the close of the college session in September. He was fond of retirement and study; the incomes of the professorship were greater than he could expect from the ministry—in the view of many it was more honorable to be a learned professor in a rising college, than to be the humble pastor of a country congregation: but judging that he was called to preach Christ, Mr. Anderson conferred not with flesh and blood. He laid aside his professorship and gave himself to the work of the ministry. After preaching in the vacant congregations of Chartiers, Allegheny, and Ohio Presbyteries, he passed, in pursuance of Synodical appointment, into the Presbytery of the Carolinas, in the spring of 1822. He preached in all the vacancies of the latter Presbytery, and in all with acceptance to all the people. In July, 1822, he was unanimously called by the united congregations of Bethany and Steel Creek, in Mecklenburgh county, North Carolina, to be their pastor. The call occasioned great thoughts of heart. Mr. Anderson had not anticipated a settlement in the Carolina Presbytery. He was not inclined, but on the contrary, averse, to a settlement in a slave State. But the people were very needy, having been without pastoral care from the time of the death of Rev. James Pringle, in 1817; and they were very earnest and urgent in their application to him, individually. After carefully and prayerfully considering what duty demanded in the case, he accepted their call. His ordination trials were delivered in Pisgah meeting-house, Lincoln county, North Carolina, about the 10th of September, and being approved, he was ordained and installed at Steel Creek meeting-house, on Thursday, the 3d of October, 1822.

The writer of this sketch was in attendance on the Presbytery at Pisgah, while Mr. Anderson submitted his trials for ordination, and there began an acquaintance, which was afterwards cultivated on long journeys, to and from different meetings of the Associate Synod — in frequent meetings of the Carolina Presbytery — in frequent meetings to dispense the Lord's Supper — in several meetings as Delegates to the Convention of Reformed churches — in many meetings of the Theological Board, and in numberless meetings in our respective habitations, both in the South and in the North. The acquaintance for which Providence afforded such ample opportunity, soon ripened into the most intimate and cordial friendship — a friendship that was never interrupted while Mr. Anderson lived; and will not be interrupted, it is confidently hoped, through the numberless ages that are yet to come. At the commencement of this acquaintance and friendship, Mr. Anderson was in the meridian of life, being about thirty-three years of age. It seems proper therefore in this place, to give some account of his personal appearance. He was a tall man, six feet and two inches in height, with a well extended frame and heavy muscular limbs. Whether standing or walking, he bore himself altogether erect, having acquired the habit of doing so, it is believed, in his military trainings. The hair of his head was quite black, and yet his complexion was uncommonly florid. His forehead was white, smooth and lofty; his cheeks not round, but long, and rather lank; his eyes were bright and penetrating. When much interested in what he was saying himself, or hearing from the lips of another, his eyes seemed to flash and twinkle, like bright stars in a clear night. His general appearance told at once and distinctly, that he was a man of intelligence, honesty and courage. Perhaps the camp had made an abiding impression on his person. But however this may be, there was the appearance of stern, solemn dignity, and a stranger meeting him on the highway, might reasonably have conjectured that he was the general of an army on a private jaunt.

He was regarded from the first not merely by the people that called him to be their pastor, but by the ministers and people of the Presbytery in general, as a great acquisition. Such a man is indeed an acquisition in any Presbytery, at any time. But when Mr. Anderson was settled in the Presbytery of the Carolinas, his gifts and abilities were eminently needful. The Presbytery included three ministers, Messrs. Dixon, Mushat, and Heron, and twenty congregations scattered over the Western Territories of Virginia, and the two Carolinas. From the congregations of Rockbridge county, Virginia, to those in Fairfield district, South Carolina, is fully three hundred miles. But the greater part of the twenty congregations are more convenient to each other, having their locality in the contiguous counties of Lincoln, Iredell, and Mecklenburgh, North Carolina, and in the adjoining districts of York, Lancaster, Chester, and Fairfield, South Carolina. The people were mostly Irish and Scotch, or their descendants; and, as is common with these races wherever found, they were zealous for the religion of their father. They had gone with their ministers into the union which gave rise to the Associate Reformed church, but about the year 1804, they withdrew from that ecclesiastical connexion, and came under the inspection of the Associate Synod of North America. The occasion was as follows —Rev. John Mason, D. D., of New York, began in 1801 or '2, to advocate through the Christian Magazine the frequent observance of the Lord's Supper, and to arraign and condemn the customary sacramental fast days, and thanksgiving days, as not required nor warranted by the word of God. The Associate Reformed Synod of the South having met (1804 or '5,) in Bethany, York District, South Carolina, took up the subject of frequent communion, and after a long and animated discussion they approved and adopted the views of Dr. Mason, in all their extent. Two ministerial members of the Synod, viz: Rev. William Dixon and Rev. Peter M'Millan, and several elders protested against the reformation resolved upon, as a serious and pernicious deformation. Their remonstrances not being regarded by their brethren, they withdrew and forwarded a petition to the Associate Synod, requesting admission to fellowship with them. In answer to this petition, the Associate Synod sent two of their members to the Carolinas, viz: Rev. John Anderson, D. D., and Rev. William Wilson, with power to constitute as a Presbytery, and receive the accession of Messrs. Dixon and M'Millan, and their adherents. The appointees fulfilled their mission in 1805 or '6, and so founded the Presbytery of the Carolinas in subordination to the Associate Synod of North America.

In a few months after the perfecting of this ecclesiastical revolution, Mr. ——— became openly and grossly intemperate, and being laid aside, the care of all the Secession congregations in the South devolved for several years on Mr. Dixon alone. At length (about the year 1810,) Mr. John Mushat, of Cambridge Presbytery, New York, accepted the call of the congregations of Cambridge and Stirling, in Iredell county, North Carolina, and was installed as their pastor. About the same time, Mr. Andrew Heron, from the same Presbytery of New York, was settled in the congregations of Ebenezer and Timber-ridge, Rockbridge county, Virginia. And not long after, Mr. James Pringle, licensed by the Presbytery of Philadelphia, undertook the pastoral charge of Bethany and Steel Creek congregations, in Mecklenburgh county, North Carolina. The measure of ministerial gifts and abilities possessed by these young ministers was very considerable — greater than falls to the lot of many who officiate acceptably and usefully. The people of the Carolina Presbytery, rejoiced in them, as bright and shining lights, and rejoiced in the hope that the principles for which they were witnesses would prevail in the land, and exert a happy influence. But the prospect was soon darkened. Mr. Mushat opened an Academy in Statesville, Iredell county, in 1815, and made teaching his principal business, abandoning the work of the ministry in a good measure: and in the Autumn of 1817, Mr. Pringle was by an inscrutable Providence removed to the land of silence. The Presbytery was brought very low, and so continued till 1821, when Mr. T. Kitchen, from the Secession church of Scotland, was settled in the pastoral charge of Shiloh and Neely's Creek congregations; the former in Lancaster, and the latter in York district, South Carolina. This addition to the Presbytery revived the spirits of the people. But Mr. Dixon being now far advanced in life, and compassed about with infirmities, the ministerial force of the Presbytery was altogether inadequate, and Mr. Anderson's services at the time of his settlement were greatly needed.

He appears to have been fully aware from the first moment of his settlement, that he was called not to enjoy *otium cum dignitate*, but to work in the Master's vineyard, and accordingly he gave himself to work. He took boarding with Col.

Thomas Grier and lady, of Steel Creek, with whom also his predecessor had lodged. The Colonel and his lady were not possessed of great wealth, but they were animated by a liberal, generous spirit, and furnished their pastor with every needful accommodation gratuitously; accounting his presence and company a sufficient remuneration. In the pastoral charge which he had been induced to accept, Mr. Anderson found one considerable advantage, which young ministers generally lack for a season — a supply of books appropriate to his studies. His predecessor, Mr. James Pringle, during the short course of his ministry, had collected for his own use a considerable library, amounting perhaps to three hundred volumes, and having neither wife nor child to provide for, he had left the whole collection to the congregation of Steel Creek, for the use of his successors in the pastorate of the congregation. As Mr. Anderson was his first successor, and came not only into Mr. Pringle's pulpit, but into his very study and bed-chamber, the books were all in their respective places as if waiting to be consulted.

It is a time of severe trial when the front ranks of an army are cut down, and those in the rear march forward to fill their places, and see their brethren silent in death, or agonized with pain. It is wonderful that a man can maintain the control of himself, in such circumstances. Mr. Anderson's position was not so appalling, but it was solemn. There was a voice in the chamber, bed and books, and the voice gave utterance to the words, *Ministers must die even as others. Remember that thou shalt die, and whatsoever thy hand findeth to do, do it with thy might.* Whether Mr. Anderson in fancy heard these words or not, he was attentive to the warning and counsel contained in them. He addicted himself to meditation and prayer. He searched the Scriptures and read commentaries and systems of Theology, that he might attain to a more perfect understanding of the Scriptures. He labored in preparing sermons and in preaching them. He held quarterly diets of examination, and general meetings of the youth in the church for examination and instruction. He attended also to parochial visitation, and exhorted from house to house. As his people were scattered over a parallelogram of thirty miles in length, and twelve in breadth, the last mentioned department of labor was very tedious and exhausting, yet he persisted in it, judging that it was an important and necessary part of his work: for how else could he know the spiritual wants of his people? and if he knew them not, how could he give to each his portion in due season?

Mr. Anderson's situation had some advantages, as has been noticed. But there were also disadvantages connected with his charge. He was subjected to a great deal of labor in the way of traveling. Each tour to Bethany, to which he repaired every second Sabbath, was a journey of forty miles, and if called to visit the sick, or engaged in visiting from house to house, the journey was increased fifteen or twenty miles, making a circuit of more than a thousand miles in the course of the year. In addition to this large domestic traveling, he had long journeys of a more public nature, in attending Presbytery, meeting with brethren to assist in dispensing the Lord's Supper, supplying vacant congregations with preaching, repairing to the meetings of Synod, &c. These public jaunts being added to his common domestic traveling, the whole would amount to twenty-five hundred, or perhaps three thousand miles *per annum;* involving a great deal of labor, and much loss of time.

Mr. Anderson soon found that traveling on horse-back subjected him to febrile excitement, and other unpleasant symptoms. With the view of preventing the irritation, he furnished himself with a vehicle; the remedy was not effectual, but still he went on with his work, and sought relief by other means. In the campaign of 1812, an attack being threatened, the army of which Mr. Anderson was a part, was put in order for the battle. Mr. Anderson being a large man and of reputation for courage, the officer in command singled him out, and calling him from the rear, where he was when the alarm was given, conducted him to the front rank and stationed him there. In like manner the Presbytery continually assigned to him the very front of ministerial exposure and hardship, and yet he did not pray to be excused because he had already done more than others, nor because the labor and exposure would probably be prejudicial to his health and comfort. Some one should go to this place and the other to dispense the Lord's Supper, or to moderate a call, or to install a minister, or to share in the deliberations of Synod: and the question being raised, who will go? often did Mr. Anderson volunteer as at Fort Meigs, or quietly submit to the appointment of Presbytery under a sense of duty.

To convince his hearers of their lost, undone estate by nature, and persuade them to trust in Christ for salvation, and to take his holy precepts for their guide and directory, was that at which Mr. Anderson aimed in all his ministrations, whether at home or abroad. He desired and endeavored to bring about a reformation in accordance with the word of God, and in conformity with the attainments of the church of Scotland in her happiest days. In carrying out this design, he preached the truth with simplicity and plainness, and assailed error directly and boldly, and yet with such calm dignity and scriptural force, that hearers who had been of a different opinion were not exasperated. His labors had not all the effect which he desired, but they were not in vain. His own members were generally awakened and stirred up to give more earnest heed to the things belonging to their peace. Many individuals were turned from irreligion and ungodliness; family worship was established in many dwellings; the Sabbath was observed with increased solemnity; intemperance and profaneness were abandoned, or practiced clandestinely, and with shame. Mr. Anderson's influence was felt in the neighboring congregations. Mr. William Dixon, the father and founder of the Presbytery, a man of earnest, solid piety, had some way fallen into the practice of baptizing the children of parents who gave attention to the preaching of the word, though they did not seek fellowship with Christ and his people, in the use of the Lord's Supper. With much kindness and with great respect, Mr. Anderson remonstrated against this practice of the venerable father as disorderly and pernicious in its effects, and his remonstrance was effectual. In some of the neighboring congregations, members of the Masonic Fraternity were church members in full communion at the time of Mr. Anderson's settlement in the Presbytery. But in the course of a few years such members, and chiefly through Mr. Anderson's influence, were called before their session and required to dissolve their connexion with the Masonic body. Most of them did so, and such as refused to comply were suspended from the fellowship of the church, as the discipline of the Associate body requires. The leaven of sound doctrine had then by various means made its way into some of the contiguous congregations. Mr. Anderson desired it to spread quickly through all the congregations of the Presbytery, and through the land, and with this view he moved the Presbytery in the Spring of 1824, to prepare and emit a pastoral letter. The Presbytery adopted the motion and appointed Mr. Anderson himself to prepare the contemplated letter. He accepted the appointment and prepared the draught of a letter, which being submitted was approved and published towards the close of the year. The original manuscript of this paper in Mr. Anderson's handwriting is before me. It is entitled, *a pastoral letter by the Associate Presbytery of the Carolinas, to the people under their care.* As it was the declared design of this paper to promote reformation according to the holy Scriptures, the author sets out with the position that true religion was in a low and languishing condition: he sustains this position by some instances and proof, and then addresses himself to the work of correcting errors in practice and in principle. Under the former head he treats of the great evil of intemperance, at that time extensively prevalent in the land, and quite too common among the members of the church. He passes on to the sin of profaning the Lord's day—the sin of neglecting family worship and family instruction—the sin of profaning gospel ordinances—the sin of contemning Christ and his salvation, by declining to profess the faith and partake of the holy sacraments. Under the second general head the author notices not the principal errors in Theology, but some of those popular erroneous sentiments, which in his judgment have a direct tendency to harden the hearts of professors in a course of defection from the truth and cause of Jesus Christ. The errors particularly noticed and refuted are the following: "We should not disturb the peace of the church by contending for divine truth and ordinances.—Error introduced or held by a professed believer should be spared.—Though we may oppose essential errors, we should not contend about the non-essential.—Controversy genders strife and displeasure among Christians, and it is good for nothing else.—Every man must answer for himself, and therefore, it is officious to trouble ourselves about the mistakes of others.—It is little difference what our sentiments are, if our practice be correct.—If we be sincere, it matters not about our faith or principles.—It is impossible to obtain an agreement among professed Christians, and we are therefore not to expect it, but to admit to the communion of the church those whom we in charity judge to be Christians, whatever their religious sentiments may be," &c. The several matters treated of in the letter, are handled in a plain, simple manner, as utility required, and yet with energy. Eloquence of diction is wanting, for it would have hindered the object intended. But sensible persons who may take up the pamphlet, will soon be satisfied that the pen was guided by a discerning mind, well stored with knowledge, and by a sincere honest heart. The following passage respecting the duty of family worship is very forcible, and shows an extensive acquaintance with the word: "*The matter of the duty being plain, that it should be performed by families, we have abundant evidence.* David returned to bless his house, 1 Chron. xvi: 43; Joshua resolved to serve the Lord with his house, Joshua xxiv: 15; Job sanctified his family, and thus did Job continually, Job i: 5; Abraham was commended for his fidelity in this matter, Gen. xviii: 19; Noah built an altar for his family, Gen. viii: 20; the patriarchs built altars wherever they resided, Gen. xii: 7, and xxxv: 1, 3, 7. Scripture is not silent respecting the neglect of this duty, Jeremiah x: 25:—'Pour out thy fury on the heathen that know thee not, and on the families that call not on thy name.' Would such a denunciation have been uttered for the neglect of family devotions, if God had not required the performance? That this duty should be performed daily, morning and evening, we have evidence from the appointment of the morning and evening sacrifices and services of old. Though the ceremonies of Divine worship have been changed, the worship itself has not. Former institutions of Divine worship remain in full force as to their substance and spirit, the ceremonial and typical form only being abolished. The appointment of morning and evening for Divine service was not typical—it was moral and substantial, Psalm xcii: 1, 2. The appointment of the sacrifices at the Temple was not a substitute for the moral service of the people, but a requisition of it throughout the tribes of Israel in their families, Luke i: 9, 10; 1 Kings viii: 37–40. Observe therefore and revere the Scripture admonitions on this subject; imitate in your practice the examples recommended, and you will find conformity to them and family devotions the same thing." The following passage on the delicate subject of instructing slaves, shows at once the courage and prudence of the author and his zeal for the glory of Christ and the salvation of men:

"On the subject of family education and family devotion, permit us to lay before you your obligations respecting your slaves: we do not detain you with admonitions to feed and clothe them: we are happy to say that the necessity of such admonitions is precluded as far as our observation extends. Nor is it our admonition at present to set them at unconditional liberty under present circumstances.* Nor is it our present design to discuss their natural right to liberty, or the absurdity of the supposition that this was ever forfeited by their suffering theft and sale by a barbarous conqueror, or the impossibility that a pecuniary compensation to one who never had a moral right over the person and liberty of the slave, should ever procure such a right to the purchaser; all which we hope we have no occasion to urge. Our present design is to urge what the law of God and sound reason testify, and your own consciences must acknowledge to be a duty—a present and imperative, but much neglected duty—the religious education of your slaves"

After obviating several objections to the duty, and showing by several Scriptures that the education of the poor afflicted creatures is an important duty, the author proceeds to urge to the performance in the following terms: "Your slaves have been taken from a land of moral darkness to a land of gospel light; but with what advantage to them, if in the midst of light they walk in darkness? Are they contented without gospel light? So are your children, so are all mankind by nature. But by the means of grace, and the

* That it is your duty to encourage a spirit of regular and well conducted emancipation, through the organ of civil government or otherwise, we do assert.

blessing of the Spirit, the unwilling are made willing; you cannot expect to find them willing in ignorance. Imitate then your Lord and Master, who sought the lost sheep. If you have the gospel and have tasted that the Lord is gracious, would you monopolize such a favor? Would you not be ready to say even to your servant, O taste and see that the Lord is good: come, I will teach you the fear of the Lord? Should not love to Christ induce you to extend the means of grace which you have enjoyed, in order to gain souls to him? How could you address one of them on a death bed, too ignorant to understand you? How could you put up a petition for the dying and expect a gracious hearing, when you have withheld that knowledge which the Holy Spirit blesses for the salvation of the soul? How can you see them approach their dreadful end, about to launch into eternal misery, and incapable of receiving instruction or consolation? How can you reflect on their end, without remorse and horror, remembering that they were committed to your care for instruction and government, and you betrayed your trust, using them only for your temporal interest. Brethren, ponder well these realities. Try these things by the word of God, and see what verdict conscience must return." From that part of the letter which treats of popular erroneous sentiments, a single paragraph is presented. "The position that we ought to admit those whom we judge to be Christians is plausible, but unfounded. The man is to be admonished as a brother whom we exclude from our communion, 2 Thess. iii: 14, 15. If we make grace in the heart the rule of admission, the door is set open for every deceiver—the purity of the church is denied to be an object of her regard, and the way is opened for the introduction of every error. According to this rule the gospel minister is necessitated either to reprove errors and sins from the pulpit, which he has indulged in admission to communion, or to prove unfaithful to his trust, by keeping back part of the counsel of God. Where truth is neglected and forgotten, piety must decay. How often does the Psalmist speak of his love to God's truth, and of his delight in it. But is it consistent with a holy love to Divine truth, with a knowledge of it and a sense of its importance, to neglect or yield it, because our neighbor loves it not, or does not believe it?"

The pastoral letter, at the contents of which we have glanced, was addressed to church members and others come to maturity of understanding. But he that feeds the sheep should feed the lambs also. The great Shepherd of the sheep requires this, John xxi: 15, and true policy requires it. That reformation must be ephemeral which overlooks the instruction and improvement of the rising generation. Our life on earth is but a shadow. The congregation that includes a hundred members, may, after the lapse of twenty years, have the same number or the double of it, but it will be found, on a careful comparison of the lists, that not more than one fourth of the original members are still remaining as component parts of the society. The youthful must therefore be the subjects of any improvement which it is desired to perpetuate. Assured of this, and recollecting that it is the express will of God that the fathers should make known his testimony and his law to their children, that the generation to come might know them, even the children which should be born, who should arise and declare them to their children, Mr. Anderson employed his leisure moments in preparing a system of questions on the Shorter Catechism of the Westminster Assembly. He intended by this work to assist parents in catechizing their children; but his principal object was to excite young persons seeking after the knowledge of Divine things, to think and inquire after the meaning of the words which they were accustomed to repeat. And accordingly his questions were mere questions. No answer was appended to them. Nothing at all was added to his questions, except a reference to some text of Scripture, which the pupil was under the necessity of hunting up and considering together with the text of the Shorter Catechism, that he might ascertain and return the true answer. When Mr. Anderson began this work, he perhaps intended nothing more than to prepare himself for catechizing with care the youth of his own charge. But when he had gone over the Assembly's Shorter Catechism, in the manner that has been noticed, he judged that the work might be useful to congregations and families generally, and accordingly he gave it to the public in the summer of 1826. With the questions and answers of the Shorter Catechism in large type, and Mr. Anderson's questions in smaller type, the work constitutes a volume of about two hundred pages, duodecimo. The edition published was small, comprising but eight hundred or perhaps a thousand copies, all of which were sold in a short time, except such copies as Mr. Anderson was pleased to distribute gratuitously. To what extent this little work was profitable to the people of the southern churches, it is not easy to say. The best means of instruction will not be attended with happy results, if they are neglected, and catechisms are too often treated with neglect. The writer, who about that time was commencing his ministry in the same Presbytery, is constrained to acknowledge that Mr. Anderson's Catechism was very useful to him, and in his judgment it is well calculated to assist both parents and children in the acquisition of saving knowledge. He that watereth, shall be watered himself, and no doubt Mr. Anderson was greatly benefited by his own labors. Whether he excogitated the questions, or collected them from the writings of others, on the same points, his writing down the questions, and searching out and considering the texts appended, must have resulted in increasing his familiarity with the principles of sacred truth, and with the Scripture testimonies on which they depend. The nature of the work precluded the display of keen discernment and of learned research, and all that is claimed for Mr. Anderson on the score of it, is that his heart was so set on doing good, that he condescended to become the teacher of babes, and having devised a means of aiding their studies, he carried it into execution with no inconsiderable labor, being excited and animated by no other motive besides the desire and hope of contributing to the improvement of many.

About the time that he began to prepare his Catechism, Mr. James Lyle, a licentiate of the Presbytery of Ohio, was ordained and installed as pastor of the congregations of Smyrna and Little River, the former in Chester, and the latter in Fairfield district, South Carolina. This addition to the ministerial force of the Presbytery, inured to Mr. Anderson's advantage, allowing him more time to devote to his Catechism and other studies, than he could otherwise have had. From the labor of traveling to supply the vacancies, he obtained additional relief by the ordination and installment of Mr. W. M. M'Elwee, as pastor of the congregations of Tirzah and Sharon, both in York district, South Carolina. The ordination took place at Sharon, on Thursday, the 1st day of April, 1827; Mr. Anderson preaching the sermon from John xxi: 15, 17; and leading in the prayer of consecration. In two or three weeks after this solemnity, Mr. Anderson, accompanied by the writer, set out to attend the meeting of the Associate Synod in the city of Pittsburgh. The journey was long, (the distance to Pittsburgh being five hundred and sixty or seventy miles,) and tedious, for there were no rail-roads in those days, nor even stage coaches on the required line: it was performed on horse-back, and occupied between ten and eleven weeks. But though the journey was tedious and wearisome, there was one circumstance of a redeeming character. It afforded abundant opportunities for friendly conference. Of the talk indulged in during that journey, one item is distinctly remembered. We were returning to the South. After many miles of wearisome travel among the defiles and steeps of the Blue Ridge, we mounted the last ana loftiest eminence, from which we have an extensive view of the Atlantic slope, in appearance a vast plain covered with living green, and at that juncture redolent with the flowers of the season. The writer felt and expressed delight in seeing once more the sunny South. Mr. Anderson seemed sad, and said in reply, *that it appeared to him, to be a dry and parched land.* How is that; are you not satisfied with your location? He answered, *the South has never seemed* to me as my home, but the land of my exile; and then went on to state a number of particular objections, of which the principal was the firm establishment of the peculiar institution. This item of conversation is related for the purpose of showing that though Mr. Anderson had been living in the South for several years, he was still a northern man in sentiment and feeling. We are apt to sympathize with the people among whom we dwell, and to fall in with their usages and way of thinking, and it has been supposed by some, that Mr. Anderson, by living in the South for a number of years, learned to sympathize with slave-holders, and with slavery itself. The supposition does him great injustice. He sympathized indeed with the Christian people of the South and cared for their souls, but the country he disliked, and the system of slave-holding he detested as an incubus on Church and State, and the fell destroyer of thousands. Not a great while after the conversation related above, during perhaps the following winter, slave-holding being the subject of conversation, Mr. Anderson declared to the writer, that were he the father of a family and the possessor of real estate in the Carolinas, he would regard it as his duty to prepare his will, and provide in the will that his family could have no use of his property, except in the way of selling it and conveying the proceeds beyond the limits of the slave-holding States. In the same conversation, or in some other about that time, having asked Mr. Anderson if his opposition to slave-holding was the reason of his continuing unmarried, he said in reply, that his opposition to slave-holding was one reason, and a principal reason, that he was unwilling to be more firmly tied to the South than he was at present.

In the spring of 1828 Mr. Anderson changed his lodgings from the hospitable mansion of Col. Grier, in Steel Creek, to the dwelling of Mr. John Wilson, in the congregation of Bethany. There was no dissension between Mr. Anderson and the Colonel or his family; nor were they weary of him, or he of them. Mr. Wilson was one of the elders of the Bethany branch, and remarkable for tender, fervent piety. His partner and children partook of the same spirit. Their dwelling and their company were inviting. But a regard for his health was the sole motive by which Mr. Anderson was prompted to make the exchange. He had been for some time troubled with febrile excitement, with want of appetite, and other symptoms of a diseased liver. The Colonel's habitation stood on a low, damp plain, two miles eastward of the Catawba river. Mr. Anderson thought that his location was in some measure the cause of his illness, and promised himself better health, in the more elevated site occupied by the Wilson family.

The Associate Synod of 1828 met in the city of Philadelphia, in the month of May. Neither Mr. Anderson nor any other member of the Presbytery of the Carolinas was in attendance, except the Rev. A. Heron, of Rockbridge county, Virginia. Measures were commenced in that Synodical meeting, which proved fatal to the congregations of the Carolina Presbytery—measures which might, perhaps, have been prevented, had Mr. Anderson been present. Mr. John K., a licentiate of the Presbytery of Miami, having spent the greater part of the preceding winter in the vacancies of the South, went up to the meeting; and though not entitled to a seat in Synod, he exerted a considerable influence. In conversation with the members, he told that the brethren in the South had many slaves, and that very few of the slaves were taught to read the holy Scriptures—that hardly any of them were church members—that in most of the families they were not brought into the house in the time of family worship—that the Act of 1811, in regard to slave-holding, was inoperative, &c. These reports, which were but too true, being handed from one to another, the attention of Synod was called to the subject of slave-holding by a particular member; and after some discussion, Synod appointed a committee to inquire and report at the next meeting, *whether further action in regard to slave-holding, was called for; and if in their judgment further action was called for, what that action should be.*

Mr. Anderson, though not present, was appointed one of the committee. The other members were the Rev. James Adams, of Green county, Ohio, and the Rev. David Carson, of Blount county, Tennessee. At the same meeting of Synod, Mr. Adams was appointed for five or six months on what was then called the Missouri Mission; and Mr. Anderson, with the view, perhaps, of allowing the committee an opportunity of meeting and consulting together, was appointed to supply Mr. Adams' pulpit for three months. Shortly after information of these appointments had reached the South, which was about the 1st of July, Mr. Anderson, in his new habitation, was taken with a severe bilious fever. His surviving the attack seemed for some time to be very doubtful; and his traveling, according to the appointment of Synod, was thought to be altogether impracticable. In answer to the prayers of many, the merciful Disposer of all things was pleased, however, to spare him, and to bring him up again from the gates of death. When he had regained a measure of strength, though still weak and pallid, he set out on horse-back, on a long journey of about eight hundred miles, in going out, and as many in returning. He started the last week of August, and returned towards the close of the year, much invigorated, though he had experienced several relapses in the course of his tour. Of his acceptableness to the brethren among whom he had been laboring, he was followed with a proof which was far from being pleasant to his many friends in the South. From Xenia to Massie's Creek, where he had preached statedly for three months, is but six miles. The Associate congregation of Xenia was at that time without a pastor. Many of the members resorted to Massie's Creek, and heard Mr. Anderson from Sabbath to Sabbath during his continuance there: all heard him occasionally in their own place of worship. Satisfied with his deportment, and with his ministerial gifts and qualifications, they petitioned the Presbytery of Miami for the moderation of a call, and concurred unanimously in calling Mr. Anderson to become their pastor. The call having been sustained by the Presbytery of Miami, was transmitted, in February or March, to the Presbytery of the Carolinas, for presentation. This proof of the high esteem entertained for Mr. Anderson by the brethren of the West was unpleasant to the people of the South, not because they thought him unworthy of esteem, but because they esteemed him so highly, and feared that the call from Xenia would issue in his removal. For this apprehension there were ample grounds. It was generally known that Mr. Anderson's health was not good, and that he attributed his bad health to the influence of the climate. It was known, too, that he did not regard with favor the *peculiar institution.* The writer, to whom Mr. Anderson had declared his dissatisfaction with the climate, and his dislike of slavery, frequently and earnestly, had scarcely a doubt that he would accept the call to Xenia, and be lost to the southern churches. The day of decision came round. The Presbytery of the Carolinas met at Steel Creek, on the first Tuesday of April. The members of the congregation of Steel Creek were generally in attendance. The people of Xenia were heard by their papers. The congregations of Bethany and Steel Creek were heard through their commissioners. Regarding the case as important and solemn in its consequences, the Presbytery directed a member to lead in prayer. The member designated prayed with tears and sobs, and all present were deeply affected. After prayer, the call was presented for acceptance or rejection. Mr. Anderson arose and announced, to the great relief and joy of all, *That as he did not* see that it was his duty to leave his present post, he declined the call to Xenia. From this account of the proceedings of that day, it may be inferred that Mr. Anderson reciprocated the affection of his southern friends, and was controlled in declining the call to Xenia by his feelings alone. Had the Presbytery and people of his charge manifested coldness and indifference, it is indeed probable that his determination would have been different from what it was. But from notes found among his papers, it appears that he had solemnly and prayerfully considered the matter of his removal before the Presbytery met, and had come to a determination respecting it.

In these times, ministers transfer themselves from one place to another so frequently, and with so little apparent consideration, that the ministry is fallen under reproach as a trade, which certain persons follow in one place or another, as seems most advantageous to themselves. It is but too probable that many ministers, in their removals, do not seriously consider whether they are following the line of duty or not. But Mr. Anderson examines carefully, as we would naturally expect a man of God to do. In his argumentation with himself, two principles are assumed; the one is, that it is sometimes the duty of a gospel minister to change the field of his labors; the other, that neither usefulness nor comfort can be reasonably expected unless the change be made in accordance with duty, or the will of God. Having placed himself on this foundation, doubtless a solid one, Mr. Anderson lifted his eyes to heaven, *looking to the great Counselor for light to show, and grace to choose the path of duty.* And besides praying for light, he endeavored to open his eyes and see, noticing and weighing the arguments *pro* and *con.* Among the considerations which he thought worthy of his attention, it is remarkable that there is no one respecting his own inclinations, and no one that has any reference to his worldly interest or credit. It seems to have been his judgment that such considerations should be disregarded in ordinary cases of the kind; and, beyond doubt, his determination to continue in the South was contrary to his inclination, as when he determined to tarry longer at Fort Meigs for the defence of the place.

During his tour to the West, Mr. Anderson met and conferred with the other members of the Committee on the subject of slave-holding. He had no angry disputations with the brethren, whom he esteemed very highly, yet he did not accord with them in judgment. Messrs. Adams and Carson agreed on a report to the Synod of 1829, in which Mr. Anderson could not concur. That the reader may understand how the parties stood, it is necessary to state that the Synod had carefully examined the subject of slave-holding in 1811, and had, after many prayers, concluded that slave-holding is a moral evil—that slave-holders in the Associate Church be required to emancipate their slaves, if the State in which they live admit of emancipation—that if the State forbid emancipation within its limits, masters may hold their slaves, not making merchandise of them, not ruling them with rigor, but with a parental sway, feeding and clothing them comfortably, instructing them in the principles of our holy religion, and treating them as though free, by giving them a reward for their work.

The report of the committee went further than this. It admits—

"1. That children born in a state of slavery, may be lawfully required to serve, with the consent of their parents, for a term of years sufficient to remunerate their masters for their support and education; and also, without the consent of their parents, if remuneration can be had in no other way.

"2. That persons of any color may, for their crimes, or for the payment of a just debt, be lawfully sold into a state of servitude for any term of years, or for life, yet not so as to affect posterity.

"3. That persons may be lawfully held in a state of servitude for a term of years, or for life, by virtue of a compact into which they have voluntarily entered.

"4. That persons who are held as slaves by the laws of the civil community, may be lawfully purchased, at their own request, and their services used by the purchaser, for a term of years, or for life, according to the agreement between the purchaser and the purchased.

"5. That persons who have been held as slaves may, for a term of years, be detained in a state of servitude, according to a rule of Church or State, tending to secure more effectually their emancipation, and their own or the community's future safety and prosperity."

The report maintains that the holding of human beings in bondage, is in all other cases sinful, and concludes with the following resolutions:

"1. That slavery be considered by this Synod a sin, not to be tolerated in any of the members of our communion.

"2. That the selling of a slave, as transferable property, by any person in our communion, is censurable.

"3. That the holding of a slave, in any case not specified in the above few particulars, is censurable.

"4. That measures be taken to procure the incorporation of a company, composed of certain persons to be chosen by Synod, for the purpose of legalizing the emancipation of slaves held by our members, (the duty of such incorporation to be explained in detail hereafter,) and that a committee be appointed to make arrangements to this effect."

These were the views of the majority of the committee, in which, as has been noticed, Mr. Anderson did not concur. Wherein he differed, and for what reasons, will be shown hereafter. At present I will merely state that Dr. John Anderson, whom Mr. Abraham Anderson had been accustomed from his youth to revere as a ripe scholar and a devout Christian, had vindicated that toleration of slave-holding granted in the Act of 1811 by several considerations. Dr. John Anderson had taught that private citizens should bear many hardships and wrongs, rather than disturb the peace and harmony of the society in which they live; and as citizens should pursue this meek and quiet course, so they should allow their colored neighbors to suffer wrong and temporal hardships, rather than disturb the peace and order of the community in attempts to relieve them. He had also taught that a private individual is not to be faulted for withholding civil rights and privileges from another, when it is not in his power to confer those rights and privileges on the other. These sentiments Mr. Anderson had imbibed in early life. He was by education, and perhaps by natural temperament, a conservative, and therefore slow to believe that the new wine is better than the old. It may be added, that living in the midst of the slave territory, Mr. Anderson was more fully acquainted with the obstacles in the way of emancipation than the other members of the committee could well be. They no doubt thought that their project could be carred into effect with advantage to the southern churches; but Mr. Anderson was fully apprized that the remedy, if applied, would prove the ruin of all the congregations belonging to the Presbytery of the Carolinas.

Mr. Anderson did not attend the meeting of Synod in 1829; and his objections not being known, the report of the majority of the committee was, without any considerable opposition, adopted as an overture, and handed down to the Presbyteries and Sessions for their judgment.

The overture came to the South with the minutes of 1829,

and was read by several ministers (if not all) to their congregations, though the public reading of such a paper was contrary to the law of the land. Many Seceders disapproved of the reading, and some of the citizens threatened the enforcement of the law, but no minister was molested.

The latter part of the summer of 1829 Mr. Anderson spent in Monroe county, Virginia, seeking health in the use of the mineral waters of that district. He returned before the meeting of Presbytery in October, somewhat improved. The attention of the Presbytery, at that meeting, was turned to the overture. After some remarks about the course which it was incumbent on the Presbytery to pursue, it was resolved unanimously to remonstrate against the overture, and Mr. Anderson was appointed to draught the remonstrance. In the course of the winter Mr. Anderson prepared a paper for that purpose, which, having been read in the spring meeting of 1830, the Presbytery adopted without altering so much as a word, and ordered the remonstrance to be forwarded and submitted to the Synod, to meet in the city of Philadelphia in the month of May. The writer carried up, and presented the document, and observed the impression produced by it. All attended while the paper was being read with evident interest. Irritation and dissatisfaction were visible in the countenances of some. When the reading was finished, a talented and influential member pronounced the remonstrance a very able document, said that he knew who was its author, and moved that a committee should be appointed to answer it. Others objected, and it was finally concluded to publish the remonstrance with the minutes of Synod, and to defer further action on the subject of slave-holding till the next meeting.

A great majority of the ministers and members of the Associate Church were, as they are still, earnestly opposed to slave-holding; and as he who opposes a particular method of removing an evil, is apt to be regarded by the earnest advocates of that method as favoring the evil and desiring the continuance of it, Mr. Anderson fell, in consequence of his able paper, under suspicion and reproach among the brethren in the North. It was concluded by many that the South had seduced him, and that he was bound with chains to the iron car of the slave-holders.

With the view of vindicating his reputation as an anti-slavery man, and showing at the same time his candor and courtesy in reasoning with opponents, and his great ability in handling a knotty, difficult question, the following extracts from the remonstrance are submitted for consideration:

"Far be it from us, (see minutes of 1830, page 35,) to defend either the principle or the practice of slavery, or to endeavor to effect in Synod even an unnecessary delay in removing the evil. Involuntary servitude is a sin, a heinous sin, and indefensible by the laws of nature or of revelation. It involves the nation in guilt whenever permitted by the government, but especially when it is maintained by legislative authority, and the chains of slavery are riveted by iniquitous laws. We are convinced that to our country, and especially to the slave States, slavery threatens moral, religious, and political ruin—that the native influence of this practice, and the judgments of God for this sin, have already produced many bitter fruits, and threaten much more—that even temporal happiness cannot long exist in the present state of things. We believe it is the duty of civil government to adopt measures for emancipation, and we view with grief and alarm their apathy on this subject. Infatuation has supervened; and providential threatenings only rouse our legislators, as Pharaoh of old, to multiply the chains of slavery and bind them faster.

"It may now be asked, after all these concessions, can you hesitate a moment about the duty of adopting the articles of the overture? We reply, as soon as the Synod shall find a practicable and lawful plan of emancipation, let these articles be adopted; but not till then. Sinful as slavery is, it is not more so than a plan of emancipation might be made to be. It is not every measure of escaping a sin that will acquit us of guilt. Shall we presume that our good intentions will justify whatever measures rashness, or mistake, might lead us to adopt? Shall we do evil, that good may come? The Synod, in 1811, were as anxious to effect the complete abolition of slavery as they are now; and nothing, we believe, but insurmountable obstacles, or at least what they judged such, led them to adopt the measures they did. If Divine Providence has since opened a door which they did not enjoy, or given us additional light, let us promptly improve our advantages. But it is possible we have lost sight of those obstacles which then checked their laudable designs, and obstacles which yet exist in all their force. It cannot, therefore, be improper to take a view of these impediments, that if they cannot be surmounted or removed, we may wait for Divine Providence to open our way; and if they can, that we may intelligently and deliberately lay our plans for doing so.

"In laying before Synod the difficulties to which we have alluded, we shall consider, in order, three methods of emancipation, which, as far as our knowledge extends, are the only methods that have been proposed, or that occur to us as possible:—*Colonization, transfer of the slaves to a free State, and emancipation at home.*

"The Colonization Society might afford some aid in effecting our object. But —(1.) The funds of that Society are as yet inadequate to such an extensive operation as we propose. (2.) Though some slave-holders might avail themselves of the privileges of that Society by advancing funds for the transportation of their own slaves, yet many masters could not command such funds. (3.) It is a condition with the Society, that the slaves be willing to go to their colony. Now a few might be willing to go, and if funds could be obtained, they might be emancipated. But some who are willing to go, could not be sent for want of funds; and those who are unwilling must, on this plan, remain in slavery. This method, therefore, cannot effect the complete abolition of slavery in our communion.

"The second plan of emancipation is to transfer the slaves to the free States. This plan is also attended with difficulties:

"1st. By this plan, slaves would not be free; they would be governed, but not represented; fixed by force and power in the lowest grade of society.

"2d. Many masters, who can support their slaves under their care, could not give them any means of subsistence, if put away.

"3d. There is reason to fear that such an influx of colored population into the free States as this measure proposes, would be prohibited.

"4th. Many masters would not be able to furnish the funds necessary to carry their slaves to a free State. Without some provision, therefore, by Synod to meet this difficulty, this method of emancipation must of necessity fail of effecting our object.

"5th. Though a master could afford the funds necessary to transfer his slaves to a free State, but would deny his ability, by what means could the church reduce her rules to practice? Could she undertake to examine the minuitæ of his estate, pronounce that he is able to transport his slaves at his own expense, and require him to do so under pain of suspension or excommunication? Synod could not, after aiding one master in emancipating his slaves, command another to do it at his own expense.

"6th. Many slaves are aged and infirm, and in most cases their masters could not provide for them without the services of the younger slaves.

"7th. Emancipation would not only be attended with loss, but in some cases with bankruptcy. It would place some masters on the pauper list, and make them dependent on the county funds. This might subject our measures to partial, and even to utter defeat by the State.

"8th. Many slaves are of such a character as not to warrant their masters to comply with the requisitions of free States in order to their admission; and as masters cannot be compelled to give their slaves freedom under this condition, such slaves must remain in servitude.

"9th. Many slaves would not be willing to go to Africa, or even to a free State. Not a few would be found of this description. To oblige them to go would be to interfere with their just rights, and still further curtail what the practice of slavery has curtailed too far. It would impose a punishment which the case does not seem to warrant. They would account it banishment to be removed, and would prefer perpetual slavery. To banish them from the soil and climate where all their endeared associations are, — to banish them for no crime, and when the necessity of the case is not imperious, would be substituting cruelty and injustice for kindness. They must by this measure be separated, not only from an endeared home, perhaps an endeared master, (the case is not uncommon,) but also from their relatives, when these are divided among several masters, as they generally are, and among masters who would not emancipate, and from whom the emancipator could not buy. It may, perhaps, be urged, in the spirit of the 3d preliminary of the overture, that those slaves who are unwilling to go to Africa, or elsewhere out of the slave States, having now the offer of freedom, may bind themselves to servitude, and the master be innocent. We reply, we think indeed the master would be innocent; not because he is by this compact free from the practice of slavery, but because, in taking this step, he can do no better. Therefore, though the master be innocent in such a compact, (the maxim, Of two moral evils, choose neither, to the contrary notwithstanding,) yet an object contemplated in the overture, the complete abolition of slavery in our communion, is not obtained. The slave, by whatever form of bond he obligates himself to his master while the State does not recognise his freedom, is in his master's power as much as ever, — he is a slave by the law of the State, and deprived of all his civil rights of which he was deprived before. He is, with all his offspring, liable to seizure for his master's debts, and liable to be claimed by legatees, even though by will and testament declared free in the State. Even though the master had bequeathed him privileges and immunities which the laws do not recognise, they all pass for nothing. These considerations show an inconsistency between the first five preliminaries in the overture, and a proposition which requires the Synod to take measures for putting it out of the power of any of our members to hold a slave in such a state, that he may be transferred as the property of the holder. All the cases admitted in these preliminaries leave the slave transferable, by either the master or the State.

"The third method of removing slavery from our communion, is emancipation in the State. Here we shall offer but one objection, which is, that the laws of the slave-holding States forbid such emancipation. A slave cannot be made free in a slave State. This plan, therefore, under existing laws, is impracticable, and must be rejected. But here we meet with a last resort, and if correct, an effectual measure for the complete abolition of slavery in our communion. It is proposed in the overture that if the laws of the State have cut off a rational prospect of liberating the slave, either immediately, or at any period nearly approaching, it then becomes the imperious duty of the individual slave-holder to free his own hands of the sin by relinquishing his unjust claim, and leaving teh guilt of it on the community. *By relinquishing his unjust claim,* we understand laying no claim whatsoever to the slave, — literally manumitting him. If this be not the meaning of the sentence quoted, we see no meaning in it at all. We are sorry to see this proposition seriously advanced; and still more sorry should we be, with all our abhorrence of slavery, to see it reduced to practice. We do consider it, under the circumstances with which slavery is at present connected, at war with the rules of morality. But as it may not appear to all as exceptionable as it does to us, we shall examine it more particularly.

"Let it be remembered that the inevitable consequence of quitting all claim to the slave, and leaving him in the slave State, which the proposition supposes, is perpetual slavery for him and his posterity under existing laws. Let us then examine the operation of this measure.

"1st. The measure proposed would confer no degree of favor on the slave; it would not restore his rights, render justice, nor amend his circumstances.

"2d. The measure proposed would be a profligate waste of the powers and privileges which slave-holders possess. All slave-holders have the power to use their slaves more humanely than the laws compel them to do, and more humanely than they are generally used throughout the slave States. They can teach, while others raise them in ignorance; they can feed and clothe, while others starve them. And if ever a time should come when the liberation of slaves would be possible, though not required by the State, by this one rash act in adopting the measure proposed, the power of benefiting the slave would be for ever lost. Does not moral justice require us to be more frugal of our power, than to throw it away to no purpose?

"3d. By the measure proposed we should be doing positive injury to the slave, exposing him to oppression, starvation, &c.

"4th. The proposition we are opposing virtually counteracts the second article of the overture, which forbids the sale of slaves. If we deliver over our servant to perpetual slavery, as this measure proposes, we do all that is evil in selling him.

"5th. By following the method proposed, we will not free our own hands of the sin of slavery. How shall we free our hands of this sin, by exposing our servants and their offspring to inevitable and perpetual slavery? Neither the laws of God nor of man, as far as we have discovered, have made a difference in the guilt of delivering and of receiving a stolen article, unless perhaps they furnish an inference, that the first is more criminal; nor between the guilt of inflicting an unjust punishment by our own hand, or by the hand of another. And by whatever circuitous method we do the one or the other, it is the same guilt. To deliver the slave, therefore, over to the civil law, to be sold according to its known regulations, is the same as to do it ourselves. David was as guilty of murdering Uriah by the hand of the Amorites, as though he had done it with his own hand."

After urging that the measure proposed would be unkind and cruel to the slaves, the remonstrance proceeds in the following terms, page 43—"We acknowledge that in the case under consideration the only alternatives are, to set the slave free from our hands into inevitable and perpetual slavery, or to retain him for the time in slavery to ourselves. Having rejected the former, we must adopt the latter. But here we are met by the formidable axiom, Of two moral evils, there is never a necessity to choose either. In the overture this axiom is immediately applied to the case before us. One would suppose the inference now is, Since there are two moral evils in our choice, slavery and the above alternative, we should choose neither, but adopt some other method of emancipation. This, however, does not appear to be the inference intended; but it is taken for granted that slavery, in all circumstances, is sinful, and that therefore by the axiom, this method of emancipation is not. Why not reverse the application of the axiom thus — The method of emancipation proposed is sinful, and therefore slavery, in comparison, is innocent? The truth of the axiom we do not deny, but we do think it is misapplied in the overture. The error lies in supposing an action sinful in certain circumstances, and therefore sinful in all circumstances. But some actions no circumstances can justify; others depend on circumstances for their justification or condemnation. To kill a neighbor is sinful in certain cases, and not in others; to labor on the Sabbath is sinful in certain cases, and not in others; so, while it is sinful to deprive a man of his liberty by violence, or to keep him in bondage by force and power when he might be free of his choice, it does not follow that to keep him in slavery till emancipation becomes possible, and till it may be done without cruelty and injustice, is also sinful."

What the Scriptures teach as to the matter on hand, is declared in the following language, page 46—"That the apostles did receive to the communion of the church both masters and servants, without requiring emancipation as a term of admission, we think cannot be denied. For proof of this we appeal to 1 Cor. vii: 20-24; Eph. vi: 5, 9. Now, what shall we do with these stubborn facts? Shall we evade them by saying, as in the overture, that it is not necessary to understand the name servant, so frequently used in the New Testament Scriptures, to mean slaves, while the term is frequently used to denote a hireling? This is irrelevant; for though we should acknowledge that the name servant frequently means hireling in the New Testament, yet if in any cases in which the apostles gave directions to masters and servants as such, and as members of the church, they used *it* to denote slaves, the question is decided. That the apostles did use the name servant in the latter sense, is clear from 1 Cor. vii: 21, and 1 Tim. vi: 1, 2."

On the question, How could the apostles tolerate slaveholding? the remonstrance states, page 47—"That it was not in their commission to lay the hand of miraculous power on the nations, and model their governments by the rules of holy Scripture; this work was left to the common providence of God, and the operation of moral and physical causes in his hand. While, therefore, the Roman government was permitted, in Divine Providence, to continue in the form it then had, and to maintain the laws it then did, entire emancipation was impossible. Slavery, then, was permitted in church members by the apostles, on the same principles for which we plead—on the principles of necessity; because the remedy was not in their hand."

These extracts are submitted for the purposes already mentioned, and not with any view, thought, or desire of reviving an old controversy.

The Synod of 1831 was appointed to meet in Canonsburg, Washington county, Pennsylvania. Mr. Anderson went up to the meeting, accompanied by the writer. We started about the middle of April, and traveled the same route as in 1827; but in carriages, and not on the saddle, as in 1827.

We reached Canonsburg towards the close of the third week. Our relatives and Christian friends rejoiced, and we rejoiced with them. Our joy, however, was moderated by frequent thoughts of our ecclesiastical position, and of the worse predicament in which we might, and perhaps would be, placed by the action of the coming Synod. We were not personally interested in the slave question. Neither of us claimed the distinction of being the master of a fellow-mortal. But as connected with our congregations and the congregations of our Presbytery, we were laid under a heavy charge by the overture of 1829. By a resolution of Synod adopted in 1830, we were required also to show the extent of our guilt; and from what we knew of northern sentiment, we feared that we had to encounter a vehement wind—such as would overturn and scatter our congregations, as the North-wester which fell upon us at the foot of the Blue Ridge overturned trees and fences, scattering the fragments in every direction. In this expectation we were disappointed. The Synod met on Wednesday, the 11th of May.

[Dr. Anderson's biographer then gives a full account of the action of the Synod on the subject of slavery—of the course pursued by Dr. Anderson and his southern brethren—of the final dissolution of their pastoral relations, and their removal from the southern States. Though the whole statement is interesting and affecting, and though many would read with admiration the strenuous efforts of Dr. Anderson in the Synod, and in the South, to avert the calamity of the complete breaking up of the Secession body in the southern States, we must omit this part of the narrative. Dr. Anderson, though decidedly opposed to slavery, would have guided the Secession Church to a wiser course, in the judgment of many, could his counsels have prevailed. But he conscientiously believed it his duty to submit to the decisions of his Synod. He left his large and interesting charge in Carolina, having received a call to a congregation in Washington county, New York. In his charge, consisting of Steel Creek and Bethany congregations, were two hundred and five slaves, of whom were sixty-nine readers, eight communicants, and one hundred and fifty-seven catechumens. Yet, from a sense of duty, having promised obedience to his brethren in the Lord, he withdrew, forever, from these poor sons of Ham.]

Before the meeting of Presbytery in 1833, a call came to hand from the Associate congregation of Hebron, Washington county, New York, which, being presented by the Presbytery, Mr. Anderson accepted of it, and demitted the pastoral care of Bethany and Steel Creek.

As soon as the weather and roads were in such a state as to admit of comfortable traveling, Mr. Anderson took his final leave of the South, and of his respectful, loving parishioners. No doubt there was heaviness on his part, and tears and sobs with them. Had he possessed the spirit of prophecy, he might have said as Paul did to the elders of Ephesus—"*And now, behold, I know that ye all, among whom I have gone preaching the kingdom of God, shall see my face no more;*" for such was the event. They saw him—they heard his solemn, affectionate voice no more.

He made his way to New York in safety, and commenced his ministerial career in Hebron about the 1st of June.

Mr. Anderson's new field of labor was much more limited than the former; and, of consequence, he had more time for reading and meditation, and being less exposed, his health was more uniform. He applied himself with earnestness and diligence to his proper work as a minister of Christ—preaching, visiting, catechizing, &c., as in the South; and, without any special efforts, he attained in a short time to a distinguished standing among the ministers and brethren of Cambridge Presbytery.

After the resignation of Professor John Anderson, of Service, in 1820, there were two schools of the prophets under the care of the Associate Synod,—one in Philadelphia, superintended by Rev. John Banks, D. D., and the other in Canonsburg, superintended by Rev. James Ramsey, D. D. Doctor Banks being removed by death in 1829, it was concluded to cast the two Seminaries into one, and place over the united Seminary two Professors,—the first to be called the Professor of Didactic and Polemic Theology, and the second to be styled Professor of Biblical Literature and Ecclesiastical History. The Synod of 1831 located the united Seminary in Canonsburg, and elected Dr. Ramsey to the Professorship of Didactic and Polemic Theology. The other Professorship was not filled at that time; but in the meeting of Synod at Canonsburg, in the fall of 1833, Rev. David Carson, of Blount county, Tennessee, was chosen to fill it. He acquiesced in the judgment of his brethren, and moved with his family to Canonsburg in June of 1834. He was thirty-three or four years of age. His ruddy complexion and robust form, promised a long life of usefulness. But the race is not to the swift, nor the battle to the strong. It was well, no doubt, that it was in his heart to build the house of the Lord. But he was not permitted to do the work. Before he had made an actual commencement in his department of official labor, he was removed to the land of silence. His death occurred about the 20th of September, 1834; and the Synod meeting shortly after in the city of Baltimore, proceeded to the election of another. Rev. Abraham Anderson was chosen; but he could not say that he would take the place, and discharge the duties of it according to the best of his ability. In the hope that time would remove his difficulties, the Synod allowed him to hold the call under consideration till the next meeting appointed to be held in Canonsburg, 1835. This indulgence was indicative of an earnest desire on the part of the Synod that Mr. Anderson would accept the post to which he was called, and he considered what was his duty in the case very seriously, and with earnest prayer for Divine direction. In a letter to the writer bearing date November 27th, 1834, the following language is used :—" One thing occurred at Synod in which I am much interested—my election to the Professorship. If I were to consult my own comfort only, I would decline. But I consider it a matter of weighty concern, and that its weight would require me to make greater sacrifices than any call I ever had before. The fear of a corrupt man, or a man under corrupt influence filling the place and poisoning the fountains and streams which water our vineyard, makes it no matter of indifference to me, and points out my accountability. The providences connected with the case have been remarkable. While I was in the Carolinas, and preferred almost anything to my situation there, and had nothing in these respects to hinder my acceptance of the call, it was not made. It was not made till I was settled, and in such circumstances, that I find it more difficult than I ever did, or would have found it before, to change my location. Thus Providence seems to say, that I must wade through difficulties, in duty or to duty—that I must not come to my duties with ease, or that it is not my duty to change my location at present. That it is through difficulties and trials I must engage in duty, and perform it, is, I am aware, no strange thing. It is the appointed way; and if this were all the hinderance it would be no argument against my removal, but I suspect some of my difficulties are insurmountable. Dear friend, I request both your counsels and your prayers. It is God only that can guide my judgment and my heart. I dread the influence of temptations from the world and of carnal views and affections. Such a dilemma presented, and to be determined under the influence of a carnal mind, is a fearful condition."

The great impediment was the very delicate health of Mrs. Anderson, which not changing for the better in the course of the time given for consideration, Mr. Anderson finally declined the office to which he had been appointed. Informed of his decision, the Synod of 1835 proceeded to the election of another, and fixed on the Rev. Thomas Beveridge, of Philadelphia, now Dr. Beveridge, who accepted the appointment, and is still serving the church in that office to the satisfaction of the Synod and students of theology.

The chair of Didactic Theology being vacant by the death of Dr. Martin, the Synod of 1847, sitting in Allegheny, proceeded to the choice of an incumbent. Mr. Anderson was chosen, and without hesitation accepted the office. No doubt he could have said as before, *Were I to consult my own comfort only, I would decline. But I consider this call a matter of weighty concern, and that its great weight requires me to make greater sacrifices than any call I ever had before.* (See Letter above.) The sacrifices involved in the undertaking were by no means trifling. He had to abandon a very commodious settlement at a considerable pecuniary loss. He had to forsake the society of his affectionate parishioners, of his relations in New York, and of his own family in some measure. He had to abandon that leisure and quietude which men at his stage of life (not far from sixty) generally prize, and to gird himself for labors in a new field,—labors that are difficult in their nature, and made more difficult as youthful candidates for the ministry are apt to be fastidious as to the manner in which their spiritual food is presented. Mr. Anderson, without doubt, counted the cost before he undertook the work, for such was his habit; and hence he did not afterwards draw back nor murmur at finding difficulties which he had not anticipated.

He repaired to Canonsburg about the 1st of November, the commencement of the theological session, leaving his wife, whose health was more uniform than in 1834, and his only child, a daughter twelve or thirteen years of age, with Mrs. Law, his wife's mother. He took boarding with Mr. Wm. M'Lelland, one of the companions and friends of his youth, and labored throughout the winter in his appropriate office, and in preaching the word to the congregation of Chartiers as a helper of Dr. Ramsey, now in debility through age. The writer attended the meeting of the Board at the close of the session, and spent some time with Mr. Anderson in his private study. He did not complain of his labors, nor of solicitude about his family, from which he was so distant, but seemed care-worn and heavy,—not so cheerful as in the sunny South, and I was therefore led to conclude that he felt his labors and privations, though he would not permit his lips to complain. The session closing with the month of March, Mr. Anderson returned to his family in New York. About this time the honorary degree of D. D. was conferred upon him by the Faculty and Board of Franklin College, in the State of Ohio.

Having in the course of the summer made some disposition of his property in New York, he returned with his family to Canonsburg in the month of October; and during the winter that followed he prosecuted his labors in the Seminary and in the pulpit, preaching about half the time for Dr. Ramsey, and on Sabbath nights alternately with his colleague in the hall of the Seminary.

Having procured an unimproved lot near the Seminary, he took upon himself the cares and anxieties of building in the summer of 1849. There was much to be done, and he so managed that all was done in a short time, and in good style. The result of the undertaking was a most commodious habitation, with its proper appurtenances. As we were returning from the meeting of Synod in Xenia, 1851, in a private and confidential interview the Doctor told me of one fact in regard to his bodily condition, by which I was led to apprehend that his earthly tabernacle was breaking down. He preserved, however, his usual healthy appearance, and continued to prosecute his work with unabated energy. In the fall of that year he took upon himself an additional burden of cares and labors. A small congregation on Miller's Run, five miles from Canonsburg, called him and his colleague, Dr. Beveridge, to be their conjoint pastors; and Dr. Anderson, in conjunction with Dr. Beveridge, accepted the call, and continued in the duties involved till near the end of his course. Dr. Anderson was in easy, and even affluent circumstances. He was not impelled to this undertaking by the necessities of his family, nor by the love of filthy lucre, but by a sense of duty and the delight he experienced in using his gifts for the benefit of others. He was well apprized that it was his duty to lay out his talents, and not bury them; and he delighted in preaching the word to an humble, attentive people, and in circulating among such a people and instructing them around their own hearths.

The writer remembers distinctly of his saying in a private interview, not long after the acceptance of that call—"*I do like to preach.*" His sense of duty, and the pleasure he found in pastoral duties were, then, the principal motives of that undertaking. It is probable, however, that he took into view the necessity of exercise in the open air, and thought that the exercise demanded by duty in the congregation would redound to his advantage.

Not long after Professors Anderson and Beveridge had taken upon them the pastoral care of Miller's Run, the Associate Synod reduced the theological course, which had been spread over four years, to three years of two sessions each, five months in the winter, as before, and three in the summer. This arrangement left to the Professors but little time for relaxation. But still Dr. Anderson went on in his course, and presented no visible signs of wearing out till August, 1854, when he was taken suddenly with the usual symptoms of gravel, and suffered exceedingly for twelve or fifteen days. His complaint was never removed altogether; but being partially relieved, he returned, after three or four weeks' confinement, to the duties of his calling. In October he maintained his erect attitude of body and his usual complexion. In January there was no visible change, except a certain snowy whiteness of his forehead and temples, in which, as the writer imagined, the sentence of death was legible. In a private interview at the time just mentioned, he spoke without reserve of his bodily condition, stating that he suffered daily, and that his sufferings were at times excruciating,—that the cause was not *stone*, but some other acrid humor thrown upon the tender organs. This judgment respecting the nature of his ailment was correct. It was at length fully ascertained that the immediate cause of his sufferings and death was chronic cystitis, attended with irritation and stricture of the urethra. How, under these painful circumstances, he preserved his composure of mind and energy of spirit, and went on with his duties in the Seminary, I cannot show more distinctly than in the language of Dr. Beveridge, who was with him daily. "During the last winter of his life," says the Doctor, in a letter lately received, "he suffered exceedingly from the disease which at last terminated his days, but he persevered in meeting with the students till the close of the session. Their last meeting with him was in his own house; and their general impression at the time was, that it would be the last. Towards the close of the winter, he limited himself in these meetings to an hour. Frequently, however, some of the students, who were not aware of the nature of his disease, would detain him after he had finished his lecture to obtain his instructions on some subject which was engaging their attention; and such was his kindness and self-denial, that he often allowed himself to be detained so long that when he returned to his house he would continue for some time in an agony." That in such circumstances he not only attempted his daily duties, but persevered and went through them, is a sufficient proof that he was possessed of a strong will and an indomitable spirit. As to his method of teaching theology during his last and other sessions, Dr. Beveridge states in the same letter:—"That taking Mark's Medulla for the text-book, (as his predecessors had done,) he embodied in a series of questions whatever he regarded as valuable in the Compend, adding when there seemed to be occasion for it, and correcting what he disapproved. The written questions and their answers did not, however, comprise all his instructions. As occasions appeared to require, he enlarged on different subjects. This he did especially when he found any point not thoroughly comprehended by the students, or when a question was raised by any of them respecting some point of doctrine; and these unpremeditated remarks were considered by the students as the most valuable of his instructions. His lectures were greatly esteemed by the young gentlemen for whose use they were prepared; and having been solicited by them to give them to the public, he had made some preparation for doing so." It may be stated here, though it be not chronologically in order, that the portion of Dr. Anderson's lectures which health and life did not permit him to review and correct for the press, has been re-written by the Rev. T. H. Beveridge, of Philadelphia, and the work is published. The Christian community will therefore have the opportunity of judging of Dr. Anderson's ability and soundness as a theologian, and of his aptness to teach. As a copy of the work has not yet come into the writer's hands, he cannot offer his opinion in regard to its merits. But a more competent judge speaks in terms of high commendation. "The work," says Dr. Cooper, editor of the Repository, "while it cannot fail to be a very valuable guide to theological students, will prove to them, and all others who may make use of it, a rich fund of valuable and varied information on the doctrines of our holy religion. Let no one decline purchasing the work from the fear that he may not be able to understand it, or that it is not adapted to the general reader. On some accounts it will be found peculiarly acceptable and useful to private members of the church. The interrogatory form which characterizes these lectures, is well calculated to arrest attention, and bring out the point clearly and distinctly before the mind. We feel rejoiced that it has been presented to the public, as we think it, on the whole, admirably calculated to diffuse throughout the church sound Scriptural principles, and to establish our people, and all who may read it, in the faith of our holy profession."—*Rep.* vol. xv., p. 442.

From this digression we return. It was faintly hoped at the close of the session, (March, 1855,) that being released from care and fatigue, Dr. Anderson would recover from his weakness, and see some years of comfort and usefulness. But his sufferings were not abated; and under the genial warmth of the dawning summer, his symptoms became more aggravated. Having taught others how to live and how to die, he was not amazed with horror, nor overwhelmed with grief,—he preserved his usual serenity of countenance and equanimity of mind. He manifested, however, a lively concern about eternal things. After hearing his own statement about his bodily condition in the month of January, the writer took the liberty of making some remarks about the grounds of faith and its happy influence in tranquillizing the mind and heart in trying times—observing, among other things, that if we had the lively, confiding faith of Paul, we would say as he did—"I know in whom I have believed, and that he is able to keep that which I have committed to him; I have finished my course, I have kept the faith; henceforth there is laid up for me a crown of righteousness," &c. There was no thought of being useful to the Doctor, except in the way of stirring up his pure mind by putting him in remembrance; yet he took a lively interest in the conversation, and spoke of it in the month of March, regretting that it had been interrupted by the coming of ———, a much esteemed friend, whom he said he had never been sorry to see coming into his house except in that instance.

The following statements respecting the exercise of Dr. Anderson in preparation for his approaching dissolution, are derived from the letter of Dr. Beveridge, extracts from which have been already given:—"About four weeks before his death, when I rose to leave him he requested me to sit down, that we might have some conversation in respect to spiritual things, and particularly in reference to death. He stated, in substance, that he hoped somewhat for recovery, but thought his case doubtful. Among other things which he mentioned as yielding him satisfaction as an evidence of the reality of grace, was perseverance for a long time in the way of righteousness. The righteous shall hold on his way. I recollect, also, that he expressed himself much pleased with some remarks I made to him about the determination of the will to what is right, even when there may be much disturbance of the affections, as when a man consents to the amputation of a limb, while his whole frame shudders at the thought of parting with it; his will is to lose the limb, but his feelings are all opposed to his will; so in crucifying the flesh, the will is to give up right hands and right eyes—to give up all for Christ, but the affections are often strongly drawn in a contrary direction."

We come to the closing scene, the account of which is taken chiefly from a letter of Dr. Beveridge to his son, Rev. Thomas H. Beveridge, of Philadelphia, dated the 8th of May, 1855:—

"Our dear brother, Dr. Anderson, is still living, but no one entertains the least hope of his recovery. On the last Sabbath of April, nine days ago, he was seized with a chill: he was somewhat better on Monday. He continued, however, to suffer a good deal on Tuesday and Wednesday. On Thursday morning I was sent for: he was supposed to be dying. He recovered somewhat during the day. I called as soon as I returned from Miller's Run, (where I had preached,) and found him sinking. On Tuesday I was again sent for, about noon, when he was once more thought to be dying. Stayed with him that evening and night. He was sensible, though not able to do much more than answer questions. On Friday, or perhaps Thursday, I asked him if he knew that he was dying. He replied that he did. I asked him if he found himself prepared to leave the world. His reply was that he trusted that he was ready. About 2 o'clock of Saturday morning, Dr. M'Elwee arrived. Dr. Anderson had apparently been inattentive to any thing for some time; but as his brother M'Elwee approached the bed, and asked if he knew him, Dr. Anderson raised himself up with a sudden start, calling out as he did so, 'M'Elwee, M'Elwee, M'Elwee!' he threw his arms around him, and drew him down to his breast, where he held him till we were obliged to remove his hands, to give Dr. M'Elwee his liberty." He seemed exceedingly gratified, and was induced to take some water, by which the clamminess of his mouth was removed, and he was able for some time to speak more distinctly. About 10 o'clock, Saturday afternoon, he fell into an agony of pain. His countenance became distorted, he tossed his head rapidly from one side to the other, and flung his arms violently in every direction, crying out as he did so, "Oh, me! Oh, me! What shall I do? What shall I do? I want strength — I want strength — I have no strength!" The writer presented himself before his face, and repeated the text, "My grace is sufficient for thee, for my strength is made perfect in weakness." The Doctor looked up with a steady, pleasant eye, and repeated the latter part of the text, "*My strength is made perfect in weakness.*" "Yes," said the writer, "trust in him, and you will find it so." He made no answer, but became calm, and lay quietly till about 2 o'clock in the afternoon, when the writer, having the Lord's Supper on hand, was obliged to leave. "On Saturday night," continues Dr. Beveridge, "his brother William came to see him, and he manifested a like gratification, and in the same way, when he recognised him. He appeared also gratified to find Dr. Hanna and other friends around him. I stayed with him all day on Saturday, leaving Dr. Hanna to preach and attend to the other services of the day at Miller's Run. On Sabbath I was obliged to leave him, and on Monday also I was at Miller's Run. During all this time, and indeed from Thursday till the present time, his sufferings have been extreme beyond any I have ever before witnessed, in intensity and duration. They have been such as almost to frighten one in relation to the last conflict. I hope, however, it will not last much longer. He has swallowed nothing for several days, and cannot even bear to have his parched lips wet with water.

"P. S. — 12 o'clock. Dr. Anderson breathed his last about half after 10 o'clock, and is to be buried to-morrow at 2 o'clock. He was sixty-six years of age last December."

He was accordingly interred, on the 9th of May, in the grave-yard of the Associate congregation of Chartiers, wherein his parents and some other relations had been previously laid. The company that followed his body to its long home was very large; and that home, through the affection of his family, has been marked by the erection of a rich but modest monument of marble. On the front of the shaft is "Anderson," the family name; on the south side of the basis is a simple inscription, which announces the time of his birth, and the time of his death; and on the north side is a text of Scripture expressive of the hope which animated Dr. Anderson while living, and comforts the hearts of surviving friends in regard to his death. The text is that in Rev. xiv: 13—"Blessed are the dead that die in the Lord from henceforth; yea, saith the Spirit, that they may rest from their labors; and their works do follow them."

Dr. Anderson's exterior was large, massive, and comely; and though large bodies and little souls are often conjoined, in this case the glory within was equal or superior to the expectations inspired by the outward form. He was able to accomplish much in a little time. Though twenty-four years of age when he commenced his academical studies, yet in the course of a few years he was equal and superior to many others who had been prosecuting those studies from their childhood. While others studied divinity, he studied divinity and medicine, and performed all the tedious duties of Professor of Languages in Jefferson College. This mental activity, and the fruit of it, much done in a little time, was visible in all the different stages of his career. What time he usually employed in preparing for the Sabbath I know not; but if an emergency required it, he could collect and arrange the materials of a sermon in a very short time. He was not so remarkable, however, for the activity of his mental operations, as for the compass and extent of his vision. As a man of the smallest stature, standing near an ant-hill, can survey it on all sides at one and the same time, so he seemed to tower above the subject which he had occasion to handle, and to view all its different sides at once, with all the objections which might be brought against the view which he maintained. This mounting above his subject was discernible in all his public discourses, and frequently in his conversation. An elderly man in the South, connected with the General Assembly of the Old School, heard Dr. Anderson occasionally, and compared him to a great bar-shear, which makes a wide furrow and buries all the weeds out of sight.

To a strong, well-balanced mind, were added, in the case of Dr. Anderson, a diligent spirit, and the art of gathering up fragments of time and bits of opportunity, and turning them to some good account. In camp he found time to write a little book, though he had not turned his attention to literary studies, and wanted all the common conveniences for writing. In after life his opportunities were better, and he improved them with equal diligence. It does not appear that he kept a diary; but he kept a note-book, in which he recorded, with some remarks, any text with which his mind was impressed in reading; and when his reflections did not lead him to fix on some particular subject for the Sabbath, he had recourse to this storehouse for assistance.

To an industrious spirit was added the love of order. His books and papers were kept in their proper places. The parts of his apparel were properly disposed; and his expenditures were not suffered to flow out at random. He noted in a little book the incomes and outlayings of a year. At the end of the year he marked the paper, and laid it by, and began anew. The love of order and convenience was, in short, conspicuous in every thing about him; in his garden, yard, and stable, as well as in his dwelling.

The result of his well-directed industry was riches in knowledge: his library was, indeed, not very large; but being of an observing, penetrating mind, and persevering spirit, what he studied was well studied. He could read a Latin system of divinity almost as freely as common English. He was so familiar with the Greek of the New Testament, that in family worship, in his own house, he read the chapter directly from the original text. He had a good acquaintance with the Hebrew of the Old Testament, and with ancient and modern history, with the principles of our republican government and of the common law. He was a good physician in all ordinary cases, and not ignorant of chemistry, nor of agriculture or architecture. He was well acquainted with human nature; and knew very generally, before the trial of a particular measure, whether it would be borne or rejected with indignation. Men of vigorous powers and great learning are sometimes destitute of common sense, but it was never supposed by any of his acquaintances that Dr. Anderson was deficient in that respect. Common sense and prudence were conspicuous in all that he said and did.

Great abilities and rich acquirements are often attended with a highly supercilious spirit, that unfits the possessor for usefulness in the world. But Dr. Anderson was humble and patient. He thought it no degradation to leave his seat in college, and ride through the country preaching the gospel to the poor and ignorant; and when settled in a pastoral charge, he was not above preaching from house to house, or visiting the poor in their affliction. A man whose gifts are excellent, may be in a great measure useless through lack of the principles that should guide him in the exercise of his gifts, and excite him to use them for the benefit of others. He may be without zeal for the glory of God and the cause of righteousness, and without love for his fellow-creatures. But Dr. Anderson was not in this unhappy case. He was very zealous for the Lord God of hosts, and towards men he was full of kindness. When, in the commencement of my ministry, I told him of any difficulty, or discouragement, or cause of perplexity, however trifling the thing was, he never made light of it, but listened with fixed attention; and when he had comprehended the case, he applied himself to the labor of helping me with as much earnestness as if I had been his own son. His tenderness was very visible in his intercourse with Mrs. Anderson and his daughter; and Dr. Beveridge, his colleague in the Seminary, witnesses that towards the students he showed all the kindness of a father particularly when any of them were under affliction. At first sight his lofty head and stern countenance led me to suspect that he was without tender feelings; and that though I might esteem, I could not love him. But first impressions are often fallacious. "Very pleasant hast thou been unto me, my brother. Thy love to me was wonderful, passing the love of women." Many good men will wound the feelings of a friend in pursuit of a jest and a laugh. But Dr. Anderson's tenderness forbade him to do so.

Some, who are not vicious, will through weakness or inconsiderateness, reveal what has been communicated to them in the confidence of friendship; and those who will make trouble for their friends intentionally, or inadvertently, are so many in all the walks of life, that the royal preacher inquires after a faithful man, and hints that it is hard to find such a man. "A faithful man, who can find?" Dr. Anderson obtained mercy to be faithful in all his relations. He was an intelligent, constant friend, and wise counselor; and the writer has often felt thankful that being such, Divine Providence had brought us into contact and fellowship.

The good qualities already noticed, were enhanced by honesty and sincerity. Too many magnify whatever they have occasion to speak of, but his communications were yea, yea, nay, nay; and whether he commended or faulted, his words were the just exponents of his thoughts. If he had offered a measure to the Presbytery or Synod, and a brother offered something better, he would abandon his own measure and maintain the substitute. He did nothing through strife or vainglory. He never spoke that others might hear how well he could speak, nor continued to harangue and reason for the sake of victory. He was, no doubt, pleased to possess the esteem of his fellow-men, but direct attempts to win popular favor, his honesty and sense of dignity would not allow him to make. He was free from that ambition which is ever striving to shine with such lustre as to throw all others into the shade, and from that bitterness of soul which gives birth to envy. If a brother in the ministry succeeded in riveting the attention of the people more closely than he had done himself, Dr. Anderson was not made restless and uneasy, nor stirred up to speak disparagingly of his brother, but rather to praise and thank the Most High for bestowing such gifts on men. To this nobleness of spirit, Dr. Beveridge, his colleague in the Seminary and in the pastorate of Miller's Run, bears witness, stating in a letter lately received, that some of the people of Miller's Run preferred Dr. Anderson, and some himself—that Dr. Anderson noticed their preferences, and spoke of them in private interviews with as much indifference as if he had been no way interested.

Weight was given to Dr. Anderson's instructions, public and private, by his habitual gravity. He was indeed affable and cheerful, and could laugh heartily when there was a just occasion. But by nature or grace, or both combined, he was estranged from levity. His speech was very generally seasoned with salt, and good to the use of edifying. I recollect but one laughable story of his telling, and that bore somewhat against himself.

He was lodging with a worthy pair of elderly Scotch people in Sterling congregation, Iredell county, North Carolina, on the night before the sacramental fast. He spoke during the evening of the sad declension of religion, and as an instance noticed the utter disregard of fast days by many; and the general neglect of every thing like fasting, by many who profess to sanctify the day. It did not occur to him to state, as was his belief, that on a day of fasting, worshipers should not indulge in table comforts as on other days, but take merely a little of something plain and simple, for necessary sustenance. The morning having come, he walked out to a grove, and spent an hour or more in prayer and study. He returned, expecting to be invited to the breakfast table, but was asked to lead in worship. Worship being over, he sat for some time and conversed with the head of the family. He went to the grove again, tarried a good while, and returned, confidently expecting that a frugal repast was in readiness for him. But instead of that the horses were saddled for going to the church, and the old lady had adjusted her bonnet and shawl. As soon as he entered the house, she accosted him very kindly, saying—"Now, Mr. Anderson, it is too much to go all day without eating any thing at all: having to preach two sermons, you will faint before you are through with them. Will you not have a little of something?" He replied—"To be sure I will, if I can get it." So she laid off her bonnet, and in a few moments invited him to a cold repast. While relating this bit of his experience, the Doctor laughed very heartily. It was not, however, a vain story. All may easily learn from it that the man of God should rightly divide the word of truth, showing what is right and proper, as well as that which is reprehensible and to be avoided.

That persons who have not had the happiness of seeing Dr. Anderson in the pulpit may have some idea of him as a preacher, it is necessary to state that though he was large and strong, his bodily organization was such that he could only speak in a conversational tone. His pronunciation being distinct, he was nevertheless heard with ease in a large assembly. It must be stated further, that he had one mental peculiarity: while his memory was grasping and retentive of ideas, he had less ability than the generality of men to remember and repeat sentences. At the commencement of his ministry he wrote his sermons at full length, as young ministers of the Associate Church generally do, but it took him a whole week to commit a sermon, and after so much labor he was hampered in the delivery. He concluded, after a few trials, that if he could not preach except in this way, it would be necessary for him to abandon the ministry. The plan on which he fell, was that of writing down the heads and particular divisions, with a few sentences under each division indicating the line of illustration to be pursued. In this way he preached with more ease and comfort, and in this way he continued to preach. Frequently, indeed, he wrote his sermon at full length; but in preparing to preach it, he did no more than make himself familiar with the line of thoughts; and thus, while the matter was premeditated, the language was extemporaneous.

It may be stated further, that in taste and judgment, Dr. Anderson was opposed to ornate discourses and rhetorical flourishes in the sacred desk. He often quoted, with approbation, the famous lines of Cowper:—

"What, will a man play tricks? Will he indulge
A silly, fond conceit of his fair form,
And just proportion, fashionable mien,
And pretty face, in presence of his God?
Or will he seek to dazzle me with tropes,
And play his brilliant parts before my eyes,
When I am hungry for the bread of life?
* * * * * * *
I seek divine simplicity in him
Who handles things divine; and all beside,
Though learned with labor, and though much admired
By curious eyes, and judgments ill informed,
To me is odious."

While, therefore, Dr. Anderson's preaching was, as to the matter, solid and rich, in respect of the language and style of delivery, it was very plain and simple. Epithets were not piled upon epithets, nor one bright comparison upon another. His hearers were not amused with graphic descriptions of persons and scenes, nor astonished at times with a torrent of diction and feeling. He was not flippant nor drawling, but flowed with an evenly tenor, as the clear stream of a prolific fountain. His able thoughts flowing immediately from his own mind, and enforced by the countenance of sincerity itself, generally commanded the attention of hearers, though the words were plain, and perhaps for that very reason. In the body of his sermon, what he ever aimed at was to manifest some point of truth, or to refute some error, and his arguments were plain and cogent. In the conclusion he appealed to the consciences of his hearers, and appealed conscience itself to the tribunal of the great Judge; and these appeals were always solemn, and often very impressive.

His many excellencies were more conspicuous on the floor of Synod than in the pulpit. In a time of a heat and excitement, his calm, dignified mien, and gentle voice, were as oil on the troubled waters. When darkness brooded over the Assembly, many not able to see the point at issue, his cool, judge-like statement of the matter, and plain arguments in behalf of the truth, were often as a bright light kindled up in a dark place. He was eminently fitted for the chair of Didactic and Polemic Theology. His great intellectual ability and solid learning, his dignity of appearance, and constant propriety of conduct, his condescending kindness and patience, made him all that could be desired in that important post.

It need scarcely be added that he was a man of piety; for what is Christian piety but the harmonious meeting of those fruits of righteousness which we have been contemplating? Of his sincere piety there are many other evidences besides that evidence which he mentioned himself to Dr. Beveridge as one that afforded him some consolation. Only two of the many shall be specified. He loved the truth of the gospel, and stood by it in the face of opposition and reproach; and he loved the word of truth—the Holy Scriptures. When the writer had accepted of a pastoral charge in the Presbytery of the Carolinas, though our dwelling-places were thirty miles apart, he proposed that we should meet once a month for reading a portion of Scripture, and offering such remarks as might occur to us, or we should be able to collect; and it appears that he bound himself to read so much of the word daily in private as would serve to take him quite through in the course of the year. His great sufferings in the close of his life are no sign or proof that he was not right in heart with God. Christ came to his beloved disciples in a storm, and they were exceedingly distressed; and we are informed in the word of truth that grace is given to every one to profit withal; that is, to be exercised to the glory of God and the benefit of others; and how could the excellent graces, faith, courage, and patience, be exercised and made manifest without some very sharp trials? Mr. Boston says:—"It is very rare, I suppose, that any of God's children have something more than ordinary about them to their advantage, but they get something more than ordinary to try them. Of all the patriarchs there was not one that had more divine manifestations, or so many as Jacob, nor so many and great afflictions either. Of all the sons of Jacob there was none so highly raised and useful as Joseph, and none so afflicted. Heman was a man of more than ordinary reach, and so of afflictions."—*Completed Works,* vol. vi., p. 650. What the writer saw himself of the terrible agonies of Dr. Anderson, (bodily agonies, for they were confined to the body,) led him to these reflections at the time. It is the lambs which the Good Shepherd gathers with his arms and carries in his bosom, and therefore "Let not the wise man glory in his wisdom, nor the mighty man in his power;" he will be apt to need all the wisdom and power which he possesses, and perhaps more. I was convinced, too, of the perfect folly of deferring preparation for death till death comes, and made in a manner to hear the word sounding from Heaven, "If the righteous scarcely be saved, where shall the wicked and ungodly appear?" Heaven is sometimes called rest; and if the Doctor's released spirit went to heaven, as is confidently hoped, how sweet was the perfect rest, and how light and trifling do all the labors and torments of the way now appear! John xvi: 21, 22.

That this imperfect exhibition of the life and character of one of the precious sons of Zion may serve to stir up some others to follow him even as he followed Christ, is the earnest desire and prayer of the writer.

W. M. M'ELWEE.

MEMOIR

OF THE LATE

REV. JOHN H. KENNEDY, A. M.

Professor of Mathematics and Natural History in Jefferson College, from April, 1830, till his death, December 15th, 1840.

BY THE LATE REV. M. BROWN, D. D.
President of Jefferson College.

[*First published in connection with a sermon delivered in the College Chapel, December 27th, 1840, and printed in Pittsburgh,* 1841.]

Rev. John H. Kennedy was descended from a very respectable and pious ancestry. James Kennedy, his grandfather, emigrated from Ireland, and settled, first in New Jersey, and afterwards in Pequa, Lancaster county, Pennsylvania, where some of the family still reside. Rev. Robert Kennedy, the father of the deceased, has been for many years in the ministry, and has sustained a very high standing among his brethren, for talents, learning, and respectability. In the full vigor of body and mind, he still lives to mourn the loss of his beloved son.

John Herron, Esq., the maternal grandfather, lived and died on "Herron's Branch," Franklin county. Of his numerous family, the only survivor is Francis Herron, D. D., who was the eldest child. At the house of this venerated grandfather, John H. Kennedy was born, November 11, 1801. His mother (Jane Herron) was, in the mysterious providence of God, removed by death, when John, her eldest son, was eighteen months old. After the death of his mother, he lived in his grandfather's family until his fifth year. During this period his health was very delicate, and little hope was entertained that he should attain to manhood. His recollections of his grandfather, and his residence in his family, were of the most pleasing kind. It was, he remarks, his "vale of Tempe;" and the time spent there, his "Saturnalia." About the close of his fifth year he was taken home by his father, who had married a second wife. He was early sent to school, but was not so fond of study as of play, and especially such sports as required vigorous exertion. These, though often exposing him to danger, and sometimes to injury, contributed to that remarkable health which he enjoyed until the last year of his life.

In his ninth or tenth year he commenced the Latin grammar with his fathor, under whose instruction he studied the Latin and Greek languages.

Living in a retired place in the country, and without any young associates and class-mates to stimulate him, he had great aversion to study, and attended to it as an irksome task until his fifteenth year.

As to his religious views and feelings during this period, he had not experienced any special religious impressions; but being favored with careful religious instruction, he was restrained from vicious excesses, was sometimes thoughtful, and generally conscientious in an external observance of the Sabbath, and religious institutions. He states that he does not remember ever to have told a lie in his life; nor was he ever guilty of profaneness, in the common acceptation of the term—so important and powerful is the influence of early religious instruction, even while the heart is devoid of all holy principles, and entirely destitute of all relish or taste for spiritual things. In his fifteenth year his father removed from Franklin county to Cumberland, in Maryland, where he took charge of an academy, and was at the same time pastor of a congregation. There he was introduced to new scenes, and exposed to new and various temptations, from witnessing profaneness, Sabbath-breaking, and various forms of vice and dissipation which prevailed in the place. These influences would have proved ruinous had he not experienced the restraints of a religious education; and though prevented from going to the same vicious excesses as others, yet he suffered great injury from these unhallowed influences. He became "hardened through the deceitfulness of sin." "For the space of two years," he writes, "I wholly restrained prayer before God, repined at parental authority, and was regardless of almost every thing but self-gratification."

We now come to a period of his life somewhat peculiar. "This," he remarks, "was the period when I may almost say, 'after the straitest sect, I lived a Pharisee.'" Like other sinners, he had often purposed to amend "at some more convenient season," but did not mean to commence so early and so vigorously as he now was constrained to do.

He was in his sixteenth year when "this twilight of the day-spring from on high" commenced. Immediately after going to bed, a powerful impression was made on his mind, with regard to the danger of his condition. This alarm was not occasioned by any particular sin, recently committed; but by a sense of the guilt and danger of prevailing thoughtlessness and irreligion. The necessity and nature of repentance seems not to have occurred; but the conviction was irresistible, that he must *amend*, and that without delay. The duty of immediately resuming prayer, which he had so long neglected, was presented to his mind, but he concluded it would be safest to *reform* first, else his prayers would not be acceptable. "Such," he adds, "were my reasonings and resolutions; such my entire ignorance of my own helplessness and depravity; and it may be well asked, 'can any good thing come out of an experience, in its commencement, so much at variance with every feature of true piety?' The resolutions formed did not pass away, as 'the morning cloud and early dew;' for God was verily here, though I knew it not, and had erected *no* altar to his praise." The reformation contemplated continued, and was extended much further and deeper than was at first anticipated, "though the light he had was like moon-light, devoid of heat, and which casts a disheartening gloom over whatever it partially illuminates." In the midst of all this darkness conscience was faithful at its post, and increasingly so, as he obtained more light and clearer views of the divine law in its spirituality and extent. Whilst he had no "delight in the law of God, after the inner man," but rather an increasing opposition to its strictness and purity, still he was constrained by the power of *conscience* to relinquish every practice with regard to which he entertained any misgivings, although it cost him a terrible struggle, and brought him to his knees before God.

November, 1818. About the close of his seventeenth year he became a student of this college. This was a very interesting period of his life. Whilst the greater part of the students here at that time, as they generally have been, and we hope always will be, were religious, or moral, it so happened, owing to some previous acquaintance, his first associates were of a very different character. Among them was one who was suddenly killed by a stroke of lightning, at the instant of his uttering the language of daring profanity. His wild associates endeavored to dissipate all his serious impressions; but no solicitations could induce him to engage in immoral practices. His inclination and purpose, before he came to college, was to be a lawyer; but his conscience now began to render him uneasy at the prospect of the temptations he should have to encounter in that profession.

He had not, as yet, openly professed religion by partaking of the Lord's Supper. He had designed to do so at a future period; but it was deferred, not from any sense of unfitness—for he had great confidence in his supposed piety—but felt reluctance to make so public a separation from the world.

At times he felt considerable uneasiness from those solemn declarations of Christ—"Whosoever shall be ashamed of me," &c.—Mark viii : 38. Referring to this in his notes, written some time after he entertained a hope of a saving change, he remarks, "I am now astonished how I could evade this striking declaration, while living in express opposition to it, and still flatter myself that I was a Christian. Yet such is the blindness of the heart till Jesus makes it wise." And he concludes some very judicious and penitential reflections on his case, as follows: "My case was, in many respects, more hopeless than that of any wretched sinner I ever read of. For though I had never gone to 'the same excess of riot,' as many others, yet I believe I never heard or read of one so completely, and for so long a time, and apparently so hopelessly deluded as I was during that time. Nothing now in my past history, or even in that of the world, convinces me more fully of the power of God than the fact that I now feel myself to be a sinner; for though my sense of my sinfulness is still slight, yet I can pray, in some measure, with meaning, 'God be merciful to me a sinner.'"

After he was some months at college, he determines to change his lodging, and his associates. He obtains boarding with Dr. Ramsey, (then residing a short distance in the country,) now Professor of Theology in the Associate Theological Seminary. For this venerable father and his family he always entertained a very high regard. Here he was removed from many temptations, and was rigidly punctual in attending to religious duties, in private, in the family, in the social prayer-meeting, and the house of God. Here, too, he was happily associated with Joseph Trimble, as his room-mate—a fellow-student of devoted piety and faithfulness, who appears to have been a principal instrument in his conversion to God.

March, 1819. The Lord's Supper was to be administered in Dr. M'Millan's church, where the students usually attended. His friend Trimble, mentioning the names of some of the applicants for admission, and stating their religious experience, with which he had made himself acquainted, took occasion to make a direct and personal appeal to his young friend. He expressed to him his doubts with regard to his self-righteous hopes, and his fears that he was under a dreadful delusion, and still in "the gall of bitterness, and bond of iniquity." The arrow was carried to his heart. Never before did the possibility of deception occur to him, though the same truths had been frequently presented under the searching and powerful ministry of Dr. M'Millan, and others. His friend urged the point of his danger and guilt in rejecting the Saviour, and concurring with the Jews in "murdering God's only Son." These expostulations awakened indescribable emotions, and "drew from him a flood of tears."

He felt that he must admit some of the charges, yet supposed that his friend was ignorant of the faithful manner he attended to secret duties. Still he felt himself in awful danger. Hell appeared infinitely dreadful. *Sure work* seemed to be absolutely necessary. He prayed with more frequency and earnestness; but his perplexity and distress remain. The arrows of God *stick fast* in his soul.

About this time he went to Washington, seven miles distant, where the sacrament was to be administered. He went in company with a number of pious students, several of whom had left Washington on account of difficulties that had occurred in reference to the college, but still retained a warm attachment to the *congregation*, where some of them had been born into the kingdom of Christ. This praying band frequently visited Washington, and especially on sacramental occasions, delighted to mingle with kindred spirits in pouring out their souls in prayer and praise, in the social prayer-meeting, and in the public sanctuary.

The account of this visit, and his exercises on the occasion, I give in Mr. Kennedy's own words: "I went to Washington, &c. My ears were now open; I heard several awakening sermons. I staid with Mr. Brown, then pastor of Washington congregation, now President of Jefferson College. I heard a good deal of conversation on religion. Some remarks on the responsible situation of clergymen's children, were principally made *at* me, and even personally applied to me. These I felt, but answered not. The agency of the Spirit of God was spoken of. I wondered what this meant; and I now suppose that, although I had often read of him, and been told of him, yet in reality I never before so much as thought 'whether there was a Holy Ghost.' While at Washington I was very miserable. I suspected some change to be necessary—what, I knew not, and yet was desirous of bringing myself to it. I had recourse to frequent prayer; not so much to seek the blessing of God, as from a notion of the *transforming efficacy* of prayer. I began to look upon myself as under conviction, and supposed that the time which had already elapsed, and the anxiety which I had undergone, *ought* to have brought matters to a favorable issue. I still wanted the payment of a *debt,* and not the bestowment of *grace.* I strove hard to make to myself a new heart and a right spirit; ignorant still of the life-giving spirit." While he was thus "like a helpless captive, sold under the power of sin"—a prisoner—enveloped in darkness—blind with regard to the method of relief—trusting to his own righteousness, and his own efforts, and not to the righteousness of Christ and the power of the Holy Ghost, the Lord "was leading him by a way he knew not." By this painful process he was teaching him more of his guilt, depravity, and utter helplessness, and the folly and wickedness of trusting to his own righteousness, his morality, his prayers, his religious observances, his resolutions, his *convictions* and his own unavailing efforts. In this way the awakened sinner, while still in the "gall of bitterness"—nothing better by his convictions, but growing worse and worse every hour—is by an unseen power driven from his refuges of lies—taught by his own experience the wickedness of his heart, and his utter helplessness. Thus cut off from every other hope, and despairing of all created help, he is brought to the foot of the cross, and enabled to say from the heart,

"A guilty, weak and helpless worm,
On thy kind arms I fall:
Be thou my strength and righteousness,
My Jesus and my all."

After returning to Canonsburg in this distressing state of mind, and after going to bed, the declaration of the Saviour to Zaccheus—"This day is salvation come to this house," Luke xix : 9—was brought to his mind with great force, and his mind dwelt upon it with delight, as a certain evidence that he was now an heir of glory—and probably some will be ready to say, surely this is the time of his deliverance, the hour of his conversion to God. But oh the deceitfulness of the heart, and the subtile wiles of the adversary! His hopes and joys from this source were all a delusion of Satan, "transformed into an angel of light." He was soon mercifully delivered from a delusion, by which many are ruined forever. He soon discovered that a mere suggestion of a text of Scripture, unaccompanied by a change of heart, and the appropriate fruits of holiness, is no better evidence of acceptance with God than the cast of a die, or the "flight of birds."

After continuing some days in the same state of anxiety and bondage, it occurred to him "not to *work* harder, but to believe and depend on Christ for acceptance." This dawn of light, which soon vanished, seems to have been the first view of the plan of salvation which had ever entered his darkened mind. A few days after he remarks, "that he degenerated in works, without growing in faith," until restored by the monition of his friend Trimble, who watched over him with prayerful concern.

Some days after he awoke in the morning in a very pleasing frame of mind: "I had a view of God's glory, to which I was before a stranger; all nature seemed to be directed by an omnipotent, unerring hand. The doleful melancholy which had brooded over me so long vanished in an instant, and I was enabled to 'rejoice that the Lord God omnipotent reigneth.' "

That this was the dawning of spiritual day he seems himself to have entertained some doubt, as the glory of God in *Christ* was not then distinctly the object of contemplation. But there is reason to believe, from subsequent experience, that this was indeed the "star of Bethlehem," although this pleasing calm was afterwards beclouded, and his views of a Saviour and the plan of salvation very obscure, and he might be said to "see men as trees walking." Yet there is little doubt that it was the dawn of the sun of righteousness; and although regeneration is an instantaneous change, and the precise moment difficult to be ascertained, yet with regard to the *evidence* of it, and the work of sanctification, this is progressive, and admits of various degrees, from the first dawning ray to the full blaze of noon.

At the close of the winter session, 1819, Mr. Kennedy returned home to Cumberland. Here, in the midst of his old acquaintances and companions, he felt himself as a lonely stranger, without the sympathy of kindred spirits, and rather pointed at by the finger of scorn. He was very conscientious in the discharge of known duty, which cost him sometimes painful sacrifices. His father was absent, at Philadelphia, attending the General Assembly; and he conducted family worship for the first time, not without a painful conflict. Although delivered from that deep distress which he had formerly experienced, and though evidently growing in humility and the knowledge of himself, his sinfulness and weakness, yet he had not those clear and comforting views of a Saviour, by which he could rejoice in him with confidence as "all his salvation and all his delight." At this stage of his experience he found one individual in Cumberland who, in the sovereign providence of God, was directed to "teach him the way more perfectly." This was a pious German, now an elder in the Presbyterian Church. This man, who had himself tasted of the "wormwood and the gall," understood his disease, and directed to the proper remedy. "Oh," said he, (with the German accent,) "it is good to feel the *wickedness* of the heart. We ought to be thankful that God has showed it to us. It is just what the apostle says in the 7th chapter of Romans: 'He then preached to him Christ and him crucified, as the end of the law for righteousness.'" From this time his views of the mediation of Christ, and of acceptance through him, were much altered, and his spiritual prospects proportionably brightened. He now enjoyed peace with God, and at length attained an "*assurance* of faith," which was seldom interrupted. At this time he was admitted to the communion of the church. At what particular time he experienced regeneration he could not say—he believed it took place before his admission to the Lord's Supper He remarks: "What I can principally say on this point is, 'that whereas I was blind, now I see.'"

On his return to college, the gloom which had brooded over him so long was dispelled: he became more sociable and cheerful—felt a warmer love for Christians, and a more tender concern for impenitent sinners—took an active part in the prayer-meeting—attended to his duties as a student with diligence and success. Wisdom's ways were ways of pleasantness. During his whole course at college he sustained a high standing as to talents and scholarship, and graduated with honor, May, 1820.

I have dwelt the longer on the *religious experience* of Mr. Kennedy, because it is in some respects remarkable, and in itself peculiarly instructive and *searching;* and because it appears to have been his desire that this part of his history should be useful and instructive to his family and friends, and the occasion of solemn warning and self-examination and hence in the biography of himself, which he commenced but did not finish, his experience is that which he has given most in detail.

The subsequent years of his life, though furnishing much that is interesting, must be glanced at with more brevity.

The summer of 1820 was spent at his father's, in general reading, and in efforts to do good, as he had opportunity. A Bible Society was commenced; also a *prayer-meeting*, of which we may be sure the honest German was an important member. Towards the close of the summer there was a powerful and extensive awakening in Cumberland and the vicinity. The *immediate* instruments were Nicholas Patterson, a licentiate from the Presbytery of Baltimore, and John Gloucester, a colored man, a member of the Presbytery of Philadelphia, much respected by all classes for his talents and usefulness, and his *modest*, unassuming piety. Prior to the visit of these ministers, which was providential, serious impressions had been made on the minds of many, no doubt in answer to prayer, and by other instrumentalities. These impressions were now increased and developed: "One soweth and another reapeth; and in both cases the glory should be given to God, and not to man. A narrative of this revival was published some time after by Mr. Kennedy, and extensively circulated.

In October, 1820, he started for the Theological Seminary at Princeton. On his way he tarried some time in Franklin, among his friends and acquaintances, and endeavored to improve his visits by faithful personal conversation with individuals. His youthful zeal, which probably was not always regulated by prudence and a correct knowledge of human nature, gave great offence. He soon found that "old Adam was too strong for young Melancthon." Persons altogether unaccustomed to such plain dealing, denounced him as an *enthusiast* and a *methodist.* It is not pleasant to persons destitute of true piety, and yet relying with self-complacency on an outward form or profession, to have their repose disturbed by honest appeals calculated to destroy their delusive hopes. Hence the charge against faithful reprovers, as the "troublers of Israel."

November, 1820. He arrived at Princeton, where he studied the regular term of three years. To this period he always reverted with endearing recollections. He commenced his theological studies with diligence and success, and was soon distinguished by his talents and acquirements.

In the fall vacation, on his return home, he was taken under the care of Carlisle Presbytery. He revisited his friends, who had been offended with his former *plain dealing*, and endeavored, not without success, to remove some of their prejudices. Among the various incidents which occurred while at Princeton, he has recorded the death of a dear young brother, (Turner,) to whom he was much attached, and whom he expected to be his companion and fellow-laborer as a missionary. The following I find in his notes: "When the hand of death was evidently upon him, the brethren were called into his room, and he was strengthened to utter a few sentences. 'I go,' says he, 'to the world of spirits. Be more faithful than I have been; and may the Lord make you instrumental in tearing down the strongholds of sin and satan.' He had trusted his salvation on Christ in life, and 'none but Jesus' was his cry in death. He bade them all farewell—shook hands with the professors and his physician, expressing his thanks for their kindness. Prayer was offered and a hymn sung. The scene was solemn and affecting—to see seventy young men, with the professors and physician, all melted in tears." This case, and that of another student, (Krebbs,) dying in the triumph of faith, seemed to disarm death of his terrors. "No event," says he, "ever disarmed death so much of his terrors to me. The same effect I find was produced on the minds of others."

During the winter or spring of 1821, he visited Morristown, New Jersey, where a powerful revival had commenced, which pervaded the whole country. This visit was profitable to himself, and useful to others. His own experience qualified him for being a safe and useful adviser to anxious souls, to guard them against the various refuges and delusions which he had himself experienced.

October, 1822—He was licensed to preach the gospel—aged twenty years and ten months. Deeply impressed with the responsibilities of the work to which he was to be devoted, he set apart a day for fasting and prayer, a duty which he often practiced in the succeeding years of his life. After his licensure to preach the gospel, he continued his studies another year at Princeton.

During his residence at Princeton he was frequently harassed with doubts, which he had never entertained, even in his former impenitent state. These doubts respected the very foundations of religion, the truth of the Scriptures, and even the existence of God. They were exceedingly distressing, and of long continuance. They did not arise from any want of arguments in support of the truth. These he considered conclusive; and the objections against these great fundamental truths he considered of no weight in point of argument, and yet he was often greatly distressed on account of his want of a pleasing, satisfactory conviction of the truth. It did not, indeed, influence his *conduct*, but interrupted his comfort. It was plainly a device of the enemy; and after conversing with Dr. Alexander, he found that the difficulty was not to be removed by mere *argument*, or by the exercise of his own reasoning alone, but by the effectual application of the truth to his heart by the mighty power of God. In this way he sought and found relief, and was never afterwards troubled with these doubts. During his last year at the Seminary, the doctrines denominated Hopkinsian were frequently the subject of warm discussion. In these discussions Mr. Kennedy took an active and decided part, in opposition to what he believed erroneous in these doctrines. A debate, prepared at that time on the subject of the atonement, was afterwards published in the first volume of the Christian Advocate. Its admission into that periodical by the venerable editor, Dr. Green, is no slight evidence of its intrinsic ability and excellence, though written by one who had just arrived at the years of manhood. In an *intellectual* point of view these discussions were of service to him; and whilst he contended for what he believed important truths—being a Calvinist of the real old school—it did not alienate his affections from his brethren who differed from him.

The following is from notes written soon after leaving Princeton, September, 1823:

"Our exercises before and at parting were very affecting. While sitting with my dear brethren at the last communion season, I thought affectingly of our Lord's declaration, Matt. xxvi: 29—'I will not henceforth drink of this fruit of the vine (with you) until that day,' &c. At our last Saturday evening prayer meeting, I asked a full and hearty pardon of all, whose feelings I might at any time have injured. We had a truly *melting* time. To all my brethren I was sincerely attached; and no diversity of sentiment could wean me from those in whom I perceived so much of the divine nature. I sincerely seek and love and defend the truth, but can love and rejoice in all those who maintain and adorn the leading features of the gospel. Of my brethren in the Seminary I can sincerely say,

'In such society as this, my willing soul would stay.'

Towards my class-mates I had feelings of peculiar regard—with whom a three years' intercourse made me well acquainted."

Leaving the Seminary in the fall of 1823, he intinerates in different directions about eighteen months. He preached for some time in Bedford, and Uniontown, Pennsylvania; traveled through some of the Western States; visited Madison, in Indiana, where no doubt he took occasion to weep over the grave of his friend Trimble.

He traveled also to the South, and preached for some time at Wilmington and Fayetteville, North Carolina. In the month of April, 1825, he again arrives at his father's, who had now returned to his former residence, in Franklin county. In the summer he visits Philadelphia—preaches in the Sixth Church, as a supply, for three months—receives a call from that congregation, and was ordained and installed as their pastor, November, 1825, in the twenty-fourth year of his age.

Previously to his settlement in the Sixth Church he had been appointed chaplain, to go out in the Brandywine, the government vessel, appointed to carry La Fayette back to his native land. This appointment was by some means prevented from reaching him until after his installment. Had he received it sooner it might have given a new direction to the current of his life.

His settlement in Philadelphia was unsought, as it was unexpected, by himself. The station was one of great importance and responsibility for so young a man. The Sixth Church grew out of a division of the old Pine Street Church, of which Dr. Alexander had been pastor when called to Princeton. On the settlement of Dr. Ely, this division took place, and the Sixth Church was formed. It contained a large portion of intelligence, piety and respectability; but its location in the vicinity of other churches, and certain pecuniary embarrassments, were unfavorable to its growth. It had become vacant by the resignation of Dr. Neil, who had accepted a call to the Presidency of Dickinson College. After laboring a year in this congregation, and discouraged at his prospect of usefulness, he determines to resign his charge. The Presbytery meet, and with the concurrent desire of the congregation, persuade him to remain. His intention was at this time to have gone to Liberia; and he often expressed his regret that he yielded to the advice to remain in Philadelphia, as he remarks that he then "had a burning zeal in behalf of Africa—such as he never felt in behalf of any other object." In 1828 he was married to Miss Harriet McCalmont, of Philadelphia, whose intelligence, piety, and accomplished education, qualified her eminently for being to him a prudent counselor and cheering companion. December, 1829, at his own request, his connexion with the Sixth Church was dissolved, having continued their pastor four years. During this period he discharged the duties of his office with ability and faithfulness. The *visible* fruits of his ministry were not equal to his *desires*, and hence his frequent discouragements, which resulted in his resignation; yet his labors were blessed to the edification of Christians, and a *goodly* number added to the church. The charge of a congregation in a city is one of great responsibility and hazard, especially to a young man; yet was Mr. Kennedy enabled to sustain a high and increasing reputation among his brethren, and the intelligent part of the religious community, as an able, lucid and instructive preacher of the gospel. It is known that he stood very high in the estimation of his venerable patron and friend, Dr. Green, who occupied a pew in his church, and sat with delight under the ministry of his young friend.

His connection with his congregation was dissolved, December, 1829. He now commits himself to the providence of God, without any definite object or plan as to future settlement. He is urged to make a tour to Missouri, with a view of settlement at St. Charles, and accordingly leaves Philadelphia with that intention. The severity of the season prevents him, and he is detained in Franklin county. A call is prepared for him from the congregation of Newville—one of the largest and wealthiest in Carlisle Presbytery. At this crisis, being uncertain and anxious as to the path of duty, he sets apart, as was his frequent custom, a day of fasting and prayer, to seek divine direction. It was the 11th of March,

1830. It is worthy of observation that on the evening of this same day, altogether unexpected to him, he received a letter from this place, inquiring as to his views in relation to a professorship in this college, in connection with the charge of a small congregation, about five miles distant.

He was at first startled at the proposal of a Professorship in Mathematics, for which he considered himself less qualified than for any other department. On further consideration, with the hope that by diligent exertion he might be prepared for the service, he is inclined to accept. He visits this place in May, receives and accepts the appointment from the college, and a call from the congregation of Centre. He returns to Philadelphia, and arrives here with his family, and enters on the duties of his profession, June, 1830.

Professor Miller, in view of whose resignation, on account of age, the appointment was made, still continued to officiate for some time. This afforded opportunity for Mr. Kennedy gradually to prepare himself for conducting the departments of Natural Philosophy and Mathematics, which he was enabled to do with great credit to himself, and to the entire satisfaction of all concerned. After the division of the departments of Natural Science and Mathematics, and the appointment of a distinct Professor for the latter, he devoted himself more exclusively to Natural Philosophy and Chemistry, in which he greatly excelled.

His life and history during his residence among us for ten years is known to us all, and need not here be detailed.

As an *instructor*, he was thorough, discriminating, accurate and lucid in his illustrations. As a member of the faculty, he was energetic, faithful, fearless, and always ready to share the responsibility of discipline and government.

As a *preacher*, he was *instructive*, solemn, searching and forcible.

As a *pastor*, he was laborious and faithful.

As a *writer*, he was characteristically lucid, simple and concise. "*Multum in parvo*" appeared to be his motto in all his productions. He wrote with great facility, and furnished for "the periodicals" a number of essays, which do him great credit.

His *talents* were various, and in some respects of a high order. He had more of the *intellectual* than the æsthetic—more of argumentation than poetry, in his composition—more of the instructive than the pathetic. There was one peculiarity in which he was defective. There was something in the construction of his mind which led him to attach undue importance to little things, as though he viewed them through a magnifying glass. This induced him sometimes to give a prominence to smaller matters, and to press the weaker points. This was noticed while he was a student at Princeton, and has been noticed in some of his literary productions. This constitutional peculiarity had no doubt an influence also in his worldly plans, which induced him to engage in various schemes and enterprises, which his friends considered rather unwise and visionary.

His *manner* was not always the best. There was something in this which at times had the appearance of harshness and severity. He was remarkably honest and faithful in testifying against sin, wherever it appeared. He seemed habitually to act on the principle, "thou shalt not hate thy neighbor in thine heart. Thou shalt in any wise rebuke thy neighbor, nor suffer sin upon him." It is not surprising, therefore, that he sometimes gave offence. Still it may be questioned whether offences of this kind are not to be charged to the too general unfaithfulness in this respect of professors, Christians and ministers, rather than to a want of *prudence* on the part of the faithful reprover.

Mr. Kennedy was a man of great *benevolence* and *liberality*. This feature of his character was not generally understood.

In his worldly transactions he was exact; and perhaps sometimes too particular in smaller matters. But when proper objects of benevolence were presented, no man amongst us was more liberal, according to his means. Besides the public contributions, in which he was always among the first, he performed many acts of private liberality, unknown to the world.

Finally.—Considered as a *Christian*, "the highest style of man," I need add nothing to the narrative already given. His *soul-searching* experience, his prayers and fastings, his conscientiousness and stern integrity, his self-denial, his steadfast faith on the righteousness of Christ, his abhorrence of sin, his desires and endeavors after holiness, and habitual aim to glorify God, gave "lucid proof" of sincere piety while he lived, which was confirmed in his death.

His health began seriously to decline last winter. A journey to the East during the summer proved unprofitable, and he returned home to die in the bosom of his family. He looked forward to the hour of his death without dread. Still he clung to life; and although with regard to himself he had no fears, and could say, "to be with Christ is best;" yet when he looked around on his wife and little children, and the prospect of leaving them exposed and unprotected in such a world as this, he greatly desired to live. At length, however, he was enabled with sweet acquiescence to commit the precious charge to Him who said, "Leave thy fatherless children; I will preserve them; and let thy widows trust in me."

His old enemy did not fail to assail him in his weak state, and when near the close of his life, with *doubts* as to the foundation of his hope. These, however, were soon dispelled, and he afterwards enjoyed uninterrupted calmness to the last. A few days before his release he spoke of his departure with great composure and confidence. When the weather permitted, he was usually taken out in a carriage. On returning, a day or two before his death, he said *that* was his last ride: in his next remove he "would be carried by angels into Abraham's bosom." On the 15th of December, in the thirty-ninth year of his age, he died without a struggle, and "sweetly fell asleep in Jesus." He has left behind a venerable father and beloved brothers and sisters to mourn—but they ought not to mourn as those who have no hope. He has left a beloved wife and five young children; but the God of the widow and the fatherless, to whom they have been committed in faith, will provide for them. The legacy of their father's pious example, his counsels and his prayers, is of more value to his children than all the treasures of the world.

APPENDIX

THE ORIGIN OF JEFFERSON COLLEGE.

After this work was placed in the hand of the printer, a very interesting document, containing a careful and elaborate inquiry respecting the first movements in the cause of classical and scientific education west of the mountains, was sent to us by its highly respected author, Prof. Robert Patterson, of Oakland College, Mississippi. We doubt not that it will fully meet the wishes of those who still adopt the current traditions on this subject, and who have felt aggrieved that any attempt has ever been made to call them in question. After the reader has bestowed upon it a careful perusal, we respectfully ask him to hear what we shall submit in reply.

WHERE WAS THE FIRST LITERARY INSTITUTION WEST OF THE MOUNTAINS?

Not four score years have yet elapsed since the first humble hall of learning was erected in the great Western Valley, and already has it become a subject of dispute, what spot is entitled to the honor of being regarded as its site? The fact itself is a forcible exemplification of the facility with which the Present forgets its obligations to the Past.

Three institutions only have been named, so far as the writer is aware, as competitors for this honor: established, respectively, by Rev. Joseph Smith, of Buffalo; by Rev. Thaddeus Dodd, of Ten Mile; and by Rev. John M'Millan, D. D., of Chartiers—all three congregations in Washington county, Pennsylvania.

1st. The first of these, that of the Rev. Joseph Smith, was undeniably in existence in 1785, as appears from a memorandum of Rev. Joseph Patterson, "Old Redstone," page 81, and probably continued until 1787 or 1788. There is no evidence that it was in existence either anterior or subsequent to the period named. Neither has any direct evidence been brought to the notice of the writer, to establish the fact that the Latin and Greek languages were taught at all in this institution. The object of Mr. Smith appears to have been mainly, if not exclusively, to furnish a theological education. Such is the opinion expressed in a letter to the writer, by Rev. Dr. Jacob Lindley, who was well acquainted with Mr. Smith's pupils, and a school-mate of some of them at Rev. Mr. Dodd's school; who states that he never heard Mr. Smith's school spoken of as a classical school. A similar opinion was expressed to the writer by Mrs. Harper and Mr. John M'Millan, children of Rev. John M'Millan, D. D., who had frequently heard their father and others speak of Rev. Mr. Dodd's as a classical school, but never of Mr. Smith's as such.

This minor point may perhaps have no relevancy to the question more immediately under examination, and indeed this character of Mr. Smith's school seems to be admitted on page 146 "Old Redstone;" as also in the same paragraph the priority of Mr. Dodd's school to Mr. Smith's is distinctly conceded. If this view be correct, the question will be narrowed down to the consideration of the rival claims of the seminaries of Mr. Dodd and of Mr. M'Millan.

2d. It is stated, "Old Redstone," page 145, that the building occupied by Mr. Dodd as an academy was erected in 1781, and (page 146) that "here, in 1782, began the first classical and scientific school in the West."

In this connection may be introduced the following extract from the letter already referred to from Rev. Dr. Jacob Lindley, dated June 2d, 1854:

"My parents, when I was eight years of age, imbibed the notion that I was pious, and sent me to the school of the prophets, which was kept in a large log house erected for the purpose, some fifty steps from Mr. Dodd's dwelling. It was sufficiently large for three or four beds, with room for tables, &c. I was sent there to live with Mr. Dodd and to study Latin, in A. D. 1782, and remained there till 1784. The Latin students then with Mr. Dodd, were James Hughs, John Brice, Robert Marshall, Francis Dunlavy, John Hannah, Daniel Lindley, David Smith, (father of Rev. Joseph Smith, D. D.,) Robert Marshall, Jr., (son of Col. James Marshall, of Buffalo,) and Jacob Lindley. Mathematical students, Daniel McFarland, Joseph Eddy, Thomas Stokely, and Thomas Gormly. All boarded with Mr. Dodd. Others were there for short seasons and left. Mr. Dodd never taught a common English school in Pennsylvania. Mr. Joseph Smith's school was a theological school, as I always understood from the young men above named, the most of whom were members of Mr. Smith's church. I certainly never heard of a Latin school of Mr. Smith's.

"In the latter part of 1785, as I think, Mr. Dodd sold the farm where his school was, and moved into his lower congregation. I suppose Mr. Dodd's Latin students went and studied theology under Mr. Smith, viz: Hughs, Marshall, Hannah, David Smith, and perhaps Dunlavy. Mr. Joseph Patterson studied theology partly under Mr. M'Millan, and partly under Mr. Smith. He never studied Latin or Greek.

"At the time, a little before or a little after, Mr. Dodd's school broke up,

Mr. M'Millan took in a number of students for the ministry. I do not personally know so much about them.

"From the time I was eight years old, no amusement could divert my attention from the conversation of my father and the ministers, when on the subject of religion and ministerial education. All is in memory, as nails driven in a sure place. But to proceed.

"I have said Mr. M'Millan's classical school succeeded that of Mr. Dodd. Some time in December, 1785, by the united influence of the members of Redstone Presbytery, a charter was procured for an academy in Washington, with a donation of 5,000 acres of land. Of the Trustees appointed, were Rev. Messrs. M'Millan, Dodd, Smith and Clark, of the Presbyterian Church, Rev. Matthew Henderson, of the Secession, and John Corbley, of the Baptist Church: also, Judges Edgar, McDowell, Allison, &c., &c. Messrs. Dodd, Smith and M'Millan were the movers in the plan. From the time of that charter, Mr. M'Millan and others set head and shoulders to build up a seminary in Washington. A unanimous appointment was made of Mr. Dodd to commence literary operations there. As there was no house built for the purpose, the commissioners offered the court-house to teach in. Mr. Dodd would consent to leave his congregations but for one year; and then some other one whom the Trustees might provide, was to take his place. This being agreed upon, Mr. Dodd entered on his appointment on the 1st of April, 1789. At the end of the year, as the Trustees had not yet succeeded in obtaining another teacher, Mr. Dodd remained three months longer. Mr. David Johnston succeeded Mr. Dodd. In the winter, after Mr. Johnston took charge of the academy, the court-house was burned down, and Mr. Johnston was taken to Canonsburg. The inhabitants of Washington, at that time, had but little piety, science or liberality to build a house or sustain a literary institution, and none to sustain a preacher. Through the perseverance of Mr. M'Millan, and the liberality of Col. Canon, a lot was given, moneys advanced, and Canonsburg Academy was built in short order. Dr. M'Millan turned his scholars into it; some of Mr. Johnston's came from Washington; some from Pittsburgh, and other places, and Canonsburg was respected as the literary depot of the West. It was with no small reluctance that Dr. M'Millan withdrew his patronage from Washington; but when compelled to do this, he turned his gigantic might to Canonsburg. He ought to be considered as the God-father—the Almus Pater of Jefferson College."

It would appear from the account above given that Mr. Dodd's school was commenced in 1782, continued till 1785, and then closed upon his change of residence; nor is there any evidence that it was ever resumed. No one has contended that the election of Mr. Dodd, nearly four years afterwards, to the post of Principal of the Washington Academy, as being at the time the most available man for that position, and with a distinct stipulation on his part that the appointment was only temporary, to enable the Trustees to secure a permanent teacher,—there being also no transfer of a school—in any wise constituted that academy the lineal descendant of Mr. Dodd's school; nor is it easy to conceive upon what principles of succession any such claim of connection could be maintained. If it be affirmed that the teacher constitutes the school, then Mr. Dodd's mantle, which must have descended upon his successor, Mr. David Johnston, was by him transferred to the Canonsburg Academy in 1791.

It is proper to remark that the account given by Rev. Dr. Lindley of the close of Mr. Dodd's connection with the Washington Academy differs from the one given in "Old Redstone," page 147; inasmuch as Mr. Dodd's return to Ten Mile seems to have preceded the destruction of the court-house by fire, and not to have been a consequence of that catastrophe. Dr. Lindley, as Dr. M'Millan had done many years before, assigns for the temporary suspension of the Washington Academy, and the location of a similar institution in Canonsburg, another cause than the conflagration of the court-house.

The result of our inquiries thus far appears to be that Mr. Dodd's school was commenced in 1782, was continued till 1785, and then closed; that Mr. Smith's school was commenced in 1785, was continued until 1787 or 1788, and then closed; and that the Washington Academy, which had been incorporated September 24th, 1787, was opened in 1789, closed temporarily in 1791, and its teacher transferred to the Canonsburg Academy. It only remains to investigate the claims to priority of the school taught by Rev. Dr. M'Millan.

3d. Before introducing any evidence in regard to the last-named institution, it may be proper to apprise the general reader that the prevailing opinion in the neighborhood of the school itself and at Jefferson College, so far back as the writer has been able to trace it, has been that, about the year 1780, Rev. Dr. M'Millan commenced a classical school at or near his residence; that he was then, or soon thereafter, assisted in conducting the same by Hon. James Ross, then a young man, afterwards, during the administration of Gen. Washington, a distinguished Senator of the United States; that with perhaps some intermissions the school continued until it was merged in the Canonsburg Academy, in 1791. More recently, three opinions have been broached: 1st. That Dr. M'Millan's school was not commenced till after 1785, upon the disruption of Mr. Dodd's school; 2d. Perhaps not until 1788, upon the discontinuance of Mr. Smith's school; 3d. That if there was a school at Dr. M'Millan's, taught either by himself or by James Ross, prior to 1785, it was only an English, and in no sense a classical one. The substantiation of any one of these hypotheses would establish the priority of the classical school at Ten Mile. They may therefore be classed under one general head, and the evidence for and against them respectively be considered together.

In support of these more recent opinions, in regard to Dr. M'Millan school, may be adduced—

1st. The evidence of Rev. Dr. Jacob Lindley, who states, in the extracts quoted above, that Dr. M'Millan's school succeeded that of Mr. Dodd.

2d. The impressions of Rev. Dr. James Carnahan, as contained in a letter to the writer, dated June 3d, 1854, of which the following extract contains all that is relevant to the present point:

"I have no personal knowledge of Dr. M'Millan's school in the 'Log-Cabin.' All I know is from reports heard when I was at school at Canonsburg. Part of the time I boarded at the same house (Patrick Scott's) with a young man who had lived for several years in Dr. M'Millan's family, and managed his farming operations. This man's name was Wilkins. He was from the same neighborhood east of the mountains with Dr. M'Millan. When I knew Mr. Wilkins, although above thirty years old, he was learning Latin with a view to the gospel ministry. As his progress was slow, he gave up his books and resumed his former occupation.

"The statement of this man respecting the Hon. James Ross, who taught school in the log-cabin, was, that he was the son of a pious widow lady in moderate circumstances, in the place of Dr. M'Millan's nativity; that her early wish and prayer was that her son should become a minister of the gospel; that she sent him to a grammar school; that when he had made considerable proficiency in Latin and Greek, and was nearly of age, with the advice and consent of his mother, he crossed the mountains and directed his steps to Dr. M'Millan's. As there was no school in the neighborhood, Mr. M'Millan built a small log-cabin near his residence, and engaged Mr. Ross to teach his own and his neighbor's children, while at the same time Mr. Ross continued his studies in Latin, Greek, and mathematics, under the direction of Mr. M'Millan. From the statements of Wilkins, the impression made in my mind was that Mr. Ross taught an English school. I have no recollection that Wilkins named James Hughs, John Brice, Robert Marshall, and others, as learning Latin or Greek with Mr. M'Millan. Some of them, and Samuel Porter, were spoken of as reading theology under the direction of Dr. M'Millan.

"My friend, the late Dr. M. Brown, has given another version of the school taught by Mr. Ross. He speaks of James Ross as an accomplished Latin and Greek scholar, and as having taught these languages in the 'Log-Cabin.' During my residence at Canonsburg from 1793 to 1798, I never heard Mr. James Ross spoken of as an accomplished classical scholar. As a man of uncommon talent, an eminent lawyer and an eloquent advocate, he was highly and justly celebrated. This reputation he had obtained before 1793. This fact renders it probable that he taught in the 'Log-Cabin' before 1785. Yet I have no means of fixing the precise date. Dr. Brown may have had good authority for stating that James Ross taught the first Latin school west of the mountains. My impressions to the contrary were received from Mr. Wilkins, and while at Canonsburg I never heard a different statement. Your father is perhaps the best living witness in regard to the origin of Latin schools west of the mountains. He had nearly finished his Latin and Greek studies when I went to Canonsburg, and went, I think in the autumn of 1794, to the University of Pennsylvania."

3d. The fact, as stated in "Old Redstone," page 77, that "the records of the Presbytery of Redstone show that there were no licentiates under their care, who had received their previous scholastic or theological training from Dr. M'Millan," till after the discontinuance of Mr. Smith's school, "and that all the first ministers had received their instruction either from Mr. Dodd or Mr. Smith." Further, that if there was such a school at Dr. M'Millan's, prior to 1785, in which young men were instructed in languages and sciences, it is strange that "not one of them can now be found, and there is no mention of such in the minutes of the Presbytery."

4th. The evidence of Mrs. Irwin, ("Old Redstone," page 77,) an aged lady, now residing near Marysville, Ohio, who was between twelve and fifteen years of age, and resided near Mr. Smith, during the continuance of his school. Mrs. Irwin states "that in 1785 Mr. Smith opened a school for assisting and training young men for the gospel ministry; that this was the first movement made for preparing young men for the ministry; that there was no such school at this time at Chartiers, nor until after the one at Buffalo was discontinued; that Mr. McGready came to the school from Dr. M'Millan's, with whom he had been living, not as a student, but as a laborer on his farm."

5th. The evidence ("Old Redstone," page 78,) of Rev. Dr. Cephas Dodd, of Amity, Pennsylvania, son of Rev. Thaddeus Dodd, who states that "there was an agreement made between Mr. Smith and Mr. Dodd, by which they engaged alternately to superintend the education of certain young men who had the ministry in view," and of this number that "Messrs. James Hughs, John Brice, Robert Marshall, John Hanna and David Smith, were with Mr. Dodd from about 1783 to 1786, and for the remainder of the time with Mr. Smith," but "were never under the tuition of Dr. M'Millan;" and that "others, as Messrs. Patterson, McGready, and Porter, were instructed solely by Mr. Smith."

6th. The letter of Dr. M'Millan to Dr. Carnahan, dated March 26th, 1832, ("Old Redstone," page 79,) in which he enumerates Messrs. Patterson, Hughs, Brice, McGready, Swan, Porter, Marquis, and McPherrin, as all of the second set of ministers, who were raised up in this country; which enumeration, taken in connection with what is above stated, has been considered as corroborative testimony.

7th. The authority of an original manuscript of Dr. M'Millan in the possession of the author of "Old Redstone," (see page 192,) in which the Doctor mentions Messrs. Hughs, Brice, McGready and Porter, "as his first scholars" —and as part of the material with which his school began; showing that "this school, which Dr. M'Millan collected, consisting of these young men, as he expressly states, could not possibly have begun until after 1785," inasmuch as they had been with either Mr. Dodd or Mr. Smith before that time.

8th. A memorandum of the Rev. Joseph Patterson, cited in "Old Redstone," page 81, to the following purport: "In the fall of 1785, being thirty-three years old, it was thought best, with the advice of the Presbytery of Redstone, that I should endeavor to prepare for the gospel ministry. There being no places of public education in this country, I, with a few others, studied with the Rev. Joseph Smith, of Buffalo congregation, Washington county, Pennsylvania."

9th. An extract from the letter of Rev. Robert Patterson to Rev. Dr. M. Brown, October 1st, 1846, as follows, ("Old Redstone," page 81.) "Between 1780 and 1790, and chiefly in the latter part of these ten years, some of the few Presbyterian clergymen living west of the mountains in Pennsylvania, were in the habit of giving instruction in the languages and sciences to young men, whose object in their studies was the gospel ministry. The Rev. Messrs. Joseph Smith and John M'Millan were distinguished in their devotion to this cause," &c., &c.

The above enumeration exhausts the arguments, so far as they have come to the knowledge of the writer, which would tend to show that Dr. M'Millan's was not the first classical and scientific school in the West, if a classical school at all. It may perhaps be well before advancing any reasons for an opposite opinion to review the foregoing as briefly as possible, and endeavor to ascertain how much there is of direct and positive testimony in all that has been adduced.

In the first place, the evidence of Rev. Dr. Lindley is perhaps the strongest and most direct. He is positive in regard to the clearness of his recollection since his eighth year, or since 1782, and affirms that Mr. M'Millan took in a number of students for the ministry about the time that Mr. Dodd's school closed: but adds that he has little personal knowledge in regard to them; and it will be seen that he makes no profession of any personal knowledge or recollection of events prior to 1782. There does not appear therefore to be any necessary conflict between this statement and the fact, if such fact be hereafter made to appear, that Dr. M'Millan's school was established before that time. There may have been intermissions in Dr. M'Millan's school; and that portion of its existence of which Dr. Lindley had some personal knowledge, was subsequent to, or coincident with the close of Mr. Dodd's institution. To represent Dr. Lindley as affirming positively that Dr. M'Millan's school had no existence whatever at any time prior to 1785, would not only be subjecting his language quoted above to a most violent and arbitrary construction, but would be representing him as affirming that to be true of which he denies any special personal knowledge, and for the contrary of which explicit testimony will be hereafter adduced on the part of those who enjoyed better opportunities for acquiring information. If this view of the case be not correct, it only remains for the reader to reconcile, on some other hypothesis, the reminiscences of Dr. Lindley with those of other equally competent witnesses, to be noticed hereafter.

In the second place, the evidence of Rev. Dr. Carnahan is professedly of a derivative character. Mr. Wilkins, the source of Dr. Carnahan's impressions, had been a laborer upon Dr. M'Millan's farm; but it does not appear at what time, nor what opportunities he possessed for acquiring information; facts important to be known before we can estimate the proper weight of his testimony. The period to which our attention is directed was some ten or fifteen years previous to the acquaintance of Dr. Carnahan with Mr. Wilkins; and the residence of the latter on the farm of Dr. M'Millan may have been long subsequent to the departure of Mr. Ross. It does not even appear that Mr. Wilkins affirmed that either Mr. Ross or Dr. M'Millan did not teach the languages; but only that such was the impression produced on the mind of Dr. Carnahan from the statements made. That this impression may have been erroneous, or the author of it mistaken, no one, upon proper evidence, would more readily admit than the venerable Dr. Carnahan himself.

A doubt seems to be expressed as to the character of Dr. M'Millan's school, whether the languages were taught at all; but this question is set at rest by the published letter to Dr. Carnahan himself from Dr. M'Millan, in which he expressly states that he gave instruction in Latin and Greek. If Mr. Wilkins produced an erroneous impression in this particular, he may have been equally inaccurate in other respects. The precise proficiency of Mr. Ross in the classics is a side issue, not immediately relevant to the question now under consideration, and may be dismissed.

In the third place, the records of the Presbytery of Redstone simply show that Messrs. John Brice and James Hughs were received on trial, as candidates for the ministry, August 15th, 1786; Messrs. Joseph Patterson and James McGready, April 17th, 1787; and others, in like manner, at subsequent times. The records in no instance state under whose instruction the candidates respectively were. It is difficult to comprehend, therefore, in what manner these records of themselves can be made to throw any light upon the question under examination. They simply show the dates at which certain young men were received as candidates, and they do not appear to show any thing more.

If it be agreed that the silence of the records in regard to any candidates prior to August 15th, 1786, proves that there could have been no school at Dr. M'Millan's for such candidates before that time, the circumstance proves too much; as it would equally follow for the same reason, that there could have been no such school at Mr. Dodd's prior to that time; which would be contrary to the admitted fact. And if this mode of reasoning is therefore clearly inapplicable to Mr. Dodd's school, with still less justice can it be applied to an earlier school, whose pupils, like those of Mr. Dodd, were not sufficiently advanced in their studies to submit themselves to an examination by Presbytery; more especially if the opinion be correct, that Dr. M'Millan's school was in existence for more than a year before the Presbytery of Redstone was organized.

As to the statement, that of the pupils of Dr. M'Millan prior to 1785, "not one of them can now be found," evidence will be submitted presently to show who a number of them were. Were it impossible, however, after the lapse of more than seventy years, now to designate with certainty a single pupil, that circumstance would not of itself be conclusive that there had been no such school. The present discussion has furnished abundant evidence to show how rapidly the memory of persons and events fades from the minds of men.

In the fourth place, the evidence of Mrs. Irwin, who states explicitly that Mr. Smith's school, in 1785, was "the first movement made for preparing young men for the ministry," is directly and irreconcilably in conflict with the fact that such a movement was made by Mr. Dodd three years before; and accordingly the author of "Old Redstone" has very handsomely (page 146) abandoned the false position which this testimony of Mrs. Irwin had led him to assume. Her statement that "there was no such school at Chartiers until the one at Buffalo was discontinued," is at variance with the testimony of Rev. Dr. Lindley, cited above, who states that Dr. M'Millan's school was in existence "at the time when Mr. Dodd's broke up, a little before, or a little after." Her testimony in regard to Mr. McGready, that he had been living with Dr. M'Millan, and that, too, as a laborer, and not as a student, is pointedly contradicted by the testimony of Mrs. Harper, the oldest child of Dr. M'Millan, who stated to the writer that Mr. McGready, whom she well remembers, lived with Judge M'Dowell, but studied Latin with her father, and taught an English school for him, which school Mrs. Harper herself attended, having learned to read from Mr. McGready; and that he never worked as a laborer for her father, unless in kindly giving his assistance in attending to the stock during her father's occasional absence. Mrs. Irwin's testimony in the same particular is contradicted by the evidence of Mrs. Park, the daughter of Judge M'Dowell, who, without any knowledge of Mrs. Harper's testimony, stated to the writer that she distinctly remembered Mr. McGready as living at her father's, studying Latin there, and going to Dr. M'Millan's to recite. It is equally at variance, in this particular, with the recollection of Rev. Dr. Cephas Dodd, who is also strongly of the impression, as he states in a letter to the writer, that Mr. McGready was a student of Dr. M'Millan's, though he has inadvertently expressed himself to the contrary in "Old Redstone," page 79—a very pardonable inaccuracy, which yet occasioned no little uneasiness to Dr. Dodd. It is also worthy of remark, in the same connection, that in about eighteen months after Mr. Smith's school commenced, Mr. McGready, whose name does not appear on any list of Mr. Dodd's pupils, and who, according to Mrs. Irwin's testimony, had been heretofore a farm-laborer, presented himself to the Presbytery as a candidate for the ministry, ("Old Redstone," page 350,) was examined in logic, moral philosophy, Latin and Greek,—his examinations all sustained,—and an exegesis assigned for the next meeting—"*An sit concursus Dei cum omnibus hominum actionibus?*"—and all these attainments, we are asked to believe, were made in less time, after the student left the plough, than would be requisite to qualify him, even with diligent study, for admission to the Freshman class of any respectable college at the present day. In fact Mr. McGready was licensed in about fifteen months afterwards. One of three things will be readily admitted: either that the standard of classical attainment in the Presbytery of Redstone was not of a very exalted character, or that Mr. McGready acquired knowledge with a facility which does not often fall to the lot of men; or that Mrs. Irwin must have been mistaken in affirming that he had not been a student with Dr. M'Millan. Nor could it fail to be matter of surprise, were it indeed true, that Dr. M'Millan had permitted a young man of undoubted piety and talent, brought from North Carolina and placed under his care expressly to be fitted for the ministerial office, in which his labors were afterwards so abundantly blessed, to remain for years without instruction, engaged in the menial labors of his farm.

But it is perhaps a waste of words to discuss the credibility of this testimony any further, since the author of "Old Redstone" has himself so entirely set it aside, when it came in conflict with the obstinate fact of the existence of Mr. Dodd's school; and if that fact had passed from Mrs. Irwin's memory, still more easily might the recollection of a yet earlier school escape, if she were even aware of events that are believed to have occurred at a time when she was, according to her own showing, about five years of age, and at a place from which she was some ten or fifteen miles distant. It is unnecessary to say that no one will for a moment suppose that Mrs. Irwin would willfully misstate facts of which she had either personal or indirect knowledge; but it is impossible to escape the conclusion that either she or others who have been named, must have failed in their recollections; and to which side the balance of probability inclines, the reader will decide for himself.

In the fifth place, it will be seen on examination of the evidence of Rev. Dr. Dodd, that he simply mentions the names of certain persons who were *not* pupils of Rev. Dr. M'Millan, which is not at all inconsistent with the fact, if it be made to appear, that there were other persons who were his pupils. He has expressed his conviction, as remarked above, that he was in error in regard to one of them; and it is probable, as will hereafter appear, that he was also in error in regard to others. It is due to Dr. Dodd to state that he remarks in a letter to the writer, dated May 17th, 1854, that that he "was too young and too far distant to know anything personally of Dr. M'Millan's school."

In the sixth place, in his published letter to Dr. Carnahan, Dr. M'Millan nowhere states who were his first pupils, neither does he specify who were his pupils at all, nor fix the year in which his school commenced. It is a matter both of surprise and regret, that in a letter so full of dates, he should have omitted the one most interesting of all, and that he did not by a stroke of his pen set the question now under discussion at rest forever.

In the seventh place, if the "original manuscript of Dr. M'Millan" is one which has never been published, it is greatly to be regretted that the author of "Old Redstone" has not given it to the world. It is impossible for the public to form any intelligent judgment respecting the contents of a document they have never seen, the extracts from which are given in imperfect sentences; and this is all that can be said of it.

If, however, the document in question is a transcript of the letter to Dr. Carnahan, referred to above, as the similarity of the phraseology in the extracts ("Old Redstone," pages 79, 80, and 192,) would seem to indicate, a re-perusal of that letter cannot fail to convince our candid and valued friend that he has possibly misconceived its import. In one part of his letter, Dr. M'Millan states that he had collected a few young men, whom he taught the Latin and Greek languages; and that some of them became useful, and others eminent, ministers of the gospel. In another part of his letter, entirely unconnected with the former, he states that he had survived "all the second set of ministers who were raised in this country," and enumerates them. Is there any law of construction by which, on collating these two passages, Dr. M'Millan can be made to affirm that these ministers were "his *first* scholars?" that "his school *began* with them?" Where does he "expressly state that his school consisted of these young men?" And what becomes of the allegation that some of these students were never his pupils at all? It is in perfect harmony with Dr. M'Millan's language to suppose that one or two of the persons named were among his earlier pupils, though the school may have contained a number of students who never became ministers; and that others on the list he enumerates may have been his pupils at various times during the entire progress of his school. This is a much more natural and probable view of the case than the one presented by the construction which has been placed upon these passages, if this be indeed the manuscript referred to, and does not conflict with positive testimony soon to be considered.

In the eighth place, the force of Rev. Joseph Patterson's memorandum (which bears date Pittsburgh, May 15th, 1822,) depends upon the meaning he attached to the term "public education." It is probable that he was comparing the humble seminaries of the time of which he wrote, with the more imposing ones of the time at which he was writing. He could not have meant that there were not, or had not been, other private schools like that of Mr. Smith, which he was attending; for it is admitted that there had been one at Mr. Dodd's; there may therefore have been another at Dr. M'Millan's.

In the ninth place, the extract from the letter of Rev. Robert Patterson, appears to indicate his impression, to the existence of which the writer of this can also testify, that the educational efforts of the various Presbyterian clergymen west of the mountains, had commenced as far back as 1780. Now, the school of Mr. Smith was not commenced until the latter part of 1785;

and that of Mr. Dodd was commenced in 1782. This extract therefore does not preclude, but rather favors the supposition that Dr. M'Millan's school was prior to Mr. Dodd's.

If the patience of the reader has not been already exhausted, he is invited to examine the evidence which may be furnished in support of the correctness of the more commonly received, and, until recently, the undisputed opinion that Dr. M'Millan's was the first Latin school in the West.

1st. The first place in the order of testimony is evidently due to that of Dr. M'Millan himself. In his published letter to Dr. Carnahan, already more than once referred to, (Pitts. Chr. Herald, Dec. 14th, 1833,) he gives a sketch only too brief of his life and times, which bears every appearance of a design on the part of the venerable writer to relate events in their regular chronological order. Commencing with his earliest years, and he even apologizes afterwards for not having given the date of his birth "in the proper place," he traces up his history until the arrival of his family at Chartiers, of the circumstances attending which he gives a rather minute description. The mention of his wife in this connection naturally leads him to anticipate his narrative so far as to give the date of her death, in 1819. He then resumes his history in the following manner:

"When I had determined to come to this country, Dr. Smith* enjoined it upon me to look out for some pious young men, and educate them for the ministry; for, said he, though some men of piety and talents may go to a new country at first, yet if they are not careful to raise up others, the country will not be well supplied. Accordingly I collected a few who gave evidence of piety, and taught them the Latin and Greek languages. Some of them became useful, and others eminent, ministers of the gospel. I had still a few with me when the Academy was opened in Canonsburg, and finding that I could not teach and do justice to my congregation, I immediately gave it up and sent them there."

The Doctor then goes on with every appearance of adhering to the regular succession of events to speak of the first remarkable outpouring of the Spirit in his congregation as occurring in December, 1781.

Now, in the first place, the order in which Dr. M'Millan introduces this portion of his history, furnishes a fair presumption that he is speaking of a period prior to December, 1781; in the second place, the phraseology with which he commences the paragraph, furnishes an equally fair presumption that he began his career as a teacher soon after "coming to this country;" in the third place, with what propriety — not to say with what truth — could he affirm that he had acted "according" to Dr. Smith's injunction, if he had totally neglected it for ten years after his settlement as a pastor of Chartiers, and that, too, with the materials for such a school in his immediate neighborhood, nay, as we are told, upon his own farm? — and in

*Of Pequea.

the fourth place, why should he say that there were "still a few with him," if his school had been in existence for the comparatively brief period we are asked to believe? If all this be only a presumption, yet it is so strong that it cannot well be set aside, unless upon the suggestion in "Old Redstone," page 80, that it may be a "lapsus memoriæ on the part of an octogenarian."

Again, in a report presented to the Trustees of Jefferson College in 1817, by Dr. Ramsey and Dr. M'Millan, and which appears upon the minutes of the Board in the handwriting of the latter, it is stated, in an account of Dr. M'Millan's efforts to establish the academy at Canonsburg, that "A house was built and a Latin and Greek school, which he had kept at his own house, for the purpose of supplying the church as far as was practicable, was transferred to this infant academy, the original fountain of science and literature in these western counties." Now from this passage, from Dr. M'Millan's own pen, it is an inevitable inference that in his opinion the Canonsburg Academy, either of itself, or by virtue of the school transferred to it, was the original fountain, &c. It could not have been the former, for the Washington Academy had been in existence before the one in Canonsburg, and long before the date of this report (1817) had eventuated in a college; and it is difficult to see how we can escape the latter conclusion.

But a still more explicit statement is made in the catalogue of Jefferson College, published in July, 1833, four months before the decease of Dr. M'Millan (November, 16th), he being at that time Vice-President of the college, and in the habit, it is believed, of frequently visiting the institution. It is there stated that "Jefferson College was chartered by the State, and regularly organized in 1802. Prior to that time there existed an academy, called Canonsburg Academy, which commenced soon after the first settlement of this country. This was the first literary institution west of the mountains. It originated in a small log-cabin, where the first Latin school was taught by the Hon. James Ross, of Pittsburgh, under the patronage and direction of Rev. Dr. M'Millan."

It would seem highly improbable — indeed, almost impossible — that this statement could have been put forth without the knowledge of Dr. M'Millan, and without some attempt to derive from himself personally the facts in regard to the origin and character of his school; or that, having been put forth, it should remain uncontradicted, if erroneous. It may, therefore, fairly be received as having the sanction of his authority.

2d. Next in order may be noticed the testimony of the children of Dr. M'Millan. On the 24th April, 1854, the writer, in company with Rev. William Ewing, the pastor of Chartiers, visited Mr. John M'Millan, (since deceased), who occupied the old homestead, and adjacent to whose dwelling stands the veritable "Log-Cabin" itself. This, however, was the second cabin. The first, which was burnt down, was at some distance from the dwelling; Mr. M'Millan indicated its site. He stated that he had often heard his father say—"That Mr. Ross taught Latin for him, and that this was the *first* Latin school in the country." The writer quotes from his memoranda, made at the time. Mr. M'Millan added that his father used to say—"He wished the world to forget, as soon as possible, that such a man as John M'Millan had ever lived." Unhappily, the world is too ready to forget its benefactors.

On the 3d August, 1854, the writer received a call from Mr. M'Millan, accompanied by his sister, Mrs. Harper, the oldest child of Dr. M'Millan. Mrs. Harper, who was in her seventy-seventh year, but appeared to possess an excellent memory, confirmed her brother's statements; and her testimony in other particulars has been already introduced and need not be repeated. She states that Mr. Ross, as well as Mr. McGready, studied languages with her father, whilst they were engaged in teaching for him, the former the Latin and the latter the English scholars.

3d. As the testimony of the next witness is perhaps the most direct of any, and by many will be deemed conclusive upon the subject, it will be proper to give it in full, as taken down by the writer at the time specified.

"*Canonsburg*, Saturday, June 17th, 1854.

"In company with Dr. John Weaver, I this day called upon Mrs. Sarah Park, an aged lady, residing with her son, Mr. M'Dowell Park, about five miles from Canonsburg.

"Mrs. Park's statements to Dr. Weaver and myself were as follows, she being in our judgment in perfect possession of all her mental faculties, her memory apparently unimpaired.

"She was born October 24th, 1769, and is now in her eighty-fifth year, and in the enjoyment of excellent health. Her maiden name was M'Dowell. Her father, Judge M'Dowell, removed from Eastern to Western Pennsylvania, when she was about four years of age (1773). Her father resided upon the farm now owned by Mr. Samuel Pollock, about two miles from Chartiers' meeting-house, and not quite two miles from Dr. M'Millan's. She distinctly recollects when Dr. M'Millan removed his family to Chartiers. There being no house prepared for him, he with his wife and child (now Mrs. Harper) remained for six weeks at her father's house. (Mrs. Park mentioned one or two incidents connected with Dr. M'Millan's temporary residence at her father's house, which, though trivial, show how distinct and vivid her recollection of that period is. As Dr. M'Millan removed his family to Chartiers in 1778, she must have been at that time nine years of age.)

"Mrs. Park does not remember the precise year when Dr. M'Millan's school commenced; but thinks she was about twelve years old, (1781,) and is quite sure she was not more than thirteen, (1782,) when she knew several young men who were studying with Dr. M'Millan at his own house, before the first school-house was built. These students were David Smith, John

Brice, James McGready, Francis Reno, and Thomas Reno. Mr. Smith boarded with Dr. M'Millan; all the others boarded with her father, Judge M'Dowell. She remembers distinctly that these young men were studying Latin books,—is perfectly sure of it. She recollects well their using books she could not read in. She never heard of an English school at Dr. M'Millan's house, and is quite sure he never taught one. She knows certainly that the young men named above recited to Dr. M'Millan at his own house, before any school-house was built, and she thinks, before Mr. Ross came out to the West. The students named above were all gone before Mrs. Park's marriage, which took place in 1786, when she was seventeen years of age. Upon her marriage she left the more immediate neighborhood of the school, and went to live upon the farm where she still resides. She does not therefore remember very distinctly matters connected with the school after that period, and about which she was not so well informed at the time.

"The first school-house was built at some distance from Dr. M'Millan's dwelling. It was called the 'Latin School,' and known by that name throughout the country. This building was destroyed by fire—she does not recollect in what year, but thinks it was after her marriage; of this she would not be certain. Mr. Ross was the first teacher in this school-house. She recollects him distinctly, and the fact of his being thus engaged. She does not know what his age at the time was—thinks it may have been twenty-five. Does not remember how long he remained with Dr. M'Millan; thinks it may have been two years. She thinks Mr. Ross obtained his education east of the mountains, and has no knowledge of his having studied with Dr. M'Millan.

"Mrs. Park never heard of any Latin school at Rev. Joseph Smith's, at Buffalo; though she says it might have been in existence without her knowledge.

"She remembers Mr. McGready perfectly well, and that he was in very limited circumstances when obtaining his education; but she does not recollect his boarding at Dr. M'Millan's, and thinks, if he did, it must have been after her marriage, (1786). She does not remember his teaching an English school."

As the above testimony is directly to the point, the reader will pardon the following evidence of the case which was taken that no error might be committed in recording it.

"*Canonsburg*, June 17th, 1854.

"*William Park, Esq.* Dear Sir:—On the previous pages I have written out the information given to me this morning by your mother, from notes I took at the time. I have read it to Dr. Weaver, who believes it to be a correct statement of the information we received. But as I may not have given your mother time to collect her thoughts in our brief visit, or as I may possibly, though unintentionally, have stated some things too positively, or perhaps omitted some matters that should have been mentioned; or as her thoughts have been turned to this subject by my questions, and she may have since recalled some facts which she did not think of at the time; I will consider it a great favor if you will read to her, carefully and slowly, what I have written, and if you will be so kind as to note down any modifications, alterations, or additions she may desire to make, and let me have the result whenever you conveniently can. Yours truly, R. P."

To this note a reply was received, June 30th, from a daughter of Mr. Park, returning the manuscript, stating that she had attended to the above request, and that her grandmother said her recollections were correctly represented and she had nothing to add. It is impossible, however, to convey to the reader any adequate idea of the vivacity and distinctness with which this truly venerable lady recalled and related the events of her childhood and youth, and the extreme caution with which she spoke of matters of which she was not perfectly sure.

In comparing the testimony of Mrs. Park with that of Mrs. Irwin, the reader cannot fail to notice that we have here the evidence of one who was twelve or thirteen years of age at the time of which she testifies,—who was in the immediate neighborhood of Dr. M'Millan, and intimate with his family, and who testifies respecting matters of which she had a personal knowledge, and occurrences which passed daily before her eyes, as opposed to the recollections of one who was at this period a child of six or seven years of age, upwards of ten miles distant, who had no personal knowledge of Dr. M'Millan's school, and who was certainly in error in regard to Mr. Dodd's. Also, that the question is here answered—"Who were Dr. M'Millan's pupils at this early date?" The names of at least five of them "have been found." And in the last place, it is important to observe, that as Messrs. Smith and Brice were among these students, in 1781, as Mrs. Park strongly believes, and certainly as early as 1782,—and as Dr. Lindley has stated that they were among his school-mates at Ten Mile from some time in 1782 until he left the school in 1784, it follows inevitably that they must have been pupils of Dr. M'Millan before they went to Mr. Dodd, even if we take the latest date assigned by Mrs. Park. David Smith was probably the youngest of these pupils, and about ten years of age; yet he had commenced Latin two years before, ("Old Redstone," page 443.) Mrs. Park, it will be seen, is five years older than Rev. Dr. Lindley, and enjoyed much more favorable opportunities than he, for acquiring a knowledge of the facts to which she testifies.

Of one of the students mentioned by Mrs. Park, the following information has been derived from Col. William Lea, of Allegheny county, through the politeness of Mr. J. C. Wrenshall: "Rev. Francis Reno (Episcopal minister) was a student of Mr. M'Millan, of Canonsburg. He came to the old church at Woodville, known as Chartiers Chapel, about the year 1792, and preached there until 1811. About that time he removed to Beaver, and died there about 1830."

It may seem unnecessary to add anything to testimony so explicit as that of Mrs. Park, and from a source so unimpeachable; but the reader who has taken any interest in the subject will be glad to see that her statements are not without corroborating evidence.

"*Canonsburg*, Saturday, June 24th, 1854.

"In company with John E. Black, Esq., the writer visited this day four aged persons in the vicinity of Canonsburg: Messrs. John Barr, (four miles from town,) Joseph Moss, (seven miles,) Daniel Darragh, Esq., (ten miles,) and James Thomas, (seven miles.)

4th. "John Barr was born in 1780, in Lancaster county, Pennsylvania; came West in 1785; and when about eight years of age, (1788,) was acquainted with Francis and Thomas Dunlavy, who were then going to Dr. M'Millan to school. Does not know about the Renos going to Dr. M'Millan's school, but remembers the men. One of them became an Episcopal minister, and preached about seven miles from Pittsburgh, on the Washington turnpike; the other a partner in a wholesale grocery in Pittsburgh. At least fifty years ago, Mr. Barr used to hear of Mr. Ross having taught Latin for Dr. M'Millan.

5th. "Joseph Moss was born in Chester county, Pennsylvania, in 1761, and is now in his ninety-third year. Came West in 1784, in his twenty-third year. Dr. M'Millan had been teaching some years before that time. Remembers Mr. Reno, who preached near Pittsburgh, and believes he studied under Dr. M'Millan. Mr. Reno was preaching soon after Mr. Moss came West. Mr. Moss was a surveyor in early life: attended Mr. Clarke's church, now Mr. Marshall's.

6th. "Daniel Darragh was born in Lancaster county, Pennsylvania, in 1766, and is now in his eighty-eighth year. Came West in 1786. Does not remember whether Dr. M'Millan's school was in operation then, or not. Always heard of it as the oldest school west of the mountains; never heard at that time of any other. Thinks Mr. Ross was then a lawyer in Washington. Does not remember hearing of Mr. Ross teaching. Remembers a student, named Slemens, who recited to Dr. M'Millan at his own house.

7th. "James Thomas, born in New Jersey in 1771, came West in 1773. Remembers hearing of Mr. Ross studying with Dr. M'Millan. Cannot recollect any particulars about the school.

"Mrs. Thomas remembers Rev. Samuel Porter living on Dr. M'Millan's place, and studying with him, about 1788. His son was her school-mate at that time. She remembers well that the school-house used to be called the 'Latin School.'

8th. "May 18th, 1854. Called this afternoon on Isaac White, Betsey White, and Mrs. Jane Berry, resident about a mile from Canonsburg. They are the children of George White, who died March 2, 1847, in his ninety-second year. He was one of the oldest settlers, having, with his father, John White, arrived at Chartiers April 29th, 1772. George White, being desirous to qualify himself for becoming an English teacher, repaired to Dr. M'Millan's school and attended it for some time; then re-crossed the mountains, and either taught or attended school for some time in Adams county, Pennsylvania; returned home, and after the lapse of some time again visited Adams county on the occasion of his marriage, which took place in 1786, when he was about thirty years of age.

"His children cannot fix the date of his attending school, but think it must have been some years before his marriage. They distinctly recollect having often heard him say that Latin was taught there then, though he did not study it; that Mr. Ross was there then, and was one of the Latin students; that he often spoke of the Latin students as considering themselves of a little more consequence than the other students, and as being so regarded by the others; and they have often heard him say that when the school-house was burnt, all the Latin books which had been left in it over night were consumed, and there were no more this side the mountains, which occasioned great inconvenience."

The recollection of a nephew of George White, Mr. James White, of Cecil township, who was present, coincided with that of his cousins as given above.

9th. Extract from a letter from Rev. Dr. Cephas Dodd, May 17th, 1854:—"When my father taught in Washington in 1789, Abraham Scott was there as a pupil. He was reading some of the higher classics, and had previously been at Dr. M'Millan's school. I used to hear him speak of Jemmy Ross (as he called him) as having been his teacher there. James Ross was at that time a practicing attorney in Washington, and had probably been so as early as 1787, as he was at that time one of the Trustees named in the charter of the Washington Academy."

10th. Extract from a letter from Hon. H. M. Brackenridge, a student at Jefferson College in 1805:—"Tarentum, Pennsylvania, June 12th, 1854. I have always understood that the first Latin school ever established in the Western part of Pennsylvania, was that set on foot by the Rev. John M'Millan at Canonsburg, or near that place, in a log-cabin by the road side. I have heard my father say that once, on his way from Pittsburgh to Washington court, he was induced, according to a practice almost invariable with him, to stop at the school in the log-cabin referred to, and there he found James Ross teaching a Latin class; and according to his custom, he examined the scholars, and conversed with the teacher, in whom he immediately took a great interest. He was well acquainted with the family and connections in the Barrens of York, where my father's father had also settled, and lived as friend and neighbor to the Ross family. This must have been prior to the year 1785, for this reason: my father established him self as a lawyer in Pittsburgh in 1781, and Mr. Ross must have been at least seven years at the bar before 1794, when he was a Senator of the United States. My father, on inquiring into his future prospects, advised him to study law, and gave him letters to his friends in Philadelphia, especially Mr. Coxe, with whom Mr. Ross completed his studies. From this we may form an idea of the time which must have elapsed before he came to the bar, and of the time necessary to acquire such distinction as to be elected to the Senate before the year 1794. It would seem to me that this would surely carry the period at which my father saw him teaching in the log-cabin, beyond the year 1785.

"Mr. Ross was of course a well-grounded Latin scholar, but I am not so well informed as to his proficiency in classical studies. It must have been good, judging from the high literary taste and polish of his style. James Ross, (no relative,) the celebrated teacher, and author of the grammar, was probably his teacher, as he had a Latin school at the place where the family of Mr. Ross resided in York county. This is the first time I ever heard the fact of Mr. M'Millan's being the first to establish a Latin school in the West, called in question."

11th. A reminiscence of Joseph Patterson, Esq., of Pittsburgh, is also in point. Mr. Patterson was intimately acquainted with Mr. Ross, and remembers to have heard him relate, that whilst living with Dr. M'Millan, he joined a party which was made up to go to the relief of the settlers on the Ohio, upon the occasion of an incursion of the Indians; and that upon the way they met one of the brothers Poe (mentioned in "Old Redstone," page 65) returning from his famous contest with the Indians on the banks of the Ohio, — the corpse of an Indian being slung over his horse. Now a referrence to any border history of the period will show that this celebrated encounter took place about the middle of July, 1782.*

12th. And finally the prevalence of the opinion, which appears to have been universal, and certainly has been until very recently undisputed, that Dr. M'Millan's was the first classical school in the West, is in itself, under the circumstances, strong evidence of its own correctness. Such a belief was general, long before the late Rev. Dr. M. Brown came to Canonsburg

* In a book entitled Western Adventure, will be found an account of the severe action of the Poes with the Indians, and will fix the date of that action no doubt correctly. I had an account of it from Andrew Poe himself, and also from the Rev. Thomas Marquis, who was in the engagement. In a conversation with the Hon. James Ross on the subject of that contest, he told me that he with a party of volunteers, met the Poes and their party on their return at Thomas White's, on Raccoon, bringing with them young Cherry, who was killed in the engagement, carrying him on a horse. Mr. Marquis told me he was near to him when he fell among a thicket of spice wood bushes, and soon died.

JOSEPH PATTERSON.

in 1822, and he does not seem in any wise to be justly held responsible for its existence. The writer, and those who accompanied him, can bear witness to the unfeigned surprise with which the oldest inhabitants of the country around Dr. M'Millan's residence, learned that the correctness of the opinion with which they had grown up from childhood was now called in question, — an opinion which, it had never occurred to them, could be within the reach of skepticism. That such a belief should have been entertained, apparently from the very first, by those who must necessarily have been cognizant of the facts, is altogether inexplicable on any other hypothesis than that the belief was warranted by the facts.

It is much to be regretted that the doubts which have been recently expressed had not been propounded sooner, before so many, who could have borne the amplest testimony to the facts of the case, had disappeared forever from the scene of those early trials, efforts, and difficulties, of which they loved to speak.

That such an opinion as that spoken of above was general, scarcely requires additional confirmation; but the following extract from a letter from Dr. Samuel Colver, of Jefferson, Greene county, Pennsylvania, May 28th, 1854, not only gives evidence of the state of opinion nearly forty years ago, but contains a tribute to the memory of Dr. M'Millan, so just and unstudied, and so honorable to the heart that conveys it, that the reader will readily pardon its insertion.

"My information on the subject was obtained as far back as the session of 1819–'20, at which time and subsequently I heard much relative to the early biography of Dr. M'Millan. During my first session at Jefferson College, I boarded at the house of the widow Emery, opposite the college. Mrs. Emery's house was much frequented by many of the old citizens of the town and country, who seemed to take particular pleasure in relating the remarkable incidents pertaining to the early and subsequent life of Dr. M'Millan. I afterwards boarded at the houses of William Thompson and Joseph M'Nairy. They were members of the Seceder Church, and were frequently visited by Dr. Ramsey, who was at that time pastor of that church. In all these places the early history and settlement of Dr. M'Millan was discussed and related so frequently and with such coincidence, as to make an indelible impression on my memory, so much so that they appear to me now as almost the narratives of but yesterday.

"At that time Dr. M'Millan was held in exalted veneration, not only by the citizens generally, but also by the students of the college, who not only looked upon him as the founder of that Institution, but as an oracle of wisdom and piety, from whom they might derive lessons of instruction. Dr. M'Millan must have been at that time near seventy years of age, yet the powers of his mind and body seemed in their full vigor, and the spirit of love and benevolence shone through all his actions. He regularly visited the college twice a week, excepting in bad weather, and attentively listened to the recitations of the classes in their turn. I remember well, if a student should make a mistake, that he was always the first to discover it, and would correct it by some humorous remark, which not only corrected the error but palliated it. He preached regularly at his place, and frequently at the college. His sermons were eloquent and powerful. At that time Dr. M'Millan was considered the most useful and benevolent man of his day; and I do not think that Gen. Washington was ever more beloved by the American people, than was Dr. M'Millan by those portions of Washington county, and elsewhere, where his usefulness as a preacher, and his benevolence in preparing young men for the ministry, were so extensively experienced.

"I now come to give you what information I have as regards that period of Dr. M'Millan's life in which he commenced his Latin school. This knowledge has been derived from the citizens of Canonsburg and its vicinity, many of whom were living at that time, who had been cotemporaneous with Dr. M'Millan in his early settlement. The result of this information is about this: that Dr. M'Millan first visited the western country in 1775, and preached to the border settlements of Westmoreland and Washington counties, during the summer and autumn of that year; and that he returned to the East, and removed with his family to the vicinity of Canonsburg, and immediately commenced a Latin school with the view of preparing young men for the ministry: that the celebrated James Ross was among his first students, and that he afterwards became a teacher of classics under Dr. M'Millan. Mrs. Harper remembers Ross as a teacher under her father as far back as her fifth year, which was about the year 1782: and of course Dr. M'Millan's Latin school must have commenced several years previous."

The writer of this can bear testimony to the existence of the same universal impression when he was a student in Jefferson College, some twenty years after the period referred to in Dr. Colver's letter; and when, in company with several of his class-mates, in the spirit of pilgrims to some consecrated shrine, he visited the humble "Log-Cabin" so often referred to, and heard from Mr. John M'Millan the same narrative which was repeated to him fifteen years afterwards, as recorded above, it never occurred to him that the attempt would or could be made to divest that hallowed spot of the honors it had worn so long.

But a still higher authority is that of the author of "Old Redstone," who was graduated at Jefferson College in 1815, and who states in a letter dated November 27th, 1854:—"I had always entertained the prevailing opinion about the history of the 'Log-Cabin' school, until, unexpectedly, without my seeking it, I got the statement which Mrs. Irwin, of Ohio, gave me."

The reader, who has had the patience to accompany us thus far, is in possession of all the evidence the writer has been able to collect upon the subject of our investigations. The field of his inquiries was not, however, by any means exhausted, when his progress was suddenly arrested, and circumstances unnecessary to be detailed compelled him to abandon his researches.

After the lapse of more than two years, a period of comparative leisure has at last enabled him to arrange his notes, and the reader must decide how far they render any assistance towards a settlement of the interesting question—Where was the first Literary Institution West of the Mountains?

A brief review of all that has been advanced in regard to Dr. M'Millan's school, will show that the only direct testimony in opposition to the commonly received opinion of its priority to all others, is that of Mrs. Irwin, and possibly that of Rev. Dr. Lindley. The evidence of the former is utterly irreconcilable with admitted facts; while the statements of the latter may be made to harmonize with the current belief. The opinion that Mr. Ross taught an English, and not a Latin school, is met by the repeated declaration of Dr. M'Millan, in the hearing of his children, to the contrary; by a similar declaration, as the writer understands it, on the part of one of Mr. Ross' old pupils, Abraham Scott; and by the evidence that Mr. Ross was discovered by Judge Brackenridge actually hearing a Latin class. The other arguments which have been adduced do not, upon examination, appear to carry with them even a presumption that the prevalent opinion is incorrect.

On the other hand, we have the personal recollection of an unexceptionable witness, Mrs. Park, to the effect that a Latin school was in existence at Dr. M'Millan's, as she believes, in 1781, and as she is positively certain, in 1782; the recollection of a daughter of Dr. M'Millan's, carrying the school back as far as 1782; an incident stated by Joseph Patterson, Esq., in regard to the early life of James Ross, which fixes his residence with Dr. M'Millan at least as far back as July, 1782; the circumstances related by Hon. H. M. Brackenridge, amounting to a fair presumption that Mr. Ross' residence with Dr. M'Millan was at a very early date; the statement of Mr. Moss that the school had been in existence for some years before 1784; the statement of the children of George White that in their opinion, for which they give reasons, their father must have attended Dr. M'Millan's school some years before 1786; the fact that some of the pupils of Mr. Dodd, who were with him from 1782 till at least 1784, had yet been with Dr. M'Millan also in 1782, which would appear to show conclusively that they must have been students at Chartiers before they repaired to Ten Mile; the declarations of Dr. M'Millan to his children, that his school was the first Latin school in the country; his own language, as quoted above, which it is difficult to reconcile with truth on any other hypothesis than that of the early commencement and the priority of his institution; and finally the universality of such an opinion amongst those who had the best opportunities for becoming acquainted with the facts, and for the existence and prevalence of which belief no explanation whatever has been offered, or can well be imagined, save that it coincides with the truth. The reader will judge for himself upon which side the evidence preponderates.

But further, it is alleged, ("Old Redstone," page 192,) that "The Academy did not originate in the Latin school at the 'Log-Cabin,' but was begun inde pendently of it, and superseded it, and caused its suspension." It is not enough, therefore, to maintain the honor of the parent stock: the legitimacy of the offspring must also be defended.

Now the facts of the case, as related by Dr. M'Millan in his letter and report, already quoted, and by Rev. R. Patterson, in his letter to Dr. Brown, are as follow:

That in July, 1791, upon a Monday after a sacramental season in Chartiers congregation, a consultation, at which Rev. Messrs. M'Millan and Smith, with other friends of learning, were present, was held, and a resolution adopted, to establish a Literary Institution in the West. On the question of its location, the "Log-Cabin" was proposed by Dr. M'Millan, Canonsburg by Col. Canon. It may here be remarked that if the former site had been selected, there could be no dispute as to the fact that the Academy was the successor of the Latin school. Canonsburg, however, was chosen, Dr. M'Millan concurring, and by appointment the exercises of the Academy were commenced the next morning in a field near the village, Dr. M'Millan himself taking the most prominent part in them. Mr. David Johnston was invited to attend and take charge of the Academy. Thus far the letter of Rev. R. Patterson, who made the first recitation. Must not these facts have escaped the author of "Old Redstone," when he observes, page 80, that "Dr. M'Millan had no direct agency, and took no active part in getting up the Canonsburg Academy?"

Further, Dr. M'Millan, in his letter, states:—"I had still a few with me when the academy was opened at Canonsburg, and finding that I could not teach and do justice to my congregation, I *immediately* gave it up and sent them there."—"Old Redstone," page 193.

Again, in his report to the Trustees, already quoted, Dr. M'Millan states that—"A Latin and Greek school which he had kept at his own house, for the purpose of supplying the church as far as was practicable, was transferred to this infant academy, the original fountain, &c., &c."

The only evidence to the contrary is the statement of William Darby, Esq., ("Old Redstone," page 193), that Dr. M'Millan's school was still in operation through 1789 and part of 1790, after the academy was established in Canonsburg. But in the first place, the academy was not established in Canonsburg until July, 1791; in the next place, if Mr. Darby meant the latter year, his evidence is directly contrary to that of Dr. M'Millan, who may be supposed to be better acquainted with the facts; and in the last place, it is contrary to a fair presumption from the language in which Rev. Mr. Lindley, as quoted above, describes the commencement of the Canonsburg Academy.

If the active co-operation of Dr. M'Millan in building up the academy,—the leading part he took in the very inception of the enterprise, as well as during all its progress, in selecting its teachers, in raising funds for it, in frequently visiting it, and in managing its concerns,—if all this, in connection with the immediate transfer of his pupils to the academy, a fact which he has certified under his own hand,—does not render that academy the lineal descendant of the Latin school,—it is difficult to imagine what would have constituted a legitimate succession.

If, upon the other hand, it be really incorrect to suppose that there was such an immediate succession, it is very clear that Dr. M'Millan himself labored under this mistaken impression; that the same misapprehension has always prevailed amongst those who have had the best opportunities for becoming familiar with the facts; and lastly, that the author of "Old Redstone" has himself fallen into the same error, when he states (page 77) that Mr. Smith's school, by being transferred to Dr. M'Millan's, was "the real nucleus, the larva, out of which grew eventually, first, the Canonsburg Academy, and then Jefferson College."

But with what propriety can it be said, ("Old Redstone," page 190), that an institution was "originated" by the Synod of Virginia, "located" in Canonsburg by the Presbytery of Redstone, and "merged into the academy of that place in 1791–'2," when this ecclesiastical figment never had any existence whatever, apart from that of the academy itself which had been in successful operation for two years before the Presbytery finally recognized it as an institution under their care? It has never been made to appear that the Synod of Virginia had any agency whatever in "originating" the academy at Canonsburg, that institution having been in existence some three months before the date of the Synod's resolution on the subject of western education. Why should we seek, at this late day, and without the slightest evidence, to justify such a course, to crown the Synod with the honors which for more than half a century have encircled the brow of M'Millan?

It is due to the memory of the noble-minded and self-sacrificing fathers of our western churches, to say that no spirit of jealousy could ever have found a lodgment in their bosoms. Disinterested zeal for the service of their Divine Master was all that impelled them to thread the mazes of these western forests, to follow close upon the obscure pathway of the pioneer, and almost simultaneously with the erection of his rude hut, to rear beside it the school-house and the church. It reflects the highest honor on these illustrious men, that scarce thirty years were suffered to elapse after the first daring adventurer had penetrated a hitherto pathless wilderness,—thirty years, not of prosperity and peace, but of painful vigilance and unceasing struggle, of unexampled hardships and heroic endurance,—until the poetry and eloquence of Greece and Rome, the truths of modern science, and of sacred learning, had found three humble halls, three devoted instructors, and a score of assiduous pupils,—though the war-whoop of the retreating savage still echoed within the surrounding valleys, and his council-fires still blazed upon the hills. History presents few parallels of achievements so worthy of remembrance, yet so speedily forgotten. Amidst any other people than the ungrateful descendants of such heroic sires, the consecrated spot wher learning reared her first abode had long since been distinguished by some fitting monument, inscribed with a name posterity should "not willingly let die."

It is due also to those whose evidence has been collated on the preceding pages, to say that the discrepancies which may be found to exist in their reminiscences, some of which have been passed by unnoticed, whilst of others it has been no grateful task to speak, should not affect their character for truthfulness. It is understood that they testify to the best of their remembrance; nor is it surprising that there should be some variations in the recollections of occurrences of three score years ago.

Especially is it due to the respected author of "Old Redstone," to bear testimony to the fidelity with which he has discharged the task he has undertaken, and to the value of his labors in rescuing so much of the history of Western Presbyterianism from that oblivion to which it was so rapidly hastening. With the devotion of a Tully, he has striven to remove the thistles that were so quickly concealing the monuments of the wisdom of the past: with the piety of an Old Mortality, he has endeavored to deepen the inscriptions sacred to the memory of the religion and the patriotism of our fathers. No one would shrink sooner than he, from denying praise where praise was justly due; and his hand would be the first to replace a chaplet he had unwittingly removed.

R. P.

Oakland College, Miss., *January 1st*, 1857.

To review this able and ingenious paper, in all its details, would be un-easonably taxing the patience of readers. We feel no special zeal about he issue of this question of priority in respect to the early Latin schools in Vestern Pennsylvania. It may be thought by some that this question was nnecessarily and foolishly raised in the first instance, and that the almost niversally current traditions should have been left undisturbed: — and that t was an invidious and dishonorable employment to attempt to displace a arland from the brow of Dr. M'Millan. Now we claim a veneration for the xalted character of that never-to-be-forgotten father of our Western Zion, ot inferior to that cherished by the writer of this paper. We greatly spect the memory of Dr. M'Millan. But to receive and adopt implicitly very tradition that may gather round a good man's history, is rather an uivocal way of evincing true respect. All who are familiar with history, e aware that ingenious fictions and legends have often been employed to gment the renown of distinguished men, and to throw a halo of glory ound their heads. Witness the ingenious tale about Dr. M'Millan in "Day's istorical Collection of Pennsylvania," page 668, where it is stated that "he ttled in Washington county in 1773,"—and "with the commencement of s labors, began his school at Canonsburg," and that "the number of his students having increased, a stone building was erected in 1790;" — not one sentence or clause of which is correct. Witness, again, the story told of Dr. Witherspoon: that when the Convention met to form the Constitution of the United States, the Doctor put a Confession of Faith in his pocket; and having our Presbyterian Constitution constantly ready for reference, he succeeded in getting our admirable frame of Government modeled, in its main features, after our Presbyterian form of Government. Whereas, Dr. Witherspoon, though a member of the Continental Congress that adopted and signed the Declaration of Independence, where his name is also found, and though a member of the Convention that drew up the articles of confederation in 1778, was not a member at all of the Convention that in 1786 formed the Constitution! Witness, again, the beautiful story about President Davies, the great American preacher — a story once universally told and believed among Presbyterians in Virginia — how, that when on a visit to England, and invited to preach before the court of George II., his overpowering eloquence so deeply moved the king that he said, aloud to one of his nobles, "did ever man speak like this man?" and how Mr. Davies paused, and then said, slowly and solemnly: "when the lion roars, the beasts of the forest tremble; when the king of heaven speaks, let the kings of the earth keep silence!" The whole story has been, long since, proved to be a mere fabrication. Witness the story of Lord Baltimore having first introduced the principles of religious liberty into his government of the Maryland colony — a legend which the Hon. J. P. Kennedy, late Secretary of the Navy, scattered to the winds, by showing, conclusively, that the principles of religious liberty were in the charter, granted by a British Protestant king to Lord Baltimore, and not in the Colonial Constitution of Maryland, further than the charter required. And, to cite a case of earlier history, witness the pleasant legend about Dionysius, the Areopagite: how he had stood among a group of philosophers, in Egypt, at the time of the supernatural darkness, occurring during our Saviour's crucifixion, and exclaimed, "Either the frame of nature is about to dissolve, or the God of nature is suffering!" — a story which the eloquent Saurin, having examined its claims, has told us, dies "pierced by a thousand spears." Indeed nothing is more common than fictitious and unfounded exaggerations gather ing round the character and doings of great and good men. And he who undertakes to question or refute such things, ought not to be branded a inimical or unfriendly, or lacking in a just regard to their reputation. Ye blind idolators of such men are found not only to possess an easy faith ready to receive implicitly every exaggerated tale, but to denounce, wit bitterness, all who do not possess the same ample powers of deglutition Very far from such a character, however, is Prof. Patterson. Though h has succeeded, apparently, in completely satisfying himself, as to the co rectness of the old current traditions about the "Log-Cabin," and the origi of Jefferson College, he treats with kindness and respect those who ha heretofore differed from him in their views. His paper, in our judgment, evinces eminent talents and earnest zeal; and what is better still, a kind, and conciliatory spirit. After a careful consideration of all that he has adduced in support of the several conclusions at which he has arrived, we cannot yet acknowledge ourselves convinced, or, in some particulars, even shaken. We will attempt a very brief statement of the matter, as it still appears to us.

1st. Was Jefferson College indebted for its origin to the "Log-Cabin" school at Chartiers? We answer that the true facts of the case now brought to light, as given in our introductory chapter of this work, from the testimony of Dr. C. Dodd, and Dr. M'Millan himself, show that Dr. M'Millan and his compeers, Messrs. Smith and Henderson, together with Judges M'Dowell, Allison, and others, having failed to resuscitate the Washington Academy, after the disaster of the fire, united in setting on foot a similar institution in the village of Canonsburg, encouraged especially by the effective co-operation of Col. Canon; and that the "Log-Cabin" school had nothing to do in the matter—though the contiguity of the new Academy rendered it both convenient and desirable to Dr. M'Millan to suspend the further continuance of his school. The discontinuance of the "Log-Cabin" school was a mere incidental circumstance, arising from the fact that a good Academy, in his immediate neighborhood, and partly through his agency, was now under way. If Dr. M'Millan and his brethren could have succeeded with the Academy at Washington, does any one believe that his school, in that event, would have had an outgrowth into another Academy, either at Canonsburg or Chartiers? It is probable, indeed, that had he succeeded in his wishes at Washington, he would not so soon have relinquished the school at Chartiers. For the sake of poor and pious young men boarding with him, without charge, or in the neighborhood, he would have continued the school a while longer. But now the great enterprise which had been commenced, and failed, at Washington, succeeded by their all uniting upon Canonsburg: its immediate vicinity to Dr. M'Millan brought him relief from what he felt to be a heavy charge upon his time and his resources, and an interference with his pastoral labors; and whether he gave up the school the very next day, or a week, or a month after; or even if he had closed it a few weeks before, in the certain anticipation of planting the original academical enterprise at Canonsburg, does not make the smallest difference—does not effect the question as to the *succession;* unless it be such a succession as the famous case of the Church Steeple and the Goodwin Sandbar! If any thing were wanting to confirm the view we have now given, it is found in the language of the *second memorial* which the Trustees sent to the Legislature, in which they give *their* account of the origin of the Academy, but make not the remotest allusion to the "Log-Cabin" school. Let the reader turn to this paper on page 46 of this work and see their statement. Now, this view of the whole case does not derogate one iota from the true honor of Dr. M'Millan. In fact, ever since we have more fully understood what he did for Washington Academy, and what efforts he made to arouse the people there to a noble and united movement for their Academy, and what he, with others, then proceeded to do at Canonsburg, we cannot but wonder that any concern should be felt about holding on to the story of the old "Log-Cabin" school growing into an Academy. But then it is asked, what are we to do with the apparent endorsement on the part of the Doctor, of the statement put forth by the Trustees of Jefferson College, in July, 1833? Why, how do we know that he endorsed it? He may not have seen it at all;* or he may have expressed his dissent; or he may have thought it not worth while to trouble himself about it. We know just nothing at all about the matter. And shall advantage be taken of our ignorance how that matter really was? and then, forsooth, his *endorsement* be claimed? "Nay, verily." But, then, what shall we make of the Doctor's expression in 1817? "A Latin and Greek school which he had kept at his own house, was transferred to this infant Academy, the original fountain of science and literature in these western States." It is urged that the last clause refers to the Latin school, and proves its priority to all other schools. But the natural construction of the passage connects the concluding expression with the "infant Academy." We have no doubt that it was this of which the expression was used. Is it necessary to go further than the Canonsburg Academy? Would the previous short life of the school at Washington, for some fifteen or sixteen months, make such an expression about Canonsburg Academy, near thirty years after that fountain began to flow, and at length to enlarge into Jefferson College, objectionable or untrue? And was not the *priority* of the Canonsburg Academy to Jefferson College the natural occasion of the expression, "original fountain?" We can see no reason in the world why any body now would make the "Log-Cabin" school the sire, or the grand-sire of Jefferson College. We know the author of "Old Redstone" can be quoted as favoring this view. But then the author did not know all the facts in the case—facts which place, really, greater honor on Dr. M'Millan, than the old theory.

2d. The next point of inquiry which we will briefly consider is as to the character of Mr. Smith's school, at Buffalo. For we are put to the proof of its very existence as a Latin and scientific school. It is useless to inquire about its precedence, if it is ruled out of court altogether. It is true, the new theory is that it was a *theological school;* and as in that character it takes the precedence of grammar schools, academies, and even colleges, it

* The records show that Dr. M'Millan was not present at that meeting of the Board. Even the Board itself probably entrusted the whole matter of drawing up and publishing the statement to their secretary, or a committee, and did not see it themselves till it was published. Further, the old records had been for some time mislaid, and were supposed to be lost. And those who proposed that paper were not aware that their own records contained a very different account of the birth of the Academy.

might be supposed that this would be sufficiently satisfactory. But we are compelled to decline that honor—at least as to its distinctive character—for the Buffalo school. Now to maintain that this school was altogether different from the Ten Mile or the Chartiers school, and, in fact, was no such school at all; and yet further maintain that it *succeeded* both these schools, is certainly a work of supererogation, for who does not know that *theological schools* presuppose other and previous literary institutions? But this new method of considering the case, puts one in much the same condition with the plaintiff who sought to recover damages from a man for breaking his borrowed kettle, and who was astonished to find the defendânt's counsel making three points in his defence: 1st., that the kettle was cracked when borrowed; 2d., was sound when returned, and 3d., was never borrowed at all! But seriously, was Mr. Smith's school like the others, or was it simply a *Divinity Hall?*

(1.) The Rev. Joseph Patterson's language in his memorandum ("Old Redstone," p. 81, quoted by Prof. Patterson,) clearly implies that it was, in part, at least, literary and scientific. Or why should he speak of there being "no places of public education?" Does he not obviously mean academies, colleges, &c.? This seems to us the natural meaning of his expressions. And, if so, it settles the question.

(2.) The Rev. Robert Patterson, in his letter to Dr. Brown, in 1845, as quoted also by Prof. Patterson, after stating that some of the Presbyterian clergymen were in the habit of giving instruction in the languages and sciences to young men, proceeds to mention by name Messrs. Smith and M'Millan; and makes no distinction whatever, in respect to the character of their schools. This testimony we regard as perfectly conclusive.

(3.) Dr. Cephas Dodd testifies to an agreement between the Rev. Messrs. Thaddeus Dodd and Joseph Smith, to superintend, alternately, the education of certain young men, and plainly implying that their instructions were of a similar nature—that their schools were, so far as such young men were concerned, alike. The testimony of Dr. Lindley, Mr. John M'Millan, Mrs. Harper, Mrs. Park, &c., we regard as of no weight whatever on this particular point. By such testimony, or testimony equally strong, we could annihilate the Ten Mile school, as a Latin school, altogether. But it is alleged that the author of "Old Redstone," has admitted that the Buffalo school was not a Latin school. The remark in "Old Redstone," page 146, that Mr. Smith's school at Buffalo "may have been the first with a more special and exclusive reference to the training of young men for the service of the church," was certainly not meant to convey the idea that it was rather theological than literary; but only that it was of a less mixed character than the Ten Mile school, and more exclusively with a view of educating, in their literary and scientific course, candidates for the ministry.

(4.) Mrs. Irwin's testimony is fully to this character of the school. She certainly meant that it preceded just such a school as that at Chartiers, however mistaken she may have been on the question of precedence. And her competency as a witness to this extent, though not important, may be admitted when other witnesses, much inferior, on this point, have been called into court.

(5.) The Rev. William Wylie, D. D., now in his eighty-fourth year, was born and brought up in Buffalo, not far from Mr. Smith's; and must have been in his twelfth or thirteenth year, in the fall of 1785. He says, in a letter dated March 13th, 1857: "That school was certainly occupied in furnishing young men with a classical education, more than in giving ecclesiastical instruction. I believe the testimony you have given the public from Mrs. Irwin is fully entitled to credit, interwoven as it is with many of the interesting scenes of her youth, and kept almost continually in view by the recollection of the many things with which these events were associated." The second point, then, we think, is clearly and finally settled. But now as to the third point.

3d. Where was the first school for training young men in a literary and scientific course, and especially for the gospel ministry? The author of the paper before us has evidently taken considerable pains to collect a mass of testimony in favor of the "Log-Cabin" school. And he has certainly evinced much ability in arranging it, and bringing it out in its full strength. Perhaps he will be thought right in the conclusion which he has reached. If so, we are not in the least troubled on that account. Truth, not victory, should be our aim. "Fiat justitia, ruat cœlum." But "audi alteram partem;" and let us just observe that there are some facts which seem to us stubborn, and not easily explained in harmony with the entire extent of Prof. Patterson's conclusions. We will briefly state them.

(1.) It is a fact that the Rev. Robert Patterson made the following statement, in his general narrative of his reminiscences, about the early educational enterprises — which he drew up at the request of Dr. M. Brown: "Between 1780 and 1790, and chiefly in the latter part of these ten years, some of the few Presbyterian clergymen living west of the mountains in Pennsylvania, were in the habit of giving instruction in the Languages and Sciences to young men whose object in their studies was the gospel ministry. The Rev. Messrs. Joseph Smith and John M'Millan were distinguished in their devotion to this cause. They both settled in congregations in Washington county, Pennsylvania. Mr. Smith had a small building erected in a corner of the garden, called 'the students' room,' too small to be dignified with the name of a hall. And Mr. M'Millan had a small log-cabin built, near his log dwelling house, known to this day by the appellation of the 'Log-Cabin.' In these primitive seminaries, &c." Here is certainly a statement from an important witness — by far the most competent, in the judgment of Dr. Carnahan, on the subject. For he expressly tells Prof. Patterson that his father is, perhaps, "*the best living witness in regard to the origin of Latin schools west of the mountains;*" and he gives his reasons for so regarding him. Now, in the above statement, carefully made at his leisure, in his study, without the presence of any one putting questions to him, or by any possibility guiding him unconsciously in any particular direction — this "best living witness" says "between 1780 and 1790, and chiefly in the latter part of these ten years, (that is between 1785 and 1790,) some few Presbyterian clergymen, &c." Would not any one who is not strongly committed to a foregone conclusion, infer that according to the best of Mr. Patterson's recollections these *Latin schools* were opened during and after 1785? And when he goes on *twice* to speak *first* of Mr. Smith and his school — that his impression was that *he* was at least as early as any other in this movement? that his school did not *follow* Dr. M'Millan's? that it was, at any rate, quite as early? He shows, also, that he had some minute and particular reminiscences about both schools. If after all, Dr. M'Millan's school, as a *Latin school*, was in full operation five years before this time, could he have been ignorant of that fact, when he evidently knows so much about it, in other respects? And if he was not ignorant of the earlier origin of the Log-Cabin school, how can we possibly explain the whole passage? If he had *designed* to ignore the earlier origin of Dr. M'Millan's school, and to lead us completely into a chronological error, could he have used any different or stronger language? In fine, we think this whole statement of the Rev. Robert Patterson presents a serious objection to the conclusions which the Professor has adopted. We shall not comment upon the manner in which the Professor disposes of this testimony of his father. We think that here, at least, he signally fails in his attempt to get out of this difficulty, by making the testimony, in effect, the very reverse of what it naturally means.

(2.) The Rev. Joseph Patterson's memorandum seems to us fairly to imply not only that there were no colleges, academies, &c., but that there were no similar schools or seminaries to that to which he repaired. If there was an older and larger institution, then, at Dr. M'Millan's, with young men preparing for the ministry, a log-cabin, Latin school, &c., he would not, in our judgment, have expressed himself just as he did. "There being no places of public education in this country, I, with a few others, studied with the Rev. Joseph Smith."

(3.) The statement given by Mrs. Irwin presents a strong objection to Prof. Patterson's conclusions; and so far from being weakened by his vigorous attack, has rather gathered strength from the critical ordeal through which it has passed. We would here state that we adopted a precisely similar course to that described in Prof. Patterson's paper, in the case of Mrs. Park. We took down Mrs. Irwin's statement immediately after the interview. Several months afterwards we enclosed it to the Rev. Mr. Smith, of Marysville, requesting him to read it to her, and ascertain whether it was correct. A copy of this letter and his answer are before us, but we think it unnecessary to insert them. The result was, that we obtained perfect assurance that we had her precise statement. It was to this effect: "That she was between twelve and fifteen years of age, living near Mr. Smith's, one of his spiritual children, took a great interest then in what Mr. Smith did, in this matter, and all her life after, familiarly remembered the following facts, viz: that in 1785, Mr. Smith, of Buffalo and Cross Creek congregations, opened a school for assisting and training young men for the gospel ministry; that Mr. McGready, Mr. Brice, Mr. Porter, and Mr. Patterson, began their course with him, Mr. James Hughs soon after joining them; that Mr. McGready came from Dr. M'Millan's, with whom he had been living, not as a student, but as a laborer on his farm; that five congregations, through the ladies, united in furnishing these students (with the exception of Mr. McGready) with clothing, viz: Buffalo, Cross Creek, Chartiers, Bethel and Ten Mile; that they made up summer and winter clothing for several of these young men, (coloring linen for summer wear in a dye made of new mown hay;) that this was the first movement made for preparing young men for the ministry; that there was no such school at this time at Chartiers, nor until after the one at Buffalo was discontinued; that Mr. M'Millan and the Chartiers ladies took their share in this effort to sustain the school at Buffalo, Mr. McGready coming from Dr. M'Millan's to the school." Now, this entire statement, which is only *partially* given in the paper under review, contains some remarkable points. In the first place, its singular, yet wholly undesigned coincidence with the statements of the Rev. Messrs. Joseph Patterson and Robert Patterson, are especially worthy of notice. The three statements taken together form a threefold cord, not easily broken. This is an element of its strength not heretofore noticed. In the second place, her minute and circumstantial account of the concerted measures taken in all the congregations for sustaining the school, could not possibly have been a mere fiction of her fancy. It must have been so. And it proves not only how clear was her memory in the case, but that it is exceedingly unlikely that at the same time there was a similar school at Chartiers. In the third place, the specific statement that Mr. McGready came from Dr. M'Millan's to this school, carries with it great force, as proving that a similar school was not then in operation at Chartiers. In the fourth place, Mrs. Irwin's qualifications as a witness in the case, are thoroughly endorsed by her minister and Dr. Wylie. But her testimony has been assailed, first because she knew, or at least said, nothing about the Ten Mile school; and even the author of "Old Redstone" is represented as "entirely having set it aside," on this account. Now this is a sheer mistake. The fact of her silence in reference to Mr. Dodd's school, is distinctly recognized and accounted for. The truth is, Mrs. Irwin ignores that school precisely in the same way that Mr. Doddridge, nearly forty years before, in his "Notes on the Life and Manners of the Western Settlers," giving an account of the first movements in the cause of education, ignored it; and just as Rev. Messrs. Joseph Patterson and Robert Patterson also both ignored it. When not one of these made the least allusion expressly to the

Ten Mile school, it is not strange that Mrs. Irwin does not. But, in the second place, it is thought that the error she committed about Mr. McGready being a laborer on Dr. M'Millan's farm vitiates her whole testimony. (The legal maxim is, "*Falsus in uno, falsus in omnibus;*" not "*ignarus in uno, ignarus in omnibus.*") Much pains are taken to refute this statement; and the testimony of Mrs. Harper and Mrs. Park is adduced to show how utterly erroneous it was; and quite an eloquent and moving representation is given of the odious light in which it places Dr. M'Millan—how that he, forgetting or disregarding the injunction of his preceptor, Dr. Smith, of Pequea, for near ten years took a young man that had been sent to him all the way from North Carolina, in order that he might train and educate him for the ministry, and set him to work for him on his farm! Now, we have no doubt, this was a mistake, or an inadvertence on the part of Mrs. Irwin. And yet it was not strange that she made such a statement. About that unimportant circumstance, she had heard what was true, in part, at that time, viz: that Mr. McGready was not then engaged in regular study; but was known or seen to be, sometimes, at the Doctor's, aiding in farming operations—at least in looking after the Doctor's affairs in his absence, as Mrs. Harper admits. The position of Mr. McGready, at that time, is no doubt correctly given by those ladies. We will further add, that we have learned, from a very intelligent source, that Mr. McGready, during the summer of 1785, took the small-pox and lay very low for some time, so that his life was nearly despaired of—that he slowly recovered, and that the first time he was able to go abroad, he attended a sacramental meeting in the Mingo Creek settlement, where Mr. Smith was assisting Dr. M'Millan on the occasion; and that under the preaching of Mr. Smith, Mr. McGready was brought under deep spiritual exercises of mind, which resulted in a hearty surrender of himself to his Saviour and his service; that he continued to regain his health and strength, but was still unable, for some time, to apply himself to regular studies. On the opening of Mr. Smith's school, he repaired to Buffalo. He had already made some progress in his preparatory course, even before he left North Carolina; and whilst teaching the English school for Dr. M'Millan, of which Mrs. Harper testifies, for she was his pupil. He prosecuted his studies with Dr. M'Millan, just as others did, both before and after this time; but there being no regular arrangement for classical studies at Chartiers, he went, no doubt with the consent of Dr. M'Millan, to Buffalo. Now, this circumstance of his going to Buffalo, which is not, and cannot be called in question, is a strong presumptive evidence that, as Mrs. Irwin says, "there was no such school, at this time, at Chartiers." There is not any force, in our judgment, in the attempt to show that Mrs. Irwin's statement would involve a reflection on Dr. M'Millan, as having neglected the injunction of his old teacher, Dr. Smith. We have no doubt, that as soon as ever the great revival (which began in the fall of 1781, and continued with signal power the following year,) brought out a number of pious, devoted young men, Dr. M'Millan took measures to help them in their studies for the ministry. But scarcely any of these fruits of the revival were brought out in his pastoral charge, though, in other respects, the results of this blessed season were most abundant, both in Chartiers and Pigeon Creek. But though, in subsequent years, many ministers were raised up in these congregations, it was not so during the first eight or nine years of the Doctor's ministry. Facts and records will clearly show this. Notwithstanding, we have no doubt that Dr. M'Millan opened the way and welcomed to his house any that desired to receive his instructions. But the "Latin School" was not, as we think, the prominent matter from the beginning. His English school was early organized, and generally taught by those who were reciting, at his own house, to himself, in languages and sciences. And occasionally one or more students of the same description were also with him, besides the teachers; such, perhaps, as Abraham Scott.*

(4.) Dr. Carnahan's statement, though in part "of a derivative character," furnishes much support to the testimony of the witnesses already cited. It is true, that the greater part of what Dr. Carnahan states, he got from Mr. Wilkins. But he shows how much weight is to be attached to Mr. Wilkins' account. Dr. Carnahan regarded him as an intelligent man, and perfectly reliable. For he had lived with Dr. M'Millan during the very period under consideration — during the time that Mr. Ross was there. He knew all about Mr. Ross, and his family, and his former history. He expressly stated to Dr. Carnahan that Mr. Ross was engaged to teach the Doctor's children, and those of the neighborhood, while he himself studied Latin with the Doctor. This gentleman remembered nothing of James Hughs, John Brice, R. Marshall and others studying Latin and Greek there. At least Dr. Carnahan does not remember that he ever spoke of them. But the strongest point in Dr. Carnahan's testimony is, that he never heard any thing at

---

*That Mr. Dodd and Mr. Smith should have a little preceded Dr. M'Millan in the cause of classical instruction is not only probable, from local causes, viz: that those who first began to look forward to the ministry were principally residing in their congregations; but also from the prominent characters of these two ministers. A decided turn for energetic action and for devising measures promptly for carrying on the great interests of the church, characterized these men. On the other hand, Dr. M'Millan's mind was eminently conservative. He was wise in counsel. He was an able defender of the "old paths." His mind was not of the inventive order. He was not ecclesiastically a De Witt Clinton or a Henry Clay, but much more a John Marshall. He was not the Luther or Calvin of the West, but rather the *Melancthon*, or the *Turretine*, or the *Beza*. He did not originate or lead forward the *missionary* movement in behalf of the western Indians. That honor must be assigned to Messrs. Macurdy, James and Thomas Hughs, Marquis, and others. So some of those men, with Dr. Anderson, led the way in the *temperance cause*, and in the *Sunday school* cause. The post unanimously assigned to Dr. M'Millan was to give theological instruction, and, for more than thirty years, to aid in training young men, for their great work of preaching the everlasting gospel.

variance with this general account *during all the time that he lived at Canonsburg*, — nor until he met with a different view, given by his old friend, Dr. M. Brown, and *even then he could recall nothing that shook his confidence* in Mr. Wilkins' statement.* Prof. Patterson, besides describing this testimony as "of a derivative character," (and therefore more closely resembling a large mass of his own testimony,) has taken several exceptions to this statement of Dr. Carnahan. But we shall not attempt to follow him in his criticisms. We hope the reader will give them all the force they merit. Neither do we think it necessary to travel over the whole ground in company with Prof. Patterson's witnesses, many of whom we know are of the most respectable character. The testimony of Dr. M'Millan's children claims very great respect. The statements of the late venerable Mr. John M'Millan, about what he heard his father say, are certainly strong. But it would not be difficult to show how they might all be accounted for, without, in the slightest degree, impeaching the veracity of either father or son, and yet leaving the general conclusion supported by such witnesses as Rev. Robert Patterson, Rev. Joseph Patterson, Mrs. Irwin, Mr. Wilkins, and Dr. Wylie, unshaken. And so with regard to the testimony of the late Mrs. Jane Harper. † Her testimony, indeed, is a little on both sides; for she

---

* The entire statement of Dr. Carnahan, as given by Prof. Patterson, was read over slowly and distinctly to Dr. Addison, of Pittsburgh, son of the distinguished Judge Addison, and one of Mr. Ross' executors by his will, and who is known to be more intimately acquainted with Mr. Ross' history than any one now living. He assured us that Dr. Carnahan's account might be fully relied on as perfectly true. In his vivacious manner he added: "It is, every word of it, gospel." He further confirmed Dr. Carnahan's account of Mr. Ross' scholarship. He likewise confirmed Mr. Wilkins' statement of the earlier history of Mr. Ross; and further related the circumstance that accounted for Mr. Ross' sudden and almost instantaneous rise at the bar, as soon as he commenced practice as a lawyer.

† This venerable lady has recently died. In an obituary notice, published in the "Banner and Advocate," respecting Mrs. Jane Harper, widow of the late Samuel Harper, Esq., and eldest daughter of the late Rev. John M'Millan, D. D., it is stated, (the italics are ours,): "Mrs. Harper passed through eventful times in the civil and religious history of Western Pennsylvania, of much of which her mind was an accurate repository, &c. She had a kind remembrance of James Ross and James McGready — the former of whom became an eminent lawyer and statesmen; the latter a renowned Evangelist and pastor in Kentucky. They had lived in her father's family, and *had been her teachers.* The former had taught a Latin and English school in a log-cabin, near her father's house, while he was pursuing his legal studies; which of course was prior to 1784, for in that year he was admitted to the bar, and entered at once upon a large practice. Mrs. Harper always asserted that those annalists of the Western church, who postpone her father's log-cabin school to a later date then those of the Rev. Joseph Smith, on Buffalo, and Rev. Thaddeus Dodd, on Ten-Mile, are in error. She said her father's was started before either of them, in a rude log-cabin, near the house, which was soon afterwards burnt down; whereupon Mr. Ross left, and all the pupils except Mr. M'Gready, *who remained in*

remembers about Dr. M'Millan's English school, and who taught it, &c. But the most important witness is the venerable Mrs. Park. That she, at the age of eighty-five, has given the honest impressions which she recalled of her childhood and youth, we have not the smallest doubt. It has seemed to us, however, that she has blended the reminiscences of different dates in such a manner, that, in a way perfectly natural, she has thrown back upon earlier years impressions of later periods. We appeal to all who have been conversant with very aged persons, whether this has not often been noticed. It is also surprising to find that her memory fails on certain particulars, when we might have expected as much distinctness of recollection as in other cases. She remembers nothing of Mr. Ross being a scholar as well as a teacher — nothing of Mr. McGready's teaching — nothing of Dr. M'Millan's English school. Her impressions about certain young men may possibly belong to a period a few years later than she supposes.* Her entire testimony about the *books* and about the *Latin school* may easily be accounted for in the same way. It seems to us, indeed, that her testimony warrants the conclusion that clasical studies were, at an early period, pursued by different persons at the Doctor's own house, and sometimes by the assistance of the teacher, such may have been the case in reference to Mr. Ross. As to the testimony of the Hon. H. M. Brackenridge — of the children of George White, (who went to qualify himself to teach an *English school,*) of Dr. Colver, &c., &c., we are perfectly willing to admit that much of it is forcible — though "of a derivative character," and that taken together it makes out a plausible, perhaps a strong case. † We cannot close this paper without a few additional remarks. The argument from the silence of the record of Redstone Presbytery is apparently misunderstood;

---

the family, and worked on the farm, until Mr. Smith started his school, where he went then. A few years afterwards another log-cabin for the school was erected and its labors resumed, *this* being the one upon which the chroniclers referred to based their statements. Such briefly is her explanation of the current anachronism, as given to the writer of this a few months before her death." This entire statement lends strong confirmation, in our judgment, to the view we have taken about the earlier character of Dr. M'Millan's school, and the *true* date of the *Latin school.*

* "I think Mrs. Harper was mistaken in the time she says D Smith, McGready, and Brice were at Dr. M'Millan's Log-Cabin."—*Rev. Dr. Wylie, in letter above cited.*

† Some estimate may be formed, perhaps, of the weight to be attached to the greater part of all the testimony which Prof. Patterson has collected; and to the present current traditions about Canonsburg, if we only consider how every one of these witnesses would have answered the questions: "Did Jefferson College originate in the 'Log-Cabin' school?" "Is this, to the best of your knowledge, the prevailing tradition and opinion around Canonsburg?" Would not both these questions be answered promptly and unanimously in the affirmative? And yet does not every one *now* see from the testimony of Dr. C. Dodd, and of Dr. M'Millan himself, as already given, that this was *not the case?*

and the attempt to refute it misses the point at issue. But before we bring this distinctly to view, we must first clear the way a little. Let it then be remembered that it is claimed for Dr. M'Millan, that in pursuance of the injunction of Dr. Smith of Pequea, he immediately after his settlement west of the mountains, sought out some suitable young men and began to train them in Latin and Greek, &c., — *therefore* his Latin school must have preceded all others. It is replied, in the *first place*, that Dr. M'Millan's account of that charge of his old preceptor justifies no such construction of it as is now attempted to be given to it. Let it again be carefully examined, and we are confident this will be seen. In the *second place*, Dr. M'Millan's statement, in his letter to Dr. Carnahan, of what he actually proceeded to do in order to carry out that charge, gives no intimation of the precise time when he succeeded in accomplishing this object. It is altogether an inference, arising from a foregone conclusion, — to make it refer to the first years of Dr. M'Millan's settlement. But further we allege, in reply, that when Dr. M'Millan states in his manuscript what he does *not state* in his letter to Dr. Carnahan, *who those were* that he thus gathered around him to train and instruct, he mentions several persons who had been previously with Mr. Dodd and Mr. Smith, and does not give the name of a single one that preceded them. His language in this manuscript, which is dated *January*, 1832, from which he copies extensively, but not entirely, in his letter to Dr. Carnahan, written *two months after*, viz: March 26th, is precisely this: "When I determined to come to this country, Dr. Smith enjoined it upon me to look out for some pious young men, and educate them for the ministry; for, said he, though some men of piety and talents may go to a new country at first, yet if they are not careful to raise up others, the country will not be well supplied. Accordingly I collected a few, who gave evidence of piety, and instructed them in the knowledge of the Latin and Greek languages, *some of whom* became useful, and others eminent, ministers of the gospel, viz: James Hughs, John Brice, James McGready, William Swan, Samuel Porter and Thomas Marquis. All these I boarded and taught, without any compensation, except about forty dollars which Mr. Swan gave to my wife after he was settled in the ministry. I had still a few with me when the academy was opened in Canonsburg, and finding that I could not teach and do justice to my congregation, I immediately gave it up and sent them there. For an account of the revivals of religion, which took place in the congregation, I must refer you to the Western Missionary Magazine, vol. 2d, page 353." Now, this is the record from which the Doctor gave only a part, or an extract, in his letter written *two months* afterwards to Dr. Carnahan. The italics are ours. We again affirm, that it contains not a syllable to show that Dr. Smith meant that he would have Dr. M'Millan to begin, forthwith, his efforts for training young men— but only that Dr. M'Millan should keep this object in view, and in due time when the way would be open, that he should proceed in this good work.

35

And we further affirm, that it contains not a syllable to show that Dr. M'Millan put any other construction upon it; and further still it shows, when he did set about this matter, what he did and how he proceeded, and with whom he began the whole enterprise. By his saying: "accordingly I collected a few, who gave evidence of piety, and *some of whom* became useful, &c., viz: James Hughs, John Brice," &c. we are fully warranted in saying that he speaks of these as a part of his *first students*. If this construction is not sustained by the whole drift of the passage, we are altogether at fault. Indeed, it seems to us strange, that any attempt should be made to prove the earlier date of Dr. M'Millan's school from this letter to Dr. Carnahan. It seems to assume that Dr. M'Millan was charged with beginning an enterprise, without any consideration, whether there were materials with which to begin it, or not.

Again it is suggested that his school must have been before 1781; for it is urged he is stating things in chronological order; and he introduces his account of the revivals, which began that year *after* his account of his school, and therefore the school must have preceded it. And yet in the very sentence before, he mentions the death of his wife in 1819; a statement manifestly out of chronological order. Nor can it be said that this statement about Mrs. M'Millan's death was introduced in connection with an account of his marriage, &c. For he had mentioned that some distance back in his narrative. And after that, he proceeded to tell of his removal, of his Log-Cabin, and the incidents connected with his beginning house-keeping, &c. And we have already quoted from his manuscript his manner of referring to the revivals. But he does not, as in his letter to Dr. Carnahan, give a further statement about them. Indeed, this circumstance, together with other peculiarities about the manuscript, its date, its beginning with an account of the Doctor's family, &c., lead us to believe that he had it before him when he wrote to Dr. Carnahan, transcribing some parts, altering others, and omitting others. That important "viz.," in the passage about his school is not in his letter to Dr. Carnahan. But it is in the manuscript, and gives it peculiar point and significance. Those three expressions—"accordingly I collected a few"—"some of whom"—"viz."—are all inseparably joined and fully bear us out in all that has been said about Dr. M'Millan's telling us with whom his Latin school *began*. Now, it was in view of this account of the matter that we regard the silence of the records of Redstone Presbytery as very significant, and confirming our construction of what Dr. M'Millan's account means. It is contended by our opponents that Dr. Smith meant that Dr. M'Millan must begin what he had enjoined on him very soon after he would settle in the West. It is further plead that Dr. M'Millan so understood him, and so did proceed "to look out for some pious young men and educate them for the ministry." Now, then, confronting all this strange construction and argument, we ask, that since Dr. M'Millan settled in the West, in 1778, and therefore they say, soon began his Latin school for piou young men, how comes it to pass that we hear nothing of them, nor indeed of any young men coming forward to put themselves under the care of the Presbytery, till August 15, 1786—nearly eight years after Dr. M'Millan settled at Chartiers? We think that if he were really training young men for the ministry, for some years before this, we would surely find it out by the records of the Redstone Presbytery. But they are silent. And when they do proceed to tell us of the first four or five candidates, it seems they were first students at Ten Mile and Buffalo, not at Chartiers. We really think these old records tell a very straight-forward story.

We are aware that it has been said, and testimony introduced to prove it, that Messrs. Brice and Hughs, and D. Smith, were all at Dr. M'Millan's before they were at Ten Mile or Buffalo. But we more than doubt this statement. Wilkins had no remembrance of them. Neither Dr. Cephas Dodd, nor Dr. Lindley, nor Dr. Wylie, had this impression. If D. Smith was there, he was a small boy, in the English school; which is possible. As to Messrs. Brice and Hughs, who were licensed in 1788, there is no reason to think, that in those times, they began their education seven or eight years before. Mr. McGready was not out from North Carolina long at Dr. M'Millan's, before he was taken sick—so we have been told—in the spring of 1785. As to his having been there in 1782 or 1781, we regard it as utterly improbable. By the way, if the attempt to ridicule Mrs. Irwin's expression, "laborer on the farm," by showing what a prodigious genius he must have been to have had an exegesis assigned him, April, 1787, so short a time after he left the plow,—if all this, we say, has not been sufficiently answered, we would merely add that these exegeses were, in those days, often given to young men after they had been but a short time engaged in their classical studies. As to what is said by the Hon. H. M. Brackenridge, about his father, on his way to Washington Court, calling at the Log-Cabin school, and hearing some of Mr. Ross's Latin scholars, we think there is some mistake. It is evidently supposed that this school was on or near the road-side, which was not the case. It was near two miles off the present Washington road. And if there was one that led nearer to Dr. M'Millan's, it was still quite distant from the Log-Cabin.* If he did call, turning out of his way, it is more likely, we submit, that he may have heard Mr. Ross himself, or given him some assistance in construing a passage or two.†

Let us now briefly state what we regard as resulting from this investigation, on both sides. Dr. M'Millan removed with his family to Western Pennsylvania in the fall of 1778. For some time his domestic circumstances, and

---

* We have since learned that the other old Washington road was still further from Dr. M'Millan's than the present stage road.

† Judge Brackenridge, in his "Incidents of the Western Insurrection," page 14, speaks of Mr. Ross as "just beginning at the bar in 1787." He might have been at the Log-Cabin as late as 1785 or 1786.

his arduous pastoral and missionary labors engrossed all his time; and the distracted state of the country also continuing, he did not begin his school enterprise till about 1781 or 1782. Though with the ultimate view of making it, in part, a classical school, it was, for some time, mainly an English school, taught by Mr. Ross, Mr. McGready, and others. He, nevertheless, at his own house, assisted these and others in classical studies, more or less. Mr. Dodd began his Classical, Scientific and English school in 1781 or 1782. In the fall of 1785, Mr. Smith began his school, exclusively for young men studying for the ministry, and taught them, not in theology, but in the languages and sciences, with the exception of Mr. Joseph Patterson, who, perhaps, studied part of the sciences and read theology under his direction. Mr. Smith, both from want of health and from increased demands for pastoral and ministerial labors, was led, in the course of a year or two, to give up his school; and the young men repaired to Dr. M'Millan's, together with some others. Then, for a period of three or four years, this school flourished, and was prominently what Dr. M'Millan always had in view—a Latin school. In the mean time, he and others, failing to get an academy successfully in operation, in Washington, united with the members of the Academy and Library Company, in and around Canonsburg, to get the Academy into full operation there. He then gave up his school, as the convenient neighborhood of the Academy enabled him so to do, to his great relief and satisfaction. As he was prominently instrumental, both at Washington and Canonsburg, in laying the foundation of this first Literary Institution in the Valley of the Mississippi, he may well be regarded as its *almus pater*.

We will only further add, that whether Prof. Patterson has made out his case or not, he has brought to light much that reflects the highest honor on Dr. M'Millan and his coadjutors—that the friends of Jefferson College and of education are under deep obligations to him for his able and patient researches; and for the talented effort he has made for the imperishable renown of that great and good man, who made such sacrifices of toil and expense, and of time and trouble, in the cause of education and Christianity.

There are some scores of things which we had designed to notice, but we gladly dismiss them all, and leave the reader to the result of his own reflections.

After we had prepared the preceding remarks upon Prof. Patterson's paper, we submitted them, together with that paper, to a professional friend, who has long been familiar with legal investigations, and with examining witnesses, &c. He kindly furnishes us with a paper containing the result of his impressions and conclusions, after carefully examining the testimony adduced by R. P. In this paper he has gone into a much more careful scrutiny of the whole subject, than we have been able to give it. But though it is committed to our disposal, its great length, and its rather less respectful treatment of the Professor and some of his witnesses, than we can altogether approve, forbid our insertion of it here. It is possible that with such alterations as we think it requires, it may hereafter be given to the public. This able, and, we think, conclusive document, furnishes several items that would be of special service to us *now*. But to extract or withdraw them for this purpose, would be doing injustice to the whole paper and diminish its value, should it be hereafter published. We will only add that we are now satisfied that some of the statements about the early *classical* school at Ten Mile are doubtful; and that an egregious anacronism pervades the whole testimony of the Rev. Dr. Lindley—doubtless altogether unintentional on his part. It will be observed that Dr. Cephas Dodd's account of his father's school rests almost exclusively upon what he got from Dr. Lindley.

DR. M'MILLAN'S MANUSCRIPT.

The following is a carefully copied transcript of the manuscript referred to in the previous review of Prof. Patterson's paper. It was apparently prepared with great care by Dr. M'Millan, and left along with his journal, which he had kept of his early missionary tours. When, some two months after he wrote it, he wrote his celebrated letter to Dr. Carnahan, he appears to have placed this manuscript before him; and while he omitted several portions of it, altered some passages and enlarged upon others, especially about the revivals, he copied somewhat closely a considerable part of it. It is altogether a precious document. The Rev. L. F. Leake, it will be seen, drew from it much of his interesting biographical sketch. We are not aware that it has ever been heretofore published. It will be seen that it completely vindicates all that we have heretofore said about it.

"My father's name was William M'Millan; my mother's maiden name was Margaret Rea; they were both born and lived in the parish of Carmony, in the county of Antrim, Ireland. They emigrated to America, about the year 1742, and settled in Fagg's manor, in Chester county, Pennsylvania. My mother died in the year 1768. My father married again, and during the time of the Revolutionary war he sold his property in Chester county and removed to the western country, where he died on the 2d of July, 1792, aged seventy-five years. His remains were buried at Chartiers. My parents had but six children, who grew up to be men and women, viz: three sons and three daughters; all of whom are now dead, except myself, who was the youngest but one of the family. I was born in Fagg's manor, on the 11th of November, 1752. Before my birth, my parents had some children, I think two sons, who died while they were young. My father told me that he had promised to God, that if he would give him another son, he would call his name John, and devote him to his service in the ministry of the gospel: accordingly as soon as I had acquired a sufficient degree of English literature, I was sent to a grammar school, kept by the Rev. Mr. John Blair, in Fagg's manor; where I continued until Mr. Blair was removed to Princeton, to superintend the college there. I was then sent to Pequea to a grammar school, kept by the Rev. Robert Smith. While there, the Lord poured out his Spirit upon the students; and I believe there were but few who were not brought under serious concern about their immortal souls: some of whom became blessings in their day, and were eminently useful in the Church of Christ; but they are all now gone to rest. It was here that I received my first religious impressions; though as long as I can remember, I had at times some checks of conscience, and was frequently terrified by dreams and visions in the night, which made me cry to God for mercy: but these seasons were of short duration; like the morning cloud and the early dew, they quickly passed away. I now saw that I was a lost, undone sinner, exposed to the wrath of a justly offended God, and could do nothing for my own relief. My convictions were not attended with much horror; though I felt that I deserved hell, and that in all probability that must be my portion: yet I could not feel that distress which I ought to feel, and which I thought I must feel before I could expect to obtain relief. I felt also much pride and legality, mingled with all the duties which I attempted to perform. In this situation I continued until I went to college, in the spring of 1770. I had not been long there until a revival of religion took place among the students; and I believe at one time there were not more than two or three, but what were under serious impressions. On a day which had been set apart by a number of the students to be observed as a day of fasting and prayer, while the others were at dinner, I retired into my study; and while trying to pray I got some discoveries of divine things, which I had never had before: I saw that the divine law was not only holy, just and spiritual, but also that it was good, and that conformity to it would make me happy. I felt no disposition to quarrel with the law; but with myself, because I was not conformed to it. I felt it now easy to submit to the gospel plan of salvation, and felt a calm and serenity of mind, to which I had hitherto been a stranger. And this was followed by a delight in contemplating the divine glory in all his works, and in meditating on the divine perfections. I thought that I could see God in every thing around me.

"I continued at college until the fall of 1772, when I returned to Pequea, and began the study of Theology under the direction of the Rev. Robert Smith, D. D. I had great difficulties in my own mind about undertaking the work of the gospel ministry. However, I at last came to this determination, to leave the matter wholly with God; if he opened the way, I would go on; if he shut it, I would be satisfied; and I think if ever I knew what it was to have no will of my own about any matter, it was about this. I passed through my trials in the Presbytery of New Castle, and was licensed by them to preach the gospel, October the 26th, 1774, at East Nattingham. The first winter I spent in itinerating in the vacant congregations of New Castle and Donegal Presbyteries. In the summer of '75, I took a tour through the settlements in Virginia, between the North and South mountains. In July I crossed the mountains between Staunton and the head of Tygart's Valley, preached in the various settlements which I passed through, until I came to Chartiers; preached there on the fourth Sabbath of August, and on the Tuesday following at Pigeon Creek. I then turned my course eastward, preached in the different settlements as I passed along, and came to my father's about the last of October. In the winter I again visited Augusta county in Virginia, crossed the mountains in January, and preached at Pigeon Creek and Chartiers until the latter end of March, 1776, when I returned home; and at a meeting of the Presbytery, on the 23d of April, I accepted a call, and was dismissed to join the Presbytery of Donegal, and on the 19th of June, at Chambersburg, was ordained.

"Having now determined to remove to the Western country and take charge of the congregations of Chartiers and Pigeon Creek, I thought it my duty to take with me a female companion. Accordingly, on the 6th of August, 1776, I was married to Catharine Brown, a young woman with whom I had been long acquainted, and who, I believed, was a dear child of God. She was the youngest child of Mr. William Brown, a ruling elder in the congregation of Upper Brandywine, Chester county, Pennsylvania. He was a very pious man, and lived to a great age, being about ninety when he died. It being in the time of the Revolutionary war, and the Indians being very troublesome on the frontiers, I was prevented from removing my family to my congregations until November, 1778. I however visited them as often as I could, ordained elders, baptized their children, and took as much care of them as circumstances would permit. When I came to this country, the cabin in which I was to live was raised, but there was no roof on it, nor chimney, nor floor in it. The people, however, were very kind, assisted me in preparing my house, and on the 15th of December I removed into it. But we had neither bedstead, nor table, nor chair, nor stool, nor pail, nor bucket. All these things we had to leave behind us; there being no wagon road at that time over the mountains; we could bring nothing with us but what was carried on pack-horses. We placed two boxes on each other, which served us for a table, and two kegs served us for seats; and having committed ourselves to God in family worship, we spread a bed on the floor, and slept soundly until morning. The next day, a neighbor coming to my assistance, we made a table and a stool, and in a little time had everything comfortable about us. Sometimes, indeed, we had no bread for weeks together; but we had plenty of pumpkins and potatoes, and all the necessaries of life, and as for luxuries, we were not much concerned about them. We enjoyed health, the gospel and its ordinances, and pious friends. We were in the place where we believe God would have us to be; and we did not doubt he would provide every thing necessary; and glory to his name, we were not disappointed. My wife and I lived comfortably together more than forty-three years; and on the 24th of November, 1819, she departed triumphantly to take possession of her house not made with hands, eternal in the heavens. When I determined to come to this country, Dr. Smith enjoined it upon me to look out for some pious young men, and educate them for the ministry; for, said he, though some men of piety and talents may go to a new country at first, yet if they are not careful to raise up others, the country will not be well supplied. Accordingly I collected a few who gave evidence of piety, and instructed them in the knowledge of the Latin and Greek languages, some of whom became useful, and others eminent, ministers of the gospel, viz: James Hughs, John Brice, James M'Gready, William Swan, Samuel Porter, and Thomas Marquis. All these I boarded and taught without any compensation, except about forty dollars, which Mr. Swan gave to my wife after he was settled in the ministry. I had still a few with me when the Academy was opened in Canonsburg, and finding that I could not teach and do justice to my congregation, I immediately gave it up and sent them there.

"For an account of the revivals of religion which took place in the congregation, I must refer you to the Western Missionary Magazine, vol. 2d, page 353. After the close of the revival which began in 1802, though upon every sacramental occasion some joined the church, yet nothing remarkable took place until the fall of 1823, when God again visited this dry and parched congregation with a shower of divine influences. About sixty joined the church as the fruits of this revival; a number of whom were students in the college, and are now preaching the Gospel of Christ to their fellow dying men. Since that time religion has rather been on the decline, though still we are not left without some tokens of the Divine presence; at every sacramental occasion, some have come out from the world and professed to take the Lord for their portion.

"J. M'MILLAN.

"January, 1832."

[*Added by another, but unknown hand.*]

"In April, May and June, he took what he supposed to be his last visit amongst some of the old churches in the West, which he had been instrumental in gathering from the wilderness and supplying with pastors. On the last Sabbath of April, and first Sabbath of May, he assisted in dispensing the Lord's Supper at Cross Creek and Cross Roads, and preached six Sabbaths in Racoon congregation, where he assisted in administering the Lord's Supper on the third Sabbath of June. During this journey he preached seventeen sermons, with more than usual fervency; and it has been since found that his labors during this journey were blessed to the spiritual quickening and edification of God's people, and the awakening of not less than — careless sinners, who have since joined themselves to the Lord. During the year 1832, he assisted in administering the Lord's Supper fourteen times, and preached about fifty times, on occasions leaning on his crutch, and in the eightieth year of his age. During the year 1833, up to the 16th of November, the time of his death, he assisted in administering the Lord's Supper seventeen times, and preached on these occasions about seventy-five times, frequently twice on the same day, besides attending to exhortations, &c."

IMPORTANCE OF COLLEGES AND OF CLASSICAL EDUCATION

EARLY HISTORY OF COLLEGIATE INSTITUTIONS.

It is one of the most auspicious signs of the times that the subject of education is beginning to awaken a deeper and more pervading interest throughout the civilized world. Great as has been the progress of improvement in the various methods of promoting the commerce, wealth and luxury of the nations, this progress would afford but little satisfaction to the philanthropist, did not the cause of general instruction keep pace with the other onward movements of the age. It must be acknowledged, however, that it requires more effort to sustain the interests of education before the public mind, than it does to uphold the cause of public improvements, and the various methods of accumulating dollars and cents. Yet the importance of every judicious method of diffusing science and literature is so obvious to every reflecting man, that those who have been concerned in devising and rearing to maturity institutions of learning in our country, during its earlier life, have strong claims, even now, amidst the din of slitting mills, and cotton factories, and locomotives, to be remembered with gratitude. The attempt has been made, in the foregoing pages, to erect an humble monument to the memory of those good men, who, nearly seventy years ago, constructed the first home of classical learning and science west of the mountains—the first College in the Valley of the Mississippi. We are aware that not a few call in question the claims of public educational institutions to any special regard—alleging even that such methods of instruction are neither safe nor wise, and in some cases, treating with derision all classical education. It has been long disputed, we know, even among the friends and advocates of the most thorough mental training, whether a more private, and even domestic system of instruction, may not claim the preference over the plan of public seminaries. The principal argument urged in behalf of humbler forms of institutions, is derived from alleged superior advantages in respect to the morals of youth. We are not to suppose that those who take this ground are advocates of nothing better than, or superior to, our common schools. This is not their meaning. They are for the widest curriculum of studies. But they would have it so managed as to supersede the erection of Colleges and Universities. But even were such a scheme practicable, it may well be questioned whether the superior advantages they claim for their system, are not altogether imaginary. If to preserve the youthful mind from vicious indulgences, and from exposure to moral contaminations, were equivalent to rendering it virtuous, and confirmed in habits of truth and sobriety, the question might be easily determined. But this is far from being the case. A boy may be surrounded by argus-eyed sentinels, that shall give the alarm at every approach of danger—may be confined to the society of the most virtuous and upright friends and companions—may be completely secluded from every possible access to haunts of vice and dissipation, and yet so far from enjoying a vigorous and manly expansion of his mental and moral powers, his whole nature may possess a feeble and sickly structure, easily tossed about and shaken by temptations, and exposed to complete shipwreck in the first storm it might be called to encounter. There is a striking analogy between the physical and the moral world. As the sturdy oak of the forest could never be trained and reared to perfection in a close receptacle, attempered by artificial heat; but must rise amidst the heats of summer and the storms of winter, and gather strength from the rocking of the tempest; so in general it is with man. Educate him apart from all possible lures of vice and folly, confine his social nature to a narrow inch of space, and you attempt to form an oak in a hot-house. That plan of instruction, then, appears to us to give most promise of success which assumes that youth are not to be constantly watched and dogged at every step with suspicion; but while it places before them the precepts of wisdom and virtue, and throws around them the influence of good example, plies every proper incentive to the attainment of a useful and honorable life; and yet throws them, in a considerable degree, upon the exercise of their own vigilance and caution, amidst surrounding dangers and temptations. But let these dangers and temptations be rendered as few as is at all compatible with public institutions. Such is the character of the academical training which we advocate. Such, we believe, were the views and principles of the good men who aimed to found the first college west of the Allegheny mountains, and sought for it a home in the quiet village of Canonsburg. They believed that a college is the place most favorable to draw out and excite all the powers of the mind. It is a wise and benevolent law of our mental structure, that mind is most effectually kindled by coming in contact with mind. That system of instruction which does not duly avail itself of this psychological principle, must be radically defective. Besides, emulation is, perhaps, an original principle of our nature, and not exclusively the result of moral obliquity. It is, we confess, peculiarly liable to abuse. But to call it into action, within due bounds, in the educational training of youth, is not only perfectly proper and admissible, but really important. And this can be much better effected in public than in private seminaries. Again, at colleges, young men learn their own strength and weakness—learn to stand erect and to walk; or, to express it without a metaphor, to think and act for themselves. Here *men* are formed. Here manly, independent, thinking men are "grown."*

---

* "The friendships, quarrels, and various intercourse among boys afford a thousand opportunities of exhibiting such principles which cannot be had in private. The emulation of glorious deeds inspires them more strongly in a crowd of spectators; and the pulse of honor, of course, beats higher. It is further asked if it be not a matter of great importance to inculcate ideas of society; and to imbue the mind with early notions of submission to authority and government. He sees the beauty of order, the utility of law, and the necessity of good government. School hours and school privileges have a favorable tendency also to impress upon him a love of liberty, of the value of which, a youth brought up at home cannot form an idea. He may have lessons on all these subjects; but such lessons must ever be inferior to a real intercourse with life—seeing with his own eyes and obtaining knowledge by his own experience."—*Encyclopedia Britannica. Art. College*

As to those who question the utility of the study of the dead languages, as they are called, we rest the defence of classical education mainly on the ground of its superlative, and long-tested fitness to exercise, train and develop the mental faculties; and on the ground of its peculiar adaptation to that period of human life in which it is usually pursued. Perhaps, however, not less weight should be attached to the consideration that this study eminently contributes to cultivate the imagination, and refine the taste. With few exceptions, those whom we recommend to our young men, as models of fine writing, were men that drank deeply from the Castalian fount—that were conducted by the midnight lamp over the classic pages of antiquity. Dr. Robertson, when visiting as Principal one of the classes of the University of Edinburgh, declared, for the encouragement of young men in the prosecution of their studies, that if he had acquired any fame as a historian, he owed it entirely to his acquaintance with the historians of antiquity. On these and similar grounds we vindicate the wisdom and necessity of colleges; and maintain that a lasting debt of gratitude is due to our *first western ministers,* and their coadjutors, for their early efforts in this cause. And if we have told the story of their toils and sacrifices in this good work, and of the delightful and surprising results, we shall hope to find some interested readers; especially in sections of our country where similar efforts are now in progress, or should soon be made. But "*festina lente.*"

Having, some years ago, directed our attention to the subject of the origin and history of seminaries of learning, in former ages and other lands, we have been advised by some of our literary friends to whom we submitted the matter, to place before our readers the following statement, as the result of our researches.

As we tell the story of our *first Western College,* it may not be out of place to attempt a brief historical sketch, in this place, of the rise and progress of such institutions. If such a subject appears uninviting to any of our readers, we claim no right to insist on a hearing for the remainder of this paper. A very summary account is all that we here propose. It is evident from Strabo and Diodorus, that among the Egyptians and Chaldeans, there existed colleges of priests, in which literature was cultivated among themselves, and communicated to others. The statements, however, about the seminaries of these very ancient nations, are not without much obscurity and uncertainty. Besides, there is, no doubt, a great difference between the institutions of these early ages, and our modern seats of science. The same remark will apply, perhaps, with equal force to the schools of the Magi, among the Persians; in which it would appear that considerable attention was paid to astronomy and natural philosophy. Among the Jews, from the time of Samuel, there existed certain societies, in which some were trained to wisdom and piety, and exercised themselves in mental efforts under the tuition of teachers. This may be inferred, we think, from what is mentioned respecting the companies or schools of the prophets. In the following age, we read that the sons of the prophets dwelt at Bethel, Jericho, and Gilgal. Hence it is not doubted by many writers that from the time of Samuel and the following age, schools of learning were among the Hebrew nation. There were more unequivocal marks and proofs, how ever, of schools among the Jews after the Babylonish captivity. These schools were extensively connected with their synagogues at Jerusalem, Babylon, and elsewhere; an incredible number of which sprang up and flourished for centuries among them.

It can be very clearly proved, from historical data, that there were no public schools, or institutions of learning, among the Greeks before the time of Plato. For though there were many who before that time furnished various kinds of instruction, yet that was rather the enterprise of indivi duals then a matter of public concern. It would seem indeed, says Conringius, a German writer, that the Athenians the most accomplished of the Greeks, granted to their citi zen, Plato, in order that they might atone for the crime committed against Philosophy, by their condemnation of Socrates, the privilege of a grove, in their suburbs. To this, the name of Academy was given, from Hecademus, or Academus, the name of the man who had constructed the grove. From this period, various philosophic schools successively arose to great eminence. But after the brightest period of Grecian history had passed away, the wars which followed upon the death of Alexander the Great, among those who succeeded him, had, in a manner, extinguished learning in all that part of the world. Indeed, it would seem to have been on the point of becoming utterly extinct, amidst the calamities of those times, had it not found a support under the patronage of the Ptolemies of Egypt. For the first Ptolemy, aving erected a museum, or college, for the maintenance and encouragement of learned men, and also a great library, for their use, drew most of the learned men of Greece thither. This library was afterwards augmented, by his successors, until it is said to have contained seven hundred thousand volumes.* By the detestable cruelties and oppressions of Ptolemy Physcon, about the year before Christ, 138, many learned men were driven into foreign parts, erected schools, and being poor, taught for small fees, and drew immense numbers of scholars. Learning thus revived, received a fresh impulse through all Greece and Asia Minor; much in the same way as it was in the western world, many ages afterwards, upon the final overthrow of the Byzantine Empire, by the Turks in 1453.

At Rome, schools for teaching various branches of useful knowledge, had existed from an early period; but no institutions of much note existed till the Augustan age. At this period, the Greek language was taught under the patronage of the court; much attention was bestowed upon the culture of polite learning, and the fine arts, and those who contributed with zeal and success to these studies, were eminently distinguished by Augustus Cæsar. But after his death, learning languished without encouragement, and was neglected, because the succeeding Emperors were more intent upon the arts of war and rapine then those more amiable arts and inventions, that are the fruits of leisure and peace. A long night gradually settled down upon the Roman empire—especially the western division of it; and an academical or collegiate institution became a "cycnus nigra, rara avis in terris."

---

* When Julius Cæsar invaded Egypt and plundered Alexandria, a large portion of this splendid collection was burnt. A part, however, that was in a region of the city called *Bruchium*, escaped the ravages of the ruthless soldiery, and of the flames. Cleopatra afterwards purchased the famous library of Pergamos, and added it to that of Alexandria. It was frequently afterwards plundered and greatly injured; but again repaired and replenished from time to time, until it was finally burnt and destroyed by the Saracens in 642. Johannes Grammaticus earnestly begged the Saracen general, Amrou Ebnal, for the library. He wrote to the Caliph, Omar, who sent him an answer worthy of the fanatical barbarian. "If the books agree with the Koran, then there is no need of them; if not, then they ought not to be endured." This immense collection of valuable manuscripts was employed for heating the public baths, for more than six months. It has, however, been questioned, on plausible grounds, whether the loss of this library has been any serious injury to the interests of History or Philosophy.

The state of letters in the first three centuries of the Christian era, among the Romans, was not favorable to the establishment and growth of literary institutions. These were principally in the hands of rhetoricians, sophists and grammarians. During this period an academy of some note was established or founded at Rome by the Emperor Adrian, in which all the sciences were taught. There was also a renowned seminary at Berytus in Phenicia, principally for the education of youth in the science of law. But of all the institutions which acquired any considerable notoriety, the famous school of Alexandria deserves particular mention. During the latter part of this period, Christianity obtained a controlling influence over most of those concerned in public or private instruction in this place. Clemens Alexandrinus, Pantenus and Origen acquired great celebrity in the Christian world as instructors. This last remarkable man did more than all others to bring learning into countenance and favor with the church. The question concerning the excellence and utility of learning, had been hotly contested among the Christians of this period. From the first ages of Christianity, a dislike to pagan learning was pretty general among Christians. Many of the Fathers were undoubtedly accomplished in liberal studies; and we are indebted to them for many valuable fragments of authors whose works have perished. Proscribed and persecuted as they were, the early Christians had not, perhaps, access to the public schools, nor much inclination to studies which seemed to them uncongenial to the character of their profession. Their prejudices even survived the establishment of Christianity. The fourth Council of Carthage prohibited the bishops from reading secular books. Jerome plainly condemns the study of them, except for pious purposes. Constantine and the succeeding emperors gave much to seminaries of learning. One of the most remarkable occurrences of this period was the bold and artful stroke of Julian the Apostate, in taking all the schools and seminaries out of the hands of the Christians, and putting them under the direction of the pagans, with the avowed design of effecting the destruction of Christianity, and the restoration of paganism. How far success would have crowned his efforts, had his life been prolonged, it is impossible to say. It was manifestly a masterly piece of policy, and has not been lost sight of or forgotten by many infidels to this day.

The Jews, during this time, had their schools at Tiberias, and in the province of Babylon, at Jara, Naherda and Pompeditha. Before the close of the second century, their institutions in Tiberias and Jamnia were quite famous. Milman has given an interesting account of their seminaries, under the Byzantine Empire; also, under the Caliphs, which he calls their golden age; and under the Western Governments, since the fall of the Roman Empire. In the fifth, sixth, and seventh centuries, some of the Christian Emperors, such as Justinian, and Theodosius the Great, bestowed some attention on letters. During this period there were public institutions in the principal cities, some of them with considerable claims to eminence; especially those at Constantinople, Rome, Marseilles, Edessa, Nisibis, Carthage, Lyons, and Treves. But the course of instruction was generally of the most jejune and meagre character. A general education embraced the *seven liberal arts;* that is, Grammar, Arithmetic, Rhetoric, Logic, Music, Geometry and Astronomy. There were some schools, towards the close of the sixth century, established in certain cathedrals and monasteries, but of a very low and miserable description. Nothing connected with our inquiries worthy of a moment's pause, meets us until we reach the times of Charlemagne, in the eight century. This great man, though illiterate himself, was a distinguished patron of education. When he ascended the throne, the few spots of sunshine, in respect to letters, were to be found in Britain and Ireland. To aid him in reviving learning and in conducting seminaries, he called from these Isles of the West some of their brightest luminaries. We must not omit to mention also the famous capitularies of Charlemagne, directing schools to be set up in bishoprics and abbeys "to learn the Psalms, Singing and Grammar."

About this time, the Emperor Lotharius convened the third Council of Valence, the eighteenth canon of which expressly enjoined that schools be set up "for learning and singing." Some attempts were made by other provincial Councils, and by several bishops, to erect seminaries in Catholic churches. But now gross darkness covered the people. The highest dignitaries of the church were unable to translate the Latin prayers. Few of them could sign their names. The most ridiculous blunders were continually made, in reading the Latin service of the church. We are told of one who had gotten the word "sumpsimus" changed into "mumpsimus." Upon having his error pointed out to him, he declared, in a rage, he would not give up his "mumpsimus" for all their "sumpsimuses." There is an ancient geographical chart, which now remains as a monument of the state of Geography in the middle ages. In it the three parts of the globe then known are so represented, that Jerusalem is placed in the middle of the globe; and Alexandria appears to be as near to it as Nazareth. Toward the close of the *tenth century*, scarcely one in Rome knew the first elements of letters. In England, Alfred declared he could not recollect a single priest south of the Thames, who understood the ordinary prayers or could translate them into his native tongue. One thing that seriously affected institutions of learning during these iron ages, was the scarcity of books. From the conquest of Egypt, by the Saracens, in the seventh century, to the close of the tenth century, the Egyptian papyrus almost ceased to be exported from Egypt. Parchments, prepared from skins, were dear, and difficult to be obtained. But about the latter period, paper began to be made from rags. By this admirable invention, not only the number of manuscripts increased, but the study of the sciences was wonderfully promoted. "The invention of the art of making paper out of rags," says Dr. Robertson, "and the invention of the art of printing, are two considerable events in literary history. It is remarkable that the former preceded the first dawning of letters and improvement in knowledge, toward the close of the eleventh century; the latter ushered in the light which spread over Europe at the era of the Reformation." About this period, there prevailed throughout the schools a remarkable division of the sciences into the Trivium and Quadrivium: the former embracing Grammar, Rhetoric and Logic; the latter, Arithmetic, Music, Geometry and Astronomy. But a judgment may be formed about the value of this apparently respectable course, when it is known that Music was confined to the chaunts of the church; and Geometry to the calculations of Easter; besides, that the Trivium formed the Pons Asinorum to nine-tenths of the students of those days. But while the night of ignorance brooded over Christendom with scarce a twinkling star in all the firmament, the Mohammedans of the East and of the West, for a period of five hundred years, cultivated literature and science with distinguished success. Their institutions in Spain, in Africa, and in Asia, attracted thousands of students; and the literary halls of Saragossa and Bagdad were crowded with admiring throngs, hanging upon the lips of Saracen lecturers. From the ninth to the fourteenth century, the Caliphs were patrons of science. In all parts, in every town, says Sismondi, academics and colleges were established, from all which many learned men proceeded. Bagdad was the capital of letters as well as of the Caliphs; but Bassora and Cufa almost equaled that city in reputation, and in the number of valuable treatises and celebrated poems which they produced. Balk, Ispahan, and Samarcand were equally the homes of science. The same enthusiasm had been carried by the Arabians beyond the frontiers of Asia. Benjamin of Tudela, the Jew, in his Itinerary, relates that he found in Alexandria more than twenty schools for the propagation of philosophy. Cairo also contained a great number of colleges; and that of Betzuela, in the suburbs of the capital, was so substantially built, that during a rebellion it served as a citadel for the army. In the towns of Fez and Morocco, likewise, the most magnificent buildings were appropriated to the purposes of instruction; and these establishments were governed by the wisest and most beneficent regulations. But Spain was more especially the seat of Arabian learning. It was there that it shone with superior brightness, and made its most rapid progress. Cordova, Granada, Seville and all the cities of the Peninsula rivaled one another in the magnificence of their schools, their colleges, their academies and their libraries.

The Academy of Granada was under the direction of Schedmaddin of Murcia, so celebrated among the Arabians. In various cities of Spain, seventy libraries were opened for the instruction of the public, at a period when all the rest of Europe, without books, without learning, and without cultivation, was plunged in the most disgraceful ignorance. The number of Arabic authors which Spain produced was so prodigious, that many Arabian bibliographers wrote learned treatises on the authors born in particular towns; or on those among the Spaniards who devoted themselves to a single branch of study, as philosophy, medicine, mathematics, and more especially, poetry. These Arabian scholars contributed to kindle the sparks of science through Western Europe, and to give an impulse to literature, which has been felt long since the whole Mohammedan world has plunged back into sullen and barbarous ignorance. Many persons who distinguished themselves by their proficiency in science during the *twelfth* and *thirteenth* centuries, were educated among the Arabians. Almost all who were eminent for science, during several centuries, if they did not resort in person to the schools of Africa, or Spain, were instructed in the philosophy of the Arabians. The first knowledge of the Aristotelian Philosophy, in the middle ages, was acquired by translations of Aristotle's works, out of the Arabic. The Arabian commentaries were esteemed the most skillful and authentic guides in the study of his system. From them the schoolmen derived the genius and principles of their philosophy. The germs of several academies and universities had been, in some manner, formed before the twelfth century. That of *Paris* especially, which eventually rose to the greatest pre-eminence, may be traced even to the tenth century. It had acquired such fame, even then, that a Monkish writer of that age, Peter of Blois, says: "It passed into a proverb, that those who were desirous to have any question settled, need only go to Paris, where the greatest difficulties are fairly resolved." In its rise, it was composed of *artists*, who taught the sciences and philosophy, and of *divines*, who made commentaries on Peter Lombard's Book of Sentences, and explained the Scriptures. At first the University was composed only of scholars and masters. Afterwards they distinguished several degrees, and fixed the time they ought to study. The degrees were: Bachelor, Licenciate, and Master or Doctor. Those were Bachelors who taught publicly. They began by reading and explaining the Scriptures; and afterwards composed treatises on the Master of Sentences, (Peter Lombard.) The former were called Biblici; the latter, Sententiarii. They bore the name of Bacillarii, or Bacalarii, from *bacilla;* either because they were admitted by giving them little wands, or because they so called the novices of the militia, who exercised with *sticks,* in order to learn to fight with *arms.* The University of *Bologna* also pretends to claim a foundation in the fifth century under *Theodosius II.*, and produces a sheepskin parchment, looking sufficiently old and musty! duly signed and sealed by that monarch.

The University of Cambridge also, at one time, seriously set up claims to an origin three hundred and seventy years before the Christian era! and produced Anaxagoras and Anaximander, Grecian philosophers, amongst the list of its professors! But these, and many other ridiculous pretensions, which might be mentioned, were better suited to the times when dynasties of Scottish kings could be traced back to the family of Noah, and Welsh pedigrees were regularly brought down from Adam! The establishment of colleges or universities is a remarkable era in literary history. The schools in cathedrals and monasteries confined themselves chiefly to the teaching of Grammar. There were only one or two masters employed in that office. But in colleges professors were employed to teach all the different parts of science. The course or order of education was fixed; the time that ought to be allotted to the study of each science was ascertained. A regular form of trying the proficiency of students was prescribed; and academical titles and honors were conferred on such as acquitted themselves with approbation. These new establishments for education, together with the extraordinary honors conferred on learned men, greatly increased the number of students. In the year 1262, at Bologna there were 10,000, and it appears from the history of that University, that *Law* was the only science taught in it at the time.

About the middle of the fourteenth century, there were no less than 13,000 students at this famous seminary of jurisprudence. In the year 1340, the number of students at Oxford is said to have been 30,000. In the same century, 10,000 persons voted on a question in the University of Paris; and as graduates only were admitted to that privilege, the number of students must have been very great. At the death of Charles VII., in 1453, the number is stated to have been 25,000. There were, indeed, few Universities in Europe at that time; but such a number of students may nevertheless be produced as a proof of the extraordinary ardor with which men applied themselves to the study of science in those ages. The discovery of the Pandects of Justinian, at Amalfi, in 1135, when the city was taken by the Pisans, is said to have led to the revival of the study of jurisprudence. This story, however, has been questioned of late, and seems to rest on insufficient authority. Seminaries, however, were founded at Bologna, at Modena, and at Mantua, for the express purpose of studying law. New Universities, about this time, also, arose at Naples and Padua, and other places. From this time, the golden age of universities commenced; and it is hard to say whether they were favored most by their sovereigns or by the See of Rome. With Aristotle as the master in philosophy, and Peter Lombard and Thomas Aquinas as the masters of theology, Rome had nothing to fear. Colleges were exempted from the ordinary tribunals, and even from those of the church. Their history, indeed, is full of struggles with the municipal authorities, and with the bishops of their several cities; in which they were sometimes the aggressors, and generally the conquerors. From all parts of Europe, students resorted to these renowned seats of learning with an eagerness for instruction which may astonish those who reflect how little of what we now deem useful could be imparted. The number, in some instances, may be exaggerated. We learn from Anthony Wood, the historian of Oxford, that "a company of varlets, who pretended to be scholars, shuffled themselves in, and did act much villainy in the University; thieving, quarreling, &c. They lived under no discipline; neither had they tutors; but only for fashion's sake, would sometimes thrust themselves into the schools, at ordinary lectures; and when they went to perform any mischief, then would they be accounted scholars, that so they might free themselves from the jurisdiction of the burghers." If we allow three varlets for one student, the University will still have been very fully frequented by the latter. We may here observe that the exemption of the students from military service and from municipal and ecclesiastical jurisdiction may serve to account, in part, for the throngs that attended the Universities. By the way, we are indebted to the same quaint historian, but honest writer, for the original meaning of the word "*College.*" It seems that, in earlier times, the students boarded in private families, or in hotels or inns kept by private, irresponsible individuals. The exactions of the persons who boarded them, perhaps, by collusion among themselves, were in many instances severe and oppressive. The expenses of the students awakened so much dissatisfaction with the students, their parents and others, that at length measures were taken by the legal authorities of these great Universities, or Public Schools, to furnish the students suitable houses, where considerable numbers of them could be accommodated with rooms and boarding. These were called Collegia. The literary institutions were not at first so called. They were most commonly styled schools, halls, and universities. But in process of time the seminaries themselves, when used also for lectures and recitations, got the name of colleges. When we learn its true origin—that originally it meant rather the *boarding-house*—it reminds us of the name of *Pike*, now given to paved roads, so called first from *turn-pike*; and *that* again from the fact that paved roads have generally turn-pike, or turn-pole gates placed on them, at intervals, where toll is taken. In the thirteenth and fourteenth centuries, many other universities sprang up in different countries. Among these may be mentioned those of Padua, Naples, Toulouse, Montpelier, Salamanca, Orleans, Prague, and Cambridge. A large proportion of scholars, in most of these institutions, were drawn by the love of science from foreign countries. The chief universities had each their own particular department of excellence. Paris was unrivaled for *scholastic theology;* Bologna, Orleans, and Bourges, for *jurisprudence;* Montpelier and Salamanca for *medicine.* Safe passages, even in time of war, were granted to students, and secured by solemn international treaties. Though this was the period of the *Inquisition*, that institution of religious persecution, first set up at Toulon against the Albigenses and Waldenses, yet there sprang up almost at the same time, an university in the same city. Though it was towards the close of that period rendered forever memorable by the *Crusades*, those fanatical expeditions that for near two centuries nearly emptied Europe of all its fools, and a large part of all its knaves, yet even this period, when superstition was in the ascendant, it is due to Pope Urban V. to bear testimony to his distinguished liberality, in supporting and encouraging literature, establishing several universities, and from his own resources supporting one thousand poor students at the different seminaries. The University of *Cambridge*, in England, now consisting of twelve Colleges and four *halls*, rose also at this period. Its first College or Hall, *St. Peter's*, was founded in 1257. This name it still retains. An attempt was, indeed, made to change it, in the seventeenth century. Lady Mary Ramsey offered it an additional endowment of a large and splendid property, if the name would be changed to Peter's and Mary's College. But Dr. Soame, at that time Master of the College, replied, that "Peter had been too long a bachelor to think of a female comrade in his old days." "A dear bought jest," says Fuller, "for the lady, piqued at the remark, threw her munificence into another channel." *Clare Hall*, and *Pembroke Hall* were next established, and others, in the course of the fourteenth and fifteenth centuries. There are perhaps now *twenty-five hundred* students in this distinguished University. In *Scotland*, several colleges were founded from the fourteenth to the sixteenth centuries. The University of *St. Andrews* was founded in 1411. That of Glasgow, in 1454. That of Aberdeen, in 1477. But the most brilliant luminary of old Caledonia is comparatively of recent origin. The University of Edinburgh was founded in 1560. Its establishment was violently opposed by the other Universities—viz: of Aberdeen, St. Andrews, and especially Glasgow, no doubt through jealousy. There are usually upwards of two thousand students in attendance. The Institution has no less than twenty-seven chairs or professorships: four of *law*; eleven of *medicine*, and nine of the *arts*; besides three of the Faculty of *theology*. The mode of instruction is by lectures. No particular course of academical instruction is followed; nor do the Professors exercise any control over the pursuits of the students. The young gentlemen are not distinguished by any particular costume. Each attends what lecture he pleases, and lives where and how he pleases.

Those who would make themselves acquainted with other institutions in Great Britain and on the continent of Europe, may consult Mr. Dwight, and other recent writers. In this country, the most ancient literary establishment is *Harvard University*, founded at Cambridge, Massachusetts, in 1638, less than twenty years after the landing of the Pilgrims, at Plymouth. Yale College was founded in 1700. Princeton College commenced its career in 1738, just one hundred years after Cambridge. It was originally called Nassau Hall, but is now called the College of New Jersey, or Princeton College. Why or when this change in the name was made, we have never understood. Colleges have since sprung up and multiplied over the whole land. De Bow, in his census tables for 1850, gives the whole number of colleges in the United States as amounting to *two hundred and thirty-nine*; in Pennsylvania, *twenty-two*—number of students in these 3,520; in all the colleges, 27,821. It would be aside from our purpose to give an historical survey of any of these numerous institutions which now adorn our country. The policy of multiplying public institutions of learning to such a degree as now prevails, has been much questioned. The great danger apprehended is that it tends to lower the standard of education—render more superficial the literary and scientific course. Yet it cannot be denied that by increasing the facilities of access to these fountains of science, a greater mass of mind is cultivated, and a larger number of those who are qualified to become useful and eminent in public life, are brought within the range of this more diffused, if less solid system. There are few who cannot point to instances of men now in the first ranks of the various professions, who would never have arisen to their present position, had they not availed themselves of some humble institution where tuition and boarding were so cheap as to be within the range of their once humble means. And perhaps a very large proportion of the most promising description of our youth, will ever be found among those whose circumstances compel them to practice the most constant industry and the most rigid economy, in their efforts to enter the paths of science and literature. Among this portion of our community may we look for the bone and sinew of our land. From these have arisen most of the eminent men who have rendered important service to our country. Jefferson College, in her earliest, as well as in her latest days, has ever been the patron and friend of the poor. Some of her noblest sons, in all the walks of life, did she train in the days of their poverty.

The sketch we have thus attempted to give of the history of the rise and progress of public seminaries, we have not deemed unsuitable as a pendant to this work. We have gathered the historical facts, given above, some years ago for a different purpose. But though we may be charged with pedantry in encumbering our humble History of a Western College with so long a paper, and may, perhaps, be compared to Knickerbocker, going back to the creation, in his history of New York; and may be further told that our *back porch* is too large for our *house;* we hope, nevertheless, that some readers may find some entertainment and gratification in its perusal. We found the facts we have given, widely scattered, in Brucker's "History of Philosophy," Hallam's "Middle Ages," Sismondi's "History of Literature," Mosheim's "Ecclesiastical History," Gibbon's "Decline and Fall of the Roman Empire," "The Encyclopedia Britannica," "The Quarterly Reviews," &c.

Trustees of the College.

FROM THE TIME IT WAS CHARTERED.

Appointed by the Legislature of Pa. January 15th, 1802.

Rev. John M'Millan,.........Resigned April 1802.
Rev. Joseph Patterson,.......Resigned Sept. 1805.
Rev. Thomas Marquis,.......Resigned Sept. 1817.
Rev. Samuel Ralston,........Died 1852.
Rev. John Black,...........Died 1802.
Rev. John M'Pherrin,.......Resigned Sept. 1804.
Rev. James Power,..........Resigned Sept. 1806.
Rev. James Dunlap..........Resigned April, 1803.
Alexander Cook, Esq........Resigned Oct. 1802.
James Edgar, Esq...........Resigned Sept. 1805.
John M'Dowel, Esq..........Died 1809.
James Allison, Esq.........Died Sept. 1807.
William Finley, Esq.........Died April, 1805.
John Mercer, Esq...........Resigned Sept. 1814.
Craig Ritchie. Esq..........Died 1833.
Gen. John Hamilton,........Resigned April, 1831.
William Hughes, Esq........Resigned Dec. 1817.
Joseph Vance, Esq..........Resigned Sept. 1810.
Robert Mahon Esq...........Resigned Sept. 1824.
James Kerr, Esq............Died 1835.
Aaron Lyle, Esq............Resigned April, 1822.

TRUSTEES ELECTED.

Rev. Thomas Moore,.........Elected Apr. 1802; Resigned Apr. 1814.
Rev. Samuel Porter,.........Elected Oct. 1802; Resigned Sept. 1811.
James Allison, Jr. Esq.......Elected Oct. 1802 Resigned Sept. 1817.
Rev. John Riddle............Elected Apr. 1803; Resigned Apr. 1805.
Rev. James Hughes..........Elected Sept. 1804; Resigned Sept 1814.
Rev. William Swan,..........Elected Sept 1804; Resigned Sept. 1824.
Dr. Samuel Murdock,.........Elec. Apr. 1805; Resigned April, 1817.
Rev. John Anderson,.........Elec. Apr. 1805; Resigned Sept. 1808.
Rev. James Ramsey,.........Elec. Sept. 1805; Resigned Sept. 1824.
William Rhea, Esq...........Elec. Sept. 1805; Resigned Dec. 1827.

Rev. William M'Millan........Elec. Sept. 1808; Resigned Sept. 1817.
Thomas Briceland, Esq.......Elec. Sept. 1809; Died 1819.
Gen. John Morgan,...........Elec. Sept. 1807; Resigned Sept. 1817.
James Mountain, Esq..........Elec. Sept. 1810; Died 1814.
Rev. William Wylie...........Elec. Sept. 1811; Resigned April 1818.
John M'Donald, Esq.........Elec. Apr. 1814; Died 1831.
Rev. Elisha M'Curdy.........Elec. Apr. 1814; Resigned Sept. 1820.
Rev. Moses Allen,.............Elec. Sept. 1814; Resigned Mar. 1839.
Abner Lacock, Esq............Elec. Sept. 1814; Resigned Sept. 1817.
Rev. Francis Herron,.........Elec. Sept. 1817; Resigned Mar. 1849.
Rev. Michael Law,............Elec. Sept, 1817; Died 1822.
Richard Johnston, Esq.......Elec. Sept. 1817; Died 1837.
Benjamin Williams, Esq......Elec. Sept. 1817.
Andrew Munro Esq.........Elec. Sept. 1817; Died 1841.
John Reed Esq................Elec. Sept. 1817.
Joseph Clokey, Esq..........Elec. Dec. 1817; Died ——
Samuel Logan, Esq...........Elec. Dec. 1817, Resigned Sept. 1837.
Rev. Robert Johnston,........Elec. Apr. 1818; Resigned Sept. 1835.
Rev. Joseph M'Elroy.........Elec. Sept. 1819; Resigned ——
Dr. Jonathan Letherman......Elec. Apr. 1820; Died 1844.
Rev. Elisha P. Swift,..........Elec. Sept. 1820; Resigned Aug. 1852
Rev. Thomas D. Baird.......Elec. Apr. 1822; Died Jan. 1839.
John Phillips, Esq............Elec. Apr. 1822, Died 1845.
Rev. Ashbel Green, D. D......Elec. Sept. 1824; Resigned Jan. 1828.
Rev. William Wilson,.........Elec. Sept. 1824; Resigned Apr. 1833.
James Gordon, Esq............Elec. Dec. 1825.
William M'Creery, Esq.......Elec. Apr. 1826; Resigned Mar. 1839.
Rev. William Jeffrey,.........Elec. Jan. 1828.
Dr. D. S. Stevenson,..........Elec. Sept. 1831; Died 1843.
William Patterson, Esq......Elec. Mar. 1832; Died 1835.
Rev. William M'Elwee,.......Elec. Sept. 1833.
Daniel Houston, Esq.........Elec. Sept. 1833.
Rev. Henry R. Weed,.........Elec. Sept. 1835, Resigned Sept. 1845.
Hon. Robert C. Grier.........Elec. Sept. 1835; Resigned Feb. 1855.
John Hays, Esq...............Elec. Sept. 1835.
Hon. H. H. Leavitt...........Elec. Mar. 1837; Resigned Oct. 1848.
James M'Cleland, Esq.........Elec. Sept. 1837, Resigned Mar. 1853.
Rev. John T. Pressly, D. D...Elec. Mar. 1839.
Rev. George Marshall,........Elec. Mar. 1839.
William Park, Esq............Elec. Mar. 1839.
James M'Cullough, Esq.......Elec. Sept. 1841.
Wm. M'Daniel, Esq...........Elec. Sept. 1844.
Dr. John V. Herriot,.........Elec. Sept. 1844; Resigned Aug. 1853.
Rev. James Sloan.............Elec. Sept. 1845.
William Marks, Esq..........Elec. Sept. 1845.
Thomas Nicholson, Esq.......Elec. Oct. 1848.
Rev. Alex. T. M'Gill, D. D....Elec. Mar. 1849.
Rev. Wm. M. Paxton,.........Elec. Aug. 1851.
Rev. Wm. P. Breed...........Elec. Dec. 1852; Resigned Aug. 1856.
Wm S. Calohan, Esq.........Elec. Mar. 1853.
Jas. K. Moorhead, Esq.......Elec. Aug. 1853.
Jas. P. Sterrett, Esq..........Elec. July, 1855.
Rev. Jas. Alexander. ....Elec. Aug. 1856.

Principals and Professors.

ELECTED:

April, 1802, Rev. John Watson, Pres. and Prof. Languages and Moral Philoshphy.—Died Nov. 30, 1802.

" " Rev. John M'Millan, Prof. of Divinity.

" " Samuel Miller, A. M. Prof. Mathematics and Natural Philosophy.--Resigned Sept. 1830.

April, 1803, Rev. James Dunlap, A. M. Pres. and Prof. Language and Moral Philosophy.—Resigned April, 1811.

" 1805, Rev. John M'Millan, D. D. Vice President.—Died Nov. 16, 1833.

" 1812. Rev. Andrew Wylie, D. D. President.—Resigned April, 1816.

Sept. 1817. Rev. Wm. M'Millan, A. M. President.—Resigned Aug. 1822.

" 1818. Rev. Abraham Anderson, A. M. Professor Languages.—Resigned Sept. 1821.

" 1821. Rev. Wm. Smith, A. M. Prof. Languages.

" 1822. Rev. Matthew Brown, D. D. President.—Resigned Sept. 1845.

April, 1824. Rev. James Ramsey, D. D. Prof. Hebrew.—Resigned Dec. 1852.

" 1826. Rev. Richard Campbell, A. M. Prof. Languages and Mathematics-—Resigned 1827.

" 1830. Rev. John H. Kennedy, A. M. Prof. Mathematics and Natural Philoshphy.—Died Dec. 15, 1840.

Sept. " Samuel Miller, A. M. Hon. Prof. Mathematcis.—Died '31.

March,1832. Jacob Green, M. D. Prof. Chemistry, Mineralogy, and Natural History.—Died Feb. 1851.

" 1834. C. J. Hadermann, Esq. Prof. Mathematics and Modern Languages.—Resigned Sept. 1836.

Sept. 1836. Washington M'Cartney, A. M Prof. Mathematics and Modern Languages.—Resigned Sept. 1837.

" 1837. Rev. Charles S. Dod, A. M. Prof. Mathematics and Modern Languages.—Resigned 1839.

Mar. 1838. William Darby, Esq. A. M. Prof. History, Geography, and Astronomy.—Resigned 1839.

Feb. 1841. Richard S. M'Culloh, Esq. A. M. Prof. Mathematics, Natural Philosopy and Chemistry.—Resigned Sept. 1843.

" 1841. Rev. A. B. Brown, A. M. Prof. Belles Lettres and Adjunct Prof. Languages.—Resigned Oct. 1847.

Mar. 1841. Henry Snyder, A. M. Adjunct Prof. Mathematics.

ELECTED:

Mar. 1843. Rev. Henry Snyder, A. M. Prof. Mathematics.—Resigned Aug. 1850.

Sept. 1843. S. R. Williams, A. M. Prof. Natural Philosophy and Chemistry.—Resigned Aug. 1852.

" 1844. Rev. Robert W. Orr, A. M. Prof. Civil Engineering, and Natural History.—Resigned Dec. 1845.

Jan. 1845. Rev. R J. Breckinridge, D. D. President.—Resigned June, 1847.

Dec. " Rev. A. B. Brown, A. M. Prof. Belles Lettres, Logic, Rhetoric and General History.

" " Rev. Robert W. Orr, A. M. Prof. Latin Language and Literature.—Resigned March, 1852.

Mar. 1846. Rev. Thomas Beveridge, D. D. Prof. Extraordinary, Evidences Nat. and Rev. Religion.—Resigned 1855.

" " John D Vowell, M. D. Prof. Extra. Phisiology and Comparative Anatomy.—Resigned ——

Oct. 1847. Rev. Alexander B. Brown, D D. President.—Resigned Aug. 1856.

June, 1848. Rev. Robert M. White, A. M. Prof. Extra Rhetoric.—Died Dec. 1848.

July, 1849. Rev. Joseph R. Wilson, A. M. Prof. Extra. Rhetoric.—Resigned ——

Aug. 1850. Robert Patterson, Esq. A. M. Professor Mathetics.—Resigned Nov. 1854.

" " Rev. William Wallace, D. D. Professor Extraordinary of Moral Science.—Died Jan. 1851.

" 1852. Rev. William Ewing, A. M Professor Extraordinary of History and Modern Languages.

" " Samuel R. Williams, A. M. Professor Extraordinary of Natural Science.—Resigned 1854

Sept. 1852. Samuel Jones, A. M. Prof. Nat. Philos. and Chemistry.

Dec. " Rev. Aaron Williams, A. M. Prof. Latin Language and Literature.

" " Rev. Abraham Anderson. D. D. Professor Extra. of Hebrew.—Died May, 1855.

Feb. 1855. John Fraser, A. M. Professor of Mathematics.

" " John B. Stilley, A M. Prof. Extra. of Civil Engineering.

July, 1855. Rev. John B. Clark, A. M. Prof. Extra. of Hebrew.

Jan'y 1857. Rev. Joseph Alden, D. D. President.

Mar. " Rev. A B. Brown, D. D. Professor of Political Economy and History.

Principals of the College,

FROM THE TIME IT WAS CHARTERED.

REV. JOHN WATSON, A. M.

Chosen Principal, Aug. 29, 1802; died Nov. 30th, 1802.

REV. JAMES DUNLAP, A. M.

Chosen April 27th, 1803; resigned April 25th, 1811.

REV. ANDREW WYLIE, D. D.

Chosen April 29th, 1812; resigned April, 1816.

REV. WILLIAM M'MILLAN, A. M.

Chosen September 24th, 1817; resigned August, 14th 1822.

REV. MATTHEW BROWN, D. D. LL. D.

Chosen September 25th, 1822; resigned September 27th, 1845.

REV. ROBERT J. BRECKINRIDGE, D. D. LL. D.

Chosen January 2d, 1845; resigned June 9th, 1847.

REV. ALEXANDER B. BROWN, D. D.

Chosen October 14th, 1847; resigned August 5th, 1856.

REV. JOSEPH ALDEN, D. D.

Chosen January 7th, 1857.

Present College Faculty.

REV. JOSEPH ALDEN, D. D.

President and Professor of Mental and Moral Philosophy.

REV. A. B. BROWN, D. D.

Professor of Political Economy and History.

REV. WILLIAM SMITH, D. D.

Vice President and Professor of the Greek Language.

SAMUEL JONES, A. M.

Professor of Natural Science.

REV. AARON WILLIAMS, D. D

Professor of the Latin Language.

JOHN FRASER, A M.

Professor of Mathematics.

REV. WILLIAM EWING, A. M.

Professor Extraordinary of Modern Languages.

JOHN B. STILLEY, A. M.

Professor Extraordinary of Civil Engineering.

REV. JOHN B. CLARK, A. M.

Professor Extraordinary of the Hebrew Language.

TUTOR.

MATTHEW B. RIDDLE, A. M.

LIST OF GRADUATES

OF JEFFERSON COLLEGE,

And Others, upon whom Honorary Degrees have been conferred.

EXPLANATIONS.—*m* Denotes Minister of the Gospel,—*l* Denotes Lawyer,—*p* Denotes Physician,—*t* Denotes Professional Teacher,—* Denotes Deceased,—*St Th* Denotes Student of Theology,—*St L* Denotes Student of Law,—*St M* Denotes Student of Medicine;—The ——— in the list of names, in any year, denotes that those who follow received only Honorary Degrees. Many of these may also be regarded as Alumni; having received their education at this College, but having been prevented from completing their course.

The present Post Office address, so far as known, is given.

1802.

*Reid Bracken, *m*
*Johnston Eaton, *m*
*William M'Millan, *m* D D Pres't Jeff Coll.
*Israel Pickens, *l* Governor Alabama.
*John Rhea, *m* D D 5

1803.

*Andrew M'Donald, *m*
*Alexander Montieth, *m*
*Cyrus Riggs, *m* 3

1804.

*John M'Donald, *l*
*Abraham Scott, *m*
*Daniel Stephens, *m*
*Clement Valandingham, *m*
*John White, *p* 5

1805.

*Moses Allen, *m*
*James Cunningham, *m*
*James Galloway, *m*
*Daniel Hayden, *m*
*James M'Connel,
*Carlos A. Norton.
*James Patterson, *m*
*James Scott, *m*
John B. Trevor, *l* Cashier, Philadelphia.
*James Wills, *l*
*James R. Wilson, *m* D D Prof. Theol. 11

---

*Rev John M'Millan, A M D D Vice Pres't Jefferson College.
*Samuel Miller, A. M. Prof. Jeff. Coll.
*Dr Samuel Murdock, A M
*Rev Samuel Ralston, A M D D Pres't Board of Trustees.
*Rev James Ramsey, A M D D Prof of Hebrew, Jefferson College.

1806.

*Thomas Hunt, *m*
*Jonathan Leslie, *m*
John Reed, *Farmer*, Washington Co. Pa.
*James Scott, *m*
George Vaneman, *m* Van Buren, Ohio. 5

---

*James Dunlap, A M D D Pres't Jefferson College.

1807.

*James Culbertson, *m*
*William Dunlap, *m*
*John Matthews, *m*
*Samuel Porter, Jr. *m*
*Joseph Stephenson, *m* 5

---

*Rev James Hughes, A M
*Rev William Swan, A M

1808.

*Stephen Boyer, *m*
*Ira Condit, *m*
*Joseph S. Hughes, *m*
*James Smith, *m* 4

---

*Rev John Anderson, D D
*Rev James Power, D D

1809.

*James Milligan, *m*
*Christopher Rankin, *l* Memb. Cong.
Joseph Scroggs, *m* Ligonier, Pa. 3

---

*Rev Samuel Porter, A M
*Rev Joseph Clarke, D D

1810.

*John Cannon, *m*

*Jonathan Gill, *m*
James Hervey, *m* D D Triadelphia, Va.
*William Hendricks, *l* LL D U. S. Senator, and Governor of Indiana.
*William Johnstone, *m*
James P. Kerr, *p*
Robert Lusk, *m*
*John Reed, *m*
*Andrew Wylie, *m* D D Pres't Jefferson and Wash. Colleges, and Ind. Univ. 9

1811.

George M'Cook, *p* M D Prof. Medical College. Pittsburgh, Pa.
James P. Mitchell, *p* Lynchburgh, Va.
*James Wright, *m* 3

1812.

Wells Andrews, *m* Prof. Ohio University. Washington, Ill.
*James Coe, *m* D D
Joseph M'Elroy, *m* D. D. New York City. 3

1813.

*Archibald Johnstone, *m*
George Junkin, *m* D D Pres't Lafayette College, and Miama University, and Washington College, Va.
*George Miller, *p*
John Montieth, *m* Prof Williams College, and Pres't University of Michigan.
James Rowland, *m* Mansfield, Ohio.
Jeremiah C. Wilcox, *l* 6

1815.

*James Frazier, *St. Theol.*
*Thomas Johnstone, *m*
Joseph Smith, *m* D D Pres't Frank. Coll. O. & Fred. Coll. Md. Greensburgh, Pa. 3

1816.

*Hugh Dickey, *m*
*William Graham, *m*
*William Wallace, *m* Editor. 3

1817.

*Abraham Anderson, *m* D D Prof Jeffeson Coll. and Asso. Th. Seminary.
*Daniel M'Intosh, *m*
*Andrew Todd, *m* 3

1818.

Robert Baird, *m* D D Secretary Am. and Foreign Christian Union. N. Y. City.
William C. Blair, *m* Indianola, Texas.
Salmon Cowles, *m* Pres't DesMoines College. West Point, Iowa.
Samuel Evans, *l* Uniontown, Pa.
Thomas Hanna, *m* D D Sup. Washington Female Sem. Washington, Pa.
William Jeffery, *m* D. D. Pres't Board of Trustees. Herriottsville, Pa.
*William M'Clure, *l*
*Joshua Moore, *m*
*James P. Miller, *m* D D
*Alexander Williamson, *m* 10

1819.

*James Adams, *m*
*David Carson, *m* Prof. Asso. Th. Sem.
Stephen Colwell, *l* Philadelphia.
Adam Coon, *l* Wellsburgh, Va.
John Coulter, *m* Coultersville.
John Lee, *l* New York City.
*Alexander M'Candless, *m*
John M'Kinney, *m* Oswego, Ill.
William Smith, *m* D D V. Pres't and Prof. Greek, Jeff. Coll. Canonsburgh, Pa.
*Joseph Trimble, *m*
*William Wallace, *m* 11

1820.

*Alexander Campbell, *m* D D
Robert Crooks, *m*
Charles E. Gullatt, *p*
*John H. Kennedy, *m* Prof. Jeff. Coll.
William Nesbit, *m* New Bedford, Pa.
*John Peebles, *m*
William S. Roberts, *m* D D
Alexander Sharp, *m* Newville Pa.
Thomas Williamson, *m* M D Miss. to the Dacotahs. Yellow Meadow, Minn.
M'Knight Williamson, *m* Hibbardsville, O. 10

1821.

Joseph B. Adams, *m* Hartleton, Pa.
*Lewis F. W. Andrews, *p*
George Buchanan, *l* Haysville, Ohio.
*Richard Campbell, *m* Pres. Frank. Coll. O.
Meredith Helm, *l*
*John Hunter, Tutor Jefferson College.
*William Johnston, *m*
William M'Connell, *l*
David M'Kinney, *m* D D Ed. Presb. Banner and Advocate. Pittsburgh, Pa.
John Pinkerton, *m* Mt. Solon, Va.
Samuel Reed, *m* Bealsville, Ohio.
Levin Rodgers, *p* Springfield, Ohio.
*Aaron Torrence, *p* 13

---

*Rev Obadiah Jennings, A M D D
Rev Rob. Johnston, A M New Castle, Pa.

1822.

Richard Brown, *m* New Hagerstown, O.
*Joseph Claybaugh, *m* D D Prof. Associate Reformed Theological Seminary.
Joseph Clokey, *m* Springfield, Ohio,
William J. Frazer, *m* St. Francisville, O.
Adam B. Gilliland, *m* Venice, Ohio,
James Johnstone, *m*
*Andrew D. Livingston, *l*
*Hugh Martin, *p*
John M'Cluskey, *m* D D Agent for Board of Education. Hartsville, Pa.
*James B. Morrow, *m*
*Ebenezer E. Munro, *St. Th.*
John Pitkin, *m* Milfordton, Ohio.
*Garland B. Shelladay, *l*
John G. Smart, *m* Madison, Indiana.
Benj. F. Spilman, *m* Shawnetown, Ill. 15

---

*Rev. Thomas D. Baird, A M D D

1823.

James Arbuthnot, *m* Unity, Adams Co. O.
*Jacob Beecher, *m*
Wells Bushnell, *m* Missionary to Indians. Youngstown, Pa.
*Daniel L. Carrol, *m* D D Pres't Hampden Sidney College.
*John K. Cunningham, *m*
Robert Dilworth, *m* D D Enon Valley, Pa.
*Boyd Emery, Sr. *p*
Boyd Emery, Jr. *p* Dunningsville, Pa.
Elliot Finley.
James C. Hall, *p* Prof Medical Coll.
*Robert Henry, *m*
Samuel C. Jennings, *m* Ed. Moon P. O. Pa.
John Lee, m
*William Lowry, *m*
*George Lyon, *l*
John M'Bean, *p* Cadiz, Ohio.
James May, *m* D D Prof Prot. Ep. Theo. Sem. Va. Alexandria, D. C.
Alex. H. Mecklin, *p* Washington, D. C.
*Robert C. Moody, *p*
*James Nourse, *m*
William C. Pollock, *p*
William R. Raum, *p*
*Samuel H. Rench, *p*
*John Reynolds, *m*
David H. Riddle, *m* D D Ex-Pres't Western Univ. Pa.
*Moses Roney, *m* Pres't Westminster College, Allegheny City.
*Robert Rutherford, *m*
Josiah Scott, *l* Judge Supreme Court, O. Hamilton, Ohio.
*William A. Stevenson, *St Th*
John Wallace, *m*
*Samuel White.
Andrew P. Wilson, *m*
Benjamin F. Yoe, *l* 32

Rev. A. O. Patterson, A M D D Oxford, Ohio.
*Rev. Robert Laird, A M

1824.

William Cunningham, *l* Editor.
*Thomas Espy, *m*
*John T. Ewing, *m*
John S. Galloway, *m* Agent American Bible Society. Springfield, Ohio.
*Henry Haynes, *l*
Samuel Hindman, *m* Iberia, Ohio.
John Hindman, *m* Dayton, Pa.
John D. Hughes, *m* Mogadore, Ohio.
Watson Hughes, *m* West Newton, Pa.
Absalom M'Cready, *m* N. Wilmington, Pa.
James M'Carrel, *m*
Joseph Mahon, *m* Agent for Board of Education. Shippensburgh, Pa.
*John Montgomery, *m*
*John E. Patterson, *St L*
William Sickles, m Indianapolis, Ind.
*James Templeton, *m*
G. W. Thompson, *l* Judge, Wheeling, Va.
John C. Tidball *l* Coshocton, Ohio.
Samuel Wilson, *m* D D Prof Associate Th. Sem. Xenia, Ohio. 19

---

*Rev Robert Bruce, D D
Rev Francis Herron, D D Pittsburgh, Pa.
*Rev Samuel Martin, D D

1825.

Charles M. Aten, *l* New Lisbon, Ohio.
*Robert Brotherton, *m*
A. B. Brown, *m* D D Ex. Pres't and Prof of Political Economy and Hist. Jeff. Coll.
James Campbell, *m* Principal Female Seminary. Walker P. O. Pa.
*J. B. Cochran, *p*
*William Cox, *m*
John F. Cowan, *m* Washington, Mo.
David Gilbert, *p* Prof Pa. Medical College, Philadelphia.
*Andrew D. Harris, *l*
David Hervey, *m* Wellsburg, Va.
Henry Hervey, *m* Martinsburg, Ohio.
John Hemphill, *l* Chief Justice, Texas—Austin, Texas.
Thomas E. Hughes, *m* Sommerville, Ohio.
Nathaniel Ingles, *m* Lockport, Ind.
*David Jacobs, *m*
*Thomas Livingston, *l*
John H. Marsden, *m* M D York Sulphur Springs, Pa.
William M'Murren, *l* Sheppardstown, Va.
*John M'Arthur, *m* D D Prof Miami University.
John Moore, *m* Bull Creek, Va.
Cornelius H. Mustard, *m* Lewes, Del.
*Benjamin F. Nourse, *p* Surgeon U. S. A.
Ethelbert P. Oliphant, *l* Uniontown, Pa.
*Alexander E. Patterson, *l*
*David Ritchie.
Thos. J. S. Smith, Memb. Leg. Dayton, O.
James Smith, *l* Cumberland, Md.
William A. Stevens, *m* D D 28

---

*Jonathan Letherman, M D
William Church, M D
William F. Irwin, M D Pittsburgh, Pa.
David Porter, M D

1826.

James Alexander, *m* Martin's Ferry, Ohio.
*Robert G. Bowland.
James Chamberlin, *m*
*James Crawford, *l*
John H. Dickey, *m*
*John Donald, *p*
Reuben Frame, *m* Fon du Lac, Wis.
Wm. J. Gibson, *m* D D Walker's P. O. Pa.
William Hughes, *m* Loudonville, Ohio.
John R. Hutchinson, *m* D D Prof Oakland College. Carrolton, La.
David Kiddoo, *l* Cuthbert, Ga.
Alexander T. M'Gill, *m* D D Prof Western and Princeton Theo. Seminaries. Princeton, N. J.
James G. M'Intire, *m* Elkton, Md.
Thomas Nichol, *p* Oskaloosa, Iowa.

Albert Osburn, *p* Wheeling, Va.
Hugh Parks, *m*
John Patton, *m* Philadelphia.
Alfred Patterson, *l* Uniontown, Pa.
[illegible] Pomroy, *m*
Azariah Prior, *m* Pottsville. Pa.
James D. Ray, *m* Prin. Mt. Ebenezer Academy Gallipolis, Ohio.
Aaron Williams, *m* D D Prof Ohio University and Jeff. Coll. Canonsburg, Pa
Thomas Wilson, *m*
*Robert G. White, *l* 24

John Gloninger, M D
George Reidenour, M D

1827.

Thomas Armat, *l*
*Isaac T. Bennet, *m*
William O. Boyd, *l* South Carolina.
James C. Boyd, *p* South Carolina.
*James Boyce, *St Th*
Jacob Coon, *m* Prof Franklin Coll Union Grove, Ill.
William Curran, *t* Philadelphia.
*John Glen, *m*
George W. Hampson, *m* Woodcock, Pa.
Charles W. Kelso, *l* Erie, Pa.
William W. Laird, *l*
William A. Lake, *l*
William M'Caleb, *l* Judge.
Robert M'Clave, *l* Carrollton, Ohio.
*Robert M'Crea, *l*
*John M'Ginley, *p*
*John M'Jimsey, *St Th*
*William M'Pherson, *l*
Wm C. Matthews, *m* D D Shelbyville, Ky.
Jno D. Matthews, *m* D D Lexington, Ky.
Newton May, *p* Philadelphia.
James Park, *t* Eckmansville, Pa.
James P. Ramsey, *m* New Bedford, Pa.
*Joseph Reed, *m*
John W. Scott, *m* D D Pres't Washington College, Washington, Pa.
William W. Snodgrass, *p*
David Sterret, *m* Carlisle, Pa.
Joel Stoneroad, *m* Woodvale, Pa.
James Wallace, *m*
*James M. Whitehill, *l*
William C. Worthington, *l* Charleston, Va.
Fran. Wythe, B'kseller, Harrisburg, Pa. 32

Rev Andrew K. Russell, A M

1828.

Robert J. Alexander, *l* Judge 8th Dis't O. St. Clairsville, Ohio.
*James S. Bell, *p*
Walter Brice, *p* South Carolina.
Levi Davis, *l*
William Finley, *m* Prospect, Butler Co Pa.
Robert Glenn, *m* Utica, Pa.
*Ashbel A. Green, *l*
*Stephen Haft, *St Th*
*Levin W. Handy, *p*
*W. W. Hutchinson.
Michael Jacobs, *m* Prof Pa. College, Gettysburgh, Pa.
Thomas Johnson, *p*
Henry T. Kyle, *l*
*Alexander M'Junkin, *t*
Sloan M'Intire, *m*
John M'Nair, *m* Clinton, New Jersey.
*Ebenezer M'Pherren, *St Th*
John Martin, *p* Pittsburgh.
*Thomas B. Peter, *l*
*James S. Snodgrass, *St Th*
Adam Torrance, *m* New Alexandria, Pa.
James Veech, *l* Uniontown, Pa.
James Watson, *l* Washington, Pa.
Samuel M. Whan, *l* Principal of Belle Air Academy. Belle Air, Md.
Samuel Wilson, *m* D D Merritstown, Pa.
Henry R. Wilson, *m* M D D D Missionary to India. Sewickley, Pa.
Loyal Young, *m* Butler, Pa.

A. T. Dean, M D
Rev John Hemphill, D D South Carolina.
Jonathan Pounder, M D

1829.

*William B. Barry, South Carolina.
Thomas W. Bartly, *l* Judge, Leg. Mansfield, Ohio.
Bankhead Boyd, *m* Strabane, Washington County. Pa.
James Boyce, *m* Bell's Store, South Car.
William H. Coyle *l* Washington City, D. C.
Charles Dubuisson, *l* Pres't Jefferson College, Mi. and Judge. Natchez, Mi
John Eagleson, *m* Buffalo, Pa.
William Eakins, *m* M'Connellsville, Ohio.
Richard Eberle, *p* Philadelphia.
John Eberle, *p* Philadelphia.
Robert M. Finley, *m* Wooster, Ohio.
John Flemming, *m* Earlville, Pa.
*Warren Flenniken, *m*
John B. Graham, *m* Ag't American Bible Soc Fairview, Ohio.
*William Gray, *m*
John E. Heanon, *m*
J. J. Hemphill, Farmer, Shippensburg, Pa.
Joseph P. Hoge, *l* Memb Cong San Francisco, California.
Samuel M. Howey *t* St Clairsville, Ohio.
*Robert R. Jenkins, South Carolina.
John C. Lowrie, *m* D D Miss to India. and Cor Sec'y B'd For Miss. N. Y. City.
*Matthew S. Lowrie, *l*
Charles F. M Cay, *t* LL D Prof Univ Georgia, and Pres't Coll of South Car.
*Samuel Moody, *m*
Abraham D. Pollock, *m* Warrenton, Va.
Richard Ransom, *l*
*William Reed, *m* Missionary to India.
David Ritchie, *l* Memb. of Congress. Pittsburgh, Pa.
Alexander Smith.
Charles C. Sullivan *l* Mem Leg. Butler, Pa.
*S. Calvin Tait, *l*
David I. Thompson, *m*
Samuel Williamson, *m* Ohio.

Joseph S. Wylie, *m* 34

Rev Reuben Davis, A M
Thomas J. M'Kaig, A M
Rev Henry Cook, D D Ireland.
William M'Ilvain, M D
Isaac Culbertson, M D
Thomas Johnson, M D
George Reiter, M D East Liberty, Pa.

1830.

William A. Adair, *m* Allegheny City, Pa.
Bela S. Allen, *St Th*
George W. Clark, Engineer, Chicago, Ill.
*John Cloud, Missionary to Africa.
Lorman Crawford, *l*
*John L. Dinwiddie, *m*
Arnold H. Dohrman, *m*
Matthew B. Hope, *m* M D D D, Miss. to China, and Prof. N. J. Coll. Princeton, N. J.
John W. Johnston, *m* Darlington, Pa.
Samuel P. Johnson, *l* Warren, Pa.
*Thomas S. Kendall, O. *m*
*John S Key, D C. *l*.
Joseph Kerr, *m* Miss. to Wea Indians. Fairfield, Iowa.
*Francis Laird, *m* Miss. to Africa.
*Samuel Long, *t* Prof. Newark Coll.
Richard L. Mackal, D. C. Clerk.
James J. Marks, *m* Quincy, Ill.
Phineas B. Marr, *m* Lewisburg, Pa.
*William Moffat, S. Car. *t*.
*Daniel S. Montgomery, *l*
John Newton, *m* D D Miss. to Lodiana, N. India.
James Patterson, *m* D D Pres. Westm. Coll. Institute. New Wilmington, Pa.
*James C. Porter, St. Th. *t*
Asahel P. Prior, *p*
Francis Rutherford, *m* D. C.
James C. Sharon, *m* Prof Des Moines Coll. Iowa. St. Francisville, Mo.
James Sloan, *m* D D Dunningsville, Pa.
*John Templeton, *l*
R. G. Thompson, *m* Tiro, Crawford Co. O.
David H. Turpin, *l*
James L. Vallandigham, *m* Newark, Del.
James Wilson, *m* Miss. to India Knoxville, Tenn. 32

John Brown, D D Scotland.
*Charles Ewing, LL D New Jersey.

1831.

Washington Baird, *m* D D Spartanburg, S. C.
Andrew H. H. Boyd, *m* D D Winchester Virginia.
Lewis P. Bush, *p* Wilmington, Del.
John S. Byrne, *l* Warrenton, Va.
David D. Clark, *m* M'Veytown, Pa.
*Hamilton W. Carter, *m*
James W. Coulter, *m*
Thomas Galt, *m* Springfield, Ill.
John D. Henderson, *l* merchant, New Orleans.
Isaac J. Henderson, *m* New Orleans,
John Herron, *l* Capt. Mex. War, Pittsburgh, Pa.
Anthony M. Higgins, *l* Farmer, Del.
*John L. Hoge, *t*
David X. Junkin, *m* D D Hollidaysburg.
Samuel A. M'Clain, *m*
*Reuben R. M'Dowell, *p*
Robert A. M'Murtrie, *l* Mem. Pa. Leg. Hollidaysburg, Pa.
*Alexander Mackey, D. C. *p*
George Marshal, *m* D D Upper St. Clair, Pa.
Addison May, *l* Farmer Md.
*John E. Morrison.
Joseph M. Parke, *m*
*John H. Patterson, *p*
*James H. Porter, *t*
James Ralston, *St Th.*
Samuel S. Sheddan, *m* Rahway, N. J.
*Cabell Taverner, *l*
Samuel M. Wilson, *m* Lithopolis, Ohio.
William Wilson, *m*
*John G. Witherspoon, *m* N. Carolina. 30

Rev. Luther Hasley, D D Bloomington, N. Y.

1832.

James L. Bartol, *l* Md.
Herbert Bixby, N. H.
*William Burnett, *m* Pres. Frank. Coll. Ohio.
James I. Kuhn, *l* Prof. O. Univ. Pittsburgh, Pa.
John H. Fromberger, *p* Delaware City.
John M. Galloway, *m* Steubenville, Ohio.
Samuel Hair, *m* Oxford, Ohio.
Henry Hanna, Iron Manufacturer, Hanging Rock, Ohio,
David Hull, *m* Watsontown. Pa.
*William M'Cormick, *m*
John K. M'Curdy, *p*
*Zantzinger M'Donald, *l*
William K. Marshall, *m* D D Rusk, Texas.
Clarke Moore, *m* Ohio.
William D. Ochiltree, *l* Judge, Nacogdoches, Texas.
William P. Orbison, *l* Huntingdon, Pa.
*James H. Patterson, *l* O.
*David Polk, *m* Brookville, Pa.
William Reynolds, *m* Prof. Pa. Coll. and Prest. Cap. Univ. O.
Joseph K. Riddle, *p* South Bend, Ind.
Norman Squires, *m*
Henry Williams, *m* 22

Joseph Patterson, Esq. A M
Rev. Alexander M'Cahan, A M Tipton, Ind
J. M'Kaig, Esq. A M
Rev. John T. Pressly, D D Allegheny City.
Rev. Stephen H. Tyng, DD N. York City.

1833.

William Begg, *m*
*William H. Blodget, *l* O.
Bolton Caldwell, *l* Judge, Vicksburg, Mis.
Thomas P. Gordon, *m* Pittsburgh, Pa.
David P. Graham, *p* New Lisbon, Ohio.
Alexander A. Hall, *m* N. Car.
Wm. Y. Hamilton, *m* Philadelphia.
Robert G. Hays, *m*
William R. Hemphill, Prof. Erskine Coll. Editor. Due West, S. Car.
James Hemphill, *l* Mem. Leg. Chester C. H. S. Car.
John Huber, *l*
James W. Kerr, *t* Teacher Blind Assylum, Philadelphia.
Shepherd Leffler, *l* Mem. Cong. Burlington, Iowa.
H. N. M'Calister, *l* Bellefonte, Pa.
James M'Clelland, *p* U. S. Navy, Erie, Pa.
*Charles S. Moffat *p* S. Car.
Daniel E. Nevin, *m* Farmer, Sewickleyville, Pa.
Edwin H. Nevin, *m* D D Pres. Franklin Coll. Ohio. Washington, D. C.
*Robert W. Orr, *m* Miss. to China, Prof. Jeff. Coll. Strattanville, Pa.
James L. Scott, *m* Miss. to Agra, N. India.
James P. Smart, *m* Xenia, Ohio.
Hamilton Smith, *m*
Joseph S. Travelli, *m* Miss. to China Prin'l Sewickley Academy.
John H. Williams, *l* Editor, Frederick City
Thomas S. Wilson, *l* 25

---

*Rev. Donald Frazer, D D Scotland.
*Rev. David M'Conaughy, D D
Ebenezer Daniels, M D Cannonsburg, Pa.

1834.

R. H. Allison, *p* Harrisburg, Pa.
A. A. Anderson, *l*
Chambers Baird, *l* Ripley, Ohio.
*Samuel T. Chapman, *l* Editor.
Joseph T. Cooper, *m* D E Ed. Evan. Repos. Philadelphia.
John D. Cummins, *l* M. Cong.
James Davis, *m* Blairsville, Pa.
Samuel R. Fisher, *m* D D Editor Ger Ref. Messenger, Chambersburg, Pa.
Thomas Foster, *p*
R. C. Galbraith, *m* Goranstown, Md.
Edward R. Geary, *m* Corvalis, Oregon Ter.
Thos. Gilkerson, *m* Saltsburg, Pa
Samuel M. Hamill, *m* Prin. High School, Lawrenceville, N. J.
I. W. K. Handy, *m* Portsmouth, Va.
J. C. Hawthorn, *p*
*F. K. Heisley, Engineer.
*N. N. Hurst, *l*
W. Hutchison, *m* Sparta, Tenn.
W. F. Irwin, *p* Irwin Station, Pa.
R. M. S Jackson, *p* State Geologist, Cresson, Pa.
J. Stuart Leech, *p*
S. Dexter Lecompte, *l* Chief Justice, Kansas.
W. S. Lindsey.
William M'Candlish, *m* Quincy, Ill.
*Washington M'Cartney, LL D Prof. Lafayette College, and Judge.
John L. M'Lean, *m*
William M'Gookin, *m* Sydney, Ohio.
Robert Osborn, *p* Point Pleasant, Va.
John V. Reynolds, *m* Meadville, Pa.
Stephen R. Riggs, *m* Miss. to Dacotash, New Hope, Minn. Ter.
*James D. Scott, *m*
Thomas L. Speer, *m*
James E. Stewart, *p* Baltimore, Md.
Thomas Walke, *l* Chilicothe, Ohio. 34

John F. James, A M
*D. S. Stevenson, M D

1835.

W. E. Andrews, *t* N. Car.
*F. E. Bailey, *l*
R. B. Barber, *l*
Thomas J. Bigham, *l* Pa. Sen. Pittsburgh,
James C. Brown, *m* Valparaiso, Ind.
James H. Buchanan, *m* Oxford, Ohio.
*John J. Bucher, *p*
*Nathaniel Burwell, *l*
*Joseph H. Chambers, *m*
Jonathan K. Cooper, *l* Peoria, Ill.
Elijah Criswell.
Alexander Donaldson, Prin'l. Eldersridge Academy, Clarksburg, Pa.
*John H. Done, *l* R. R. Sup.
*George H. Evans, *l*
Richard Gailey, *m* Hastings, Ohio.
W. M. Galbraith, *m* De Graff, Ohio.
Robert Gracey, *m* Pittsburgh, Pa
James Grier, *m* Noblestown, Pa.
Robert C. Grier, *m* D D Pres. Erskine Coll. Due West, S. C.
Andrew P. Happer, *m* Miss China, Canton.
Robert S. Holmes, *p* U. S Army.
Mortimer D. Johnson, *m* Prof Davidson College, N. Car.
George Johnson, *l* Portsmouth, Ohio.
J. W. Knott, *m* Shelby, Ohio.
*Shepherd Laurie, *p* D. C
William Lawrence, *l* Washington, Ohio.
Samuel C M'Cune, *m* Fairfield, Iowa.
*James Y. M'Ginnis, *m* Pres. of Acad.
*John W. Murray, *m*
C. K. Nelson, *m*
Charles H. Nourse, *m* Leesburg, Va.
Elijah Peale, Cashier, New Orleans.
*James Peebles, *p*
*Charles Ramsey, *l*
Hugh W. Reynolds, *l* Peoria, Ill.
*W H. Riley, *p* Md.
Alfred Ryors, *m* D D Pres. Ohio and Ind. Univ. and Prof. Cent. Coll. Ky. Danville.
Lawrence Stright, *m*
D. W. Swartz, *m*
Joseph Templeton, *m* St. Louis, Mo
Robert B. Walker, *m* Plaingrove, Pa.

*James Walker, *m*
Z. Yarnall, *l* Wheeling, Va. 43

William B Heiskel, Esq. A M Philadel.
Prof John E. Barbazet, A M
Rev. Rudolph Zickwolf, A M
Rev. Robert Stewart, D D Ireland.
Rev. David Elliot, D D Allegheny City.
Prof. Jacob Green, LL D

1836.

*Thomas B. Beer, *m*
H. F. Bowen, *m* Md.
P. D. Boyd, *m*
James Cameron, *m* Brunswick.
Irwin Carson, *m* Oscaloosa.
Philip Condit, *m*
Samuel M. Cooper, *m* Clearfield.
Edmund S. Doty, *l* Mifflintown, Pa,
*James C. Doty, *p*
Joseph W. Fowler, *l* Judge Sup. Ct. La.
John R. Franklin, *l* Mem. Congress, Snow Hill, Md.
William Gass, *t*
George M. Gibbs, *m* Gravelly Hill, N. C.
James R. Gilland, *m* Prof. Davidson Coll. N. Carolina.
Thomas Grier, *m* Camden, S. C.
G. B. Gray, *m* Md,
Hugh Hamilton.
*J. K. Henderson, *l*
*B. Wilbur Huntingdon, *l* Judge.
Henry Keim, *p* Pontiac, Mich.
Henry C. Knight, *l*
John Livingston, *m*
*J. Somerville Marbury, *m* D. C.
James Mason, *l*
John R. M'Fee, *l* Georgetown, Del.
D. B. M'Ginley, *p*
D. H. A. M'Lean, *m* Prof. Westm. Coll. Inst. and Prin. High School. Pittsburgh, Pa.
F. A. Muhlenburg, *m* Prof. Pa. College.—Gettysburg, Pa.
H. B. Pigman, *l*
*William Ramsey, *l*
*John C. Rankin, *p*
J. Huston Rankin.
Cyrus C. Riggs, *m* Pres't Richmond Coll. West Newton, Pa.
C. W. Russell, *l* Wheeling, Va.
Frederick A. Shearer, *m* Iowa City.
Francis S. Steel, *l*
John M. Stevenson, *m* D D Prof. Ohio Univ. Agent Cor. Sec. Amer. M. Soc. New Albany, Ind.
Frederick A. Thomas,
*Alexander Weed, *Engineer*, Va.
Samuel R. Williams, *t* Prof. Jeff. College, and Prin. Fem College, Louisville, Ky
Uriah W. Wise, *l* Prin. of Acad.
*Samuel A. Woods, *t* Va. 42

---

*Prof John Armstrong, A M
Dr. Hugh Campbell, A M
Prof Hiram Sims, A M
Peter A. Brown, Esq. LL D Philadelphia.

1837.

William G. Barnet, *p* Venice, Washington County, Pa.
Newton Bracken, *m* Portersville, Pa.
Joseph T. Buchanan, *m*
James Campbell, *l* Clarion, Pa.
*Alexander Campbell, *p*
Cyrus Dickson, *m* Baltimore, Md.
John Donaldson, *m* Salem, Ky.
William Eaton, *m* Clarksburg, Va.
George M. Eldridge, *l* Judge.
J. Buchanan Hall, *p* California.
George Hill *m* Blairsville, Pa.
B. D. Jackson, *l* Cambridge, Md.
*Thomas W. Kerr, *m*
Harrison P. Laird, *l* Leg. Penn'a. Greensburg, Pa.
David Laughlin, *t* Juniata Co. Pa.
*Robert F. Law, *St Th*
*Thomas S. Lewis, *St Th*
John Y. Lind, *p* Supt. Marine Hospital, San Francisco, Cal.
*Walter M. Lowrie, *m* Miss. to China.
*A. Martin, *p* O.
*Robert M'Murdy, *m*
Joseph E. Nourse, *m* Prof. U. S. Naval Academy. Annapolis, Md.
Griffith Owen, *m* Baltimore, Md.
John Patrick, *m* S. Car.
Jacob Pentzer, *m* Miamisburg, Ohio.
Samuel Pettigrew, *m* Ill.
George W. Purnell, *l* St. Francisville, Ia.
*Wilson Scott, *l*
Philo M. Semple, *m* Berlin, Ohio.
Joseph T. Smith, *m* D D Baltimore, Md.
Kensey John Stewart, *m*
W. M. Stewart, *l* Indiana, Pa.
Samuel Templeton, *m* Va.
John Todd, *m* Brookville, Pa.
Hilliary Williams, *l* Md.
David Wilson, *t* Prin Central Acad. Port Royal, Pa.
*Joseph Wilson, *St Th*
A. D. Wilson, *l*
John Witherow. 29

H. N. Lee, Esq. A M Kittanning, Pa.
Alfred Marks, Esq. A M
Rev Simeon Brown, A M Lebanon, Ohio.
Hon L. S. Handy, A M
William Orr, A M
M. Morgan, Esq. A M
John Millington, Prof. A M Va.
*Dr Robert Thompson, A M
*Rev John Williams, D D
Rev Isaac Grier, D D N. Car.
Rev E. P. Swift, D D Allegheny City.
Hon Lewis Cass, LL D Mich,

1838.

S. S. Blair, *l* Hollidaysburg, Pa.
*M. M. Brown, *m*
William H. Buffington,
*William Caskey, *m*

Robert Clark, *l* Prof Madison College.
Jacob Doll, *m* Prin. Fem. Sem. Yancysville, N. C.
Thomas P. Farrar, *l* Natchez, Mi.
Charles R. Fasset, *p*
Lewis Granger, *m* California.
William Mathiot, *l* Lancaster, Pa,
William H. M'Carer, *m* Evansville, Ia.
David M'Cay, *m* Callensburg, Pa.
*Benjamin G. M'Phail, *m* Snow Hill, Md.
*A. C. Miller, *m* White Rock.
James C. Miller, *l*
J. Krepps Miller, *l* Memb. Cong. Oregon.
James Montgomery, *m* Clarion, Pa.
Alfred Nevin, *m* D D Lancaster, Pa.
*Shepherd G. Patrick, *l*
Joseph H. Pressly, *m* Erie, Pa.
David F Reed, *m* Chili, Ohio.
William Rothrock, *m*
Henry Snyder, *m* Prof. Jeff. Cent. and Hamp. Sid. Coll. Hampden Sydney.
*George W. Stinson, *l*
*Thomas Sutton, *l*
*William D. Tassey, *l*
*John Watson, *l*
Felix B. Welton, Moorfield, Va. Farmer.
*E. H. C. Wilson, *l* 29

Rev James Marr, A M Lebanon, Ohio.

1839.

John E. Alexander, *m* Prin. Mill. Acad.—Washington, Ohio.
Moses Blackburn, *m* Petersburg, Ohio.
Alexander W. Brownlee, *m*
*Adley Calhoun, *m*
Peter P. Cluff, *p* Grange, Mo.
James Coulter, *m* Harmonsburg, Pa.
*George M. Dickson, *St Th*
Charles F. Divers, *m* Cedarville, N. J.
*John W. Duff, *m*
Alexander M Earle, *l*
E. J. Forsythe, *l*
J. K. Gibson, *l*
Smith F. Grier, *m* New Cumberland, Va.
Robert Hamill, *m* Boalsburg, Pa.
John V. Harbaugh, *l* Kansas.
Edwin W. Henry, Berlin, Md
John C. Kunkel, *l* Mem. Congress, Harrisburg, Pa
*John Lloyd, Miss to China,
*Samuel P. Marshall, *m*
A. Craig M'Clelland, *m* Ft. Wayne, Ind.
John M. M'Conaughy, *m* M D Lane, Ill,
Thomas Middleton, *m*
George Miles.
Norman Miller, *l* Martinsburg, Va.
*Thomas J. Murray, *p*
James Naylor, *m* Oakley, Va.
Roger Owen, *m* Prin. Chest. Hill Acad.—Chestnut Hill, Pa.
Jacob H. Patton, *m* and *t* New York City.
John Reed.
James Craig Reid, *t* Engineer, Erie, Pa.
*John H. Rittenhouse, *m*
Fitz William Sargent, *p* Philadelphia.
Owen Evans Shannon, *m*
Philander C. Smith,
William W. Stickley, *m* Spout Spring, Va.
Alexander Swaney, *m* Carrolton, Ohio.
W. Sheridan Thompson, *m* New Canton, Va
Joseph C. Wallace, *l*
George Willey, *l* Cleveland, Ohio.
M. Allen Williams, *m* Miss. to Chili. San Francisco, Cal.
Thomas M. Wilson, O.
William W. Woodend, *m* Prin. Saltsburg Acad. Saltsburg, Pa.
Samuel S Woods, *l* Lewistown. 43

Andrew F. Ross, A M
Prof James Espy, A M Washington City.
T. B. Beall, Esq. A. M
Rev Daniel Zacharias, A M, D D Frederick City, Md.
*Rev Asahel Nettleton, D D Conn.
Rev Wm. Shaw, D D Scotland.
Rev O. Stewart, D D Ireland.
Rev John W. Nevin, D D Lancaster, Pa.

1840.

J. Patton Anderson, Gov. Wash. Ter.
George E Austin, Farmer, Cambridge, Md
Samuel F. Boyd, Editor, Port Gibson, Mi.
Hugh A. Brown, *m* Miss. to China. Rockford, Ill.
James C. Carson *m* Salem X Roads, Pa.
A. G. W. Carter, *l* Judge, Cincinnati.
Samuel Coulter, *t* Editor,
Robert W. Dougherty, *l* Editor, Princess Anne, Md.
Archibald B. Earle, *l*
George Earle, *l* Elkton, Md
John Haldeman, *l* Pa Leg. Harrisburg Pa.
*Daniel S. Haich, *St Th*
Joseph M. Hays, *m*
James C. Herron, *m* Napa, Cal.
Daniel L. Hughes, *m* Stover's Place.
David Hughes, *m* M D New Plymouth, O.
Parker Jacobs, *l* Lewistown, Pa.
Samuel Mahaffey, *m* Washington, Ohio.
*David W. M'Conaughy.
Solomon M'Nair, *m* Washington, N J.
George Miller, *l*
James W. Miller, *m* Gay Hill, Tex.
John T. Moore, Planter, Port Gibson, Mi.
N. Grier Parke, *m* Pitston, Pa.
William A. Passavant, *m* Zelienople, Pa.
Robert Patterson, *t* Prof. in Jeff. College, Pa and Oakland College, Mi,
W. H. Reed.
Robert A Ross, *m* North Car.
Robert Steele, *m*
James Wason, *l* Hagerstown, Md.
G. A. Wenzel, *m* Philadelphia.
Henry A. White, *l* Princess Anne, Md. 32

Joseph Braddock, A M
Rev J. S. Dunwiddie, A M
Jacob Hall, Esq. A M Independence, Mo.

1841.

Moses Arnott *m* Hanover, Ind.
James A. Banks, *l* Lewistown, Pa.
Henry R. Bell, *p* Chicago, Ill.

William C. Bovard, Merchant, Warren, Pa
John K. Boyce, *m*
Thomas A. Bracken, *m* Independence, Mo.
James Buchanan, *m*
William Carlisle, *m* Chanceford, Pa.
*Isaac M. Cook, *m*
John B. Craighead, Farmer, Canonsburg.
Thomas M. Crawford, *m* Slate Hill.
Wilson M. Donaldson, *m* Bluffton, Ind.
David Donaldson, *p* Allegheny Co. Pa.
Ralph Douglass, *m*
*James C. Duncan.
*Joshua Elder, *m*
Edward J. Elliott.
John Hunter, *m*
*John F. Kean, *m*
J. M'D. Leavitt, *m* Prof. Ohio University. Athens, Ohio.
James B. M'Bride, *m*
Isaiah M'Junkin, *p* Butler. Pa,
Ebenezer M'Junkin, *l* Butler, Pa.
Isaac G. M'Laughlin, *m* Charlotte, N. C.
Andrew D. Mitchell, *m* Harrisburg, Pa.
John Oliphant, *l*
William Ottinger, *m* Grandview, Iowa.
John J. Patterson, Harrisburg, Pa.
*John H. Pottinger, *p*
*William L. Richards, *m* Miss. to China.
William M. Robinson, *m* Newark, Ohio.
Henry E. Sayre, *l* Waynesburg, Pa.
John A. Scott, *m* Prin. Female Sem. Halifax, C H Va.
W. M'K. Scott, *m* D D Prof Centre College Ky. Cincinnati, Ohio.
John Y. Scouller, *m* Fairhaven, Ohio.
William L. Shoemaker, *e*
Robert R. Sloan, *m* Prin Female Seminary Mt, Vernon, Ohio.
R. B. Sterling, Iron Manufacturer, Pittsburgh, Pa
Alexander Story, *m* Columbus, Iowa.
John M. Strong, *p*
Thomas R. Stewart, *l* Cambridge, Md.
John R. Taylor.
Joseph N. Watson, *m* Lewistown, Pa.
E. King Wilson, *l* Snow Hill, Md. 43

Prof L. Gaussen, D D
Prof Adolphe Monod, D D France.
Rev Andrew Marshal, D D Scotland.
Rev John Jameson, D D Scotland.
Rev Thomas J, Biggs, D D Cin. O.
Hon Robert C. Grier, LL D Philadelphia.

1842.

*Abraham Anderson, *m*
*D. Woods Baker, Coast Survey.
Dwight W. Bell, *l* Pittsburgh, Pa.
Algernon S. Bell *l* Pittsburgh, Pa.
John C. Biser, Md.
B. E. Chain, *m*
David R. Campbell, *m* Wintersville.
William Coleman, *l* Diamond Springs, Cal
*J. K. Cornyn, *m*
Henry U. Davis, *m*
D. W. Downer, *l* Uniontown, Pa.
Rees C. Evans, *m* Doylestown, Pa.
Andrew B. Frazier, *m*
Jared D. Fyler.
*James Gallatin, *m*
John W. Hazlett, *m* Carrick, Pa.
S. K Hughes, *m* Chestreville, Ohio.
John Lewis, *p* Ogden, Ind,
*A. M. Linn, *l*
J R. Lowrie, *l* Hollidaysburg, Pa.
Charles Martin, Prof Hamp. Sid. Coll. Va. Hampden Sid. Va.
B. F. M'Keehen, *p* Romines Mills.
Isaac S. M'Micken *l*
Ulysses Mercur; *l* Towanda, Pa.
Robert P. Nevin, Druggist, Pittsburgh.
Samuel I. Reid, *m* Prin. Chalm. Inst.—Holly Springs, Mi.
Robert King Reid, *p* Sup. Insane Asylum. Stockton, Col.
William Roseburgh, Cashier, Pittsburgh.
Isaac O. Sloan.
John F. Smith, *m* Richmond, Ind,
Robert Stanton, Planter, Natchez, Mi.
William Stanton, Planter Natchez, Mi.
John Steele, *m* Macomb, Ill,
*Samuel F. Sterling, *l*
*John Sturgeon, *p*
Darius Thomas *m*
William G. Van Lear, *l* Williamsport Md.
W. C. Van Bibber, *p* Md.
Joseph R. Whitham, *m*.
William L. Wingate, *p*
John Weaver, *p* Cannonsburg.
Daniel R. Wolfe, *l* New Castle, Del.

T. D. Baird, Jr. A B A M St. Louis, Mo.
Rev J. D. Mitchell, A B Wyoming, Pa.

1843.

*Richard Allison, *p*
J. Trooper Armstrong, *p* Ark.
James H. Baird, *m* Upper Sandusky, Ohio.
*John Barr, *m*
*J. K Bingham, *l*
William R. Bingham, *m* Warren Tavern Pa
*Thomas Black, St Th.
David C. Boal, *l* Bellefonte, Pa.
John Boyd, *l*
Cornelius Byles, *p* Franklin Grove, Pa.
James C. Clarke, *l* Greensburg, Pa.
Andrew Cochran, *m* Durhamville, N. Y.
J. Alexander Coulter, Civ. Eng. Greensburg, Pa.
James Cummings, *p* California.
William Edgar, *m* Murraysville, Pa.
*R. S. Elliott, St Th
Ebenezer Erskine, *m* Columbia, Pa.
William Ferguson, *l* Cincinnati, Ohio.
James H. Fife, *m* Mt. Pleasant, Pa.
J. Gregg Gibson, *p*
George W. Gunnison, *m* Prin. Burlington Univ. Iowa, and of Erie Academy. Erie, Pa.
S. W. Gilson. *l* Canfield, Ohio.
Jacob S. Haldeman, *l* Pa. Legislature, Harisburg, Pa.

John Hamilton, *t* Prin. of Acad. Mt. Zion, Simp. Co. Mi.
A. W. Hendricks, *l* Madison, Ind.
William M. Houston, *p* Santa Fee, Mo.
John Humerickhouse, *p* Coshocton, Ohio.
*Aaron H. Kerr, *m* Prof Alex. College.—St. Peter, Minn.
Richard T. Merrick, *l* Baltimore, Md.
William J. M'Culloch, Engineer, Washington, D. C.
James Matthews, *m* Prof. Cent, College.—Danvilie, Ky.
Joseph P. Moore, *m t* East Liberty, Pa.
John P. Penny, *l* Pittsburgh, Pa.
Jonathan Rennick, *l* Circleville, Ohio.
Abner O. Rockwell *m* Finleyville, Pa.
John Rowe, *m* Gallipolis, Ohio.
A. A. Scott, *p*
W. C. Sheets, *m* Morgantown; N. C.
James Smith, *m* Rochester, Pa.
S. Hume Smith, *m*
Francis A. Stewart, *l* Pittsburgh, Pa.
John M. Sullivan, *l* Ass't Sec. of State.
Elliott E. Swift, *m* New Castle, Pa.
J. Bowman Switzer, *l* Pittsburgh, Pa.
*George W. Watson, *p*
*Keever Wharton, *p*
N. D. Wright. 47

Rev E. Thompson Baird, A M D D Columbus, Mi.
Hon James Thompson, A M Erie, Pa.
William Reynolds, Esq. A M Meadville.
*Rev Wm. Atkinson, D D Va.
Rev James Peddie, D D Scotland.
Rev James Harper, D D Scotland.
*Rev James Martin, D D Prof.
*Hon Henry Baldwin, LL D

1844.

John Adair Anderson, *l*
*Samuel P. Berry, *m*
Andrew M. Beveridge, m Hoosack Falls.
Ebenezer E. Boyce, *m* North Car.
R. P. Crawford, *l* Kittanning, Pa.
George A. Hoffman, Cumberland, Md.
William Horner, *t*
R. C. Irwin, *p* Hollidaysburg, Pa.
James S. Jackson, *l* Lexington, Ky.
John J. Lane, *m* Prof Franklin College O. Wrightsville, Pa.
*James Leiper, St Th.
James E. Marquis, *m* Shelby, Ohio.
*Thomas M'Cague *m*
Nesbit M'Donald, *p* Pittsburgh, Pa.
Walter R. Macdonald, *l* Ogdensburg, N. Y.
Rodney Mason, *l* Springfield, Ohio.
*John R. Miller,
Ephraim Ogden, *m* Glade Mills, Pa.
S. Duncan Oliphant, *l* Uniontown Pa.
*Erastus S. Scott. *l*
George W. Shaiffer, *m* Prin. Female Sem. Shirleysburg, Pa.
James A. Shankland. *m* Detroit, Mich.
John C. Telford, *m* Mahoning, Pa.
Samuel Torrance, Farmer, Allegheny Co.
George Vaneman, *m* Florida.
George S. Walker, *p* California.
George L. Washington, *l* Va.
*Robert A. White, *l* Ed. South, Lit. Mess.
W. Biddle Wilkins, *l*
Joseph R. Wilson, *m* Prof. Jeff. Coll. and Hamp. Sid. Coll.

W. S. Lane, Esq, A M
Henry D Maxwell, Esq. A M Easton Pa.
*Hon. Daniel Duncan, A M
Rev, James L, Dinwiddie, D D
Rev Nathan L. Rice, D D St Louis, Mo.

1845.

James Allison, *m* Sewickleyville, Pa.
A. S. Baldwin, *p* M'Sherrysville, Pa.
James W. Bell, *p*
Robert Burgess, *m* Poland, Ohio.
J. Walton Cameron, *p*
James C. Campbell, *m* Paris, Pa.
William Doyle, Steubenville Ohio.
John W. Duncan, Iron Manufacturer, Pittsburgh, Pa.
Samuel J, Mills Eaton, *m* Franklin, Pa.
James C. Fleming, *p* Monongahela City.
James W. Fry.
J. W. Henderson, *p*
John H. Jackson, *p* Ky.
Thomas P. Johnston, *m* Clark P. O. Pa.
William F. Kean, *m* Freeport Pa.
Milton S. Latham, *l* Mem. Cong. and Col. Customs. San Francisco, Cal.
John Letherman, *p* Surg. U. S. Army. Fort Devine, New Mex.
C. Ritchie Letherman, Farmer, Palmyra, Missouri.
Darius D. M'Cluer, *l* Mi.
D. S. M'Henry. *m* Commerce, Mich.
John D. M'Nay, *m*
R. B. Minton.
R. S. Morton, *m* Hookstown, Pa.
Daniel Motzer, *m* Middlebrook, Md.
J. A. Murphy, *p*
Joshua T. Owen, *l t* Chestnut Hill, Pa.
Louis F. Baichley, *l* Marion Ohio,
Samuel P. Ross, *l* Pittsburgh, Pa.
John Shane, *l* Steubenville, Ohio.
Samuel A. Speer, Finley, Ohio.
James P. Sterrett, *l* Pittsburgh, Pa.
S Calhoun Stewart Merchant, St. Louis.
John Stuart, *m* Montgomery Ohio.
John R. Sturgeon, *m* Noblestown, Pa.
P Stryker Talmage, *m* Bloomfield, N. J.
Josiah Thompson, *m* Cherry Valley, Pa.
James Thompson, *m* N. Y. City.
A. R. Vance, Engineer, Ripley, Ohio,
Augustus A. Watson, *p*
Jacob Winters, *m* Brownsburg, Va. 40

Prof S C. Gray, A B
Hon James Ross Snowden, A M Philadelphia, Pa.
David Strother, Esq A M Martinsburg Va.
Dr J. E Snodgrass, A M
Rev James H. Thornwell, D D S. Car.
Rev James Rodgers, D D Allegheny City.

Rev. Ezra Keller, D D Ohio.
Rev. James Carlisle, D D London.
Rev. Robert Ferguson, LL D London,
*Hon. Henry Clay, LL D Ky.
*Rev. Matthew Brown, LL D

1846.

*James B. Allison.
Samuel Brown, *m* O.
Wm. L. Baird, *l* Prof Westm. Coll. Mo.
*Vincent Cockins, *m*
George W. Elder, *l* Lewistown, Pa.
Thomas R. Gilmore, Cadiz, Ohio.
Taylor L. Graham, *p*
John Haft, Druggist, Pittsburgh, Pa,
*James Kelso, *m*
J. Milton Kirkpatrick, *l* Pittsburgh, Pa.
Robert P. Lake, Druggist, Baltimore, Md.
J. Irwin Marks, *p*
*William Martin, Farmer.
James Martin, Bank Teller, Albany, N Y
*J. A. M'Curley.
William G. M'Elhaney, *m* Hoboken, N. J.
Thomas V. Milligan. *t* Prin of Academy, New Hagerstown, Ohio.
James H. Orbison, *m* Missionary to Ambala, N. I.
Michael Parkinson, *m* Island Creek, Ohio
Henry M. Pettibone, Planter, Woodville, Mi.
Joseph S. Pomroy, *m* Fairview, La.
James Ross Ramsey, *m* Miss. Creek Ind. Micco, Ark,
*James B. P. Robinson, *l*
James L. Rogers, *m* Prin. Female Inst. Florence, Ala.
Alexander Scott, *m* Savannah. Ohio.
Isaac N. Shannon, *m* Mt, Vernon, O.
Alexander E. Sharpe, *p* Newville, Pa.
A. Brady Sharpe, *l* Chambersburg, Pa.
Hugh Sturgeon, Cedar Rapids, Iowa.
*Elijah Van Buskirk, *m*
John W. Walker, *m* West Fairfield, Pa.
*Isaac A. Walker, *t* Farmer, Shirland, Pa.
Wm. H. West, *l* Prof Hamp, Sid. College. Bellefontaine, Ohio.
*J. H. West.
Frederick N. Whaley, *m* Clarksburg, Va.
O. H. Williams, *m*
George W. Zahnizer, *m* Conneautville, Pa.
37

W. S. Sterrett, A M Antrim, Ohio.
Enoch Lanning, A B N. J.
Rev Robert Steel, D D
Rev Samuel Steel, D D Hillsboro, Ohio.
Rev Charles C. Jones, D D South Car.
Rev John Stockton, D D Cross Creek Village.
*Hon Kensey Johns LL D Del.
Hon John J. Crittenden, LL D Frankfort, Ky.

1847.

John Adams, *l* Mt Vernon, Ohio
George D. Archibald, *m* Cincinnati, Ohio.
Thomas H. Beveridge, *m* Philadelphia.
Amos S. Billingsly, *m* Wirtemburg, Pa.
James Braden, *p*
George B. Brandon, *l* Mi.
W. Biays Brown. *m* Prof Transyl. Univ; Lexington, Ky.
Dwight Brown, Farmer, Lexington, Ky.
Leander Browning, *l* Va.
George Cairns, *m* Slate Lick, Pa.
John Campbell, *p*
*Hugh M. Campbell, *l*
David W. Carson, *m* Service, Pa.
*Lewis Castleman, Farmer, Ky.
S. Newell Cochran, *t* Canonsburg, Pa.
James S. Coulter.
John L. Craig, *m* Princeton, Ind.
George A. Crawford, *p* Editor, Lock Haven, Pa.
E. Van Ness Dean, *l* Wooster, Ohio.
J. G. Dickson, p Canonsburg, Pa.
Blanton H. Duncan, *l* Louisville, Ky
Henry Clay Dunlap, Far. Lexington, Ky.
J. Todd Edgar, *t* Prin Female Sem. Shelbyville, Tenn.
*James L Finley.
William C. Gilson, *p*
Albert G. Graham, *l* Jonesboro, Tenn.
Laverty Grier, *m*
John Hamilton, East Springfield, Ohio.
Isaac. N. Hays, *m* Shippensburg, Pa.
Henry H. Hornsby, Farmer, Ky.
James Huston, *t*
John R. Irwin, O
Robert D. Lilley, *l* Hillsboro, Ohio.
A. B. Maxwell, *m* Alliance, Ohio,
James H. M'Bride, *t* Philadelphia.
John M'Intosh, O.
David M'Kee, *m* Philadelphia, Pa.
John M'Nutt, Farmer, Dunacn's Falls, O.
Jacob Myers, Editor.
Henry M. Painter, *m* Brownsville, Md.
Luther M. Reynolds, *l* Dover, Del.
J Bingham Ripley, *m* Philadelpha.
James Levin Rogers, *m* Springfield, Ohio.
*William Sample, *St Th*
*Mead Satterfield, *m*
*Hamilton Scott, *m* O.
Leonidas W Sexton, *l* Rushville, Ind.
*James H. Shaiffer, *St Th*
Samuel Simmons, *l* St. Louis, Mo.
J. R. W. Sloan, *m* New York City.
W. Graydon Smith, Engineer. Carrollville, Md.
Edmund Snair, Jeweler, Huntingdon, Pa.
Robert Sutton, *l* Clarion, Pa.
William G. Taylor, *m* Tarentum, Pa.
Andrew C. Todd, *m* St Louis, Mo.
Alexander G Wallace, Irwin Station, Pa.
Thomas Ward, *m* O.
William H. Wilson, *m* Washington, Iowa.
William W. Wilson, Land Agent, Council Bluffs, Iowa.
Thomas S. Woods, *l* New Lisbon, Ohio.

Rev. Stephen Yerkis, A M Baltimore, Md.
*Rev. P. S. Spencer, D D Va.

Rev. James Smith, D D Ky.
Rev. James C. Watson, D D Milton, Pa.
Rev. Robert J. Breckenridge, LL D Danville, Ky.
Rev. James Dennum, D D Ireland.

1848.

Alexander H. Amerine, *m* Martins' Ferry Ohio,
W. J. Bertolette *p* Shreeve, Ohio.
William Y. Brown, *m* Omaha City.
Wilton W. Brown, *m* Williamsburg, Ohio
J. Woods Brown.
George W. Clarke. *l* Iowa City.
Matthew Clarke, *m* Blairsville, Pa.
Archibald B. Cook, *p* Med. College, Ky.—Louisville, Ky.
J. Irwin Cox, Farmer, Shippensburg, Pa.
John K. Cramer, *m* Williamsport, Md.
*Daniel W. Crofts, *l* O
Robert Curry, Prin. Female Sem. New Brighton, Pa.
John R. Duncan, *m* Moundsville, Va.
James Elliott, *l* Steubenville, Ohio.
John M. Geary, *m* Plain's Store, La,
*Ellis B. Gregg, *l*
*John Harbison, Printer.
*T. Moore Hill, *m*
Thomas J. Jenkins, Farmer, Va.
*William A. Jenkins, *p* Va.
Albert G. Jenkins, *l* Va.
Calvin P. Johnston, O.
Joshua F. Lawrence, Louisville, Ky.
William F. Livingston, Duncan's Falls, O.
*John Lyons, *St Th* O.
Walter Lowrie Lyons, Iowa.
William G. March, *m* Canfield, Ohio.
John M'Ewen, Merchant, Philadelphia.
John T. M'Carty, *l* Yuba, Cal.
H. C. M'Farland, *m* Carrick, Pa,
I. Newton M'Kinney, Flemington, Pa.
Jacob H. Miller, *l* Pittsburgh, Pa.
Josiah Milligan, *m* Princeton, Ill.
John J Patterson, Editor "Telegraph," Harrisburg, Pa.
J. Wilson Paxton, *m* Cannon Falls, Minn.
Cyrus L. Pershing, *l* Johnstown, Pa.
William A Pugh, *p*
William A. Rankin, *m* Belle Air, Md.
Joseph G. Reaser, *m* Inst. in Theol. Sem. Danville, Ky.
James W. Robinson, *l* Marysville, Ohio.
A. Denny Rogers, *l* Springfield, Ohio.
William P. Ruthrauff, m Canton, Ohio.
Soloman A. Sharp, *l* San Francisco, Cal.
J. M'Dowell Sharp, *l* Chambersburg, Pa.
William C. Smith, *m* Bell's Landing.
G. W. Strain, *m*
J. Russel Thompson, *m* Hickory, Pa.
Andrew Virtue, *m* Monroeville, Pa.
Sam. Tom. Wilson, *m* Rock Island, Ill.
Samuel B Wilson, *l* Beaver, Pa.
Joseph H. Wilson, *l* Beaver, Pa.
Richard C. Woods.
Edward E. Young, *l*
G. Ivester Young, *l* Probate Judge. Canfield, Ohio 54

Rev. J. B. Spotswood D D Del.
William Rogers, Esq. A M Ohio.
Hon Samuel Hepburn, LL D,
*Hon. Thomas M. T. M'Kennan, LL D
Hon. Samson Mason, LL D Ohio.

1849.

Butler P. Anderson, Astroia, Oregon.
*William R. Anderson.
George C. Arnold, *m* Philadelphia.
John M. Barnett, *m* Superior, Wis.
Samuel B. Barton, *t* Prof Cent. Coll. Ky. Louisville, Ky.
*Augustus Burt, *l*
Joseph H. Calvin, *m* Boligee, Ala.
William Porter Carson, *m* Marengo, Ill.
James G. Carson, *m* Claysville, Pa.
James Linn Cochran, *p* Sterling, Ill.
*Samuel H. Dickie, *p*
James M. Edmunds, Absecon, N. J.
John Elliott, *m* Alexandria, Pa.
N. Fletcher, *l* Editor, Massilon, Ohio.
George Frazer, Nicholasville, Ky.
James Mason Grier, *l* Philadelphia.
John P. Gilchrist, *l* Wheeling, Va.
*John T. Gibson, *l* Ill.
William R. Hamilton, *p*
Joseph A. Hanna, *m* Oregon Ter.
*Adam Harris, *m*
Cristopher Ingle, *l* Washington City,
John Q. A. Jones, *t* Prin of Academy. Elkton, Md.
I. N. Keller, *l* Wheeling, Va.
John Boal Laird, *p*
W. D. Leiper, *t* Tenn.
*J. A. Leiper, *m*
Alonzo Linn, *m* Prof Lafay. College. Easton, Pa.
James W. Logan, *l* Editor, Muscatine, Ia.
John H. Mathers, *l* Richland Centre, Wis
David M'Kinney, Merchant, Peoria, Ill.
William M'Culloch, *m* Fairview.
John B. M'Nay, *m* Muncie, Ind.
Charles A. Munn, *m*
*Joseph Murray.
C. H. Perkins, *m* Milford Centre, Ohio.
H. C. Piatt, *l* Tipton, Iowa.
Benjamin F. Ray, Merchant, Galena, Ill.
A. M. Reid, *t m* Steubenville Female Sem. Steubenville, Ohio.
S. C. Reid, *m*
J. W. Robinson, *p* Gettysburg, Pa.
Robert F. Sample, *m* Bedford, Pa.
G. M. Sloan, *l*
*Hiram M. Smith, *St Th*
D. F. Smith, *m*
J. M. Snodgrass, *m* Leipsic, Ohio
*Hugh Swan, *St Th*
William R. Vincent *m* Uniontown, Ohio.
William G. Walker, *t* Prin Female Sem. Owensboro, Ky.
Thomas B. Wilson, *m* Xenia, Ohio.
T. Scott Witherow, *m*
John A. Wolf, *p*
James F. Woodrow, *t* Prof. Oglethorpe Univ. Milliageville, Ga.
William G. Woods, *p* Ky.

Rev. Huey Newell, A B Fort Madison. Ia.
Rev. Nathaniel G. North, A M Charlestown, Va.
Rev. W. S. Emory, A M
Rev. J. Lochren, A M Waynesburg, Pa.
John Swan, Esq. A M Cumberland, Md.
S B. Hempstead, A M Hanging Rock, O.
J. Naff M'Guffin, Esq. A M New Castle Pa
Doctor M'Gugen, A M Mt. Vernon, Ohio.
Dr. J. H. M. Peebles, A M New Castle, Pa.
J. J. Aiken, A M Pittsburgh, Pa.
Rev, William D. Howard, A M Pittsburgh.
Richard Coulter, Esq. A M Greensburg Pa.
Rev. J. W. Dickie, A M Mansfield, Ohio.
Rev. George A. Lyon, D D Erie, Pa.
Rev. J. P. Pressly, D D Due West, S. Car.
Hon. Thomas Bradford, LL D
Hon. Thaddeus Stevens, LL D Lancaster.

1850.

N. W. Bankston, *l* Hinds Co. Mi.
*Thomas M Barber, *l*
John C. Barr, *m* Princeton, Ill.
*Josiah D. Brown, *l*
John Allen Brown, *m* Ligonier, Pa.
John C. Calohan, R. R. Contractor, Canonsburg, Pa.
William Campbell, *m*
Samuel L. Campbell, *t* Uniontown, Pa.
John W. Chalfant, Merchant, Pittsburgh.
William H. Covert.
Robert N. Dick, *m*
Caleb W. Finley, *m* London Ohio.
J. M. Gallagher, *l* Editor, Pittsburgh, Pa
David H. Goodwillie, *m* Supt. Pub. Schools Stamford, C. W.
*James M. Gorsuch, *m*
Alexander C. Graff, Iron Manufacturer, Milroy, Pa.
William F. Green, *l* Lewisburg, N. C.
Thomas F. Griffin, *l* Galveston, Texas.
David Hall, *m* Brady's Bend, Pa.
William Hartley, Farmer
Archibald D. Hawkins, *l* N. C.
John Smith Hays, *m* Charlestown, Ind.
George Hayward, Farmer, Snow Hill, Md.
Benjamin F. Hill, *p* Candor, Pa.
J. F. Hutchison, *m* Kenton, Ohio.
Samuel R. Latta.
*Joseph M Lippincott, *m*
John S. Love, *p* Pine Swamp, P. O. Pa.
Isaac M'Bride. *p* Philadelphia, Pa.
David L. Machesney, *p*
Robert M'Cullough, *m* Chinese Camp, Cal.
Samuel N. M'Cullough.
William M'Kay, *m*
Robert M'Millan, *m* Canonsburg, Pa.
Joseph H. Mathers, *m* Richland Cent. Wis.
David Minnis, *p* Beaver, Pa.
T. E. Morgan, *l* Keokuck, Iowa.
William Okeson, *l* Debuque, Iowa.
Franklin Orr, *m* Kent, Pa.
W. W. Patrick, *l* Pittsburgh, Pa.
*Levi Penny.
Israel C. Pershing, *m* Steubenville, Ohio.
John R. Purnell, *l* Snow Hill, Md.
M. Stanley Quay, *l* Beaver, Pa.
George Sherman Rice, *m*
David J. Rogers, R. R. Contractor, Mansfield, Pa.
William P. Saunders, *m*
John P. Scott, *m* Millersburg, O.
A. O. Scott.
Henry Martyn Smith, Engineer, Toledo, O
John Spence, *l* Bastrop, Texas.
Thomas B. Stewart, Farmer, Ohio Co. Va.
George H. Stone, *l* Springfield, Ill.
W. H. Sturgeon, *p*
D. M. Taliaferro, *p* Ky,
Robert F. Wilson, *m* M'Keesport, Pa. 56

Peter Hayden, A B, A M Pittsburgh, Pa.
W. W. Stewart, A B Huntingdon Co. Pa.
S. S. Lyon, A B Huntingdon Co. Pa.
James Orr, A B
Samuel Long, A B Pittsburgh, Pa.
William P. Harvison, A B, A M Amity Pa.
William Dickey, Esq. A M Elkton, Ky.
Rev. James Clark, D D Pres't Wash. Coll. Lewisburg, Pa.
Rev. Charles W. Nassau, D D Lawrenceville, N. J.
*Rev. Daniel M'Kinley, D D
Hon. Thomas H. Baird, LL D Monongahela City.
Hon. James Allison, LL D Beaver, Pa.

1851.

James W. Anderson, *m*
C. B. Betts, *m*
*Crosby M. Boggs.
Cyrus G. Braddock, *m* Herriottsville, Pa.
Aaron S. Brandon, Planter, Ft. Adams, Mi.
Benjamin S. Bristow, Ky,
James Caldwell, *m* Libertyville. Iowa.
John A. Campbell, *m* St. Mary's, Ohio.
Archibald Cook, *l* Mercer, Pa,
Jonathan R. Coulter, *m* Coultersville.
Henry B. Cozzens, Vicksburg, Mi.
William F. Culbertson, *m* Danville, Ky.
Samuel Duncan, *l* Dubuque, Iowa.
John F. Fife, *t* Land Agent, Mt. Pleasant, Tenn.
James W. Hanna, *m* Canal Fulton O.
Andrew D. Hepburn, *st Th* Princeton, New Jersey.
Andrew J. Johnston, Druggist, Baltimore, Md.
Sinclair Johnson, Teacher, O.
John Jordon, Farmer.
William D. Kearns, *p* Pittsburgh, Pa.
Robert P. Kennedy, Engineer, Canonsburg.
Alexander Kennedy, Hagerstown, Md.
Samuel M. L. Keir, *m* Xenia, Ohio.
Thomas M'Cague, *m* Miss. to Cairo, Egypt.
R. B. M'Cann, *l* O.
John L. M'Cartney, *St Th* Prof Musk Coll. Allegheny City.
William G. M'Creary, *t* New Brighton, Pa.
William C. M'Cune, *m* Cincinnati, Ohio.
John M. M'Elroy, *m* Ottumwa, Iowa
William E. M'Laren, Editor, Pittsburgh.

S. G. M'Neil, *m* Pittsburgh, Ind.
Henry S. Martin, *l* Prin. Un. Sch, Canton, Ohio.
S. M. Matheny, *p*
Simon B. Mercer, Prin. Dunlaps Cr. Acad. Merritstown, Pa.
F. M. Michie, Mi.
William F. Morgan, *m* Rural Valley, Pa.
Richard H. Morrow, *m* Cedar Rapids, Ia.
George B. Newell, *m*
James H. Potter, *m*
W. Hamilton Pyle, *p* Henderson, Texas.
L. B. W. Shryock, *m* Crittenden, Ky.
J. Irwin Smith, *m* Ontonagon, Mich.
J. Henderson Smith,
Henry Martyn Smith, *m* New Orleans.
R. C. G. Sproul, *l* Pittsburgh, Pa.
Samuel M Swan, *p* Waverly Station, Ill.
Thomas B. Vaneman, *m* Canonsburg, Pa.
A. M'Lean White, *p* Hartstown, Pa.
Jonathon Wilson, *m* Spencer Acad. Choctaw Nation.
William Swan Wilson, *m* Warsaw, Ind.
James L. Wilson, *m* Cascade, Iowa. 52

George W. Marquis, Esq. A M Tuscagee.
Matthew I. Stewart, Esq. A M Pittsburgh
Benjamin Rush Bradford, Esq. A M New Brighton, Pa.
Dr Jno. B. Stilley, A M Upper St.Clair Pa.
Rev. William Grimes, A M
Rev. William Richards, D D Reading. Pa.
Rev. Thos. Woodrow, D D Worthington, O.
Rev. Charles Forbes Buchan, D D Scot.
Rev. John Clark, D D Scotland.
Rev. A. P. Goudy, D D Irelsnd.
Rev. James Steel, D D Ireland.

1852.

William J. Alexander, *m* Perry, Pa.
Johnston Armstrong, *p* Alliance, Ohio.
David Bacon, *l* Niles, Michigan.
A. B. Beamer, *m* Va.
R. K. Campbell, *m* 20 mile Stand, O.
William M. Christy *l* Kittanning, Pa.
John H. Clark, *St Th* Allegheny, Pa.
Silas M. Clark, *l* Indiana, Pa.
Joseph L. Cook, *St Law* Greensburgh, Pa.
William Cunningham, *St Th* Princeton, New Jersey.
John B. Davidson, *t* Langley, Va.
E. L. Dodder, *m* Fort Dodge, Iowa.
James A. Duff, *m* Darlington, Pa.
William J Edie, Lewistown, Ill.
William H. French, Brush Run, Washington Co Pa.
Chas. K. Geddes, *St Law* Kittanning, Pa.
J. C. Grier, *m* Mechanicsburg, Pa.
George Hammond, Clerk, Baltimore, Md.
Thomas J. Himes, Druggist, Rock Island, Illinois.
Albert O. Johnson, *m* Miss. at Futtegurh, India.
Jacob W. Lanius, *m* Waveland, Ind.
James L. Marshall, Merchant, Pittsburgh
*James Mathers, *l*.
Henry M'Cormick, *p* Clinton, Iowa.
*W. W. Miller, *p*.
Thos. F. Otwell, *p* Planter, Georgetown, Ky.
Robert W. Playford, *p* Brownsville.
Matthew B. Riddle, *St Th t* Canonsburg.
James F. Robinson, *l* Columbia, Ark.
Alexander Scott, *t*.
Joseph Shaw.
A. B. Simmons, *l* Texas.
*J. Rowland Stewart, *t*.
Francis L. Stewart, Prof. Missouri.
Lewis M. Stewart, *l*.
D. W. Templeton, *l*.
John W. Van Lear, Somerset.
B. C. Ward, *t*.
Eugene M Wilson, *l* Wynona, Minn.
John E. Woods *m* Bentonsport, Ia.
John N. Young, *m* 41

Rev. Matthew H. Wilson, A M Kent, Pa.
J. Booth, Esq. A M Bucyrus, Ohio.
W. P. Pearson, Esq. A M.
Rev. Melancthon W. Jacobus, D D Allegheny City, Pa.
Rev. John Ekin, D D Pittsburgh, Pa.
Rev. John Marsh, D D N. Y.
Rev. Septimus Tuston, D D D. C.
Rev. James Johnston, D D Ohio.
Dr. R. Dunglison, LL D Philadelphia.
Rev. David Davidson, LL D Scotland.

1853.

J. A. Amis, *p* N Car.
Charles Berryman.
Samuel Boon, *t* Owenstown, Ky.
Henry M. Bracken, Pleasant Hill, Mo.
J. R. Burgett, *m* Allegheny City.
John D. Caldwell, *m*.
Rush Clark, *t* Iowa City, Iowa.
William B. Craig, *m* Shippensburgh, Pa.
John B. Dunn, *m* Andes N. Y.
James S. Eckles, *St Law t* Albany, N. Y.
Thomas Ewing, *l* Prin. Natchez Institute, tion, Natchez, Mi.
John G. Frow, *p*.
Ebenezer Haft, Surveyor, N. Albany Oregon.
Alfred W. Haines, *m*
I Newton Himes, *p*.
William E. Hunt, *m* Coshocton, Ohio.
Augustus S. Landis, *St Law* Hollidaysburg, Pa.
William H. Letherman, *p* Surg. U. S. Navy, Baltimore, Md.
William L. M'Connell, *m* Canonsburg, Pa.
George W. M'Murran, Shepherdstown, Va.
George W. Mechlin, *m* Prin. Glade Run Academy, Dayton, Pa.
William Mitchell, Assist. Prin. Academy, Morgantown, Va.
Samuel Patterson, *m* Urichsville, Ohio.
Alfred Pearson, *l* Harrisburgh, Pa.
D. H. Scott, *p* Chilicothe, Ohio.
Julius A. Smith, *t* Charlestown, Ill.
James H. Stokes, *t*.
James C. Sturgeon, *t* Prin. High School, Lafayette, Ala.

John W Sutherland, t Prin. Fem. Sem. Jefferson City, Mo.
Francis Taliiaferro. p Ky.
John C. Thom, St Th Natchez, Mi.
Albert E Thompson, m
Isaac Vanmeter, Farmer, Piketon, Ohio.
William Wight, St Th Delhi, N, Y.
David M. Wilson, Merchant, Baltimore, Md.
Martin Luther Wortman, m West Newton, Pa. 36

Alexander Taylor, Esq A B Indiana, Pa.
Dr. Joseph Connelly, A B Triadelphis, Va.
Dr. John V. Herriott, A M Philadelphia, Pa.
Hon. John W. Howe, A M Franklin.
P. L. Grim, Esq. A M Beaver, Pa,
Rev. David Kirkpatrick, D D Poke Run, Pa.

1854.

John M'Leary Adair, St Th Xenia, Ohio.
Thomas Alexander, Allegheny City, Pa.
F. Barnett, St Law Ashland, Ohio.
Joseph L. Bitner, Merchant, Harrisburg, Pa.
J. C. Boyd, St Th Allegheny City.
Gerard C. Crandon, p Natchez, Mi.
David S. Brandon. Merchant, Natchez, Mi
William A. Burchfield, St Th Allegheny C.
Joseph H. Campbell, t.
Robert Carothers, m Turtle Creek, Pa.
William Clark, Prince George, Md.
David A. Cunningham, m Allegheny City.
T. R. Elder, m Superior, Wis.
James I Frazer, St Th Xenia, Ohio.
W. Nevin Geddes, t.
N. Hallock Gillett, Prin. Acad. Owengsville, Ky.
Walter L. Graham; l Butler, Pa.
R. St. Clair Graham, St Law Greensburg.
Addison Henry, St Th Allegheny City.
W. B. Herriott, St Law Pittsburgh.
Campbell T. Jamieson. Clerk, N. Orleans.
William A. Jeffery, Waynesburg, Pa.
William Johnson, t Hookstown, Pa.
John P. Kennedy, m Allegheny City.
T. Ruston Kennedy, l Meadville.
*Thomas Kerr, St Th O.
John T. Kyle, l.
David Lenox, t.
D. S. Logan, Prin Enon Academy, Pa.
A. Lowman, St Th Allegheny City.
John S. M'Culloch, St Th Allegheny City.
Matthew M'Featers, St Th Danville, Ky.
W. Morrow M'Kee, t Urbana, Ohio.
William L. Mitchell, Greenfield, Mo.
Alexander M. Moore, Tenn.
Benjamin F. Myers.
J. B Negley, Surveyor, Butler, Pa.
J. C. Nevin, St Th Allegheny City, Pa.
Benson J. Orsborn, l Texas.
Henry W. Patterson, St Law Uniontown, Pa.
R. H. Peterson, t.
John A. Pinkerton, m Allegheny City, Pa.
William H. Playford, St Law Brownsville, Pa.
John W. Polk, Nicaragua.
William H. Pretlow, Va.
Thomas E. Roberts St Th Andover, Mass.
George Shotwell Roudebush, St Th.
Walter B. Smith, Merch't, Pittsburgh, Pa.
Jamas C. Snodgrass, St Law Greensburgh, Pa.
John M. Stevenson. t.
Calvin W. Stewart, St Th Princeton, N. J.
A. A. Stewart, St Law Greensburgh, Pa.
Edward P. Swift, St Th Allegheny, City.
John M. Vanmeter, l Portsmouth, O.
J. D. Walkinshaw, St Th Saltsburg, Pa.
John H. Young, St Th Pittsburgh, Pa. 56

E. J. Pershing, Esq. A M Rock Island, Ill.
*Edward P. Hunter, Esq. A M Va.
B. M. Kerr, Esq. Mansfield, Pa.
P. A. Cregar, Esq. A M Philadelphia.
Rev. H. B. Cunningham, D D N. Car.
Rev. A. D. Clark, D D As. Ref. Th. Seminary, Allegheny City.
Rev John H. Brown, D D Lexington, Ky.
Rev A. M'Farlane, D D Scotland.
Rev D. D. Heather, D D Ireland
Dr Thomas D. Mutter, LL D Philadelphia.

1855.

Abraham Anderson, St Th Xenia, Ohio.
T. Coulter Anderson, St Th Allegheny City, Pa.
Wm Wilson Barr, St Th Xenia, Ohio.
D. Henry Barron, St Th Allegheny City.
John H. Bast, t Reading, Pa.
J. A. Carrothers, Farmer, Iowa.
John S. Chapman, St L Lebanon, Tenn.
Ira M. Condit St Th Allegheny City.
James S. Elder, m Clarksburgh, Pa
Thomas B. Elder, Farmer Eldersridge, Pa.
James A. Ewing, St Th Allegheny City.
Charles S. Foresman, St Law.
James T. Fredericks, St Th Allegheny City, Pa.
Geo. Graham, St Th Allegheny City, Pa.
Jesse W. Hamilton, St Th Allegheny City, Pa
Daniel W. Hanna, Paper Manufacturer, Steubenville, Ohio,
S. M. Hickman, m Teaching.
Alpheus H. Holloway, St Th Danville Ky
William Hutchinson, Teaching, Natchez,
John C. Irwin, St Th Allegheny City, Pa.
Richard H. Jackson, Prin Oakwood Acad. Hamilton, Hancock, Co Ill.
B Oliver Junkin, St Th Allegheny City.
William B. Keeling, St Th Allegheny City
J. Moffit Kennedy, Teaching, Chester County, Pa.
Andrew W. Kerr, Teaching, Clarksville, Minn.
Adam Kimple, St Law Franklin Centre, Ia
David Nelson Lapsley, St Med St Francisville, Mo.

Samuel P. Large, *St Med* Elizabeth, Pa.
John Y. M'Cartney, *St Th* Allegheny City
William M'Gregor, *St Law* Lake Providence, La.
John M'Kinley, *St Law*
A. Smith M'Kinney, Merchant. Peoria, Ill
James M'Master, *St Med* Pittsburgh, Pa.
Robert R. Moore, *St Th* Allegheny City.
William P. Moore, *St Th* New Derry, Pa.
S. T. Murray, *St Law*
John Purviance, *St Law*
R. G Ralston, Teaching,
Samuel M. Sharp, *St Th* Steubenville, O.
John A. E. Simpson, *St Th* Noblestown Pa
J. E. Thomas, Prin. Aca. Pine Grove Mills,
Daniel W. Townsend, *St Th* Allegheny City, Pa.
Allan Wall, *St Med* Indianapolis, Ind.
Samuel Watson *St Th* Allegheny City, Pa
Samuel Wead, *St Law* Dayton, Ohio,
Isaac N. White, *St Th* Xenia, Ohio.
Philip Williard, *St Th* Lancaster, Pa.
John S. Woods, Engineer.

---

*Rev. Patrick F. Jones, A M
Rev. William H. Andrews, A M Ohio.
Rev. James Chrystie, D D, N. Y.
Rev. William M. Hetherington, D D Scotland.

1856.

William E. Allison, Hancock Co. Va.
Thomas Andrews, *St Th* Allegheny City.
David W. Ballantine, *St Law* Temperanceville, Pa.
James A. Beaver, *St Law* Bellefonte, Pa.
William J. Burchinal, *St Th*
Thomas C. Campbell, *St Th* Allegheny City, Pa.
David T. Campbell, *st Th* Princeton, N. J.
Milton Campbell, Teaching, Springfield X Roads
G. Wilson Chalfant, Monongahela City.
John F. Craig, *st law*, Clarion, Pa.
J. M. Cummins, *st med* Ligonier, Pa.
John D. Elder, Teaching.
Sam'l C. Ewing, Farming, Irwin's Sta. Pa.
J. E. Garretson, Teaching.
James C. Gillam, *st th* Allegheny City, Pa.
J. S. Gilmore, *St Th* Princeton, N. J.
Wm C. Gordon, Teaching, Black Lick, Pa.
David D. Green, *st Th* Allegheny City, Pa.
Francis B. Guthrie, Water Proof, La
William W. Hays, Victoria, Texas.
John P Houston, Texas
J. Dagg Howey, *st th* Allegheny City, Pa.
Wm. G. Keady, Teaching, Jonesboro Tenn.
Geo. Hays Kennedy, Teaching, Chicago,
Orr Lawson, *st th* Lawsonville, Clarion Co. Pa.
A. Brown Lewis, Natchez, Mi.
Joseph L. Lower, *st th* Princeton, N. J.
William M. M'Curdy, Washington, Ohio.
Charles W. M'Daniel, Clerk, Philadelphia.
Jno. K. M'Ilheny, *st law* Hunterstown, Pa.
James Y. M'Kee, Washington, Ohio.
S. Davidson M'Pherson, *st th* Shippensburg, Pa.
W. Stanhope Marshall, Natchez, Mi.
Jas H. Matthews, Maysville, Ky.
James E. Morrow, Clover Port, Ky.
Nicholas V. Morrow, *st th* Allegheny City.
Andrew J. Murry, *t* Murrysville, Pa.
Wilson Paxton, Teaching, Owensboro, Ky.
H. R. Peairs, *st th* Allegheny City, Pa.
Joseph L. Polk, Teaching.
James A. Reed, *st th* Allegheny City, Pa.
Thomas F. J. Rider, *t* Princess Anne, Md.
Samuel A. Riggs; *st law* Pittsburgh, Pa.
George Scott, *st th* Allegheny City, Pa.
C. S. Scroggs, Marshall, Texas.
Joseph D Smith, *st th* Princeton, N. J.
John M. Smith, *st th* Allegheny City, Pa.
Tom Stockdale, *st law* Greene Co. Pa.
Samuel B. Taggart, *st th* Allegheny City.
Robert S. Townsend, Teaching.
M. M. Travis, *st th* Allegheny City, Pa.
Theophilus Weaver, Teaching, Bowsburg, Pa.
A. G. Wilson, Teaching, Beaver, Pa.
Miles C. Wilson, *st th* Lafayette, Ala.
J. Charles Young, *st law* Pittsburgh, Pa.
John Bishop Young, *st law* Chicago, Ill. 56

Rev. Charles W. Baird, A M Yonkers, N Y.
Rev. A. W. Course, A M Rockville, Ind.
W. Whitton Redick, Esq. A M Allegheny City, Pa.
Rev. Reese Happersett, D D Philadelphia.
Hon. Thomas H. Burrows, LL D Lancaster, Pa.

Present Board of Trustees.

CATALOGUE OF BOOKS

Published and for sale by J. T. Shryock, Pittsburgh.

Traveling agents can be supplied with most of the following named Books at a large Discount; and they are not generallg for sale in Book Stores. Copies mailed prepaid, for an advaance of 1 6 of the Price named for each Book.

THE DISCOURSES AND DIALOGUES OF THE REV. SAMUEL PORTER, WITH A BIOGRAPHICAL SKETCH BY THE REV. DR. ELLIOTT.

These Discourses are upon very important subjects:

The first is "A Discourse on the Decrees of God, the Perseverance of the Saints, and Sinless Perfection, being the substance of two Sermons, delivered at Congruity, June 16, 1793."

The Second, "A Revival of True Religion delineated on Scriptural and Rational Principles, in a Sermon delivered at the opening of the Synod of Pittsburgh, October 2 1805.

The Third, "A Discourse relative to the Atonement of Christ; delivered in the First Presbyterian Church, Pittsburgh, October 1, 1811, at the opening of the Synod of Pittsburgh."

The Dialogues between DEATH and the BELIEVER and DEATH and the HYPOCRITE, are written in a somewhat peculiar style, and worthy the attention of every professing Christian. This Book contains 250 pages. Bound in Cloth. Price 50 cts.

SACRED FOUNTAINS; OR OBSERVATIONS, *Historical and Practical, on the Streams, Lakes, and Fountains, of the Holy Land. By the Rev. David Wilson, of Harpers' Ferry, Va.*

This work is well suited for the young, and would be suitable as a present to a Son, Daughter, or Friend. It is interesting and instructive; contains 211 pages, and three Engravings, Cloth binding; Price 60 cts.

THE PASTOR'S MANUAL; a Selection of Tracts on Pastoral Duty; containing Baxter's Reformed Pastor; Mason's Student and Pastor; Qualifications for Teachers; Rules for Preachers' Conduct; Booth's Pastoral Cautions; &c. 418 12mo. pages, b'd in Cloth, price $1.

THE CHRISTIAN INSTRUCTOR; CONTAINING a summary explanation and defence of the Doctrines and Duties of the Christian Religion, by Rev. J. Hopkins, D. D. 357 12mo. pps cloth Binding; price $1.

THE READY RECKONER, IN DOLLARS AND Cents, to which are added forms of notes, Bills, Receipts Petitions, &c. together with useful interest and other tables. Price 50 Cents.

MESSIANIC PROPHECY AND LIFE OF CHRIST: The prophecies concerning, and History of Christ compared. 484 12mo. pages, cloth binding, price $1

THE LIFE AND DISCOURSES OF SIR JOSHUA REYNOLDS, first President of the Royal Academy. First American Edition, 286 12mo. pages, price 75 cents.

www.ingramcontent.com/pod-product-compliance
Lightning Source LLC
LaVergne TN
LVHW021121110826
845150LV00005B/908

* 9 7 8 1 4 2 5 5 5 1 7 2 8 *